Born in 1712, the son of a Swiss watch-maker, Jean-Jacques Rousseau lived sixty-six years of unparalleled contrast between noble and ignoble, good and evil.

His influence in literary history is unique and unrivaled. Furthermore, this incredible man who is the father of Romanticism is also one of the most important figures in political history. Every modern political theory from democracy to fascism owes a debt to the mind and pen of Jean-Jacques Rousseau.

THE CONFESSIONS OF
JEAN-JACQUES
ROUSSEAU

•

Edited, revised and prefaced by
LESTER G. CROCKER

THE POCKET LIBRARY

The Confessions of Jean-Jacques Rousseau

1957

•

This book is one of a Distinguished Series
The Pocket Library
offering to the reader outstanding literary
landmarks of all time and all languages
in an inexpensive, well-designed format.

L
Published by Pocket Books, Inc. • 630 Fifth Avenue • New York, N. Y.

The translation used in the POCKET BOOK edition
of *The Confessions* is based on the standard
version, first published (anonymously) in 1783,
and corrected by the editor of this volume.

PREFACE

"I was determined to make it a work unique of its kind, by an unexampled truthfulness, which, for once, at least, would enable the outside world to behold a man as he really was in his inmost self. . . . I, who have always believed, and still believe myself to be, all things considered, the best of men, felt that there is no human heart, however pure it may be, which does not hide some odious vice."

Thus Rousseau describes the self-revelation that poured from his wrenched and tortured heart. For here is more than a book; here is a man, uncovered in the nakedness of body and soul. It is a stirring tale he unfolds: a picaresque story of incredible adventures and mad loves, an imbroglio of plots and intrigues. We are vagabonds with this man, and lovers; we grow up with him, suffer with him the spasms of pleasure and pain, of weakness and triumph. And behind the actor who fills the foreground, we see the stage he treads, an unrolling panorama of the eighteenth-century world, the cottages of the humble, the *cafés* and *salons* of the literati, the empty lives and pale gestures of the aristocracy, withered leaves on a dying branch. But all these—adventures, plots, people—are overtowered by the figure who reacts so drastically to them, by the character they serve to illuminate in a raw, unfiltered light.

To reveal oneself in one's inmost self—no task is more difficult than this. Many have tried it; none has succeeded so well as Rousseau in making the reader feel that the last curtain has been lifted, that he is really looking on that innermost recess in his heart of hearts, the one where we all hide ourselves, not only from the world, but from our own selves. This is the recess where we store the little episodes and feelings we are most ashamed to call our own, the secrets from ourselves that the need for self-protection and self-respect bids us envelop in shadows.

What is it that makes a man able to perform this feat? Not honesty, for honesty alone—how many memoirs and confessions prove it!—falters before this very last of all curtains. Jean-Jacques' triumph comes from his very weaknesses and defects, which for this purpose are unparalleled virtues. If he had not been a sexual exhibitionist, he could not have found satisfaction in the sublimated exhibitionism that makes his *Confessions* so successful. If he had not been a monstrous egoist, he would not have experienced the exhilaration of doing what no other man had done (so he says), nor the conviction that everything about himself was supremely important. Honesty is not, in fact, the stamp of these confessions. Sincerity, yes, that of a paranoid who sincerely warps facts and motives into the pattern of reality he can accept. For Rousseau, sinned against as he was, was equally a sinner. We must beware of accepting his account as the truth—despite sincerity. Rousseau never admits he is wrong, never believes he is wrong, always twists, always lies to himself when he is at fault—except in cases where admission of guilt does not involve giving credit to his enemies, but leads instead to greater credit for himself, for the unexampled honesty of admitting it. This is what so enraged his adversaries, who accused him of making small confessions to throw the cloak of truth over his greater distortions.

Rousseau's life and character will unfold themselves, better than any biographer has yet described them. If the man is formed in the child, if the physical determines the moral—we shall witness the plant growing from the seed, gradually twisted (partly by problems of sexuality) and then diseased, racked by pain and by torment, pitiful in its struggle against an environment it cannot cope with. If the good can be allied with the bad, the noble with the corrupt, we shall witness this, too. For Rousseau was naïve and oversubtle, forgiving and rancorous, generous and petty, able to possess women and never to enjoy them. He loved man, and quarreled with all men. Suspicious and overconfiding, trembling with insecurity, arrogant, too, neurotic above all things, he could write with clairvoyance: "As soon as I lost sight of men, I ceased to despise them; as soon as I lost sight of the wicked, I ceased to hate them. . . . I became again shy, courteous and timid; in a word, the same Jean-Jacques as I had been before."

Rousseau is a great writer. He brought back to French literature the voices of lyricism and eloquence, a new spring in the winter of classicism. The romantic age owed him much. He restored nature to literature, not only by his descriptive powers, but by a living act of communion. He expressed man's profoundest need: to experience his own existence, and the anguish that springs from it. The unashamed display of his inner world, his introspection and self-analysis, led the way toward the exaltation of individuality that characterized romantic literature. For he was a man like unto no other; this was his pride and his worth. ". . . I dare to believe that I am not made like any of those . . . in existence. If I am not better, at least I am different." And all the world outside was not something to which he should bend this sacred individuality, but something that had reality and meaning only in his own inner self.

Doubtless Rousseau has been even more influential, and of more continuing importance, as a thinker. In the fermenting Age of Enlightenment, he was both of his time and against it. Like most of his contemporaries, he dreamed longingly of a "state of nature," for men were most virtuous when most natural. Montesquieu, Voltaire, Diderot and their followers, like Rousseau, saw that our society had failed to solve its great problems. They, too, contrary to what is often said, believed man had been corrupted by his institutions, that natural law must be rediscovered. But they envisioned man struggling closer to his goals through the development of rational truth and scientific culture.

It was on this score that Rousseau broke with them, in a thunderous quarrel. Fighting against his time—and against ours—he proclaimed the supreme value of the intuitions and the inner life, in a culture which subjugated them more and more to the impersonality of objective facts. His protest fore-cast the modern revolt of men like Kierkegaard, Bergson and Gabriel Marcel. Rousseau did not tell us to go back to a prim-itive life, but he warned us to change our road. He foresaw all our "progress" putting us in weightier chains; he sensed that the course of our mechanistic culture would stifle the free, inner world, making us the slaves and victims of our own contrivings. Ever emptier within, ever less the masters of our destinies—not in this way could we satisfy our deep need for freedom, happiness, justice, self-realization.

And so, he stood alone. He had powerful enemies on the right and on the left, in the liberal-capitalistic *philosophes*, and in the dominating feudal institutions. He stood up with stubborn honesty and pride against two powerful streams, and these were the flood tides that broke his life and swept away his sanity. But his work remains. Rousseau is still a living force, extolled or damned as the apostle of democracy, an-archy, or totalitarianism by men who have failed to see he wanted none of these.

Rousseau's philosophy is not a part of his *Confessions*. The reader who is interested in his thought must turn to other writings. Here we shall meet and penetrate the spirit and the flesh out of which his philosophy grew, and from which we cannot cut it off.

And now, *ecce homo*—behold the man!

—LESTER G. CROCKER
Goucher College

BALTIMORE, MD.

CONTENTS

Part the First

Part the Second

THE CONFESSIONS OF
JEAN-JACQUES
ROUSSEAU

PART THE FIRST

BOOK ONE

[1712-1719]

I AM commencing an undertaking, hitherto without precedent, and which will never find an imitator. I desire to set before my fellows the likeness of a man in all the truth of nature, and that man myself.

I alone. I know my heart, and I know men. I am not made like any of those I have seen; I dare to believe that I am not made like any of those who are in existence. If I am not better, at least I am different. Whether Nature has acted rightly or wrongly in destroying the mould in which she cast me, can only be decided after I have been read.

Let the trumpet of the Day of Judgment sound when it will, I will present myself before the Sovereign Judge with this book in my hand. I will say boldly: "This is what I have done, what I have thought, what I was. I have told the good and the bad with equal frankness. I have neither omitted anything bad, nor interpolated anything good. If I have occasionally made use of some immaterial embellishments, this has only been in order to fill a gap caused by lack of memory. I may have assumed the truth of that which I knew might have been true, never of that which I knew to be false. I have shown myself as I was: mean and contemptible, good, high-minded and sublime, according as I was one or the other. I have unveiled my inmost self even as Thou hast seen it, O Eternal Being. Gather round me the countless host of my fellow-men; let them hear my confessions, lament for my unworthiness, and blush for my imperfections. Then let each of them in turn reveal, with the same frankness, the secrets of his heart at the foot of the Throne, and say, if he dare, '*I was better than that man!*' "

1

I was born at Geneva, in the year 1712, and was the son of Isaac Rousseau and Susanne Bernard, citizens. The distribution of a very moderate inheritance amongst fifteen children had reduced my father's portion almost to nothing; and his only means of livelihood was his trade of watchmaker, at which he was really very clever. My mother, a daughter of the Protestant minister Bernard, was better off. She was clever and beautiful, and my father had found difficulty in obtaining her hand. Their affection for each other had begun almost as soon as they were born. When only eight years old, they walked every evening upon the Treille;° at ten, they were inseparable. Sympathy and union of soul strengthened in them the feeling produced by intimacy. Both, naturally full of tender sensibility, only waited for the moment when they should find the same disposition in another—or, rather, this moment waited for them, and each abandoned his heart to the first which opened to receive it. Destiny, which appeared to oppose their passion, only encouraged it. The young lover, unable to obtain possession of his mistress, was consumed by grief. She advised him to travel, and endeavour to forget her. He travelled, but without result, and returned more in love than ever. He found her whom he loved still faithful and true. After this trial of affection, nothing was left for them but to love each other all their lives. This they swore to do, and Heaven blessed their oath.

Gabriel Bernard, my mother's brother, fell in love with one of my father's sisters, who only consented to accept the hand of the brother, on condition that her own brother married the sister. Love arranged everything, and the two marriages took place on the same day. Thus my uncle became the husband of my aunt, and their children were doubly my first cousins. At the end of a year, a child was born to both, after which they were again obliged to separate.

My uncle Bernard was an engineer. He took service in the Empire and in Hungary, under Prince Eugène. He distinguished himself at the siege and battle of Belgrade. My father, after the birth of my only brother, set out for Con-

---

* A fashionable promenade in Geneva.

stantinople, whither he was summoned to undertake the post of watchmaker to the Sultan. During his absence, my mother's beauty, intellect and talents gained for her the devotion of numerous admirers. M. de la Closure, the French Resident, was one of the most eager to offer his. His passion must have been great, for, thirty years later, I saw him greatly affected when speaking to me of her. To enable her to resist such advances, my mother had more than her virtue: she loved her husband tenderly. She pressed him to return; he left all, and returned. I was the unhappy fruit of this return. Ten months later I was born, a weak and ailing child; I cost my mother her life, and my birth was the first of my misfortunes.

I have never heard how my father bore this loss, but I know that he was inconsolable. He believed that he saw his wife again in me, without being able to forget that it was I who had robbed him of her; he never embraced me without my perceiving, by his sighs and the convulsive manner in which he clasped me to his breast, that a bitter regret was mingled with his caresses, which were on that account only the more tender. When he said to me, "Jean-Jacques, let us talk of your mother," I used to answer, "Well, then, my father, we will weep!"—and this word alone was sufficient to move him to tears. "Ah!" said he, with a sigh, "give her back to me, console me for her loss, fill the void which she has left in my soul. Should I love you as I do, if you were only my son?" Forty years after he had lost her, he died in the arms of a second wife, but the name of the first was on his lips and her image at the bottom of his heart.

Such were the authors of my existence. Of all the gifts which Heaven had bestowed upon them, a sensitive heart is the only one they bequeathed to me; it had been the source of their happiness, but for me it proved the source of all the misfortunes of my life.

I was brought into the world in an almost dying condition; little hope was entertained of saving my life. I carried within me the germs of a complaint which the course of time has strengthened, and which at times allows me a respite only to make me suffer more cruelly in another manner. One of my father's sisters, an amiable and virtuous young woman, took such care of me that she saved my life. At this moment, while I am writing, she is still alive, at the age of eighty, nursing a husband younger than herself, but exhausted by excessive drinking. Dear aunt, I forgive you for having preserved my life; and I deeply regret that, at the end of your days, I am unable to repay the tender care which you lavished upon me at the beginning of my own.* My dear old nurse Jacqueline is also still alive, healthy and robust. The hands which opened my eyes at my birth will be able to close them for me at my death.

I felt before I thought: this is the common lot of humanity. I experienced it more than others. I do not know what I did until I was five or six years old. I do not know how I learned to read; I only remember my earliest reading, and the effect it had upon me; from that time I date my uninterrupted self-consciousness. My mother had left some romances behind her, which my father and I began to read after supper. At first it was only a question of practising me in reading by the aid of amusing books; but soon the interest became so lively, that we used to read in turn without stopping, and spent whole nights in this occupation. We were unable to leave off until the volume was finished. Sometimes, my father, hearing the swallows begin to twitter in the early morning, would say, quite ashamed, "Let us go to bed; I am more of a child than yourself."

In a short time I acquired, by this dangerous method, not only extreme facility in reading and understanding what I read, but a knowledge of the passions that was unique in a child of my age. I had no idea of things in themselves, although all the feelings of actual life were already known to me. I had conceived nothing, but felt everything. These confused emotions which I felt one after the other, certainly did not warp the reasoning powers which I did not as yet pos-

* The name of this aunt was Madame Gonceru. In March, 1767, Rousseau settled upon her an income of one hundred *livres,* and, even in the time of his greatest distress, always paid it regularly.

sess; but they shaped them in me of a peculiar stamp, and gave me odd and romantic notions of human life, of which experience and reflection have never been able wholly to cure me.

[1719-1723.]—The romances came to an end in the summer of 1719. The following winter brought us something different. My mother's library being exhausted, we had recourse to the share of her father's which had fallen to us. Luckily, there were some good books in it; in fact, it could hardly have been otherwise, for the library had been collected by a minister, who was even a learned man according to the fashion of the day, and was at the same time a man of taste and intellect. The "History of the Empire and the Church," by Le Sueur; Bossuet's "Treatise upon Universal History"; Plutarch's "Lives of Famous Men"; Nani's "History of Venice"; Ovid's "Metamorphoses"; La Bruyère; Fontenelle's "Worlds"; his "Dialogues of the Dead"; and some volumes of Molière—all these were brought over into my father's room, and I read to him out of them while he worked. I conceived a taste for them that was rare and perhaps unique at my age. Plutarch, especially, became my favourite author. The pleasure I took in reading him over and over again cured me a little of my taste for romance, and I soon preferred Agesilaus, Brutus, and Aristides to Orondates, Artamenes, and Juba. This interesting reading, and the conversations between my father and myself to which it gave rise, formed in me the free and republican spirit, the proud and indomitable character unable to endure slavery or servitude, which has tormented me throughout my life in situations the least fitted to afford it scope. Unceasingly occupied with thoughts of Rome and Athens, living as it were amongst their great men, myself by birth the citizen of a republic and the son of a father whose patriotism was his strongest passion, I was fired by his example; I believed myself a Greek or a Roman; I lost my identity in that of the individual whose life I was reading; the recitals of the qualities of endurance and intrepidity which arrested my attention made my eyes glisten and strengthened my voice. One day, while I was relating the history of Scaevola at table, those present were alarmed to see me come forward and hold my hand over a chafing-dish, to illustrate his action.

I had a brother seven years older than myself, who was learning my father's trade. The excessive affection which was lavished upon myself caused him to be somewhat neglected, which treatment I cannot approve of. His education felt the consequences of this neglect. He took to evil courses before he was old enough to be a regular profligate. He was put with another master, from whom he was continually running away, as he had done from home. I hardly ever saw him; I can scarcely say that I knew him; but I never ceased to love him tenderly, and he loved me as much as a vagabond can love anything. I remember that, on one occasion, when my father was chastising him harshly and in anger, I threw myself impetuously between them and embraced him closely. In this manner I covered his body with mine, and received the blows which were aimed at him; I so obstinately maintained my position that at last my father was obliged to leave off, being either disarmed by my cries and tears, or afraid of hurting me more than him. At last, my brother turned out so badly that he ran away and disappeared altogether. Sometime afterwards we heard that he was in Germany. He never once wrote to us. From that time nothing more has been heard of him, and thus I have remained an only son.

If this poor boy was carelessly brought up, this was not the case with his brother; the children of kings could not be more carefully looked after than I was during my early years—worshipped by all around me, and, which is far less common, treated as a beloved, never as a spoiled child. Till I left my father's house, I was never once allowed to run about the streets by myself with the other children; in my case no one ever had to satisfy or check any of those fantastic whims which are attributed to Nature, but are all in reality the result of education. I had the faults of my age: I was a chatterbox, a glutton, and, sometimes, a liar. I would have stolen fruits, bonbons, or eatables; but I have never found pleasure in doing harm or damage, in accusing others, or in tormenting poor dumb animals. I remember, however, that I once urinated in a saucepan belonging to one of our neighbours, Madame Clot, while she was at church. I declare that, even now, the recollection of this makes me laugh, because Madame Clot, a good woman in other respects, was the most confirmed old grumbler I have ever known. Such is the brief and true story of all my childish offences.

How could I become wicked, when I had nothing but examples of gentleness before my eyes, and none around me but the best people in the world? My father, my aunt, my nurse, my relations, our friends, our neighbours, all who surrounded me, did not, it is true, obey me, but they loved me; and I loved them in return. My wishes were so little excited and so little opposed, that it did not occur to me to have any. I can swear that, until I served under a master, I never knew what a fancy was.

[The tender memory of his aunt, whose singing gave him a fondness for music, is still fresh in his heart.]

Would anyone believe that I, an old dotard, eaten up by cares and troubles, sometime find myself weeping like a child, when I mumble one of those little airs in a voice already broken and trembling? One of them, especially, has come back to me completely, as far as the tune is concerned; the second half of the words, however, has obstinately resisted all my efforts to recall it, although I have an indistinct recollection of the rhymes. Here is the beginning, and all that I can remember of the rest:

> Tircis, je n'ose
> Écouter ton chalumeau
> Sous l'ormeau:
> Car on en cause
> Déjà dans notre hameau.
>
> . . . . . .
> . . . . . un berger
> . . . . s'engager
> . . . . . sans danger
> Et toujours l'épine est sous la rose.

I ask, where is the affecting charm which my heart finds in this song? it is a whim, which I am quite unable to understand; but, be that as it may, it is absolutely impossible for me to sing it through without being interrupted by my tears. I have intended, times without number, to write to Paris to make inquiries concerning the remainder of the words, in case anyone should happen to know them; but I am almost certain that the pleasure which I feel in recalling the air would partly disappear, if it should be proved that others besides my poor aunt Suson have sung it.

Such were my earliest emotions on my entry into life; thus began to form or display itself in me that heart at once so proud and tender, that character so effeminate but yet indomitable, which, ever wavering between timidity and courage, weakness and self-control, has throughout my life made me inconsistent, and has caused abstinence and enjoyment, pleasure and prudence equally to elude my grasp.

[A quarrel leads to the exile of Jean-Jacques' father. The boy is sent, together with Uncle Bernard's son, to board with Pastor Lambercier and his sister, at Bossey. He learns to love the countryside, and a simple life.]

As Mademoiselle Lambercier had the affection of a mother for us, she also exercised the authority of one, and sometimes carried it so far as to inflict upon us the punishment of children when we had deserved it. For some time she was content with threats, and this threat of a punishment that was quite new to me appeared very terrible; but, after it had been carried out, I found the reality less terrible than the expectation; and, what was still more strange, this chastisement made me still more devoted to her who had inflicted it. It needed all the strength of this devotion and all my natural docility to keep myself from doing something which would have deservedly brought upon me a repetition of it; for I had found in the pain, even in the disgrace, a mixture of sensuality which had left me less afraid than desirous of experiencing it again from the same hand. No doubt some precocious sexual instinct was mingled with this feeling, for the same chastisement inflicted by her brother would not have seemed to me at all pleasant. But, considering his disposition, there was little cause to fear the substitution; and if I kept myself from deserving punishment, it was solely for fear of displeasing Mademoiselle Lambercier; for, so great is the power exercised over me by kindness, even by that which is due to the senses, that it has always controlled the latter in my heart.

The repetition of the offence, which I avoided without being afraid of it, occurred without any fault of mine, that is to say, of my will, and I may say that I profited by it without any qualm of conscience. But this second time was also the last; for Mademoiselle Lambercier, who had no doubt noticed something which convinced her that the punishment did not have the desired effect, declared that it tired her too much, and that she would abandon it. Until then we had slept in her room, sometimes even in her bed during the winter. Two days afterwards we were put to sleep in another room, and from that time I had the honour, which I would gladly have dispensed with, of being treated by her as a big boy.

Who would believe that this childish punishment, inflicted upon me when only eight years old by a young woman of thirty, disposed of my tastes, my desires, my passions, and my own self for the remainder of my life, and that in a manner exactly contrary to that which should have been the natural result? When my feelings were once inflamed, my desires so went astray that, limited to what I had already felt, they did not trouble themselves to look for anything else. In spite of my hot blood, which has been inflamed with sensuality almost from my birth, I kept myself free from every taint until the age when the coldest and most sluggish temperaments begin to develop. In torments for a long time, without knowing why, I devoured with burning glances all the pretty women I met; my imagination unceasingly recalled them to me, only to make use of them in my own fashion, and to make of them so many Mlles. Lambercier.

Even after I had reached years of maturity, this curious taste, always abiding with me and carried to depravity and even frenzy, preserved my morality, which it might naturally have been expected to destroy. If ever a bringing-up was chaste and modest, assuredly mine was. My three aunts were not only models of propriety, but reserved to a degree which has long since been unknown amongst women. My father, a man of pleasure, but a gallant of the old school, never said a word, even in the presence of women whom he loved more than others, which would have brought a blush to a maiden's cheek; and the respect due to children has never been so much insisted upon as in my family and in my presence. In this respect I found M. Lambercier equally careful; and an excellent servant was dismissed for having used a somewhat too free expression in our presence. Until I was a young man, I not only had no distinct idea of the union of the sexes, but the confused notion which I had regarding it never presented itself to me except in a hateful and disgusting form. For common prostitutes I felt a loathing which has never been effaced: the sight of a profligate always filled me with contempt, even with affright. My horror of debauchery became thus pronounced ever since the day when, walking to Little Sacconex by a hollow way, I saw on both sides holes in the ground, where I was told that these creatures carried on their intercourse. The thought of the one always brought back to my mind the copulation of dogs, and the bare recollection was sufficient to disgust me.

This tendency of my bringing-up, in itself adapted to delay the first outbreaks of an inflammable temperament, was assisted, as I have already said, by the direction which the first indications of sensuality took in my case. Busying my imagination solely with what I had actually felt, in spite of most uncomfortable effervescence of blood, I knew how to turn my desires only in the direction of that kind of pleasure with which I was acquainted, without ever going as far as that which had been made hateful to me, and which, without my having the least suspicion of it, was so closely related to the other. In my foolish fancies, in my erotic frenzies, in the extravagant acts to which they sometimes led me, I had recourse in my imagination to the assistance of the other sex, without ever thinking that it was serviceable for any purpose than that for which I was burning to make use of it.

In this manner, then, in spite of an ardent, lascivious and precocious temperament, I passed the age of puberty without desiring, even without knowing of any other sensual pleasures than those of which Mademoiselle Lambercier had most innocently given me the idea; and when, in course of time, I became a man, that which should have destroyed me again preserved me. My old childish taste, instead of disappearing, became so associated with the other, that I could never banish it from the desires kindled by my senses. This madness, joined to my natural shyness, has always made me very unenterprising with women, for want of courage to say all or power to do all, inasmuch as the kind of enjoyment, of which the other was only for me the final consummation could neither be appropriated by him who longed for it, nor guessed by her who was able to bestow it. Thus I have spent my life in idle longing, without saying a word, in the presence of those whom I loved most. Too bashful to declare my taste, I at least satisfied it in situations which had reference to it and kept up the idea of it. To lie at the feet of an imperious mistress, to obey her commands, to ask her forgiveness—this was for me a sweet enjoyment; and, the more my lively imagination heated my blood, the more I presented the appearance of a bashful lover. It may be easily imagined that this manner of making love does not lead to very speedy results, and is not very dangerous to the virtue of those who are its object. For this reason I have rarely possessed, but have none the less enjoyed myself in my own way—that is to say, in imagination. Thus it has happened that my senses, in harmony with my timid disposition and my romantic spirit, have kept my sentiments pure and my morals blameless, owing to the very tastes which, combined with a little more impudence, might have plunged me into the most brutal sensuality.

I have taken the first and most difficult step in the dark and dirty labyrinth of my confessions. It is easier to admit that which is criminal than that which is ridiculous and makes a man feel ashamed. Henceforth I am sure of myself; after having ventured to say so much, I can shrink from nothing. One may judge what such confessions have cost me, from the fact that, during the whole course of my life, I have never dared to declare my folly to those whom I loved with the frenzy of a passion which deprived me of sight and hearing, which robbed me of my senses and caused me to tremble all over with a convulsive movement. I have never brought myself, even when on most intimate terms, to ask women to grant me the only favour of all which was wanting. This never happened to me but once—in my childhood, with a girl of my own age; even then, it was she who first proposed it.

While thus going back to the first traces of my inner life, I find elements which sometimes appear incompatible, and yet have united in order to produce with vigour a simple and uniform effect; and I find others which, although apparently the same, have formed combinations so different, owing to the co-operation of certain circumstances, that one would never imagine that these elements were in any way connected. Who, for instance, would believe that one of the most powerful movements of my soul was tempered in the same spring from which a stream of sensuality and softness has entered my blood? Without leaving the subject of which I have just spoken, I shall produce by means of it a very different impression.

One day I was learning my lesson by myself in the room next to the kitchen. The servant had put Mademoiselle Lambercier's combs in front of the fire-place to dry. When she came back to fetch them, she found one with a whole row of teeth broken. Who was to blame for the damage? No one except myself had entered the room. On being questioned, I denied that I had touched the comb. M. and Mademoiselle Lambercier both began to admonish, to press, and to threaten me; I obstinately persisted in my denial; but the evidence was too strong, and outweighed all my protestations, although it was the first time that I had been found to lie so boldly. The matter was regarded as serious, as in fact it deserved to be. The mischievousness, the falsehood, the obstinacy appeared equally deserving of punishment; but this time it was not by Mademoiselle Lambercier that chastisement was inflicted. My uncle Bernard was written to, and he came. My poor cousin was accused of another equally grave offence; we were involved in the same punishment. It was terrible. Had they wished to look for the remedy in the evil itself and to deaden forever my depraved senses, they could not have set to work better, and for a long time my senses left me undisturbed.

They could not draw from me the desired confession. Although I was several times brought up before them and reduced to a pitiable condition, I remained unshaken. I would have endured death, and made up my mind to do so. Force was obliged to yield to the diabolical obstinacy of a child—as they called my firmness. At last I emerged from this cruel trial, utterly broken, but triumphant.

It is now nearly fifty years since this incident took place, and I have no fear of being punished again for the same thing. Well, then, I declare in the sight of heaven that I was innocent of the offence, that I neither broke nor touched the comb, that I never went near the fire-place, and had never even thought of doing so. It would be useless to ask me how the damage was done: I do not know, and I cannot understand; all that I know for certain is, that I had nothing to do with it.

Imagine a child, shy and obedient in ordinary life, but fiery, proud, and unruly in his passions: a child who had always been led by the voice of reason and always treated with gentleness, justice, and consideration, who had not even a notion of injustice, and who for the first time becomes acquainted with so terrible an example of it on the part of the very people whom he most loves and respects! What an upset of ideas! what a disturbance of feelings! what revolution in his heart, in his brain, in the whole of his little intellectual and moral being! Imagine all this, I say, if possible. As for myself, I feel incapable of disentangling and following up the least trace of what then took place within me.

I had not yet sense enough to feel how much appearances were against me, and to put myself in the place of the others. I kept to my own place, and all that I felt was the harshness of a frightful punishment for an offence which I had not committed. The bodily pain, although severe, I felt but little: all I felt was indignation, rage, despair. My cousin, whose case was almost the same, and who had been punished for an involuntary mistake as if it had been a premeditated act, following my example, flew into a rage, and worked himself up to the same pitch of excitement as myself. Both in the same bed, we embraced each other with convulsive transports: we felt suffocated; and when at length our young hearts, somewhat relieved, were able to vent their wrath, we sat upright in bed and began to shout, times without number, with all our might: *Carnifex! carnifex! carnifex!**

While I write these words, I feel that my pulse beats faster; those moments will always be present to me though I should live a hundred thousand years. That first feeling of violence and injustice has remained so deeply graven on my soul, that all the ideas connected with it bring back to me my first emotion; and this feeling, which, in its origin, had reference only to myself, has become so strong in itself and so completely detached from all personal interest, that, when I see or hear of any act of injustice—whoever is the victim of it, and wherever it is committed—my heart kindles with rage, as if the effect of it recoiled upon myself. When I read of the cruelties of a ferocious tyrant, the crafty atrocities of a rascally priest, I would gladly set out to plunge a dagger into the heart of such wretches, although I had to die for it a hundred times. I have often put myself in a perspiration, pursuing or stoning a cock, a cow, a dog, or any animal which I saw tormenting another merely because it felt itself the stronger. This impulse may be natural to me, and I believe that it is; but the profound impression left upon me by the first injustice I suffered was too long and too strongly connected with it, not to have greatly strengthened it.

With the above incident the tranquillity of my childish life was over. From that moment I ceased to enjoy a pure happiness, and even at the present day I feel that the recollection of the charms of my childhood ceases there. We remained a few months longer at Bossey. We were there, as the first man

* Executioner.

is represented to us—still in the earthly paradise, but we no longer enjoyed it; in appearance our condition was the same, in reality it was quite a different manner of existence. Attachment, respect, intimacy, and confidence no longer united pupils and guides: we no longer regarded them as gods, who were able to read in our hearts; we became less ashamed of doing wrong and more afraid of being accused; we began to dissemble, to be insubordinate, to lie. All the vices of our age corrupted our innocence and threw a veil of ugliness over our amusements. Even the country lost in our eyes that charm of gentleness and simplicity which goes to the heart. It appeared to us lonely and sombre: it seemed as if it were covered with a veil which concealed its beauties from our eyes. We ceased to cultivate our little gardens, our plants, our flowers. We no longer scratched up the ground gently, or cried with joy when we saw the seed which we had sown beginning to sprout. We were disgusted with the life, and the others were disgusted with us; my uncle took us away, and we separated from M. and Mademoiselle Lambercier, having had enough of each other, and feeling but little regret at the separation.

Nearly thirty years have passed since I left Bossey, without my recalling to mind my stay there with any connected and pleasurable recollections; but, now that I have passed the prime of life and am approaching old age, I feel these same recollections springing up again while others disappear; they stamp themselves upon my memory with features, the charm and strength of which increase daily, as if, feeling life already slipping away, I were endeavouring to grasp it again by its commencement. The most trifling incidents of that time please me, simply because they belong to that period. I remember all the details of place, persons, and time. I see the maid or the manservant busy in the room, a swallow darting through the window, a fly settling on my hand while I was saying my lesson: I see the whole arrangement of the room in which we used to live; M. Lambercier's study on the right, a copperplate engraving of all the Popes, a barometer, a large almanack hanging on the wall, the raspberry bushes which, growing in a garden situated on very high ground facing the back of the

house, shaded the window and sometimes forced their way
through it. I am quite aware that the reader does not want
to know all this; but I am bound to tell him. Why have I not
the courage to relate to him in like manner all the trifling
anecdotes of that happy time, which still make me tremble
with joy when I recall them? Five or six in particular—but let
us compromise. I will spare you the five, but I wish to tell
you one, only one, provided that you will permit me to tell
it in as much detail as possible, in order to prolong my enjoyment.

If I only had your pleasure in view, I might choose the story
of Mademoiselle Lambercier's backside, which, owing to an
unfortunate somersault at the bottom of the meadow, was
exhibited in full view to the King of Sardinia, who happened
to be passing by; but that of the walnut-tree on the terrace is
more amusing for me who took an active part in it, whereas
I was merely a spectator of the somersault; besides, I declare
that I found absolutely nothing to laugh at in an accident
which, although comic in itself, alarmed me for the safety of
a person whom I loved as a mother and, perhaps, even more.

[Lambercier plants a walnut-tree. Rousseau and his cousin
plant their own tree, and divert some of their uncle's irrigation
water. But their delight leads to discovery, and destruction of
the tree. Two years at Bossey° are followed by three more at
Uncle Bernard's house in Geneva, in close friendship with his
cousin, whom he defended against the other urchins. In 1723
Rousseau is put out to apprenticeship. He is dismissed from
a lawyer's office as an incompetent "jackass." Next he is sent
to an engraver.]

[1723–1728.]—Thus the most valuable time of my boyhood
was wasted in follies, before my future career had been decided upon.

My new master, M. Ducommun, was a rough and violent
young man, who in a short time succeeded in tarnishing all
the brightness of my childhood, stupefying my loving and
lively nature, and reducing me, in mind as well as in position,

* In reality less than a year. Rousseau's memory is at fault. The whole
episode took place in 1722, not 1724.

to a real state of apprenticeship. My Latin, my antiquities, my history, were all for a long time forgotten; I did not even remember that there had ever been any Romans in the world. My father, when I went to see him, no longer found in me his idol; for the ladies I was no longer the gallant Jean-Jacques; and I felt so certain myself that the Lamberciers would not have recognised their pupil in me, that I was ashamed to pay them a visit, and have never seen them since. The vilest tastes, the lowest street-blackguardism took the place of my simple amusements and effaced even the remembrance of them. I must, in spite of a most upright training, have had a great propensity to degenerate; for the change took place with great rapidity. . . .

My master's tyranny at length made the work, of which I should have been very fond, altogether unbearable, and filled me with vices which I should otherwise have hated, such as lying, idleness and thieving. The recollection of the alteration produced in me by that period of my life has taught me, better than anything else, the difference between filial dependence and abject servitude. Naturally shy and timid, no fault was more foreign to my disposition than impudence; but I had enjoyed an honourable liberty, which hitherto had only been gradually restrained, and at length disappeared altogether. I was bold with my father, unrestrained with M. Lambercier, and modest with my uncle; I became timid with my master, and from that moment I was a lost child. Accustomed to perfect equality in my intercourse with my superiors, knowing no pleasure which was not within my reach, seeing no dish of which I could not have a share, having no desire which I could not have openly expressed, and carrying my heart upon my lips—it is easy to judge what I was bound to become, in a house in which I did not venture to open my mouth, where I was obliged to leave the table before the meal was half over, and the room as soon as I had nothing more to do there; where, incessantly fettered to my work, I saw only objects of enjoyment for others and of privation for myself; where the sight of the liberty enjoyed by my master and companions increased the weight of my servitude; where, in disputes about matters as to which I was best informed, I did not venture to open my mouth; where, in short, everything that I saw became for my heart an object of longing, simply because I was deprived of all. From that time my ease of manner, my gaiety, the happy expressions which, in former times, when I had done something wrong, had gained me immunity from punishment—all were gone. I cannot help laughing when I remember how, one evening, at my father's house, having been sent to bed without any supper for some piece of roguery, I passed through the kitchen with my melancholy piece of bread, and, seeing the joint turning on the spit, sniffed at it. All the household was standing round the hearth, and, in passing, I was obliged to say good-night to everybody. When I had gone the round, I winked at the joint, which looked so nice and smelt so good, and could not help bowing to it as well, and saying in a mournful voice, "Good-night, roast beef!" This naïve sally amused them so much that they made me stop to supper. Perhaps it might have had the same effect with my master, but I am sure that it would never have occurred to me, and that I should not have had the courage, to say it in his presence.

In this manner I learnt to covet in silence, to dissemble, to lie, and, lastly, to steal—an idea which, up to that time, had never even entered my mind, and of which since then I have never been able to cure myself completely. Covetousness and weakness always lead in that direction. This explains why all servants are rogues, and why all apprentices ought to be; but the latter, in a peaceful state of equality, where all that they see is within their reach, lose, as they grow up, this disgraceful propensity. Not having had the same advantages, I have not been able to reap the same benefits.

It is nearly always good, but badly directed principles, that make a child take the first step towards evil. In spite of continual privations and temptations, I had been more than a year with my master without being able to make up my mind to take anything, even eatables. My first theft was a matter of obliging some one else, but it opened the door to others, the motive of which was not so praiseworthy.

[To please an older companion, Rousseau steals asparagus for him to sell. He gets nothing for it.]

And yet, if I had been caught, what blows, abuse, and cruel treatment should I have had to endure, while the wretch, who would have been sure to give me the lie, would have been believed on his word, and I should have suffered double punishment for having had the impudence to accuse him, seeing that he was a journeyman, while I was only an apprentice! So true it is that, in every condition of life, the strong man who is guilty saves himself at the expense of the innocent who is weak.

In this manner I learned that stealing was not so terrible a thing as I had imagined, and I soon knew how to make such good use of my discovery, that nothing I desired, if it was within my reach, was safe from me. I was not absolutely ill-fed, and abstinence was only rendered difficult to me from seeing that my master observed it so ill himself. The custom of sending young people from the table when the most appetising dishes are brought on appears to me admirably adapted to make them gluttons as well as thieves. In a short time I became both the one and the other; and, as a rule, I came off very well; occasionally, when I was caught, very badly.

I shudder, and at the same time laugh, when I remember an apple hunt which cost me dear. These apples were at the bottom of a storeroom, which was lighted from the kitchen by means of a high grating. One day, when I was alone in the house, I climbed upon the kneading-trough, in order to look at the precious fruit in the garden of the Hesperides, which was out of my reach. I went to fetch the spit to see if I could touch the apples; it was too short. To make it longer, I tied on to it another little spit which was used for small game, for my master was very fond of sport. I thrust several times without success; at last, to my great delight, I felt that I had secured an apple. I pulled very gently; the apple was close to the grating; I was ready to catch hold of it. But who can describe my grief, when I found that it was too large to pass through the bars? How many expedients I tried, to get it through! I had to find supports to keep the spit in its place, a knife long enough to divide the apple, a lath to hold it up. At last I managed to divide it, and hoped to be able to pull the pieces towards me one after the other; but no sooner were they separated than they both fell into the storeroom. Compassionate reader, share my affliction!

I by no means lost courage; but I had lost considerable time. I was afraid of being surprised. I put off a more lucky attempt till the following day, and returned to my work as quietly as if I had done nothing, without thinking of the two tell-tale witnesses in the storeroom.

The next day, finding the opportunity favourable, I made a fresh attempt. I climbed upon my stool, lengthened the spit, adjusted it, and was ready to make a lunge . . . but, unfortunately, the dragon was not asleep; all at once the door of the storeroom opened, my master came out, folded his arms, looked at me, and said, "Courage!" . . . the pen falls from my hand.

In consequence of continuous ill-treatment I soon became less sensitive to it, and regarded it as a kind of compensation for theft, which gave me the right to continue the latter. Instead of looking back and considering the punishment, I looked forward and thought of revenge. I considered that, if I were beaten as a rogue, I was entitled to behave like one. I found that stealing and a flogging went together, and constituted a sort of bargain, and that, if I performed my part, I could safely leave my master to carry out his own. With this idea, I began to steal more quietly than before. I said to myself: "What will be the result? I shall be flogged. Never mind; I am made to be flogged." . . .

I am a man of very strong passions, and, while I am stirred by them, nothing can equal my impetuosity; I forget all discretion, all feelings of respect, fear and decency; I am cynical, impudent, violent and fearless; no feeling of shame keeps me back, no danger frightens me; with the exception of the single object which occupies my thoughts, the universe is nothing to me. But all this lasts only for a moment, and the following moment plunges me into complete annihilation. In my calmer moments I am indolence and timidity itself; everything frightens and discourages me; a fly, buzzing past, alarms me; a word which I have to say, a gesture which I have to make, terrifies my idleness; fear and shame overpower me to such an extent that I would gladly hide myself from the sight of my fellow-creatures. If I have to act, I do not know what to do; if I have to speak, I do not know what to say; if anyone looks at me, I am put out of countenance. When I am strongly moved I sometimes know how to find the right words, but in ordinary conversation I can find absolutely nothing, and my condition is unbearable for the simple reason that I am obliged to speak.

Add to this, that none of my prevailing tastes centre in things that can be bought. I want nothing but unadulterated pleasures, and money poisons all. For instance, I am fond of the pleasures of the table; but, as I cannot endure either the constraint of good society or the drunkenness of the tavern, I can only enjoy them with a friend; alone, I cannot do so, for my imagination then occupies itself with other things, and eating affords me no pleasure. If my heated blood longs for women, my excited heart longs still more for affection. Women who could be bought for money would lose for me all their charms; I even doubt whether it would be in me to make use of them. I find it the same with all pleasures within my reach; unless they cost me nothing, I find them insipid. I only love those enjoyments which belong to no one but the first man who knows how to enjoy them.

Money has never appeared to me as valuable as it is generally considered. More than that, it has never even appeared to me particularly convenient. It is good for nothing in itself; it has to be changed before it can be enjoyed; one is obliged to buy, to bargain, to be often cheated, to pay dearly, to be badly served. I should like something which is good in quality; with my money I am sure to get it bad. If I pay a high price for a fresh egg, it is stale; for a nice piece of fruit, it is unripe; for a girl, she is spoilt. I am fond of good wine, but where am I to get it? At a wine merchant's? Whatever I do, he is sure to poison me. If I really wish to be well served, what trouble and embarrassment it entails! I must have friends, correspondents, give commissions, write, go backwards and forwards, wait, and in the end be often deceived! What trouble with my money! my fear of it is greater than my fondness for good wine.

Times without number, during my apprenticeship and afterwards, I have gone out with the intention of buying some delicacy. Coming to a pastrycook's shop, I notice some women at the counter; I think I can already see them laughing amongst themselves at the little glutton. I go on to a fruiterer's; I eye the fine pears; their smell tempts me. Two or three young people close by me look at me; a man who knows me is standing in front of his shop; I see a girl approaching in the distance: is it the housemaid? My short-sightedness causes all kinds of illusions. I take all the passers-by for acquaintances; everywhere I am intimidated, restrained by some obstacle; my desire increases with my shame, and at last I return home like a fool, consumed with longing, having in my pocket the means of satisfying it, and yet not having had the courage to buy anything.

I should enter into the most insipid details if, in relating how my money was spent by myself or others, I were to describe the embarrassment, the shame, the repugnance, the inconvenience, the annoyances of all kinds which I have always experienced. In proportion as the reader, following the course of my life, becomes acquainted with my real temperament, he will understand all this, without my taking the trouble to tell him.

This being understood, it will be easy to comprehend one of my apparent inconsistencies—the union of an almost sordid avarice with the greatest contempt for money. It is a piece of furniture in which I find so little convenience, that it never enters my mind to long for it when I have not got it, and that, when I have got it, I keep it for a long time without spending it, for want of knowing how to make use of it in a way to please myself; but if a convenient and agreeable opportunity presents itself, I make such good use of it that my purse is empty before I know it. Besides this, one need not expect to find in me that curious characteristic of misers—that of spending for the sake of ostentation; on the contrary, spend in secret for the sake of enjoyment; far from glorying in my expenditure, I conceal it. I feel so strongly that money is of no use to me, that I am almost ashamed to have any, still more to make use of it. If I had ever had an income sufficient to live comfortably upon, I am certain that I should never have been tempted to be a miser. I should have spent it all, without attempting to increase it; but my precarious circumstances made me careful. I worship freedom; I abhor restraint, trouble, dependence. As long as the money in my purse lasts, it assures my independence; it relieves me of the trouble of finding expedients to replenish it, a necessity which always inspired me with dread; but the fear of seeing it exhausted makes me hoard it carefully. The money which a man possesses is the instrument of freedom; that which we eagerly pursue is the instrument of slavery. Therefore I hold fast to that which I have, and desire nothing.

My disinterestedness is, therefore, nothing but laziness; the pleasure of possession is not worth the trouble of acquisition. In like manner, my extravagance is nothing but idleness; when the opportunity of spending agreeably presents itself, it cannot be too profitably employed. Money tempts me less than things, because between money and the possession of the desired object there is always an intermediary, whereas between the thing itself and the enjoyment of it there is none. If I see the thing, it tempts me; if I only see the means of gaining possession of it, it does not. For this reason I have committed thefts, and even now I sometimes pilfer trifles which tempt me, and which I prefer to take rather than to ask for; but neither when a child nor a grown-up man do I ever remember to have robbed anyone of a farthing, except on one occasion, fifteen years ago, when I stole seven *livres* ten *sous*. The incident is worth recording, for it contains a most extraordinary mixture of folly and impudence, which I should have found difficulty in believing if it concerned anyone but myself.

It took place in Paris. I was walking with M. de Francueil in the Palais-Royal about five o'clock. He pulled out his watch, looked at it, and said: "Let us go to the Opera." I

agreed; we went. He took two tickets for the amphitheatr
gave me one, and went on in front with the other. I follow
him; he went in. Entering after him, I found the door locke
I looked, and seeing everybody standing up, thought it wou
be easy to lose myself in the crowd, or at any rate to make
de Francueil believe that I had lost myself. I went out, to
back my check, then my money, and went off, without thin
ing that as soon as I had reached the door everybody h
taken their seats, and that M. de Francueil clearly saw th
I was no longer there.*

As nothing was ever more foreign to my disposition th
such behaviour, I mention it in order to show that there a
moments of semi-delirium during which men must not
judged by their actions. I did not exactly want to steal t
money, I wanted to steal the employment of it; the less of
theft it was, the greater its disgracefulness.

I should never finish these details if I were to follow all t
paths along which, during my apprenticeship, I descend
from the sublimity of heroism to the depths of worthlessne
And yet, although I adopted the vices of my position, I cou
not altogether acquire a taste for them. I wearied of t
amusements of my companions; and when excessive restrai
had rendered work unendurable to me, I grew tired of ever
thing. This renewed my taste for reading, which I had
some time lost. This reading, for which I stole time fr
my work, became a new offense which brought new puni
ment upon me. The taste for it, provoked by constraint, l
came a passion, and soon a regular madness. La Tribu,
well-known lender of books, provided me with all kinds
literature. Good or bad, all were alike to me; I had no choi
and read everything with equal avidity. I read at the wo
table, I read on my errands, I read in the water-closet, a
forgot myself for hours together; my head became giddy w
reading; I could do nothing else. My master watched m
surprised me, beat me, took away my books. How many v
umes were torn, burnt, and thrown out of the window! he

* According to George Sand, M. de Francueil, who was her grandfath
always denied the truth of this story.

many works were left in odd volumes in La Tribu's stock! When I had no more money to pay her, I gave her my shirts, neckties and clothes; my three sous of pocket-money were regularly taken to her every Sunday. . . .

In consequence of quarrels, blows, and secret and ill-chosen reading, my disposition became savage and taciturn; my mind became altogether perverted, and I lived like a misanthrope. However, if my good taste did not keep me from silly and insipid books, my good fortune preserved me from such as were filthy and licentious; not that La Tribu, a woman in all respects most accommodating, would have made any scruple about lending them to me; but, in order to increase their importance, she always mentioned them to me with an air of mystery which had just the effect of making me refuse them, as much from disgust as from shame; and chance aided my modest disposition so well, that I was more than thirty years old before I set eyes upon any of those dangerous books which a fine lady finds inconvenient because they can only be read with one hand.

In less than a year I exhausted La Tribu's little stock, and want of occupation, during my spare time, became painful to me. I had been cured of my childish and knavish propensities by my passion for reading, and even by the books I read, which, although ill-chosen and frequently bad, filled my heart with nobler sentiments than those with which my sphere of life had inspired me. Disgusted with everything that was within my reach, and feeling that everything which might have tempted me was too far removed from me, I saw nothing possible which might have flattered my heart. My excited senses had long clamoured for an enjoyment, the object of which I could not even imagine. I was as far removed from actual enjoyment as if I had been sexless; and, already fully developed and sensitive, I sometimes thought of my crazes, but saw nothing beyond them. In this strange situation, my restless imagination entered upon an occupation which saved me from myself and calmed my growing sensuality. This consisted in feeding myself upon the situations which had interested me in the course of my reading, in recalling them, in varying them, in combining them, in making them so truly my own that I became one of the persons who filled my imagination, and always saw myself in the situations most agreeable to my taste; and that, finally, the fictitious state in which I succeeded in putting myself made me forget my actual state with which I was so dissatisfied. This love of imaginary objects, and the readiness with which I occupied myself with them, ended by disgusting me with everything around me, and decided that liking for solitude which has never left me. In the sequel we shall see more than once the curious effects of this disposition, apparently so gloomy and misanthropic, but which is really due to a too affectionate, too loving and too tender heart, which, being unable to find any in existence resembling it, is obliged to nourish itself with fancies. . . .

In this manner I reached my sixteenth year, restless, dissatisfied with myself and everything, without any of the tastes of my condition of life, without any of the pleasures of my age, consumed by desires of the object of which I was ignorant, weeping without any cause for tears, sighing without knowing why—in short, tenderly caressing my chimeras, since I saw nothing around me which counterbalanced them. On Sundays, my fellow-apprentices came to fetch me after service to go and amuse myself with them. I would gladly have escaped from them if I had been able; but, once engaged in their amusements, I became more excited and went further than any of them; it was as difficult to set me going as to stop me. Such was always my disposition. During our walks outside the city I always went further than any of them without thinking about my return, unless others thought of it for me. Twice I was caught: the gates were shut before I could get back. The next day I was treated as may be imagined; the second time I was promised such a reception if it ever happened again, that I resolved not to run the risk of it; yet this third time, so dreaded, came to pass. My watchfulness was rendered useless by a confounded Captain Minutoli, who always shut the gate at which he was on guard half-an-hour before the others. I was returning with two companions. About half a league from the city I heard the retreat sounded:

I doubled my pace: I heard the tattoo beat, and ran with all my might. I arrived out of breath and bathed in perspiration; my heart beat; from a distance I saw the soldiers at their posts; I rushed up and cried out with a voice half-choked. It was too late! Twenty paces from the outposts, I saw the first bridge raised. I shuddered when I saw those terrible horns rising in the air—a sinister and fatal omen of the destiny which that moment was opening for me.

[Frightened, tired of punishments, Jean-Jacques decides to run away.]

Before I abandon myself to the fatality of my lot, allow me to turn my eyes for a moment upon the destiny which, in the nature of things, would have awaited me if I had fallen into the hands of a better master. Nothing was more suitable to my disposition or better adapted to make me happy than the quiet and obscure lot of a respectable artisan, especially of a certain class such as that of the engravers of Geneva. Such a position, sufficiently lucrative to afford a comfortable livelihood, but not sufficiently so to lead to fortune, would have limited my ambition for the rest of my days, and, leaving me an honourable leisure to cultivate modest tastes, would have confined me within my own sphere, without offering me the means of getting out of it. My imaginative powers were rich enough to beautify all callings with their chimeras, and strong enough to transport me, so to speak, at will from one to another; so it would have been immaterial to me in what position I actually found myself. It could not have been so far from the place where I was, to my first castle in the air, that I could not have taken up my abode there without any difficulty. From this alone it followed that the simplest vocation, that which involved the least trouble and anxiety, that which allowed the greatest mental freedom, was the one which suited me best: and that was exactly my own. I should have passed a peaceful and quiet life, such as my disposition required, in the bosom of my religion, my country, my family and my friends, in the monotony of a profession that suited my taste, and in a society after my own heart. I should have been a good Christian, a good citizen, a good father of a family, a good friend, a good workman, a good man in every relation of life. I should have loved my position in life, perhaps honoured it; and, having spent a life—simple, indeed, and obscure, but calm and serene—I should have died peacefully in the bosom of my family. Though, doubtless, soon forgotten, I should at least have been regretted as long as anyone remembered me.

Instead of that—what picture am I going to draw? Let us not anticipate the sorrows of my life; I shall occupy my readers more than enough with this melancholy subject.

BOOK TWO

[1728-1731]

HOWEVER mournful the moment, when terror suggested to me the idea of flight, had appeared—the moment when I carried it into execution appeared equally delightful. While still a child, to leave my country, my parents, my means of support, my resources; to give up an apprenticeship half-served, without a sufficient knowledge of my trade to earn my livelihood; to abandon myself to the horrors of want, without any means of saving myself from it; to expose myself, at the age of innocence and weakness, to all the temptations of vice and despair; to seek, in the distance, suffering, error, snares, servitude, and death, beneath a yoke far more unbending than that which I had been unable to endure—this was what I was going to do, this was the prospect which I ought to have considered. How different was that which my fancy painted! The independence which I believed I had gained was the only feeling which moved me. Free, and my own master, I believed I could do everything, attain to everything; I had only to launch myself forth, to mount and fly through the air. I entered the vast world with a feeling of security; it was to be filled with the fame of my achievements; at every step I was to find festivities, treasures, adventures, friends ready to serve me, mistresses eager to please me; I had only to show myself, to engage the attention of the whole world—and yet not the whole world; to a certain extent I could dispense with it, and did not want so much. Charming society was enough for me, without troubling myself about the rest. In my modesty I limited myself to a narrow, but delightfully select circle, in which my sovereignty was assured. A single castle was the limit of my ambition. As the favourite of the lord and the lady, as the lover of the daughter, as the friend of the son and protector of the neighbours, I was content—I wanted no more.

[Rousseau falls into the hands of a Catholic priest, M. de Pontverre, who directs him to the house of a new convert, Madame de Warens, at Annecy.]

At last I arrived: I saw Madame de Warens. That epoch of my life decided my character; I cannot bring myself to pass lightly over it. I was in the middle of my sixteenth year. Without being what is called a handsome lad, I was well set up, I had a pretty foot, a fine leg, an easy manner, lively features, a pretty little mouth, black hair and eyebrows, small and even sunken eyes, which, however, vigorously darted forth the fire with which my blood was kindled. Unhappily, I knew nothing of that, and it has never occurred to me during my life to think about my personal appearance except when it was too late to profit by it. With the timidity of my age was united that of a very loving disposition, always troubled by the fear of displeasing. Besides, although my mind was tolerably well formed, I had never seen the world, and was entirely wanting in manners, and my knowledge, far from supplementing this defect, only served to intimidate me still more by making me feel how sadly I needed them.

Fearing, therefore, that my first appearance would not prejudice Madame de Warens in my favour, I had recourse to other expedients. I composed a beautiful letter in oratorical style, in which, intermingling phrases out of books with the language of an apprentice, I displayed all my eloquence in order to gain her goodwill. I enclosed M. de Pontverre's letter in my own, and set out for the dreaded interview. Madame de Warens was not at home. I was told that she had just gone to church. It was Palm-Sunday in 1728. I ran after her. I saw her; I overtook her; I addressed her. I ought to remember the spot. Since then I have often wetted it with my tears and covered it with my kisses. I should like to surround this happy spot with a railing of gold. I should like to draw upon it the homage of the world. Whoever loves to honour the monuments of the salvation of men should only approach them on his knees.

It was in a passage behind her house, leading between a brook on the right, which separated the house from the garden, and the court wall on the left, through a back-gate to the Franciscan church. Just as she was going to enter, Madame de Warens, hearing my voice, turned round. How did the sight of her strike me! I had pictured to myself an old, grim, religious enthusiast; in my opinion, M. de Pontverre's pious lady could be nothing. else. Instead, I beheld a face full of charm, beautiful blue eyes—full of gentleness—a dazzling complexion, the contour of an enchanting bosom. Nothing escaped the rapid glance of the young proselyte—for at that moment I became hers, feeling convinced that a religion preached by such apostles must inevitably lead to paradise. With a smile, she took the letter which I presented to her with a trembling hand, opened it, glanced at that of M. de Pontverre, returned to mine, read it through, and would have read it again, had not her servant reminded her that it was time to go in. "Well, my child," she said to me in a tone which made me tremble, "so you are wandering about the country at your age; that is indeed a pity." Then, without waiting for me to answer, she added, "Go and wait for me; tell them to give you some breakfast. After mass I will come and talk to you."

[Madame de Warens was twelve years older than Jean-Jacques. He relates her earlier adventures and describes her character.]

It was a question what was to become of me; and, in order to discuss my future more at leisure, she kept me to dinner. It was the first meal in my life at which my appetite failed me;

and her maid, who waited upon us, said that I was the first traveller of my age and class that she had ever seen in such a condition. This remark, which did me no harm in the eyes of her mistress, struck home to a great lout who was dining with us, and who devoured by himself quite a respectable dinner for six. As for myself, I was in a state of rapture which did not allow me to eat. My heart fed upon an entirely new feeling, with which my whole being was filled, and which left me no inclination for doing anything else.

Madame de Warens wanted to know the details of my little history; and in relating them I recovered all the fire and vivacity which I had lost during my apprenticeship. The more I interested this excellent soul in my favour, the more she lamented the lot to which I intended to expose myself. She did not venture to advise me to return to Geneva; in her position that would have been an act of treason to the Catholic faith; and she knew only too well how she was watched and how her words were weighed. But she spoke to me so touchingly of my father's affliction, that it was easy to see that she would have approved of my going to console him. She did not know how strongly, without knowing it, she was pleading against herself. I think I have already said that my mind was made up; the more eloquent and persuasive her words, the more they went to my heart, the less I was able to make up my mind to separate from her. I felt that to return to Geneva would be to put an almost insurmountable barrier between herself and me, unless I again took the step which I had already taken, and by which it was better to abide once and for all. I accordingly remained firm. Madame de Warens, seeing that her efforts were unavailing, did not persist in them, to avoid compromising herself, but she said to me, with a look of compassion, "Poor little one, you must go where God calls you; but when you are grown up, you will think of me." I believe she herself had no idea how cruelly this prediction was to be fulfilled.

[It is decided that Rousseau will journey to Turin, to be received at a hospice for Catholic converts.]

My father was not only a man of honour, he was a man of

proved uprightness, and he had one of those strong souls which are capable of great virtues; in addition to which, he was a good father, especially towards myself. He loved me very tenderly, but he also loved his pleasures, and, since I had lived apart from him, other tastes had rendered his paternal affection somewhat lukewarm. He had married again at Nyon; and although his wife was no longer of an age to present me with brothers, she had relations. This created another family, other aims, a new establishment, which no longer so frequently recalled the memory of myself. My father was growing old, and had nothing to live upon; but my brother and myself had a small property from our mother, the interest of which could be claimed by my father during our absence. This idea did not present itself to him directly, and by no means prevented him from doing his duty; but it exercised a secret influence without his being aware of it, and sometimes moderated his zeal, which he would have pushed further had it not been for that. That, I believe, was the reason why, having originally gone to Annecy to find me out, he did not follow me as far as Chambéri, where he would have been morally certain to find me. That again was the reason why, when I went to pay him a visit, as I frequently did after my flight, he always received me with the caresses of a father, but without making any serious efforts to keep me with him.

This behaviour on the part of a father, whose tenderness and uprightness I knew so well, led me to reflections upon myself, which have in no small degree contributed to keep my heart in a healthy condition. From these I have drawn the great moral lesson, perhaps the only one of any practical value, to avoid those situations of life which bring our duties into conflict with our interests, and which show us our own advantage in the misfortunes of others; for it is certain that, in such situations, however sincere our love of virtue, we must, sooner or later, inevitably grow weak without perceiving it, and become unjust and wicked in act, without having ceased to be just and good in our hearts.

This principle, deeply imprinted on the bottom of my

heart, which, although somewhat late, in practice guided my whole conduct, is one of those which have caused me to appear a very strange and foolish creature in the eyes of the world, and, above all, amongst my acquaintances. I have been reproached with wanting to pose as an original, and different from others. In reality, I have never troubled about acting like other people or differently from them. I sincerely desired to do what was right. I withdrew, as far as it lay in my power, from situations which opposed my interests to those of others, and might, consequently, inspire me with a secret, though involuntary, desire of injuring them.

Two years ago my Lord Marshal wanted to put my name in his will; I strongly opposed this. I told him that I would not for the world know that my name was down in anyone's will, least of all in his. He gave in; but insisted upon bestowing upon me a pension for life, to which I offered no opposition. It will be said that I gain by this alteration; that may be so, but I know, oh! father and benefactor, that, if I unhappily survive you, in losing you I have everything to lose and nothing to gain.

That, in my opinion, is the true philosophy, the only philosophy which is really suited for the human heart. I am more impressed every day by its profound solidity, and in all my recent writings I have presented it under various aspects; but the public is superficial, and has not known how to recognise it. If, after I have finished my present task, I live long enough to undertake another, I propose to give, in the sequel to "Émile,"* so attractive and striking an example of this maxim, that the reader will be compelled to notice it. But enough reflections for a traveller; it is time to continue my journey!

[The leisurely journey to Turin turned out to be a delightful experience.]

This recollection has left me the liveliest taste for everything connected with it, especially for mountains and walks. I have never journeyed on foot except in my younger days, and then always with the greatest pleasure. Duties, business,

* In the "New Héloïse," Part III, letter xx.

luggage, soon obliged me to play the gentleman and take a carriage; gnawing cares, perplexities, and discomfort got in with me, and from that moment, instead of feeling, as before, nothing but the pleasure of travelling, my only anxiety was to reach the end of my journey. For a long time I endeavoured to find in Paris two companions of the same tastes as myself willing to spend fifty *louis* of their money and a year of their time upon a walking tour through Italy with me, with only a single lad to carry our travelling-bags. Many appeared enchanted with the idea, but in reality considered it as nothing but a castle in the air, only fit to talk about without any idea of putting it into execution. I remember that Diderot and Grimm, with whom I once discussed the idea with enthusiasm, at last became enamoured of it. Once I thought the matter settled, but it all ended in their wanting to make a journey on paper, in which Grimm found nothing so delightful as making Diderot commit a number of impieties and handing me over to the inquisition in his stead.

My regret at arriving so soon at Turin was lessened by the pleasure of seeing a large city, and by the hope of soon playing a part worthy of myself; for already the fumes of ambition were mounting to my brain; already I regarded myself as infinitely raised above my former condition of apprentice, and I was far from suspecting that, in a short time, I was destined to fall far below it.

I had some letters. I presented them, and was immediately conducted to the hospice for catechumens, to be instructed in the religion with which I was to purchase my livelihood. On my arrival, I beheld a large gate with iron bars, which was double-locked behind me as soon as I had passed through it. This introduction struck me as more imposing than agreeable, and was beginning to afford me food for reflection, when I was conducted into a tolerably large room. All its furniture consisted of a wooden altar, surmounted by a large crucifix, at the end of the room, in front of which stood four or five chairs, also made of wood, which looked as if they had been polished, but in reality had become shiny merely from constant use and rubbing. In this assembly-room were four or five frightful villains—my fellow-students—who seemed to be rather the devil's constables than aspirants to the honour of sons of God. Two of these rascals were Slavònians, who called themselves Jews or Moors, and, as they confessed to me, spent their life in wandering through Spain and Italy, embracing Christianity and submitting to be baptised where they found it worth their while. Another iron door was then thrown open, which divided into two a large balcony running along the courtyard. Through this door our sisters entered, catechumens who, like myself, were to be born again, not by means of baptism, but by a solemn abjuration of their faith. They were certainly the greatest sluts and the most disgusting vagabonds who ever contaminated the sheepfold of the Lord. Only one appeared to me pretty and attractive; she was about my own age, perhaps two or three years older. She had roguish eyes, which sometimes met mine. This inspired me with a desire to make her acquaintance; but, during nearly two months, which she spent in the house after my arrival— she had already been there three months—I found it absolutely impossible to speak to her, so strictly had she been recommended to the care of our old jaileress, and so carefully was she watched by the holy missionary, who laboured with more zeal than diligence to convert her. She must have been extremely dull, although she did not appear so, for never did tuition require so long a time. The holy man always found her unfit for the act of abjuration; but she grew weary of her confinement, and declared that she wanted to leave—Christian or no Christian. They were obliged to take her at her word, while she still showed herself ready to become one, for fear she might become refractory and refuse.

The little community was assembled in honour of the newcomer. A short address was delivered to us, in which I was exhorted to consent to respond to the favour which God extended to me, while the others were invited to pray for me and edify me by their example. After this, our virgins returned to their seclusion, and I had time to meditate with astonishment upon my own situation to my heart's content. . . .

If I have said that we ought not to speak about religion to children, if we wish them to possess any, and, further, that they are incapable of knowing God, even according to our ideas, I have drawn this conviction from my observations, not from my own experience, for I knew that no conclusion could be drawn from it in regard to others. Find me Jean-Jacques Rousseaus, six years old, and speak to *them* of God when they are seven; I will guarantee that you run no risk.

I think it will be admitted that, in the case of a child, and even of a man, to have religion means to follow that in which he is born. This faith is sometimes lessened, rarely enlarged; dogmatic belief is one of the fruits of education. Besides this general principle which attached me to the religious creed of my fathers, I had the aversion for Catholicism peculiar to our village, which represented it as a frightful idolatry, and painted its priests in the blackest colours. This feeling was so strong in me, that at first I never looked into the inside of a church, never met a priest in a surplice, never heard the processional bell, without a shudder of terror and alarm, which soon left me in the towns, but has often come upon me again in country parishes, more like those where I had first felt it. It is true that this impression contrasted singularly with the recollections of the caresses which the priests of the environs of Geneva were fond of bestowing upon the children of the city. While the bell announcing supreme unction alarmed me, the bell for mass and vespers reminded me of breakfast, collation, fresh butter, fruit, and milk-food. M. de Pontverre's good dinner still produced a great effect. Thus I had easily driven all such thoughts out of my mind. Seeing papism only in its connection with amusement and good living, I had readily accustomed myself to the idea of living in its midst; but the idea of solemnly going over to the Church of Rome had only presented itself to me for a moment, as possible in a distant future. At the present moment it was no longer possible to deceive myself; I saw with horror the kind of consent which I had given, and its inevitable consequences. The future neophytes around me were not calculated to sustain my courage by their example, and I could not conceal from myself that the holy work, which I intended to carry out, was in the main the action of a bandit; for, young as I was, I felt that, whatever religion might be the true one, I was going to sell my own, and that, even though I made a good choice, in the bottom of my heart I should lie to the Holy Spirit and deserve the contempt of men. The more I thought of it, the more indignant I became with myself; and I sighed over the destiny which had brought me to this pass, as if this destiny had not been my own work. There were moments when these reflections became so strong, that, if I had found the door open for a moment, I should certainly have run away; but this was impossible, and my resolution was not strong enough. Too many secret desires combated it not to overcome it. Besides, my fixed determination not to return to Geneva, shame, the difficulty of crossing the mountains again, the embarrassment of finding myself far from my country, without friends and without resources—all these feelings combined to make me regard my prickings of conscience as a too tardy repentance; I pretended to reproach myself for what I had done, in order to excuse what I was going to do. While aggravating the errors of the past, I regarded the future as their necessary result. Instead of saying to myself, "Nothing is done yet, and you can be innocent if you wish," I said, "Sigh for the crime of which you have made yourself guilty, and which you have made it necessary for yourself to carry out." . . .

The sophism which ruined me, is that common to most men who complain of want of strength when it is already too late to make use of it. Virtue only becomes difficult by our own fault; if we could always be prudent, we should rarely need to be virtuous. But inclinations, easily surmountable, hurry us along without resistance; we yield to trifling temptations, the danger of which we despise. Imperceptibly we fall into perilous situations, from which we could easily have protected ourselves, but from which we can no longer extricate ourselves without heroic efforts which appal us; and at last we fall into the abyss, reproaching God, "Why hast Thou made me so weak?" But, in spite of ourselves, He replies to our consciences, "I have made you too weak to save yourself from the abyss, because I made you strong enough not to fall into it."

I did not exactly resolve to become a Catholic; but, seeing the time still far off, I profited by the occasion to accustom myself gradually to the idea, and in the meantime I hoped for some unforeseen circumstance which would get me out of the difficulty. In order to gain time, I resolved to make the best defence of which I was capable. But soon my vanity relieved me from thinking of my resolution; and, as soon as I observed that I sometimes embarrassed those who desired to instruct me, that was sufficient to make me endeavour to floor them altogether. I even exhibited ridiculous eagerness in this undertaking; for, while they were working upon me, I wanted to work upon them. I honestly believed that I had only to convince them, to make them turn Protestants.

Consequently, they did not find in me nearly as much tractability as they had expected, either in regard to my knowledge or good will. Protestants are generally better instructed than Catholics. This is only natural; the doctrine of the one requires discussion, that of the other submission. The Catholic is obliged to embrace the decision that is put before him; the Protestant must learn to decide for himself. This was well known; but no great difficulties were expected for persons of experience from one of my age and position. Besides, I had not yet received my first Communion, nor received the instructions connected with it; that, too, was known. But what they did not know was that, to make up for this, I had been well taught at M. Lambercier's, and that, in addition, I had by me a little storehouse, very inconvenient for these gentlemen, in the history of the Church and the Empire, which, while living with my father, I had learnt almost by heart, and since then almost forgotten, but which came back to me in proportion as the dispute grew warmer

A little, old, but somewhat venerable priest held the first meeting of all of us together. For my companions this meeting was rather a catechism than a discussion, and he had more to do with instructing them than with removing their objections n my own case it was different. When my turn came, I topped him at every point, and spared him no single difficulty which I was able to throw in his way. This protracted he meeting, and made it very tedious for those who were resent. My old priest spoke much, grew excited, wandered rom his subject, and got himself out of the difficulty by declaring that he did not know French well. The next day, for ear that my indiscreet objections might give offence to my ompanions, I was put into another room with another priest, who was younger and a good speaker—that is to say, a coiner f fine phrases—and satisfied with himself, if ever a teacher vas. I did not, however, allow myself to be too much cowed y his imposing manner; and feeling that, after all, I was ble to hold my own, I proceeded to answer him with tolrable confidence, and to press him on all sides to the best of ay ability. He thought to overwhelm me with St. Augustine, t. Gregory, and the other fathers, but found, to his incredible urprise, that I handled all the fathers nearly as readily as he lid; not that I had ever read them, as neither perhaps had e, but I remembered several passages out of my "Le Sueur"; nd, as soon as he quoted one, without stopping to dispute it, answered it by another from the same Father, which frequently caused him considerable embarrassment. However, in he end he gained the victory, for two reasons. In the first lace, he was the stronger, and, feeling that I was, so to peak, at his mercy, I correctly judged, young as I was, that : would not do to press him—to drive him to extremities; for I aw clearly enough that the little old priest had conceived o great affection for myself or my learning. In the second lace, the young priest was an educated man, while I was ot. This caused him to employ in his manner of argument a aethod which I was unable to follow, and, as soon as he felt imself pushed by some unforeseen objection, he put it off ntil the next day, declaring that I was wandering from the oint. Sometimes he even refused to accept my quotations, eclaring that they were false; and, offering to go and fetch he book for me, defied me to find them. He felt that he did ot risk much, and that, with all my borrowed learning, I was

not sufficiently experienced in handling books, and did n[o]
know enough Latin to find a passage in a large volume, eve[n]
though I might be certain that it was there. I even suspecte[d]
him of making use of the same dishonesty of which he accuse[d]
our ministers, and of sometimes inventing passages, in orde[r]
to extricate himself from a difficulty which embarrassed hi[m]

While these petty disputes about trifles lasted, and the tim[e]
was spent in arguing, mumbling prayers, and doing nothin[g,]
a disgusting little adventure happened to me, which ve[ry]
nearly turned out very badly for me.

There is no soul so vile, no heart so barbarous, that it [is]
not susceptible of some kind of attachment. One of the tw[o]
vagabonds who called themselves Moors conceived an affe[c]
tion for me. He was fond of accosting me, talked to me in h[is]
jargon, rendered me slight services, sometimes gave me pa[rt]
of his food, and frequently kissed me with an ardour whic[h]
was very annoying to me. In spite of the natural alarm whic[h]
I felt at his gingerbread face decorated with a long scar, an[d]
his inflamed countenance which appeared more furious tha[n]
tender, I endured his kisses, saying to myself: "The poor fe[l]
low has conceived a lively friendship for me. I should [be]
wrong to repulse him." He gradually began to take great[er]
liberties, and sometimes made such curious proposals to m[e]
that I thought he was mad. One night, he wanted to slee[p]
with me. I refused, saying that my bed was too small. H[e]
pressed me to go to his, but I again refused, for the wret[ch]
was so dirty and stunk so strongly of chewed tobacco, that [it]
made me quite sick.

Early on the following morning, we were both alone in t[he]
assembly-room. He recommenced his caresses, but with su[ch]
violent movements, that it became quite alarming. At la[st]
he wanted to take the most disgusting liberties with me, an[d]
taking hold of my hand, tried to make me take the same wi[th]
him. I uttered a loud cry, and, jumping back, freed myse[lf]
from him; and, without exhibiting anger or indignation, for [I]
had not the least idea what it was all about, I expressed m[y]
surprise and disgust so energetically, that he left me where [I]
was; but, while he was finishing his efforts, I saw somethi[ng]

gluey and whitish shoot towards the fireplace and fall upon the ground, which turned my stomach. I rushed upon the balcony, more moved, more troubled, more frightened than I had ever been in my life, and prepared to find myself ill.

I could not understand what had been the matter with the wretch. I believed that he was attacked by epilepsy, or some other madness even more terrible; and in truth, I know nothing more hideous for any cool-blooded person to see than such filthy and dirty behaviour, and a frightful countenance inflamed by brutal lust. I have never seen another man in a similar condition; but if we are like it when we are with women, their looks must certainly be bewitched, for them not to feel disgusted at us.

I was in a great hurry to go and tell everyone what had just happened to me. Our old stewardess bade me hold my tongue; but I saw that my story had greatly affected her, and I heard her mutter: *Can maledet! brutta bestia!**

Not understanding why I ought to hold my tongue, I went my own way in spite of her prohibition, and I talked so much that, the next day, one of the governors came at an early hour to administer a sharp reproof to me, accusing me of compromising the honour of a holy house, and of making a great fuss about a trifle.

He spun out his lecture by explaining to me many things of which I was ignorant, but which he did not believe he was teaching me, for he was convinced that I had defended myself because I was unwilling to consent, not because I did not know what the Moor wanted from me. He told me gravely that it was an action forbidden as highly immoral, the desire of which, however, was not an affront to the person who was the object of it, and that there was no need to be so annoyed at having been considered worthy of affection. He told me plainly that he himself, during his youth, had had the same honour paid to him, and that, having been surprised when he was not in a condition to offer any resistance, he had not found it particularly painful. He was so shameless as to make use of plain language; and, imagining that the reason of

* Cursed dog! filthy beast!

my resistance was the fear of pain, he assured me that I need have no fear, and that I ought not to be alarmed where there was no reason for it.

I listened to this wretch with an astonishment which was increased by the fact that he did not speak for himself, but only appeared to be instructing me for my good. The subject appeared to him so simple, that he did not even attempt to ensure privacy; and our conversation was heard by a third party in the person of an ecclesiastic who seemed no more frightened by it than himself. This air of naturalness so imposed upon me, that I was convinced that it was no doubt a custom recognised in the world, as to which I had not had the opportunity of being instructed sooner. This made me listen without anger, but not without disgust. The image of what had happened to me, but above all of what I had seen, remained so deeply impressed upon my memory that, when I thought of it, I still felt disgusted. Without knowing any more about it, my aversion for the thing itself extended to its apologist; and I could not restrain myself sufficiently to prevent him seeing the bad effect of his lessons. He cast a glance at me that was by no means affectionate and from that time spared no efforts to make my stay in the hospice disagreeable. He succeeded so well that, seeing that there was only one way of getting away, I hastened to take it with as much eagerness as I had up till then exhibited in order to keep away from it.

[Rousseau is finally accepted into the Church, is paraded through the streets and makes public abjuration.]

This was not all. I was next obliged to go to the Inquisition to receive absolution from the crime of heresy, and to re-enter the bosom of the Church with the ceremony to which Henry IV. was subjected in the person of his ambassador. The behaviour and look of the reverend father inquisitor were not calculated to remove the secret terror which had seized upon me when I entered the house. After several questions about my belief, my position, and my family, he abruptly asked me whether my mother was damned. Fright caused me to repress the first movement of my indignation. I contented myself with answering that I ventured to hope that she was not, and that God might have enlightened her at her last hour. The monk was silent, but made a grimace which by no means appeared to me a sign of approval.

When all was over, at the moment when I expected to be provided for in accordance with my hopes, I was put out of doors with a little more than twenty francs in small money—the result of the collection made for me. I was recommended to live as a good Christian, to remain true to grace; they wished me good luck, shut the door upon me, and I saw no more of them.

Thus, in an instant, all my great expectations disappeared, and the only result of the self-seeking step that I had just taken, was the consciousness of having been an apostate and a dupe at the same time. It may be easily imagined what a sudden revolution took place in my ideas, when I saw myself dashed down from my brilliant dreams of fortune into utter misery, and when, after having deliberated in the morning upon the choice of the palace I should inhabit, I found myself in the evening obliged to go to bed in the street. It will be imagined that I began by abandoning myself to a feeling of despair, the more cruel in proportion as regret for my errors was aggravated by the reproach that all my misfortune was my own work. Nothing of the kind. For the first time in my life, I had just been shut up for more than two months. My first sensation was one of joy at the recovery of my liberty. After a long period of slavery, again master of myself and my actions, I beheld myself in the midst of a large city, abounding in resources, full of persons of distinction, by whom I could not fail to be welcomed in consequence of my good qualities and my talents as soon as I became known. Besides, I had plenty of time to wait, and the twenty francs, which I had in my pocket, appeared to me an inexhaustible treasure. I could spend them as I pleased, without being accountable to anybody. It was the first time that I had ever been so well off. Far from becoming disheartened or shedding tears, I only changed my hopes, and my *amour-propre* lost nothing by the exchange. I had never felt so confident and secure; I believed my fortune already made, and I considered it a fine thing to have no one but myself to thank for it.

[He spends the next days wandering around the city, enjoying his freedom and independence. But his limited funds quickly diminish.]

While waiting for something better, I took to going from shop to shop to offer my services for engraving figures or coats-of-arms on silver, hoping to tempt customers by my cheapness, since I left the amount of payment to them. This plan did not prove very successful. I was generally shown the door; and the work I got was so little, that I scarcely earned enough to pay for two or three meals. One day, however, as I was walking at an early hour through the *Contrada nova*, I saw through a shop window a young woman of so kindly and attractive an appearance, that, in spite of my shyness with women, I entered without hesitation and placed my humble talents at her disposal. She did not repulse me, but made me sit down and tell her my little history, pitied me, bade me cheer up, since assuredly good Christians would not desert me, and, having sent to a neighbouring goldsmith for the tools which I told her I wanted, she went into the kitchen and fetched me some breakfast with her own hands. This beginning appeared to me to promise well; the result did not give the lie to it. She appeared satisfied with my bit of work, and still more with my humble chatter, when I was a little more at my ease; for she was brilliant and handsomely dressed, and, in spite of her gracious manner, her appearance had inspired me with awe. But her kindly reception, her compassionate voice, her gentle and caressing manners, soon put me at my ease. I saw that I was successful, and this increased my success. But, although she was an Italian and too pretty not to be somewhat of a coquette, she was at the same time so modest, and I was so shy, that it was difficult for it to lead to anything further. We were not allowed to finish the adventure. I remember with the greater rapture the brief moments which I spent by her side, and I can declare that in their first beginnings I tasted the sweetest and purest joys of love.

She was an extremely piquant brunette, whose liveliness was rendered somewhat touching by the expression of good nature on her pretty face. Her name was Madame Basile. Her husband, who was older than herself and somewhat jealous, left her, while he was travelling, under the care of a clerk, who appeared too disagreeable to be seductive, and yet was not without pretensions of his own, which he only showed by his bad temper. This he visited upon me, although I was very fond of hearing him play the flute, on which he was a tolerably good performer. This new Aegisthus grumbled whenever he saw me enter the place, and treated me with a contempt which his mistress returned in full. It even seemed as if it delighted her to caress me in his presence, in order to plague him; and this kind of revenge, although very much to my taste, would have been still more agreeable in a *tête-à-tête*. But she never pushed matters to that extent, or, at least, not in the same manner. Whether it was that she found me too young, or did not know how to make advances, or really intended to be discreet, she exhibited at that time a kind of reserve, which, while not repellent, intimidated me without my knowing the reason why. Although I did not feel for her the real and tender respect that I felt for Madame de Warens, I was more timid and less familiar with her. I was embarrassed and confused; I did not venture to look at her or to breathe by her side; and yet I dreaded to leave her worse than death. I devoured with a greedy eye everything I could look at without being observed: the flowers in her dress, the tips of her pretty feet, the glimpse of a firm white arm which I caught between her glove and her cuff, and of her bosom, which was sometimes visible between her tucker and her neckerchief. Each object strengthened the impression made by the rest. From looking at what I could see, and even further than that, my eyes became troubled, my breast felt oppressed; my respiration became every moment more choked, I could scarcely breathe, and all I could do was to heave a succession of noiseless sighs, which were very embarrassing in the complete stillness in which we often found ourselves. Luckily Madame Basile, busy with her work, did not notice it, as far as I could see. However, I sometimes saw the bosom of her dress heave as if in sympathy. This dangerous sight made me lose my head completely; but, when I was ready to give way to my transports, she quietly said something to me which immediately brought me to my senses again.

I saw her several times alone in this manner, without a word, or gesture, or even a too expressive look indicating the least understanding between us. This state of things, very tormenting for myself, was nevertheless extremely delightful, and in the simplicity of my heart I could scarcely understand why I felt so tormented. It appeared that these little *tête-à-têtes* were not unpleasant to her either; at any rate, she provided opportunity for them pretty frequently—certainly a very harmless endeavour on her part, for all the use which she made of them herself, or allowed me to make.

One day, tired of the clerk's silly conversation, she had gone upstairs to her room. I hastily finished my little task in the room behind the shop, and followed her. The door of her room was half open. I entered without being seen. She was working at her embroidery near a window, with her back turned towards the door. She could neither see me nor hear me come in, owing to the noise of the carriages in the street. She was always well dressed; on that day her toilet was almost coquettish. Her attitude was graceful; her head, slightly bent, allowed the whiteness of her neck to be seen; her hair, elegantly fastened up, was ornamented with flowers. Over her whole form was spread a charm, which I had time to consider, and which made me beside myself. I threw myself on my knees on the threshold, stretching out my arms towards her with passionate movements, feeling certain that she could not hear me, and not thinking it possible that she could see me; but over the mantelpiece was a looking-glass, which betrayed me. I do not know what effect my attack of madness produced upon her; she neither looked at me, nor said a word; but, half-turning her head, with a simple movement of her finger she pointed to the mat at her feet. To tremble, to utter a cry, to fling myself down on the spot she had indicated, was for me the work of a moment; but it will scarcely be believed that, in this position, I did not venture to attempt anything further, to say a single word, to lift my eyes to her, or even to touch her, in my uncomfortable attitude, to support myself for an instant upon her knees. Although unable to speak or move, I was certainly not tranquil; everything about me betrayed my agitation, my joy, my gratitude, my ardent desires, which, without definite aim or object, were restrained by the fear of displeasing, in regard to which my youthful heart could not make itself easy.

She appeared no less moved and no less shy than myself. Disturbed at seeing me there, disconcerted at having drawn me thither, and beginning to feel the full consequences of a sign which she had no doubt made without due reflection, she neither drew me towards her nor repulsed me. She did not take her eyes from her work; she tried to behave as if she had not seen me at her feet; but all my stupidity could not prevent me from concluding that she shared my embarrassment, perhaps even my desires, and that she was restrained by the same feeling of shame as myself, although this did not assist me to overcome it. Being five or six years older than myself, she ought, as I considered, to have had all the boldness on her side; and I said to myself that, as she did nothing to awaken mine, she could not wish me to show any. Even now I think I was right, and certainly she was too clever not to see that a novice, such as I was, needed to be not only encouraged, but also instructed.

I do not know what would have been the end of this lively dumb show, nor how long I should have remained without moving in my ridiculous and yet delicious situation, if we had not been interrupted. At the moment of my most violent excitement, I heard the door of the kitchen, which was close to the room where we were, open, and Madame Basile, in lively alarm which showed itself in her words and gestures, said, "Get up! here comes Rosina." Hastily rising, I seized the hand which she held out to me, and imprinted two burning kisses upon it, at the second of which I felt this charming hand pressed lightly against my lips. Never in my life had I enjoyed so sweet a moment; but the opportunity which I had lost never came again, and our youthful loves stopped at that point.

This is, perhaps, the very reason why the image of that amiable woman has remained imprinted on the bottom of my heart in such charming outlines. It has even grown in beauty in proportion as my knowledge of the world and women has been enlarged. If she had only had a little experience, she would have behaved differently in order to encourage a lad; but, if her heart was weak, it was upright; she yielded involuntarily to the inclination which carried her away; it was, according to all appearance, her first infidelity, and I should perhaps, have found more difficulty in overcoming her shyness than my own. Without having gone so far, I found in her presence indescribable happiness. None of the feelings caused by the possession of women have ever equalled the two minutes which I spent at her feet without even venturing to touch her dress. No; there is no enjoyment equal to that which a virtuous woman, whom one loves, can afford. Everything is a favour with her. A sign with the finger, a hand pressed lightly against my mouth—these are the only favours that I ever received from Madame Basile, and the recollection of these trifling tokens of regard still enchants me when I think of them.

For the two next days it was in vain that I looked out for the chance of another *tête-à-tête*; it was impossible for me to find the opportunity, and I did not observe any anxiety on her part to bring it about. Her manner, although not colder, was more reserved than usual; and I believe that she avoided my looks, for fear of being unable to control her own sufficiently. Her confounded clerk was more unbearable than ever; he even joked and bantered me, saying that I should get on with the ladies. I trembled at the thought of having been guilty of some indiscretion; and, already considering that there was an understanding between Madame Basile and myself, I wished to keep secret an inclination which, until then, had not greatly needed it. This made me more careful in seizing opportunities to satisfy it; and, as I wished them to be safe, I no longer found any at all.

This is another romantic folly of which I have never been able to cure myself, and which, combined with my natural shyness, has strikingly falsified the clerk's predictions. I loved too sincerely, too completely, I venture to say, to be able to be happy easily. Never have passions been at once more lively and purer than mine; never has love been tenderer, truer, more disinterested. I would have sacrificed my happiness a thousand times for that of the person whom I loved; her reputation was dearer to me than my life, and I would never have wished to endanger her repose for a single moment for all the pleasures of enjoyment. This feeling has made me employ such carefulness, such secrecy, and such precaution in my undertakings, that none of them have ever been successful. My want of success with women has always been caused by my excessive love for them.

[The lady's husband returns, and informed by the clerk, puts Rousseau out. He then becomes a lackey in the service of the Comtesse de Vercellis, who is wasting away with cancer. She dictates letters to him.]

I believe that from that time I suffered from the malicious sport of secret intrigue which has ever since thwarted me, and which has inspired me with a very natural aversion for the apparent order of things which produces it. The heir of Madame de Vercellis, who was childless, was her nephew, the Comte de la Roque, who assiduously paid court to her. Besides, her chief servants, who saw that her end was near, did not neglect their own interests; and there were so many devoted attendants round her, that it would have been difficult for her to give a thought to myself. At the head of the establishment was a certain M. Lorenzi, a clever man, whose still more clever wife had so insinuated herself into her mistress's good graces, that she stood rather on the footing of a friend than of a paid servant. She had bestowed the post of lady's-maid upon her own niece, Mademoiselle Pontal, a sly creature, who gave herself the airs of a maid of honour, and so successfully helped her aunt to get round her mistress, that she only saw through their eyes and only acted through their hands. I had not the good fortune to please these three persons; I obeyed them, but I did not serve them; I did not consider that, besides serving our common mistress, I was obliged to be a servant to her servants. Besides, I was the kind of person who caused them uneasiness. They saw clearly that I was not in my place; they were afraid that Madame saw it as well, and that what she might do to put me in my proper position, might diminish their share of her money; for people of this class, too greedy to be just, look upon every legacy left to others as stolen from their own property. They accordingly conspired to remove me from her sight. She was fond of writing letters; it was an amusement for her in her state of health; they made her lose her taste for it, and had her physician turn her away from it, persuading her that it was too tiring for her. On the pretence that I did not understand my duty, two loutish sedan-chair carriers were employed in my place; in short, they managed so cleverly that, when she made her will, I was not allowed to enter her room for eight days. It is true that I subsequently went in as before, and I showed her even more attention than anyone else; for the sufferings the poor woman endured tore my heart; the firmness with which she bore them inspired me with extreme reverence and affection for her, and I often shed tears of genuine sorrow in my room, unperceived by her or anyone else.

At length we lost her. I saw her die. Her life had been the life of a woman of talent and intelligence; her death was that of a philosopher. I can say that she inspired me with a feeling of esteem for the Catholic religion, by the cheerfulness of soul with which she fulfilled its instructions, without carelessness and without affectation. She was naturally of a serious disposition. Towards the end of her illness, she assumed a sort of gaiety, which was too regular to be unreal, and which was only a counterpoise to her melancholy condition and was the gift of reason. She only kept her bed the two last days, and continued to converse quietly with everybody to the end. At last, speaking no more, and already in the agonies of death, she broke wind loudly. "Good!" she said, turning round, "a woman who can let out wind is not dead!" These were the last words she uttered.

She left a year's wages to her underservants. I received nothing, not having been entered on the list of her establishment. However, the Comte de la Roque ordered thirty *livres* to be given me, and left me the new suit which I was wearing, and which M. Lorenzi wanted to take from me. He even promised to try and find a place for me, and gave me leave to go and see him. I went there two or three times without being able to speak to him. Being easily rebuffed, I did not go again. It will soon be seen that I was wrong. Would that I had finished all that I had to say about my stay at Madame de Vercellis's! But, although my condition apparently remained the same, I did not leave the house as I entered it. I carried away from it lasting recollections of crime and the insupportable weight of remorse, which, after forty years, still lies heavy on my conscience; while the bitterness of it, far from growing weaker, makes itself more strongly felt with my advancing years. Who would believe that a childish fault could have such cruel consequences? For these more than probable consequences my heart is inconsolable. I have, perhaps, caused the ruin of an amiable, honest, and estimable girl, who certainly was far more worthy than myself, and doomed her to disgrace and misery.

It is almost unavoidable that the break up of an establishment should cause some confusion in the house, and that several things should get lost; however, the servants were so honest, and the Lorenzis so watchful, that nothing was missing when the inventory was taken. Only Mademoiselle Pontal had lost a piece of old red and silver-coloured ribbon. Many other things of greater value were at my disposal; this ribbon alone tempted me; I stole it, and, as I took no trouble to conceal it, it was soon found. They wanted to know how it had come into my possession. I became confused, stammered, blushed, and at last said that Marion had given it to me. Marion was a young girl from Maurienne, whom Madame de Vercellis had taken for her cook, when she left off giving dinners and discharged her own, as she had more need of good soup than of fine stews. Marion was not only pretty but had a fresh colour, only found on the mountains, and, above all, there was something about her so gentle and modest, that it was impossible for anyone to see her without loving her; in addition to that, she was a good and virtuous girl, and of unquestionable honesty. All were surprised when I mentioned her name. We were both equally trusted and it was considered important to find out which of us two was really the thief. She was sent for; a number of people were assembled, amongst them the Comte de la Roque. When she came, the ribbon was shown to her. I boldly accused her; she was astounded, and unable to utter a word; looked at me in a manner that would have disarmed the Devil himself, but against which my barbarous heart was proof. At last, she denied the theft firmly, but without anger, addressed herself to me, exhorted me to reflect, and not to disgrace an innocent girl who had never done me any harm; but I, with infernal impudence, persisted in my story, and declared to her face that she had given me the ribbon. The poor girl began to cry, and only said to me: "Ah! Rousseau, I thought you were a good man. You make me very unhappy, but I should not like to be in your place." That was all. She proceeded to defend herself with equal simplicity and firmness, but without allowing herself to utter the slightest reproach against me. This moderation, contrasted with my decided tone, did her harm. It did not seem natural to suppose, on the one side, such devilish impudence, and, on the other, such angelic mildness. Although the matter did not appear to be absolutely settled, they were prepossessed in my favour. In the confusion which prevailed, they did not give themselves time to get to the bottom of the affair; and the Comte de la Roque, in dismissing us both, contented himself with saying that the conscience of the guilty one would amply avenge the innocent. His prediction has been fulfilled; it fulfills itself every day.

I do not know what became of the victim of my false accusation; but it is not likely that she afterwards found it easy to get a good situation. She carried away with her an imputation upon her honesty which was in every way cruel. The theft was only a trifling one, but still it was a theft, and, what is worse, made use of to lead a young man astray; lastly, lying and obstinacy left nothing to be hoped from one in whom so many vices were united. I do not even consider misery and desertion as the greatest danger to which I exposed her. At her age, who knows to what extremes discouragement and the feeling of ill-used innocence may have carried her? Oh, if my remorse at having succeeded in making her unhappy is unendurable, one may judge what remorse I feel at the thought of having, perhaps, made her worse than myself!

This cruel remembrance at times so sorely troubles and upsets me, that in my sleepless hours I seem to see the poor girl coming to reproach me for my crime, as if it had been committed only yesterday. As long as I have lived quietly, it has tormented me less; but in the midst of a stormy life it robs me of the sweet consolation of persecuted innocence, it makes me feel what I think I have said in one of my books, that "Remorse goes to sleep when our fortunes are prosperous, and makes itself felt more keenly in adversity." However, I have never been able to bring myself to unburden my heart of this confession to a friend. The closest intimacy has never led me so far with anyone, not even with Madame de Warens. All that I have been able to do has been to confess that I had to reproach myself with an atrocious act, but I have never stated wherein it consisted. This burden has remained to this day upon my conscience without alleviation; and I can affirm that the desire of freeing myself from it in some degree, has greatly contributed to the resolution I have taken of writing my Confessions.

I have behaved straightforwardly in the confession which I have just made, and it will assuredly be found that I have not attempted to palliate the blackness of my offence. But I should not fulfil the object of this book, if I did not at the same time set forth my inner feelings, and hesitated to excuse myself by what is strictly true. Wicked intent was never further from me than at that cruel moment; and when I accused the unhappy girl, it is singular, but it is true, that my friendship for her was the cause of it. She was present to my thoughts; I threw the blame on the first object which presented itself. I accused her of having done what I meant to

do, and of having given me the ribbon, because my intention
was to give it to her. When I afterwards saw her appear, my
heart was torn; but the presence of so many people was
stronger than repentance. I was not afraid of punishment, I
was only afraid of disgrace; and that I feared more than
death, more than crime, more than anything else in the world.
I should have rejoiced if the earth had suddenly opened, swallowed me up and suffocated me; the unconquerable fear of
shame overcame everything, and alone made me impudent.
The greater my crime, the more the dread of confessing it
made me fearless. I saw nothing but the horror of being
recognised and publicly declared, in my own presence, a
thief, liar, and slanderer. Complete embarrassment deprived
me of every other feeling. If I had been allowed to recover
myself I should have assuredly confessed everything. If M.
de la Roque had taken me aside and said to me: "Do not ruin
this poor girl; if you are guilty, confess it to me," I should
have immediately thrown myself at his feet, of that I am
perfectly certain. But, when I needed encouragement, they
only intimidated me. And yet it is only fair to consider my
age. I was little more than a child, or rather, I still was one.
In youth real crimes are even more criminal than in riper
years; but that which is only weakness is less so, and my
offence was at bottom scarcely anything else. Thus the recollection of it afflicts me not so much by reason of the evil in
itself as on account of its evil consequences. It has even done
me the good of securing me for the rest of my life against
every act tending to crime, by the terrible impression which
I have retained of the only offence that I have ever committed; and I believe that my horror of a lie is due in great
measure to my regret at having been capable myself of telling
one so shameful. If it is a crime that can be expiated, as I
venture to believe, it must be expiated by all the unhappiness
which has overwhelmed the last years of my life, by forty
years of honourable and upright conduct in difficult circumstances; and poor Marion finds so many avengers in this
world, that, however great my offence against her may have

been, I have little fear of dying without absolution. This is what I have to say on this matter: permit me never to speak of it again.

BOOK THREE

[1728-1731]

HAVING left Madame de Vercellis's house in almost the same state as I had entered it, I went back to my old landlady, with whom I remained for five or six weeks, during which health, youth, and idleness again rendered my temperament troublesome. I was restless, absent-minded, a dreamer. I wept, I sighed, I longed for a happiness of which I had no idea, and of which I nevertheless felt the want. This state cannot be described; only few men can even imagine it, because most of them have forestalled this fulness of life, at once so tormenting and so delicious, which, in the intoxication of desire, gives a foretaste of enjoyment. My heated blood incessantly filled my brain with girls and women; but, ignorant of the relations of sex, I made use of them in my imagination in accordance with my distorted notions, without knowing what else to do with them; and these notions kept my feelings in a state of most uncomfortable activity, from which, fortunately, they did not teach me how to deliver myself. I would have given my life to have found another Mademoiselle Goton for a quarter of an hour. But it was no longer the time when childish amusements took this direction as if naturally. Shame, the companion of a bad conscience, had made its appearance with advancing years; it had increased my natural shyness to such an extent that it made it unconquerable; and never, neither then nor later, have I been able to bring myself to make an indecent proposal, unless she, to whom I made it, in some measure forced me to it by her advances, even though I knew that she was by no means scrupulous, and felt almost certain of being taken at my word.

My agitation became so strong that, being unable to satisfy my desires, I excited them by the most extravagant behaviour. I haunted dark alleys and hidden retreats, where I might be able to expose myself to women in the condition in which I should have liked to have been in their company. What they saw was not an obscene object, I never even thought of such a thing; it was a ridiculous object. The foolish pleasure I took in displaying it before their eyes cannot be described. There was only one step further necessary for me to take, in order to gain actual experience of the treatment I desired, and I have no doubt that some woman would have been bold enough to afford me the amusement, while passing by, if I had had the courage to wait. This folly of mine led to a disaster almost as comical, but less agreeable for myself.

One day, I took up my position at the bottom of a court where there was a well, from which the girls of the house were in the habit of fetching water. At this spot there was a slight descent which led to some cellars by several entrances. In the dark I examined these underground passages, and finding them long and dark, I concluded that there was no outlet, and that, if I happened to be seen and surprised, I should find a safe hiding-place in them. Thus emboldened, I exhibited to the girls who came to the well a sight more laughable than seductive. The more modest pretended to see nothing; others began to laugh; others felt insulted and cried out. I ran into my retreat; someone followed me. I heard a man's voice, which I had not expected, and which alarmed me. I plunged underground at the risk of losing myself; the noise, the voices, the man's voice, still followed me. I had always reckoned upon the darkness; I saw a light. I shuddered, and plunged further into the darkness. A wall stopped me, and, being unable to go any further, I was obliged to await my fate. In a moment I was seized by a tall man with a big moustache, a big hat, and a big sword, who was escorted by four or five old women, each armed with a broom-handle, amongst whom I perceived the little wretch who had discovered me, and who, no doubt, wanted to see me face to face.

The man with the sword, seizing me by the arm, asked me

roughly what I was doing there. It may be imagined that I had no answer ready. However, I recovered myself; and, in desperation, at this critical moment I invented a romantic excuse which proved successful. I begged him in a suppliant voice to have pity upon my age and condition; I said that I was a young stranger of good birth, whose brain was affected; that I had run away from home, because they wanted to shut me up; that I was lost if he betrayed me; but that, if he would let me go, I might some day be able to reward him for his kindness. Contrary to all expectation, my words and demeanour took effect; the terrible man was touched by them, and, after administering a short reproof, he let me go quietly without questioning me further. From the demeanour of the girl and the old women, when they saw me go, I judged that the man whom I feared so much had been of great service to me, and that I should not have got off so easily with them alone. I heard them murmur something or other to which I hardly paid attention; for, provided that the man and his sword did not interfere, I felt confident, active and vigorous as I was, of escaping from them and their cudgels.

A few days afterwards, while walking down a street with a young Abbé, my neighbour, I nearly ran into the man with the sword. He recognised me, and, imitating me mockingly, said: "I am a prince, I am a prince, and I am a coward; but don't let his highness come back again!" He said no more, and I sneaked away, not venturing to look up, and thanking him in my heart for his discretion. I judged that the confounded old women had made him ashamed of his credulity. Anyhow, Piedmontese as he was, he was a good man, and I never think of him without a feeling of gratitude; for the story was so funny that, merely from the desire of creating a laugh, anyone else in his place would have shamed me. This adventure, without having the consequences which I dreaded, nevertheless made me careful for a long time.

My stay with Madame de Vercellis had gained me some acquaintances, whom I cultivated in the hope that they might prove useful to me. Amongst others, I sometimes went to visit a Savoyard Abbé, named M. Gaime, tutor to the children

of the Comte de Mellarède. He was still young and went little
into society, but was full of good sense, honour and intelligence, and one of the most honourable men that I have
known. He was not the least use to me for the object which
took me to him; he had not sufficient influence to get me a
situation; but I gained from him still more precious advantages, which have been of use to me all my life, lessons of
healthy morality and principles of sound reason. In my alter-
nating tastes and ideas, I had always been too high or too
low—Achilles or Thersites: now a hero, now a good-for-
nothing. M. Gaime undertook to put me in my place, and to
show me to myself in my true colours, without sparing or
discouraging me. He spoke to me with due recognition of my
natural talents, but added that he saw obstacles arising from
them which would prevent me from making the best use of
them; so that, in his opinion, they would be less useful to me
as steps to fortune than as a means to enable me to do
without it. He put before me a true picture of human life, of
which I had only false ideas; he showed me how, in the
midst of contrary fortune, the wise man can always strive
after happiness and sail against the wind in order to reach it;
that there is no true happiness without prudence, and that
prudence belongs to all conditions of life. He damped my
admiration for external grandeur, by proving that those who
ruled others were neither happier nor wiser than the ruled.
He told me one thing, which I have often remembered since
then—that, if every man could read the hearts of all other
men, there would be found more people willing to descend
than to rise in life. This reflection, the truth of which is striking, and in which there is no exaggeration, has been of great
service to me during the course of my life, by helping to make
me quietly content with my position. He gave me the first
true ideas of what was honourable, which my inflated genius
had only grasped in its exaggerated forms. He made me feel
that the enthusiasm of lofty virtues was rarely shown in society; that, in trying to climb too high, one was in danger of
falling; that a continued round of trifling duties, always well
performed, required no less effort than heroic actions; that

from them a man gained more in the matter of honour and happiness; and that it was infinitely better to enjoy the esteem of one's fellow men at all times, than their admiration occasionally.

In order to define the duties of man, it was necessary to go back to their principles. Besides, the step which I had just taken, and of which my present condition was the result, led us to speak of religion. It will be already imagined that the honourable M. Gaime is, in great part at least, the original of the "Savoyard Vicar." Only, as prudence constrained him to speak with more reserve, he expressed himself less openly upon certain points; but, for the rest, his maxims, his sentiments, his opinions were the same, and, his advice to return home not excepted, everything was just as I have publicly represented it. Therefore, without enlarging further upon the conversations, the substance of which is accessible to everyone, I will only say that his lessons, the wisdom of which was at first without effect, became in my heart a germ of virtue and religion which was never choked, and which only needed the care of a dearer hand in order to bear fruit.

[Comte de la Roque obtains a position for Rousseau in the household of the Comte de Gouvon. He admires the count's grand-daughter, Mademoiselle de Breil.]

Mademoiselle de Breil was a young lady of nearly my own age, well formed, tolerably good-looking, fresh-complexioned, with very dark hair, and, although a brunette, she had the expression of gentleness which is peculiar to blonde women, and which my heart has never been able to resist. Her court dress, so becoming to young people, showed her beautiful figure to advantage, uncovered her bosom and shoulders, and made her complexion still more dazzling by reason of the mourning which was worn at the time. It will be said that a servant has no business to notice such things; I was wrong, no doubt, but I noticed them all the same, and I was not the only one who did so. The *maître d'hôtel* and the *valets de chambre* sometimes spoke of them at table with a coarseness which made me suffer cruelly. My head was not, however, so turned that I fell in love without more ado. I did not forget

myself; I kept myself in my place, and even my desires were
not allowed too much freedom. I liked to see Mademoiselle de
Breil, to hear her say a few words which showed her intelligence, good sense and modesty; my ambition, limited to the
pleasure of serving her, never went beyond my rights. At table
I was always on the look out to assert them. If her footman
left her chair for a moment, I was behind it immediately;
otherwise I stood opposite to her; I looked in her eyes to see
what she was going to ask for, and watched for the moment
to change her plate. What would I not have done if she
would only have deigned to give me some order, to look at
me, to address a single word to me! but no! I had the mortification of being nothing to her; she did not even notice that I
was there. However, on one occasion, when her brother, who
sometimes spoke to me at table, addressed a somewhat uncivil
remark to me, I gave him an answer, so neat and so well expressed, that she noticed it and turned her eyes upon me. This
glance, rapid as it was, nevertheless enchanted me. The next
day, the opportunity of winning a second glance presented
itself, and I took advantage of it. A big dinner was given on
that occasion, at which for the first time I saw the *maître
d'hôtel,* to my great astonishment, waiting with his hat on his
head and a sword at his side. By chance the conversation
turned upon the motto of the house of Solar, which was em-
broidered under the coat-of-arms, *Tel fiert qui ne tue pas.* As
the Piedmontese are not, as a rule, masters of the French
language, someone detected in this motto a mistake in spell-
ing, and declared that there should be no *t* in the word *fiert.*

The old Comte de Gouvon was just going to answer, but,
happening to look at me, saw that I was smiling without venturing to say anything, and ordered me to speak. I thereupon
said that I did not believe that the *t* was unnecessary; that
fiert was an old French word, not derived from *ferus,* proud,
threatening, but from *ferit,* he strikes, he wounds; so that the
meaning of the motto appeared to me to be, not, Many a man
threatens, but, Many a man strikes and does not kill.

All the company looked first at me and then at themselves
without saying a word. I had never seen such astonishment

in my life. But what flattered me more was to see from
Mademoiselle de Breil's face that she was evidently much
pleased. This disdainful young lady condescended to cast a
second glance at me, which, at least, was equal to the first;
then, turning her eyes towards her grandfather, she appeared
to be waiting with a sort of impatience for the compliment
which was my due, and which he, in fact, paid me so fully
and completely, and with the appearance of such satisfaction,
that the whole table hastened to join in the chorus. The
moment was brief, but in every respect delicious. It was one
of those moments, only too rare, which replace things in their
natural order, and avenge depreciated merit for the insults of
fortune. A few minutes afterwards, Mademoiselle de Breil,
lifting her eyes to me again, asked me, in a timid and affable
voice, to give her something to drink. I need not say that I
did not keep her waiting; but, as I came near to her, I trembled so violently that, having filled the glass too full, I spilt
some of the water over her plate, and even over herself. Her
brother asked me thoughtlessly why I was trembling so?
This question did not serve to reassure me, and Mademoiselle
de Breil blushed up to the whites of her eyes.

Here ended the romance, in which it will be observed, as
in the case of Madame Basile and during all the rest of my
life, that I am not happy in the conclusion of my amours. In
vain I paid special attention to Madame de Breil's ante-room;
I did not obtain another mark of attention from her daughter.
She went in and out without looking at me, and, as for myself,
I hardly ventured to cast eyes upon her. I was even so stupid
and awkward that, one day, when she dropped her glove
while passing, instead of darting upon this glove which I
should have liked to cover with kisses, I did not dare to leave
my place; and I allowed it to be picked up by a great lout of a
valet, whom I would gladly have throttled. To complete my
nervousness, I perceived that I had not the good fortune to
please Madame de Breil. She not only gave me no orders, but
never accepted my services; and on two occasions, finding me
in her ante-room, she asked me coldly if I had not something
to do. I was obliged to renounce this dear ante-room; at first I

regretted it, but distractions intervened, and soon I thought no more of it.

The kindness of her stepfather, who at last perceived that I was there, consoled me for the coldness of Madame de Breil. During the evening after the dinner of which I have spoken, he held a conversation with me for half-an-hour, with which he appeared satisfied, and I was delighted. This good old man, although less gifted than Madame de Vercellis, had more heart, and I got on better with him. He told me to attach myself to his son, the Abbé de Gouvon, who had conceived a regard for me; that this regard, if I made good use of it, might be useful to me, and assist me in acquiring what I still lacked, in order to promote what they had in view for me. Next morning, I hastened to the Abbé. He did not receive me as a servant, but made me sit down by the side of the fire, and, questioning me with the greatest gentleness, soon discovered that my education, which had been commenced in so many things, was complete in none. Finding, especially, that I knew very little Latin, he undertook to teach me more. It was arranged that I should go to him every morning, and I commenced the following day. Thus, by one of those curious coincidences, which will often be found in the course of my life, I was at once above and below my station—I was pupil and valet in the same house; and, while still a servant, I had a tutor of such noble birth that he ought to have been the tutor of none but kings' sons. . . .

I spent a good part of the morning with him, both for my own instruction and for his service—not personal service, for that he never allowed me to perform, but to write from his dictation and to do copying; and my duties as secretary were more useful to me than my studies as pupil. In this manner I not only learnt Italian in its purity, but I imbibed a taste for literature, and acquired some knowledge of good books which had been impossible at La Tribu's, and which proved very serviceable to me afterwards when I began to work by myself.

This was the period of my life when, without romantic projects, I might most reasonably have hoped for success. The Abbé, who was well satisfied with me, told everybody; and his father had conceived so special a regard for me that the Comte de Favria told me that he had spoken of me to the King. Even Madame de Breil had laid aside her contemptuous demeanour towards me. In short, I became a sort of favourite in the house, to the great jealousy of the other servants, who, seeing me honoured by receiving instruction from their master's son, well understood that I was not long intended to remain one of themselves.

As far as I was able to judge of the views entertained for me from a few words hastily dropped, upon which I only reflected later, it seems to me that the house of Solar, eager for ambassadorial, and possibly, in the future, ministerial offices, would have been very glad to educate in advance a trustworthy and talented person, who being entirely dependent upon it, might have been received into its confidence and have served it faithfully. This project of the Comte de Gouvon was noble, judicious, generous, and truly worthy of a great nobleman, beneficent and far-seeing; but, not to mention that, at the time, I did not see its entire range, it was too sensible for me to understand, and required too long a period of submission. My foolish ambition only looked for good fortune in the midst of adventures; and, as no woman had anything to do with it, this means of succeeding seemed to me slow, wearisome, and dull; whereas I ought to have considered it safer and more honourable, for the very reason that no women were mixed up in it, seeing that the kind of merit which they take under their protection was assuredly not so honourable as that which I was supposed to possess.

Everything was going on admirably. I had gained, almost taken by storm, the respect of all; the time of probation was over, and in the house I was looked upon generally as a young man of great promise who was not in his proper place, but whom everyone expected to see promoted to it. But my place was not that which was generally assigned to me, and I was destined to reach it by a very different road. I now come to one of those characteristic traits which are peculiar to me, and which I need only put before the reader without further discussion.

[Rousseau falls under the influence of a rascally companion named Bâcle, and despising all counsel, sets out with him on a vagabond tour of Switzerland and France. But on approaching Madame de Warens' home at Annecy, he suddenly bids Bâcle adieu.]

How my heart beat as I drew near to her house! My legs trembled beneath me; my eyes seemed covered with a veil; I saw nothing, I heard nothing, I should not have recognised anybody; I was obliged to stop several times to recover my breath and compose myself. Was it the fear of not obtaining the assistance I needed that troubled me so? does the fear of starvation cause such alarm to a person of my age? No! that I can declare with as much truth as pride; never, at any moment of my life, has self-interest or want been able to open or shut my heart. In the course of a life, uneven and memorable for its vicissitudes, often without shelter and bread, I have always looked with the same eye upon wealth and poverty. In time of need I could have begged or stolen like anybody else, but never distressed myself in consequence of being reduced to do so. Few men have sighed so much as I, few have shed so many tears in their life; but never has poverty or the fear of being reduced to it made me utter a sigh or shed a tear. My soul, proof against fortune, has never known true blessings or misfortunes other than those which do not depend upon her; and, when I am in want of nothing that is needful, that is just the time when I feel myself the unhappiest of mortals.

No sooner had I shown myself to Madame de Warens, than her manner reassured me. I trembled at the first sound of her voice. I threw myself at her feet, and, in transports of liveliest joy, I fastened my lips upon her hand. I do not know whether she had heard any news of me, but her face showed little surprise and no displeasure. "Poor little one," she said, in a caressing voice, "here you are again then? I knew you were too young for the journey. I am glad, at any rate, that it has not turned out so badly as I had feared." Then she made me tell my story, which was not a long one, and which I faithfully related, suppressing a few details, but otherwise neither sparing nor excusing myself.

It was a question where I was to sleep. She consulted her maid. I hardly ventured to breathe during the discussion; but when I heard that I was to sleep in the house I could scarcely contain myself, and I saw my little bundle carried into the room appointed for me with much the same feelings as St. Preux saw his chaise taken into Madame de Wolmar's° coach-house. To increase my delight, I learned that this favour was not to be a passing one, and, at the moment when I was believed to be thinking of something quite different, I heard her say: "Let them say what they like; since Providence sends him back to me, I am resolved not to abandon him."

Thus I was at last settled in her house. This settlement, however, was not as yet that from which I date the happy days of my life, but it served to pave the way for it. Although this sensibility of the heart, which makes us truly enjoy ourselves, is the work of Nature, and, perhaps, a product of the organism, it requires certain situations to develop it. Without such developing causes, a man born with powerful susceptibilities would feel nothing, and would, perhaps, die without ever having known his real self. Up to that time, it had been so, or nearly so, with me: and I should, perhaps, have always remained such, if I had never known Madame de Warens, or if, having known her, I had not lived with her long enough to contract the sweet habit of affectionate feelings with which she inspired me. I venture to say that he who only feels love does not feel what is sweetest in life. I know another feeling, less impetuous, perhaps, but a thousand times more delightful, which is sometimes combined with love, but is frequently separated from it. This feeling is not simple friendship either; it is more voluptuous, more tender. I do not believe that it can be felt for a person of the same sex; at any rate, I was a friend, if ever a man was, and I never felt it in the presence of any of my friends. This is somewhat obscure, but it will become clear in the sequel; feelings can only be satisfactorily described by their effects.

* Characters in the "New Héloïse."

Madame de Warens lived in an old house, large enough to contain a pretty spare room, which she made her drawing-room; in this I was lodged. It overlooked the passage of which I have already spoken, where our first interview took place; on the other side of the brook and the gardens the country could be seen. This view was not a matter of indifference to the youthful occupant. Since I had lived at Bossey, it was the first time that I had seen anything green before my windows. Always surrounded by walls, I had nothing before my eyes except the roofs of houses or the dull grey of the streets. How vividly I felt the charm of novelty, which strengthened my inclination to tender emotions! I looked upon this enchanting landscape as another of my dear patroness's kindnesses; it seemed to me that she had put everything there on purpose for me; I placed myself in it by her side full of peaceful contentment; I saw her everywhere, in the midst of the flowers and verdure; her charms and those of spring melted together insensibly before my eyes. My heart, until then restricted, expanded in this unconfined space, and my sighs found freer vent amongst the fruit-gardens. . . .

From the first day, the most complete intimacy was established between us, which has continued during the rest of her life. "Little one" was my name; "Mamma" was hers; and we always remained "Little one" and "Mamma," even when advancing years had almost obliterated the difference between us. I find that these two names give a wonderfully good idea of the tone of our intercourse, of the simplicity of our manners, and, above all, of the mutual relation of our hearts. For me she was the tenderest of mothers, who never sought her own pleasure, but always what was best for me; and if sensuality entered at all into her attachment for me, it did not alter its character, but only rendered it more enchanting, and intoxicated me with the delight of having a young and pretty mamma whom it was delightful to me to caress—I say caress in the strictest sense of the word, for it never occurred to her to be sparing of kisses and the tenderest caresses of a mother, and it certainly never entered my mind to abuse them. It will be objected that, in the end, we had relations of a different character; I admit it, but I must wait a little—I cannot say all at once.

The moment of our first meeting was the only really passionate moment which she has ever made me feel; yet this moment was the work of surprise. My looks never ventured to peep indiscreetly beneath her neckerchief, although an ill-concealed *embonpoint* might very well have attracted them. I felt no transports or desires in her presence. I was in a state of charming repose and enjoyment, without knowing in what the enjoyment consisted. I could have spent all my life in this manner, and eternity as well, without a moment's weariness. She is the only person with whom I have never felt that dearth of conversation which makes the obligation of keeping it up a martyrdom. Our *tête-à-têtes* were not so much conversations as an inexhaustible gossip, which never came to an end unless it was interrupted. There was no need to invite me to talk; it was far more necessary to impose silence upon me. From constantly thinking over her plans, she often fell into a reverie. Well, then I let her alone; I held my tongue, I looked at her, and was the happiest of men. I had still a singular fancy. Without claiming the favour of a *tête-à-tête*, I incessantly sought one; and enjoyed it with a passion which degenerated into madness when troublesome visitors disturbed it. As soon as anyone came—whether man or woman, it did not matter which—I left the room grumbling, being unable to remain with her in the presence of a third party. I counted the minutes in her ante-room, cursing these eternal visitors a thousand times, and unable to imagine how it was that they had so much, because I myself had still more, to say.

I only felt the full strength of my attachment when I no longer saw her. When I saw her, I was only content; but, during her absence, my restlessness became painful. The need of living with her caused me outbreaks of tenderness which often ended in tears. I shall never forget how, on the day of a great festival, while she was at vespers, I went for a walk outside the town, my heart full of her image and a burning desire to spend my life with her. I had sense enough to see that at present this was impossible, and that the happiness which I enjoyed so deeply could only be short. This gave to my reflections a tinge of melancholy, about which, however, there was nothing gloomy, and which was tempered by flattering hopes. The sound of the bells, which always singularly affects me, the song of the birds, the beauty of the daylight, the enchanting landscape, the scattered country dwellings in which my fancy placed our common home—all these produced upon me an impression so vivid, tender, melancholy and touching, that I saw myself transported, as it were, in ecstasy, into that happy time and place, wherein my heart, possessing all the happiness it could desire, tasted it with inexpressible rapture, without even a thought of sensual pleasure. I never remember to have plunged into the future with greater force and illusion than on that occasion; and what has struck me most in the recollection of this dream after it had been realised, is that I have found things again exactly as I had imagined them. If ever the dream of a man awake resembled a prophetic vision, it was assuredly that dream of mine. I was only deceived in the imaginary duration; for the days, the years, and our whole life were spent in serene and undisturbed tranquillity, whereas in reality it lasted only for a moment. Alas! my most lasting happiness belongs to a dream, the fulfilment of which was almost immediately followed by the awakening.

I should never have done, if I were to enter into the details of all the follies which the remembrance of this dear mamma caused me to commit when I was no longer in her presence. How often have I kissed my bed, since she had slept in it; my curtains, all the furniture of my room, since they belonged to her, and her beautiful hand had touched them; even the floor, on which I prostrated myself, since she had walked upon it! Sometimes, even in her presence, I was guilty of extravagances, which only the most violent love seemed capable of inspiring. At table one day, just when she had put a piece of food into her mouth, I exclaimed that I saw a hair in it; she put back the morsel on her plate, and I eagerly seized and swallowed it. In a word, between myself and the most passionate lover there was only one, but that an essential, point of distinction, which makes my condition almost unintelligible and inconceivable.

I had returned from Italy not quite the same as I had entered it, but as, perhaps, no one of my age had ever returned from it. I had brought back, not my mental and moral, but my bodily virginity. I had felt the progress of years; my restless temperament had at last made itself felt, and its first outbreak, quite involuntary, had caused me alarm about my health in a manner which shows better than anything else the innocence in which I had lived up to that time. Soon reassured, I learned that dangerous means of assisting it, which cheats Nature and saves up for young men of my temperament many forms of excess at the expense of their health, strength, and, sometimes, of their life. This vice, which shame and timidity find so convenient, possesses, besides a great attraction for lively imaginations—that of being able to dispose of the whole sex as they desire, and to make the beauty which tempts them minister to their pleasures, without being obliged to obtain its consent. Seduced by this fatal advantage, I did my best to destroy the good constitution which Nature had restored to me, and which I had given time to strengthen itself. Add to this habit the circumstances of my position, living as I was with a beautiful woman, caressing her image in the bottom of my heart, seeing her continually throughout the day, surrounded in the evening by objects which reminded me of her, sleeping in the bed in which I knew she had slept! What causes for excitement! Many a reader, who reflects upon them, no doubt already considers me as half-dead! Quite the contrary; that which ought to have destroyed me was just the thing that saved me, at least for a time. Intoxicated with the charm of living with her, with the ardent desire of spending my life with her, I always saw in her, whether she were absent or present, a tender mother, a beloved sister, a delightful friend, and nothing more. I saw her always thus, always the same, and I never saw anyone but her. Her image, ever present to my heart, left room for no other; she was for me the only woman in the world; and the extreme sweetness of the feelings with which she inspired me did not allow my senses time to awake for others, and protected me against her and all her sex. In a word, I was chaste, because I loved her. Considering these results, which I can only imperfectly describe, let him who can say what was the nature of my attachment for her. For myself, all that I can say about it is that, if it already seems to be very extraordinary, in the sequel it will appear far more so.

[Rousseau busies himself helping Madame de Warens in her herb business. He continues his reading.]

In the room which I occupied I had found a few books: the "Spectator," "Pufendorf," "St. Évremond," the "Henriade." Although I no longer had my old mania for reading, I read a little when I had nothing else to do. The "Spectator," especially, pleased me and proved beneficial to me. The Abbé de Gouvon had taught me to read less greedily and with more reflection; and, accordingly, my reading did me more good. . . .

We read La Bruyère together; he pleased her better than La Rochefoucauld, a gloomy and comfortless author, especially for the young, who do not care to see men as they are. When she moralised, she sometimes lost herself in lengthy discourses; but, by kissing her mouth or hands from time to time, I managed to endure it, and her prolixity ceased to weary me. . . .

Two things, almost incompatible, are united in me in a manner which I am unable to understand: a very ardent temperament, lively and tumultuous passions, and, at the same time, slowly developed and confused ideas, which never present themselves until it is too late. One might say that my heart and my mind do not belong to the same person. Feeling takes possession of my soul more rapidly than a flash of lightning; but, instead of illuminating, inflames and dazzles me. I feel everything and see nothing. I am carried away by my passions, but stupid; in order to think, I must be cool. The astonishing thing is that, notwithstanding, I exhibit tolerably sound judgment, penetration, even finesse, if I am not hurried; with sufficient leisure I can compose excellent impromptus; but I have never said or done anything worthy of notice on the spur of the moment. I could carry on a very clever conversation through the post, as the Spaniards are said to carry on a game of chess. When I read of that Duke of Savoy, who turned round on his journey, in order to cry, "At your throat, Parisian huckster," I said, "There you have myself!"

This sluggishness of thought, combined with such liveliness of feeling, not only enters into my conversation, but I feel it even when alone and at work. My ideas arrange themselves in my head with almost incredible difficulty; they circulate in it with uncertain sound, and ferment till they excite and heat me, and make my heart beat fast; and, in the midst of this excitement, I see nothing clearly and am unable to write a single word—I am obliged to wait. Imperceptibly this great agitation subsides, the confusion clears up, everything takes its proper place, but slowly, and only after a period of long and confused agitation. Have you ever been to the opera in Italy? During the changes of scene, there prevails upon the stage of those vast theatres an unpleasant disorder which continues for some time: all the decorations are mixed up, things are pulled about in different directions in a manner most painful to see, which produces the impression that everything must be upset. Gradually, however, complete order is restored, nothing is wanting, and one is quite astounded to see an enchanting spectacle succeed this long continued disorder. This mode of procedure is almost the same as that which takes place in my brain when I attempt to write. If I had known how to wait first and then to restore in all their beauty the things represented therein, few writers would have surpassed me.

Hence comes the extreme difficulty which I find in writing. My manuscripts, scratched, smeared, muddled and almost illegible, bear witness to the trouble they have cost me. There is not one of them which I have not been obliged to copy four or five times before I could give it to the printer. I have never been able to produce anything, pen in hand, in front of my table and paper; it is during a walk, in the midst of rocks and forests, at night in my bed while lying awake, that I write in my brain; one may judge how slowly, especially in the case of a man utterly without verbal memory and who has never been able to learn six lines by heart in his life. Many of my periods have been turned and turned again five or six nights in my head before they were fit to be set down on paper. This, also, is the reason why I succeed better in works which require labour than in those which require to be written with a certain lightness of style, such as letters—a style of which I have never been able to properly catch the tone, so that such occupation is a perfect torture to me. I cannot write a letter on the most trifling subject, which does not cost me hours of fatigue; or, if I try to write down immediately what occurs to me, I know neither how to begin nor how to end; my letter is a long and confused mass of verbosity, and, when it is read, my meaning is difficult to make out.

Not only is it painful for me to put my ideas into shape: I also find a difficulty in grasping them. I have studied mankind, and believe that I am a fairly shrewd observer; nevertheless, I cannot see clearly anything of all that I see; I only see clearly what I remember, and only show intelligence in my recollections. Of all that is said, of all that is done, of all that goes on in my presence, I feel nothing, I see through nothing. The outward sign is the only thing that strikes me. But, later, all comes back to me: I recall place, time, manner, look, gesture, and circumstance: nothing escapes me. Then, from what people have said or done, I discover what they have thought; and I am rarely mistaken.

If, when alone with myself, I am so little master of my intellectual capacity, it may be imagined what I must be in conversation, when, in order to speak to the purpose, it is necessary to think of a thousand things at the same time and at once. The mere idea of all the usages of society—which it is so necessary to observe, and of which I am certain to forget one or the other—is enough to frighten me. I do not even understand how anyone can dare to speak at all in society, where, at every word, it is essential to pass in review all those who are present; it is essential to be acquainted with all their characters and histories, in order to make sure of saying nothing which can give offence. In this respect, those who live in the world have a great advantage; since they know better than others what ought not to be spoken about, they are more confident of what they say; and yet, even they frequently let fall awkward and ill-timed remarks. How must it fare with one who drops into their midst as it were from the clouds! It is almost impossible for him to speak for a minute with impunity. In a *tête-à-tête*, there is another inconvenience which I find even worse; the necessity of talking perpetually. When one is spoken to, one is obliged to answer, and, when silence ensues, to take up the conversation again. This unbearable constraint would alone have disgusted me with society. I find no compulsion more terrible than the obligation of speaking continuously and on the spur of the moment. I do not know whether this has anything to do with my mortal aversion to constraint of any kind; but to be absolutely obliged to speak is enough to make me infallibly talk nonsense.

A still more fatal defect of mine is that, instead of being able to hold my tongue when I have nothing to say, that is just the time when, in order to discharge my debt sooner, I am mad to speak. I hasten to stammer out a few words destitute of ideas, and am only too happy when they have no meaning at all. When attempting to overcome or conceal my stupidity, I rarely fail to show it. . . .

This detailed explanation, to which a special circumstance has led me, is not without its use in reference to what follows. It contains the solution of many extraordinary things which I have done, and which are attributed to an unsociable disposition which I by no means possess. I should be as fond of society as anyone else, if I was not sure of appearing in it, not only to my own disadvantage, but quite a different person from what I really am. My resolution to write and live in seclusion, is exactly that which suits me. If I had been present, my powers would never have been known, or even suspected.

[It is decided that Jean-Jacques is to be made into a priest. Sadly he leaves for the seminary, where he studies under the Abbé Gâtier.]

I have never seen a more touching expression than M.

Gâtier's. He was fair, and his beard inclined to be red; he had the ordinary appearance of those who came from his province, who all conceal considerable intelligence under a heavy exterior; but what truly distinguished him was a tender, affectionate and loving heart. There was in his large blue eyes a mixture of gentleness, tenderness and sadness, which made it impossible for anyone to see him without being attracted by him. From the looks and manner of this poor young man, one would have said that he foresaw his destiny, and that he felt he was born to be unhappy.

Some years afterwards, I learned that, while *vicaire* of a parish, he seduced a girl, the only one whom, in spite of a very tender heart, he had ever loved. The girl had a child by him, which caused a terrible scandal in a parish which was very strictly managed. The priests, being under good regulations, are not allowed to have children—except by married women. For his offence against this rule of propriety, he was imprisoned, disgraced, and deprived of his benefice. I do not know whether he afterwards regained his position, but the thought of his misfortune, deeply graven on my heart, returned to me when I wrote "Émile"; and, uniting M. Gâtier with M. Gaime, I made of these two worthy priests the original of the "Savoyard Vicar." I flatter myself that the imitation has not disgraced its originals. . . .

I was destined to be the reject of all professions. Although M. Gâtier had given the least unfavourable account of my progress that he possibly could, it was easily seen that it was out of proportion to my efforts, and that was no encouragement to make me study further. Accordingly, the bishop and the Superior refused to have any more to do with me, and gave me back to Madame de Warens as a person not even good enough for a priest; in other respects, a good enough lad, they said, and free from vice: which was the reason why, in spite of so many discouraging prejudices against me, she did not desert me.

I brought back to her in triumph her volume of music, of which I had made such good use. My air of *Alpheus and Arethusa* was nearly all that I had learnt at the seminary. My marked taste for this art gave her the idea of making me a musician; the opportunity was favourable; she had music at her house at least once a week, and the choir-master of the cathedral, who directed these little concerts, was a frequent visitor. He was a Parisian, named Le Maître, a good composer, very lively, very gay, still young, tolerably good-looking, not very intelligent, but, on the whole, a good fellow. Mamma introduced me to him. I took a fancy to him, and he was not displeased with me; the fee was discussed and settled. In short, I went to live in his house, where I passed the winter the more agreeably, as it was only twenty yards distant from mamma's; we were with her in a moment, and very often supped there together.

It will be readily imagined that life in the choir-master's house, where singing and gaiety prevailed, together with musicians and choir-boys, pleased me far better than life in the seminary with the fathers of St. Lazare. However, this life, although more unrestrained, was not less orderly and regular. I was born to love independence, without abusing it. For six whole months, I never went out once, except to visit mamma or to attend church, nor did I ever feel tempted to do so. This period is one of those during which I have enjoyed the greatest calm, and which I recall with the greatest pleasure. Of the various situations in which I have found myself, some have been distinguished by such a feeling of comfort, that, in recalling them, I am as affected by them as if I were still similarly situated. I not only recall times, places, persons, but all the surrounding objects, the temperature of the air, its smell, its colour, a certain local impression only felt there, the lively remembrance of which stirs my old transports anew. For instance, all that was repeated in the choir-master's house, all that was sung in the choir, everything that took place there, the beautiful and majestic dress of the canons, the chasubles of the priests, the mitres of the chanters, the faces of the musicians, an old lame carpenter, who played the counterbass, a fair little Abbé who played the violin, the ragged cassock which, after laying down his sword, M. le Maître put on over his lay-coat, and the beautiful fine surplice with which he covered his rags when he went to the choir; the pride with which, holding my little flageolet, I took my place in the orchestra in the gallery, to assist in the end of a recitative which M. le Maître had composed on purpose for me; the good dinner waiting for us afterwards, the good appetite we took to it—all these objects together, recurring most vividly a hundred times to my memory, have enchanted me as much or even more than the reality had ever done.

I lived at Annecy for nearly a year without the least reproach; everybody was satisfied with me. Since my departure from Turin I had committed no follies, nor was I guilty of any as long as I was under mamma's eyes. She guided me, and always guided me well; my attachment to her had become my only passion, and, a proof that it was not a foolish passion, my heart formed my reason. It is true that a single sentiment, absorbing, so to speak, all my faculties, put it out of my power to learn anything, even music, although I did my utmost. But it was not my fault; the most perfect goodwill was there, and steady application. But I was distracted, a dreamer; I sighed. What could I do? Nothing that depended upon me was wanting to ensure my progress; but, in order for me to commit fresh follies, I only needed a subject to put them into my head. This subject presented itself; chance arranged matters, and, as will be seen in the sequel, my stupid head knew how to profit by it.

One evening during the month of February, in very cold weather, while we were all seated round the fire, we heard a knock at the street door. Perrine took her lantern, went down and opened it; and returned with a young man, who came upstairs, introduced himself with an easy air, paid M. le Maître a short and well-turned compliment, and told us that he was a French musician, obliged by the low state of his finances to offer his services to churches, in order to pay his way. When he heard the words "French musician," Le Maître's good heart leaped for joy; he was passionately fond of his country and his profession. He received the young wayfarer, offered him a night's lodging, of which he seemed sorely in want, and which he accepted without much ceremony. I examined him while he was warming himself and chattering, while waiting for supper. He was short of stature, but broad-shouldered. There was something misshapen about his figure, without any special deformity; he was, so to speak, a hunch-back with straight shoulders, and I fancy that he limped a little. His black coat was worn out by constant use rather than old, and was falling to pieces; his shirt, made of very fine linen, was very dirty; he wore beautiful fringed ruffles and gaiters, in either of which he could have put both his legs; and, by way of protection against the snow, he had a little hat only fit to carry under his arm. In this whimsical attire, however, there was something noble, to which his general demeanour did not give the lie. His expression was pleasant and intelligent: he spoke readily and well, although his language was rather too free. Everything about him showed him to be a young libertine of good education, who did not go begging like a beggar, but like a madcap. He told us that his name was Venture de Villeneuve, that he came from Paris, that he had lost his way, and, forgetting for the moment his *rôle* of musician, he added that he was going to Grenoble to see one of his relations who was a member of the parliament.

During supper the conversation turned upon music, and he spoke well upon the subject. He was acquainted with all the great virtuosi, all the famous works, all the actors and actresses, pretty women, and great noblemen. He appeared familiar with everything that was alluded to; but, directly a subject was broached, he upset the discussion with some broad joke, which made us laugh and forget what had been said. It was Saturday; on the following day there was music in the cathedral. M. le Maître proposed to him to take part in the singing; "With pleasure," he replied. Being asked what part he took, he answered, "Alto," and went on to speak of something else. Before church, his part was given him to look through; but he never even glanced at it. This piece of swagger surprised Le Maître. "You will see," he whispered to me, "that he doesn't know a note." "I am very much afraid so," I replied. I followed them full of uneasiness. When the singing began, my heart beat violently, for I was greatly interested in him.

I soon found I had no reason for uneasiness. He sang his two parts with the greatest correctness and the best taste imaginable, and, what was more, in a charming voice. I have rarely experienced a more agreeable surprise.

[But "mamma" does not take to Jean-Jacques' new friend, and the dangers of a bad influence are averted. M. le Maître decides to run away, and Rousseau accompanies him on this adventure as far as Lyons, then deserts Le Maître when he is seized by an epileptic fit.]

Of all the incidents I have related up to the present time some traces have remained in all the places where I have lived; those which I shall relate in the next book are almost entirely unknown. They are the greatest extravagances of my life, and it is fortunate that they have not led to worse results. But my head, raised to the pitch of a foreign instrument, was out of its proper key; it recovered it of itself, and I abandoned my follies, or at least only committed such as were more in agreement with my natural disposition. This period of my youth is the one of which I have the most confused idea. During this time scarcely anything occurred of sufficient interest to my heart for me to preserve a lively recollection of it; and it is almost unavoidable that, amidst so many wanderings backwards and forwards, so many successive changes, I should transpose times or places. I am writing entirely from memory, without notes, without materials to assist my recollection. There are events in my life which are as fresh in my mind as if they had just happened; but there are also gaps and voids, which I can only fill up by the aid of a narrative which is as confused as the recollection of it which has remained to me. It is, therefore, possible that I have sometimes made mistakes, and I may do so again, in unimportant matters, up to the time when I possess surer information regarding myself; but, in all that is really of essential importance, I feel sure of being an accurate and faithful chronicler, as I shall always endeavour to be in everything—of that the reader may rest assured.

[Returning to Annecy, Rousseau finds that Madame de Warens has left for Paris, engaged in one of her mysterious intrigues.]

BOOK FOUR

[1731-1732]

I ARRIVED at Annecy, where I no longer found her. Imagine my surprise and grief! Then, for the first time, my regret at having abandoned Le Maître in so cowardly a manner made itself felt. It became keener still, when I heard of the misfortunes that had befallen him. His box of music, which contained all his worldly goods, the precious box, which had cost such trouble to save, had been seized on its arrival at Lyons, in consequence of a letter, in which the Chapter had informed Comte Dortan of its secret removal. Le Maître in vain claimed his property, his means of livelihood, the work of his whole life. The ownership of the box was at least open to dispute; but the question was not raised. The matter was decided on the spot by the law of the stronger, and poor Le Maître thus lost the fruit of his talents, the work of his youth and the resource of his old age.

Nothing was wanting to the blow which fell upon me to make it overwhelming. But I was at an age when great sorrow takes little hold, and I soon found means of consolation. I expected soon to hear news of Madame de Warens, although I did not know her address and she was ignorant of my return; and, as for my desertion of Le Maître, all things considered, I did not find it so blameworthy. I had been of service to him in his flight; that was the only service I could render him. If I had remained with him in France, I could not have cured him of his illness, I could not have saved his box, I should only have doubled his expenditure without being able to help him. This was the light in which I then regarded the matter: I regard it differently now. A mean action does not torture us when we have just committed it, but long afterwards, when we recall it to mind; for the remembrance of it never dies.

[He moves in with Venture, whom he admires more than ever.]

Madame de Warens had only taken Anet with her; she had left Merceret behind, her maid of whom I have already spoken, and whom I found still occupying her mistress' room. Mademoiselle Merceret was a little older than myself, not pretty, but sufficiently agreeable; a good Fribourgeoise, free from vice, in whom I discovered no other failing except that at times she was somewhat insubordinate to her mistress. I went to see her pretty often; she was an old acquaintance, and the sight of her reminded me of another still dearer, for whose sake I loved her. She had several friends, amongst them a certain Mademoiselle Giraud, a Genevese, who, for my sins, took it into her head to take a fancy to me. She continually pressed Merceret to take me to see her, which I allowed her to do, because I was fond of her, and there were other young persons there whose company was very agreeable. As for Mademoiselle Giraud, who made up to me in every possible way, nothing could add to the aversion I felt towards her. When she put her withered black snout, filthy with snuff, near my face I could hardly keep from spitting on it. But I bore it patiently; besides, I enjoyed myself very much with all the girls, all of whom, either to pay court to Mademoiselle Giraud, or for my own sake, vied with one another in making much of me. In all this I saw nothing but friendship. Since then, I have sometimes thought that it only rested with myself to see something more; but it never occurred to me, I never even gave it a thought.

Besides, seamstresses, chambermaids, and shop girls had not much temptation for me; I wanted young ladies. Everyone has his fancies; this has always been mine, and my ideas on this point are not those of Horace. However, it is certainly not the vanity of rank and position that attracts me; it is a well preserved complexion, beautiful hands, a charming toilet, a general air of elegance and neatness, better taste in dress and expression, a finer and better made gown, a nattier pair of shoes, ribbons, lace, better arranged hair—this is what attracts me. I should always prefer a girl, even of less personal attractions, if better dressed. I myself confess this preference is ridiculous; but my heart, in spite of myself, makes me entertain it.

Well! once again these advantages offered themselves, and it only rested with myself to profit by them. How I love, from time to time, to come suddenly upon the delightful moments of my youth! They were so sweet to me; they have been so brief, so rare, and I have enjoyed them so cheaply! Ah! the mere remembrance of them brings back to my heart an unmixed pleasure which I sorely need to reanimate my courage and to sustain the weariness of my remaining years.

One morning, the dawn appeared so beautiful that I threw on my clothes and hurried out into the country to see the sun rise. I enjoyed this sight in all its charm; it was the week after the festival of St. John. The earth, decked in its greatest splendour, was covered with verdure and flowers; the nightingales, nearly at the end of their song, seemed to delight in singing the louder; all the birds, uniting in their farewell to Spring, were singing in honour of the birth of a beautiful summer day, one of those beautiful days which one no longer sees at my age and which are unknown in the melancholy land* in which I am now living.

Without perceiving it, I had wandered some distance from the town; the heat increased, and I walked along under the shady trees of a little valley by the side of a brook. I heard behind me the sound of horses' hoofs and the voices of girls, who seemed in a difficulty, but, nevertheless, were laughing heartily at it. I turned round, and heard myself called by name; when I drew near, I found two young ladies of my acquaintance, Mademoiselle de Graffenried and Mademoiselle Galley, who, being poor horsewomen, did not know how to make their horses cross the brook. Mademoiselle de Graffenried was an amiable young Bernese, who, having been

* Rousseau was at this time at Wootton, in Staffordshire.

driven from her home in consequence of some youthful folly, had followed the example of Madame de Warens, at whose house I had sometimes seen her; but, as she had no pension, she had been only too glad to attach herself to Mademoiselle Galley, who, having conceived a friendship for her, had persuaded her mother to let her stay with her as her companion until she could find some employment. Mademoiselle Galley was a year younger than her companion, and better-looking; there was something about her more delicate and more refined; at the same time, she had a very neat and well-developed figure, the greatest charm a girl can possess. They loved each other tenderly, and their good nature could not fail to keep up this intimacy, unless some lover came to disturb it. They told me that they were on their way to Toune, an old château belonging to Madame Galley; they begged me to assist them to get their horses across, which they could not manage by themselves. I wanted to whip the horses, but they were afraid that I might be kicked and they themselves thrown off. I accordingly had recourse to another expedient. I took Mademoiselle Galley's horse by the bridle, and then, pulling it after me, crossed the brook with the water up to my knees; the other horse followed without any hesitation. After this, I wanted to take leave of the young ladies and go my way like a fool. They whispered a few words to each other, and Mademoiselle de Graffenried, turning to me, said, "No, no; you shan't escape us like that. You have got wet in serving us, and we owe it as a duty to our conscience to see that you get dry. You must come with us, if you please; we make you our prisoner." My heart beat; I looked at Mademoiselle Galley. "Yes, yes," added she, laughing at my look of affright; "prisoner of war. Get up behind her; we will give a good account of you." "But, mademoiselle," I objected, "I have not the honour of your mother's acquaintance; what will she say when she sees me?" "Her mother is not at Toune," replied Mademoiselle de Graffenried; "we are alone; we return this evening, and you can return with us."

The effect of electricity is not more rapid than was the effect of these words upon me. Trembling with joy, I sprang upon Mademoiselle de Graffenried's horse; and, when I was obliged to put my arm round her waist to support myself, my heart beat so violently that she noticed it. She told me that hers was beating too, since she was afraid of falling. In the situation in which I was, this was almost an invitation to me to verify the truth for myself; but I had not the courage; and, during the whole of the ride, my two arms surrounded her like a belt, which certainly held her tight, but never shifted its place for a moment. Many women who read this would like to box my ears—and they would not be wrong.

The pleasant excursion and the chatter of the young ladies made me so talkative that we were never silent for a moment until evening—in fact, as long as we were together. They had put me so completely at my ease, that my tongue was as eloquent as my eyes, although not in the same manner. For a few moments only, when I found myself alone with one or the other, the conversation became a little constrained; but the absent one soon returned, and did not allow us time to investigate the reason for our embarrassment.

When we reached Toune, after I had first dried myself, we breakfasted. Next, it was necessary to proceed to the important business of dinner. The young ladies from time to time left off their cooking to kiss the farmer's children, and their poor scullion looked on and smothered his vexation. Provisions had been sent from the town, and all that was requisite for a good dinner, especially in the matter of delicacies; but, unfortunately, the wine had been forgotten. This was no wonder, since the young ladies did not drink it; but I was sorry for it, since I had counted upon its assistance to give me courage. They also were annoyed, possibly for the same reason, although I do not think so. Their lively and charming gaiety was innocence personified; besides, what could the two of them have done with me? They sent all round the neighbourhood to try and get some wine, but without success, so abstemious and poor are the peasants of this canton. They expressed their regret to me; I said that they need not be so concerned about it, that they did not require wine in order to intoxicate me. This was the only compliment I ventured to pay them during the day; but I believe that the roguish creatures saw clearly enough that the compliment was sincere.

We dined in the farmer's kitchen, the two friends seated on benches on either side of the long table, and their guest between them on a three-legged stool. What a dinner! what an enchanting remembrance! Why should a man, when he can enjoy pleasures so pure and real at so little cost, try to find new ones? No supper at any of the *petites maisons* of Paris could be compared to this meal, not only for gaiety and cheerfulness, but, I declare, for sensual enjoyment.

After dinner we practised a little economy. Instead of drinking the coffee which remained over from breakfast, we kept it for our tea with the cream and cakes which they had brought with them; and, to keep up our appetites, we went into the orchard to finish our dessert with cherries. I climbed up the tree, and threw down bunches of fruit, while they threw the stones back at me through the branches. Once Mademoiselle Galley, holding out her apron and throwing back her head, presented herself as a mark so prettily, and I took such accurate aim, that I threw a bunch right into her bosom. How we laughed! I said to myself, If my lips were only cherries how readily would I throw them into the same place!

The day passed in this manner in the most unrestrained enjoyment, which, however, never overstepped the limits of the strictest decency. No *double-entendre*, no risqué jest was uttered; and this decency was by no means forced, it was perfectly natural, and we acted and spoke as our hearts prompted. In short, my modesty—others will call it stupidity—was so great, that the greatest liberty of which I was guilty was once to kiss Mademoiselle Galley's hand. It is true that the circumstances gave special value to this favour. We were alone, I was breathing with difficulty, her eyes were cast down; my mouth, instead of giving utterance to words, fastened upon her hand, which she gently withdrew after I had kissed it, looking at me in a manner that showed no irritation. I do not know what I might have said to her; her friend came into the room, and appeared to me distinctly ugly at that moment.

At last, they remembered that they ought not to wait till night before returning to the town. We only just had time to get back while it was daylight, and we hastened to set out in the same order as we came. If I had dared, I would have changed the order; for Mademoiselle Galley's looks had created a profound impression upon my heart; but I did not venture to say anything, and it was not for her to make the proposal. On the way, we said to ourselves that it was a great pity that the day was over; but, far from complaining that it had been too short, we agreed that we had possessed the secret of lengthening it by the aid of all the amusements with which we had known how to occupy it.

I left them almost at the spot where they had found me. With what regret we separated! with what delight we planned to meet again! Twelve hours spent together were for us as good as centuries of intimacy. The sweet remembrance of that day cost the young girls nothing; the tender union between us three was worth far livelier pleasures, which would not have suffered it to exist; we loved one another openly and without shame, and were ready to love one another always in the same manner. Innocence of character has its enjoyment, which is certainly equal to any other, since it knows no relaxation and never ceases. As for me, I know that the memory of so beautiful a day touches and charms me more, and goes straighter to my heart, than the recollection of any pleasures that I have ever enjoyed. I did not exactly know what I wanted with these two charming persons, but both of them interested me exceedingly. I do not say that, if I had had control of the arrangements, my heart would have been equally shared between them. I had a slight feeling of preference; I should have been quite happy to have Mademoiselle de Graffenried as a mistress; but, if it had depended entirely upon myself, I think I should have preferred her for an intimate friend. Be that as it may, it seemed to me, when I left them, that I could no longer live without them both. Who would have said that I was never to see them in my life again, and that our love of a day was to end there?

My readers will not fail to laugh at my love adventures, and to remark that, after lengthy preliminaries, even those which made greatest progress, end in a kiss of the hand. Oh, my readers, do not be mistaken! I have, perhaps, had greater enjoyment in my amours which have ended in a simple kiss of the hand, than you will ever have in yours, which have begun with at least that!

[Through Venture, Jean-Jacques becomes acquainted with a government official, M. Simon.]

I must not omit to say something about his personal appearance, of which, considering his magisterial capacity and the *bel esprit* on which he prided himself, it would otherwise be impossible for anyone to form an idea. His height was certainly not three feet. His legs, straight, thin, and tolerably long, would have made him look taller, if they had been vertical; but they formed an obtuse angle like those of a wide-opened pair of compasses. His body was not only short, but thin and in every way indescribably small. When naked, he must have looked like a grasshopper. His head, of ordinary size, with a well-formed face, noble features, and nice eyes, looked like a false head set upon a stump. He might have spared himself much expense in the matter of clothing, for his large wig alone covered him completely from head to foot.

He had two entirely different voices, which, when he spoke, continually mingled together, and contrasted in a manner which at first was very amusing, but soon became disagreeable. One was grave and sonorous; if I may say so, it was the voice of his head. The other—clear, sharp, and piercing —was the voice of his body. When he was very careful, spoke very deliberately, and husbanded his breath, he could always speak with his deep voice; but as soon as he became ever so little animated and spoke in a livelier tone, his accent resembled the whistling of a key, and he had the greatest difficulty in recovering his bass.

With the appearance which I have described, and which is not in the least exaggerated, M. Simon was polite, a great courtier, and careful in his dress even to foppishness. As he desired to make the most of his advantages, he liked to give audience in bed; for no one, who saw a fine head on the pillow, was likely to imagine that that was all. This sometimes caused scenes, which I am sure all Annecy still remembers.

One morning, when he was waiting for some litigants in, or rather upon, this bed, in a beautiful fine white nightcap, ornamented with two large knots of rose-coloured ribbon, a countryman arrived and knocked at the door. The maid-servant had gone out. M. Simon, hearing the knock repeated, cried out, "Come in," and the word, spoken a little too vigorously, came out of his mouth with his shrill utterance. The man entered, looked to see where the woman's voice came from, and, seeing in the bed a woman's mob-cap and a top-knot, was going to retire with profound apologies. M. Simon became angry, and cried out in a still shriller voice. The countryman, confirmed in his idea and considering himself insulted, overwhelmed him with abuse, told him that he was apparently nothing but a prostitute, and that the Juge-Mage set anything but a good example in his house. M. Simon, full of fury, and having no other weapon but his chamberpot, was going to throw it at the poor man's head, when his house-keeper came in.

[Mademoiselle Merceret decides to return to her family at Fribourg, and Jean-Jacques is appointed to chaperone her.]

I am sorry to be obliged to describe so many girls in love with me; but, as I have very little reason to be vain of the advantages I have gained from these amours, I think I may tell the truth without scruple. Merceret, younger and not so cunning as Giraud, never made such lively advances; but she imitated the tone of my voice and accent, repeated my words, showed me the attention which I ought to have shown to her, and, being naturally very timid, always took care that we slept in the same room; an intimacy which rarely stops at such a point in the case of a young man of twenty and a young woman of twenty-five who are travelling together.

On this occasion, however, such was the case. My simplicity was such that, although Merceret was not disagreeable to me, not only did the slightest attempt at gallantry never occur to my mind, during the whole journey, but I never even had the remotest idea of anything of the kind; and, even if the idea had occurred to me, I should have been too foolish to know how to take advantage of it. I could not imagine how a young man and a young woman could ever sleep together; I believed that it required ages to prepare for this terrible arrangement. If poor Merceret, when she offered to defray my expenses, reckoned upon some equivalent, she was deceived; we reached Fribourg exactly as we had left Annecy.

When we passed through Geneva, I did not go to see any-one; but I almost had a serious attack of illness on the bridges. I have never seen the walls of this happy city, never entered its gates, without feeling a certain heart-sinking, the result of excessive emotion. While the noble image of liberty elevated my soul, thoughts of equality, union, and gentleness of manners moved me even to tears, and inspired me with a lively regret at having lost all these blessings. How mistaken I was, and yet how naturally I thought I saw all this in my native land, because I carried it in my heart.

We were obliged to pass Nyon. Pass without seeing my good father! Had I been able to bring myself to do this, I should afterwards have died of grief. I left Merceret at the inn, and went at all risks to see him. Ah! how wrong I was to be afraid of him! When I approached him, his heart opened itself to those feelings of a father with which it was filled. How he wept while we embraced! He at first thought that I had returned to him. I told him my story and my resolution. He feebly opposed it. He pointed out to me the dangers to which I was exposing myself, and told me that the briefest follies were the best. For the rest, he did not feel the slightest temptation to detain me by force, and in that I am of opinion that he was right; but it is none the less certain that he did not do all that he might have done to bring me back, whether it was that he himself was of the opinion that I ought not to retrace the step that I had already taken, or, perhaps, did not quite know what he could do with me at my age. I have since learned that he had formed a very unjust and entirely false, although very natural, opinion of my travelling companion. . . .

We arrived without accident at Fribourg. Towards the end of the journey, my companion's advances became less pronounced. After our arrival, she showed me nothing but coldness, and her father, who was not rolling in money, did not give me a very favourable reception; and I went to an inn to sleep. The following day I went to see them; they invited me to dinner; I accepted. Then we separated with dry eyes. In the evening I returned to my beershop, and left the place two days after my arrival, without exactly knowing which way I intended to go.

Here again was an incident in my life when Providence offered me exactly what I wanted, in order to spend my days in happiness. Merceret was a very good girl, certainly not brilliant or handsome, but neither was she ugly; she possessed little animation, and, but for occasional exhibitions of temper, which passed off with tears and never led to any stormy results, was very sensible. She was really attached to me; I might have married her without any difficulty, and followed her father's trade; my taste for music would have made me fond of it. I should have settled at Fribourg—a little town, not pretty, certainly, but inhabited by very good-natured people. I should, no doubt, have lost much pleasure, but I should have lived in peace to my last hour; and I, better than anyone else, ought to know that there was no reason for a moment's hesitation about such a bargain.

Why is it that, having found so many good people in my youth, I find so few in my later years? Is their race extinct? No; but the class in which I am obliged to look for them now, is no longer the same as that in which I found them. Among the people, where great passions only speak at intervals, the sentiments of nature make themselves more frequently heard; in the higher ranks they are absolutely stifled, and, under the mask of sentiment, it is only interest or vanity that speaks. . . .

Behold me a teacher of singing, without knowing how to decipher an air; for even had I profited by the six months spent with Le Maître, they would never have been sufficient; besides, I had been taught by a master, and that was enough to make me learn indifferently. A Parisian from Geneva, and a Catholic in a Protestant country, I considered I ought to change my name as well as my religion and my country. I always adhered as closely as possible to my great model. He had called himself Venture de Villeneuve; out of the name Rousseau I made the anagram Vaussore, and called myself Vaussore de Villeneuve. Venture knew how to compose, although he had said nothing about it; I, without any knowledge of this, boasted of my skill before all the world; and, without being able to score the most trifling vaudeville, I gave myself out as a composer.

[He undertakes to compose a piece for a chamber concert.]

The company assembled to perform my piece. I explained to each how the time was to be taken, the manner of execution, and the signs of repetition of the parts. I was extremely busy. They spent five or six minutes in trying their voices and instruments, which seemed five or six centuries. At last all was ready; I gave five or six beats of "Attention!" with a beautiful roll of paper upon my conductor's desk. Silence having been obtained, I solemnly began to beat time, the performance commenced. . . . No, since the days of French opera, never has such a caterwauling been heard! Whatever they might have thought of my pretended talent, the effect was worse than anything that seemed to be expected. The musicians were ready to choke with laughter; the audience opened their eyes wide, and would gladly have stopped their ears, but did not know how. The musicians, who played the part of my executioners, wishing to amuse themselves, scraped horribly enough to split the drum of a deaf man's ear. I had the hardihood to keep on without stopping, my forehead covered with large drops of sweat, but prevented by shame from running away and leaving them all in the lurch. By way of consolation, I heard those who were present whispering to themselves, or rather to me, "Intolerable! What mad music! What a witches' Sabbath!" Poor Jean-Jacques! in this cruel moment, little did you think that one day, in the presence of the King of France and all his Court, your music would excite murmurs of applause and astonishment, and that, in all the boxes round you, charming women would whisper to themselves, "What enchanting music! What charming notes! All these airs go straight to the heart!"

But what put everyone in good humour was the minuet. No sooner had a few notes been played, than I heard on all sides bursts of laughter. Everybody congratulated me on my refined taste; they assured me that this minuet would make a name for me, and that my composition deserved to be sung everywhere. I need not describe my anguish, nor confess that I well deserved it.

[He manages to eke out a miserable living with his music lessons.]

I have not spoken of poor mamma for some time; but it would be a mistake to think that I also forgot her. I never ceased to think of her and to long to find her again, not only to satisfy the needs of existence, but still more those of my heart. My devotion to her, lively and tender as it was, did not prevent me from loving others, but not in the same way. All alike owed my tenderness to their charms; but, whereas in the case of others these were the only cause of it, and it would have disappeared with them, mamma might have grown old and ugly, and I should have loved her as fondly as ever. My heart had completely transferred to her person the homage which it at first rendered to her beauty; and, whatever change she might have suffered, my feelings towards her could never have changed, provided that she had still remained herself. I knew very well that I owed her my gratitude; but in reality I did not think of that. Whatever she might have done for me or not, it would always have been the same. I loved her neither from a feeling of duty or self-interest, nor from motives of convenience; I loved her because I was born to love her. When I fell in love with any other woman, I admit that it distracted my attention, and I thought of her less frequently; but I thought of her with the same feelings of pleasure, and, whether in love or not, I never occupied my thoughts with her without feeling that there could never be any real happiness for me in life as long as I was separated from her.

[Jean-Jacques makes a four-day walking tour to Vevay.]

Whenever I approach the Canton of Vaud, I am conscious of an impression in which the remembrance of Madame de Warens, who was born there, of my father who lived there, of Mademoiselle de Vulson who enjoyed the first fruits of my youthful love, of several pleasure trips which I made there when a child and, I believe, some other exciting cause, more mysterious and more powerful than all this, is combined. When the burning desire for this happy and peaceful life, which flees from me and for which I was born, inflames my imagination, it is always the Canton of Vaud, near the lake, in the midst of enchanting scenery, to which it draws me. I feel that I must have an orchard on the shore of this lake and no other, that I must have a loyal friend, a loving wife, a cow, and a little boat. I shall never enjoy perfect happiness on earth until I have all that. I laugh at the simplicity with which I have several times visited this country merely in search of this imaginary happiness. I was always surprised to find its inhabitants, especially the women, of quite a different character from that which I expected. How contradictory it appeared to me! The country and its inhabitants have never seemed to me made for each other.

During this journey to Vevay, walking along the beautiful shore, I abandoned myself to the sweetest melancholy. My heart eagerly flung itself into a thousand innocent raptures; I was filled with emotion, I sighed and wept like a child. How often have I stopped to weep to my heart's content, and, sitting on a large stone, amused myself with looking at my tears falling into the water!

At Vevay I lodged at *La Clef*, and, during the two days that I remained there without seeing anyone, I conceived an affection for this town which has followed me on all my journeys, and which, finally, made me fix the abode of the heroes of my romance there. I would say to all persons of taste and feeling: Go to Vevay, explore the country, contemplate the scenery, row on the lake, and then say if Nature has not made this beautiful country for a Julie, a Claire and a St. Preux; but do not expect to find them there!

I insensibly learned music by teaching it. My life was tolerably pleasant; a sensible man would have been content with it, but my restless heart wanted something more. On Sundays and other days when I was at liberty, I roamed the country and forests in the neighbourhood, ever wandering, musing, and sighing; and, when once out of the city, I never returned till the evening. One day, being at Boudry, I went into an inn to dine; I saw there a man with a long beard, a violet-coloured coat after the Greek style, a fur cap, of somewhat noble appearance and presence, who often had great difficulty in making himself understood, since he spoke an almost unintelligible jargon, which resembled Italian more than any other language. I understood nearly everything he said, and I was the only person who did. He could only express his meaning by making signs to the landlord and the country people. I said a few words to him in Italian, which he understood perfectly; he got up and embraced me with delight. The acquaintance was soon made, and from that moment I acted as his interpreter. His dinner was a good one, mine was barely tolerable; he invited me to share his, and I accepted without ceremony. Drinking and chattering, we became quite intimate, and at the end of the meal we were inseparable. He told me that he was a Greek prelate and Archimandrite of Jerusalem, and that he had been commissioned to make a collection in Europe for the restoration of the Holy Sepulchre. He showed me beautiful patents from the Czarina and the Emperor; he had several more from other sovereigns. He was well satisfied with the amount he had already collected, but he had found incredible difficulties in Germany, since he did not understand a word of German, Latin, or French, and was reduced to his Greek, Turkish, and the *lingua franca,* as his sole resource, which had not helped him much in the country in which he had made so bad a beginning. He proposed that I should accompany him as secretary and interpreter. Although I had just bought a new violet coat, which was not ill-suited to my new employment, I looked anything but smart, so that he thought it would be an easy matter to secure my services, and in this he was not mistaken. Our agreement was soon made; I asked nothing, and he promised much. Without security, without bond, without knowing anything about him, I submitted myself to his guidance, and the next morning behold me on my way to Jerusalem!

[After some successful extortions, the "Archimandrite" is unmasked by the French ambassador and imprisoned. Rousseau wins the favor of the ambassador, who sends him to Paris, where he is to be companion to the nephew of a M. Godard.]

When anyone offered me an empty seat in a carriage, or accosted me on the road, I made a wry face when I saw that fortune overthrown, the edifice of which I reared during my walk. This time my ideas were warlike. I was going to be attached to a military man and to become a soldier myself; for it had been arranged that I should begin by being a cadet. I already saw myself in an officer's uniform, with a beautiful white plume. My breast swelled at this noble thought. I had a smattering of geometry and fortification; I had an uncle an engineer; I was, in a manner, a soldier born. My short sight was a slight obstacle, which, however, did not trouble me much; and I hoped, by dint of coolness and intrepidity, to make up for this defect. I had read that Marshal Schomberg was very short-sighted; why should not Marshal Rousseau be the same? I grew so warm in pursuit of these foolish ideas, that I saw nothing but troops, ramparts, gabions, batteries, and myself, in the midst of fire and smoke, calmly giving my orders with my field-glass in my hand. However, when I passed through beautiful scenery, when I saw groves and rivulets, this touching sight made me sigh regretfully; in the midst of my glory, I felt that my heart was not made for such din and noise; and soon, without knowing how, I found myself in the midst of my beloved sheepfolds, renouncing for ever the toils of Mars.

How greatly did the entrance into Paris belie the idea I had formed of it! The external decorations of Turin, the beauty of its streets, the symmetry and regularity of the houses, had made me look for something quite different in Paris. I had imagined to myself a city of most imposing aspect, as beautiful as it was large, where nothing was to be seen but splendid streets and palaces of gold and marble. Entering by the suburb of St. Marceau, I saw nothing but dirty and stinking little streets, ugly black houses, a general air of slovenliness and poverty, beggars, carters, menders of old clothes, criers of decoctions and old hats. All this, from the outset, struck me so forcibly, that all the real magnificence I have since seen in Paris has been unable to destroy this first impression, and I have always retained a secret dislike against residence in this capital. I may say that the whole time, during which I afterwards lived there, was employed solely in trying to find means to enable me to live away from it.

Such is the fruit of a too lively imagination, which exaggerates beyond human exaggeration, and is always ready to see more than it has been told to expect. I had heard Paris so much praised, that I had represented it to myself as the ancient Babylon, where, if I had ever visited it, I should, perhaps, have found as much to take off from the picture which I had drawn of it. The same thing happened to me at the Opera, whither I hastened to go the day after my arrival. The same thing happened to me later at Versailles; and again, when I saw the sea for the first time; and the same thing will always happen to me, when I see anything which has been too loudly announced; for it is impossible for men, and difficult for Nature herself, to surpass the exuberance of my imagination.

[In Paris, Rousseau is not well treated. Learning that Madame de Warens has returned to Switzerland, he sets out again on her trail. On the way, he gives free rein to his love of nature and the chimeras of his imagination.]

One day, amongst others, having purposely turned out of my way to get a nearer view of a spot which appeared worthy of admiration, I was so delighted with it, and went round it so often that, at last, I completely lost myself. After several hours of useless walking, tired, and dying of hunger and thirst, I entered a peasant's hut, not much to look at, but the only dwelling I saw in the neighbourhood. I expected to find it the same as in Geneva, or Switzerland, where all the well-to-do inhabitants are in a position to show hospitality. I begged him to give me dinner, and offered to pay for it. He offered me some skimmed milk and coarse barley bread, saying that that was all he had. I drank the milk with delight, and ate the bread, husks and all; but it was not very invigorating fare for a man exhausted by fatigue. The peasant, who examined me closely, estimated the truth of my story by my appetite, and immediately afterwards declared that he could see that I was a good and honourable young man,* who had not come there to betray him for money. He opened a little trapdoor near the kitchen, went down, and came up a minute afterwards with a nice brown wheaten loaf, a very tempting-looking ham, although considerably cut down, and a bottle of wine, the sight of which rejoiced my heart more than all the rest; to this he added a substantial omelette, and I made a dinner such as none but a pedestrian ever enjoyed. When it came to the question of payment, his uneasiness and alarm returned; he would take none of my money, and refused it with singular anxiety; and the amusing thing was that I could not imagine what he was afraid of. At last, with a shudder, he uttered the terrible words, "Revenue-officers and excise-men." He gave me to understand that he hid his wine on account of the excise, that he hid his bread on account of the tax, and that he was a lost man, if anyone had a suspicion that he was not starving. All that he said to me on this subject, of which I had not the least idea, made an impression upon me which will never be forgotten. It was the germ of the inextinguishable hatred which subsequently grew up in my heart against the oppression to which these unhappy people are subject, and against their oppressors. This man, although in good circumstances, did not dare to eat the bread which he had obtained by the sweat of his brow, and could only escape utter ruin by displaying the same poverty as prevailed

---

* At that time, apparently, my features did not as yet resemble those of my later portraits [Rousseau].

around him. I left his house, equally indignant and touched, lamenting the lot of these beautiful countries, upon which Nature has only lavished her gifts to make them the prey of barbarous farmers of taxes.

[At Lyons, Jean-Jacques finds himself without money.]

One evening, I was sitting in Bellecour, after having partaken of a very light supper, musing how I should get out of my difficulties, when a man in a cap came and sat by my side. He looked like one of those silk-workers who, at Lyons, are called *taffetatiers*. He spoke to me; I answered him. After we had talked for about a quarter of an hour, with the same coolness and without any alteration in the tone of his voice, he proposed that we should amuse ourselves together. I waited for him to explain what amusement he meant, but, without another word, he made ready to give me a practical illustration. We were almost touching each other, and the night was not too dark to prevent me from seeing what he was going to do. He had no designs upon my person; at least, nothing seemed to show that he meditated anything of the kind, and the place would not have been adapted for it; just as he had told me, he only wanted each of us to amuse himself separately. This appeared to him so simple a matter, that it never occurred to him that I should not look upon it in the same light. I was so terrified at this disgraceful proposal, that, without replying, I got up in a hurry, and ran away as fast as I could, fancying the wretch was at my heels. I was so confused that, instead of making for my lodging, I ran in the direction of the quay, and did not stop till I had crossed the wooden bridge, trembling as if I had just committed a crime. I was addicted to the same vice; the recollection of this incident cured me of it for a long time.

During this journey I met with an adventure of an almost similar kind, but which exposed me to greater danger. Finding that my funds were nearly exhausted, I economised the miserable sum that remained. At first I took my meals less frequently at my inn; soon I gave up taking them there altogether, since, for five or six *sous*, I could satisfy myself quite as well at the tavern, as for twenty-five *sous* at the inn. As I no longer took my meals there, I did not feel justified in sleeping there, not that I was much in debt, but I was ashamed to occupy a bedroom without putting any profit into my landlady's pocket. It was beautiful weather. One very hot evening I decided to pass the night in the public square. I had already settled myself upon a bench, when an Abbé, who was passing by, saw me lying down, came up to me, and asked me if I had anywhere to sleep. I confessed the state of my affairs, and he seemed touched. He sat down by my side and we conversed. He was an agreeable talker; all he said gave me the highest possible opinion of him. When he saw that I was favourably inclined, he told me that he had not very extensive quarters himself; that he had only one room, but that he certainly would not leave me to sleep in the square; that it was too late to find a lodging, and he offered me half his bed for the night. I accepted his offer, for I already had hopes of finding in him a friend who might be useful to me. We went. He struck a light. His room seemed neat and clean, and he did the honours with great politeness. He took some cherries steeped in brandy out of a glass jar; we each ate two, and went to bed.

This man had the same tastes as my Jew of the hospice, but did not show them so brutally. Either because he knew that I should be heard and was afraid to force me to defend myself, or because he was really less determined in his designs, he did not venture to propose their accomplishment openly, and tried to excite without alarming me. Taught by my former experience, I soon understood what he wanted, and shuddered. Not knowing in what kind of house or in whose hands I was, I was afraid to make a noise for fear of being murdered. I pretended not to know what he wanted of me; but, appearing greatly annoyed at his caresses, and quite decided not to let them go on, I managed so well that he was obliged to restrain himself. Then I spoke to him with all the gentleness and firmness of which I was capable; and, without appearing to suspect anything, I excused my uneasiness on the score of my recent adventure, which I made a show of relating to him in terms so full of horror and disgust, that I believe I disgusted him, and he altogether abandoned his filthy designs. We spent the rest of the night quietly; he even gave me some good and sensible information; certainly he was a man of some intelligence, although a great rascal.

In the morning, the Abbé, not wishing to appear dissatisfied, spoke of breakfast, and asked one of his landlady's daughters, who was a pretty girl, to send some to him. She answered that she had no time. He turned to her sister, who did not deign to give him an answer. We still waited; no breakfast. At last, we went into these young ladies' room. They received the Abbé in a manner that was anything but cordial. I had still less reason to congratulate myself on my reception. The elder, turning round, stepped upon my toes with the pointed heel of her boot, where a very painful corn had obliged me to cut a hole in my shoe; the other abruptly pulled away from behind me a chair on which I was just going to sit down; their mother, while throwing water out of the window, splashed my face; wherever I sat down, they made me move that they might look for something. I had never in my life been at a party like that. In their jeering and insulting looks I saw concealed rage, which I was so stupid as to fail to understand. Astounded, stupefied, and inclined to think they were all bewitched, I began to feel seriously alarmed, when the Abbé, who pretended to see and hear nothing, judging correctly that no breakfast was to be expected, decided to leave the house. I hastened to follow him, thinking myself lucky to escape from the three furies. As we were walking along, he proposed that we should go and have breakfast at the café. Although I was very hungry, I declined his offer, which he did not press me to accept, and we separated at the third or fourth turning. I was delighted to get out of sight of everything connected with that accursed house; and I believe that he was very glad to have taken me so far from it that I should have found great difficulty in recognising it. No similar adventures have ever happened to me either in Paris or any other city. They have given me so disagreeable an impression of the people of Lyons, that I have always looked upon this city as the most frightfully corrupt in all Europe.

[Rousseau fills his stomach and his purse by copying some music—very badly—at a monastery, then sets out again for Chambéri—and Madame de Warens.]

My heart beat with joy when I drew near to my dear mamma, but I walked no faster. I like to walk at my ease, and to stop when I like. A wandering life is what I want. To walk through a beautiful country in fine weather, without being obliged to hurry, and with a pleasant prospect at the end, is of all kinds of life the one most suited to my taste. My idea of a beautiful country is already known. No flat country, however beautiful, has ever seemed so to my eyes. I must have mountain torrents, rocks, firs, dark forests, mountains, steep roads to climb or descend, precipices at my side to frighten me. I had this pleasure, and enjoyed it in all its charm, as I approached Chambéri. Not far from a precipitous mountain wall, called Le Pas de l'Échelle, below the military road cut out of the rocks, at the place called Chailles, a little stream rushes and foams in some fearful precipices, which it seems to have spent millions of ages in hollowing out. Along the side of the road is a parapet to prevent accidents, which enabled me to look down and be as giddy as I pleased; for the amusing thing about my taste for steep places is, that I am very fond of the feeling of giddiness which they give rise to, provided I am in a safe position. Leaning securely over the parapet, I stretched forward, and remained there for hours together, from time to time catching a glimpse of the foam and dark water, the roaring of which I heard in the midst of the screams of the ravens and birds of prey which flew from rock to rock, and from bush to bush, a hundred fathoms below me. In places where the slope was fairly even, and the brushwood was not too thick to allow stones to pass through, I collected from a distance a large number, as big as I could carry, and piled them up on the parapet; then, hurling them down, one after the other, I amused myself with watching them roll, rebound, and shiver into a thousand pieces, before reaching the bottom of the abyss. . . .

At length I arrived; I saw her again. She was not alone.
The Intendant-General was with her when I entered. Without
a word, she took me by the hand and introduced me to him
with that graceful manner which gained her the affection of
all, saying: "Here is the poor young man, sir; deign to protect
him as long as he deserves it, and I shall feel no further
anxiety about him for the rest of his life." Then she turned to
me; "My child," she said, "you belong to the King; thank
Monsieur l'Intendant, who offers you the means to live." I
opened my eyes wide and said nothing, without knowing
exactly what to think of it; my growing ambition nearly turned
my head, and already I saw myself a young Intendant. My
fortune certainly did not prove as brilliant as I had expected
from such a start; but, for the moment, it was enough to keep
me, and that, for me, was a good deal.

[Rousseau is put to work on the compilation of a tax reg-
ister.]

These lengthy details of my early youth will naturally have
seemed puerile, and I regret it; although born a man in certain respects, I long remained a child, and in many respects
I am one still. I have never promised to introduce a great
character to the public; I have promised to describe myself
as I am; and, in order to know me in my riper years, it is
necessary to have known me well in my youth. Since, as a
rule, objects make less impression upon me than the remembrance of them, and since all my ideas assume the form of
the representations of objects in my mind, the first traits which
have stamped themselves upon my mind have remained, and
those which have since imprinted themselves there have
rather combined with them than obliterated them. There
is a certain sequence of mental conditions and ideas that
exercise an influence upon those which follow them, and with
which it is necessary to be acquainted, in order to pass a
correct judgment upon the latter. I endeavour in all cases to
develop the first causes, in order to make the concatenation
of effects felt. I should like to be able to make my soul to a
certain extent transparent to the eyes of the reader; and, with
this object, I endeavour to show it to him from all points of

view, to exhibit it to him in every aspect, and to contrive that none of its movements shall escape his notice, so that he may be able by himself to judge of the principles that produce them.

If I made myself responsible for the result, and said to him, "Such is my character," he might think that, if I am not deceiving him, I am at least deceiving myself. But, in simply detailing to him everything that has happened to me, all my acts, thoughts, and feelings, I cannot mislead him, except wilfully, and even if I wished to do so I should not find it easy. It is his business to collect these scattered elements, and to determine the being which is composed of them; the result must be his work; and if he is mistaken, all the fault will be his. But for this purpose it is not sufficient that my narrative should be true; it must also be exact. It is not for me to judge of the importance of facts; it is my duty to mention them all, and to leave him to select them. This is what I have hitherto aimed at with all my best endeavours, and in the sequel I will not depart from it. But the recollections of middle-age are always less vivid than those of early youth. I have begun by making the best possible use of the latter. If the former return to me with the same freshness, impatient readers will, perhaps, grow tired; but I myself shall not be dissatisfied with my work. I have only one thing to fear in this undertaking; not that I may say too much or what is not true, but that I may not say all, and may conceal the truth.

BOOK FIVE

[1732-1736]

[JEAN-JACQUES is again living with his beloved "mamma," but in a dark room, in a gloomy house. She reveals to him that Claude Anet, her servant, is also her lover.]

However, it was not without pain that I discovered that

another could live with her on terms of greater intimacy than myself. I had never even thought of desiring such a position for myself; but it was hard for me to see it filled by another, and my feeling was a very natural one. Notwithstanding, instead of conceiving an aversion to him who had robbed me of her, I actually found that my attachment to her extended itself to him. Before all things I desired her happiness; and, since he was necessary to it, I was content that he should be happy likewise. On his part, he entered completely into his mistress's views, and conceived a sincere friendship for the friend whom she had chosen. Without claiming the authority over me to which his position entitled him, he naturally exercised that which his superior intelligence gave him over mine. I never ventured to do anything of which he appeared to disapprove, and he only disapproved of what was bad. Thus we lived in a union which made us all happy, and which could only be dissolved by death. One of the proofs of the excellent character of this admirable woman is, that all those who loved her loved one another. Jealousy, even rivalry, submitted to the predominant feeling which she inspired, and I have never seen any of those who surrounded her ill-disposed towards one another. Let my readers pause a moment at this panegyric, and if they can think of any other woman of whom they can say the same, I advise them to attach themselves to her, if they value their repose.

Here commences, from the time of my arrival at Chambéri to my departure from Paris in 1741, a period of eight or nine years, during which I shall have few events to relate, because my life was as simple as it was pleasant. This uniformity was exactly what I most wanted to complete the formation of my character, which continual troubles had prevented from becoming settled. During this precious interval, my miscellaneous and disconnected education acquired consistency, and made me what I have never ceased to be, amidst all the storms which awaited me. . . .

The colouring of the maps of our geometricians had also given me a taste for drawing. I bought some colours, and began to paint flowers and landscapes. It was a pity that I found I possessed but little talent for this art, for I was entirely devoted to it. I could have spent whole months in the midst of my crayons and pencils without going out. As this occupation occupied too much of my attention, they were compelled to drag me away from it. It is always the same with all the pursuits to which I begin to devote myself; they grow upon me, become a passion, and soon I see nothing else in the world but my favourite amusement. Age has not cured me of this fault, it has not even diminished it; even while I write this, I sit like an old twaddler, infatuated with another study, which is useless to me and of which I understand nothing, which even those who have devoted themselves to it during their youth, are obliged to give up at the age when I want to begin it.

At that time, it would have been in its right place. The opportunity was favourable, and I had some temptation to make use of it. The satisfaction that I saw in Anet's eyes, when he came home loaded with new plants, two or three times nearly made me go out botanising with him. I am almost certain that, if I had only gone once, I should have been captivated by it, and I should, perhaps, now be a famous botanist; for I know no study in the world better suited to my natural tastes than that of plants; and the life which I have now been leading for ten years in the country is hardly anything but a continual botanising, although certainly without purpose, or progress; but, at that time, having no idea of the science of botany, I conceived a kind of contempt—even of aversion—for it, and only considered it an occupation fit for an apothecary. Mamma, who was very fond of it, made no other use of it herself; she only looked for common plants, such as she could make use of in her remedies. In this manner, botany, chemistry, and anatomy, confused in my mind under the general term medicine, only served to provide me throughout the day with a subject for humorous sarcasms, and, from time to time, brought upon me a box on the ears. Besides, a different and most opposite taste gradually developed itself in me, and soon supplanted all the others. I mean music. I must certainly have been born for this art, since I began to love it from my earliest childhood, and it is the only one that I have loved constantly at all times. The remarkable thing is, that an art, for which I was intended by Nature, has nevertheless cost me so much trouble to learn, and that my progress in it has been so slow, that, although I have practised it all my life, I have never been able to sing with any certainty at sight. What at that time made this study particularly a pleasure, was that I could pursue it together with mamma. With very different tastes in other respects, we found in music a bond of union, which I gladly made use of. She made no objection; I was at that time almost as advanced as she was; after two or three attempts we could decipher an air. Sometimes, when I saw her busy round a furnace, I used to say: "Mamma, here is a charming duet, which seems to me just the thing to make your drugs smell of burning." "On my honour," she would reply, "if you make me burn them, I will make you eat them." While the dispute was going on, I pulled her to her piano, where we soon forgot everything else; the extract of juniper or absinthe was reduced to powder; she smeared my face with it—and how delightful it all was! . . .

[He studies Rameau's "Treatise on Harmony," soon organizes monthly concerts, and resigns from his post to devote himself to music. He gives singing lessons, and is admitted "into the fashionable world." He is more attracted by his pupils' figures than by their voices.]

I also had some pupils among the middle classes, amongst others, one who was the indirect cause of a change in my relations, of which I have to speak, since I must tell everything. She was a grocer's daughter, named Mademoiselle Lard; a perfect model for a Greek statue, and whom I should quote as the most beautiful girl I have ever seen, if true beauty could exist without life and soul. Her indifference, coldness, and want of feeling were almost incredible. It was as impossible to please as it was to annoy her; and I am convinced that, if any man had made an attempt upon her virtue, she would have allowed him to succeed, not from inclination, but from sheer stupidity. Her mother, who did not wish to run the risk, never left her for a moment. In having her taught singing, in providing her with a young master, she did all she could to rouse her, but without success. While the master tried to fascinate the daughter, the mother tried to fascinate the master, with equally bad success. Madame Lard united with her natural vivacity all the sprightliness which her daughter should have possessed. She was a lively, pretty little woman, although her features were somewhat irregular and marked with the small-pox. She had small, fiery eyes, which were rather red, and nearly always sore. Every morning, on my arrival, I found my coffee and cream ready; the mother never failed to salute me with a hearty kiss on the lips, which I should have liked to return to the daughter, merely out of curiosity to see how she would have taken it. All this was done so simply and naturally, that, even when M. Lard was there, the kissing and caressing went on as usual. He was a good fellow, the true father of his daughter, whom his wife never deceived, since she had no need to do so. . . .

Madame Lard showed me too much attention for me to show none to her. These attentions touched me greatly. I spoke about them to mamma, as something which was no secret; and, even if there had been any mystery, I should have spoken to her all the same, for it would have been impossible for me to keep a secret of any kind from her; my heart was as open before her as in the sight of heaven. She did not consider the matter quite as harmless as I did. She saw advances where I had only seen friendship; she thought that, if Madame Lard made it a point of honour not to leave me as great a fool as she had found me, she would somehow or other succeed in making herself understood, and, apart from the consideration that it was not fair that another woman should undertake the instruction of her pupil, she had motives, which were more worthy of her, in a desire to protect me from the snares to which my age and calling exposed me. At the same time, a more dangerous snare was set for me, which I indeed escaped, but which showed her that the dangers, which continually threatened me, rendered necessary all the measures of protection which she could employ.

The Comtesse de Menthon, the mother of one of my pupils, was a woman of great wit, and had the reputation of being equally malicious. It was reported that she had caused several quarrels, amongst others, one which had had fatal consequences for the house of Antremont. Mamma was sufficiently intimate with her to be acquainted with her character; having quite innocently taken the fancy of someone upon whom Madame de Menthon had designs, mamma was charged by her with the offence of the preference shown towards her, although she had neither sought nor accepted it; and, from that time, Madame de Menthon sought to do her rival several ill turns, none of which succeeded. By way of sample, I will relate one of the most laughable. They were together in the country, with several gentlemen of the neighbourhood, amongst whom was the suitor in question. Madame de Menthon one day told one of these gentlemen that Madame de Warens was very affected, and she had no taste, dressed badly, and kept her bosom covered like a tradesman's wife. "As for the last point," answered the gentleman, who was fond of a joke, "she has her reasons for it; I know she has a scar on her breast, just like an ugly rat, so perfectly natural that it looks as if it was moving." Hatred, like love, causes credulity. Madame de Menthon resolved to make capital out of this discovery; and one day, when mamma was playing cards with the lady's ungrateful favourite, she seized the opportunity to step behind her rival, and, almost upsetting her chair, cleverly turned back her neckerchief; but, instead of the large rat, the gentleman saw something very different, which it was easier to see than to forget, and this was certainly not what the lady had intended.

I was not calculated to attract Madame de Menthon, who only liked to see brilliant company around her; nevertheless, she paid me some attention, not on account of my personal appearance, about which she certainly did not trouble herself, but because of my supposed wit, which might have made me serviceable to her. She had a lively taste for satire, and was fond of composing songs and verses about those who displeased her. If she had found me sufficiently gifted to assist her in composing her verses, and sufficiently obliging to write them, between us we should soon have turned Chambéri upside down. These lampoons would have been traced back to their source; Madame de Menthon would have got out of it by sacrificing me, and I should, perhaps, have been imprisoned for the rest of my life, as a reward for playing the Apollo of the ladies.

Happily, nothing of the kind happened. Madame de Menthon kept me to dinner two or three times, to make me talk, and found that I was only a fool. I was conscious of this myself, and sighed over it, envying the accomplishments of my friend Venture, whereas I ought to have been grateful to my stupidity for saving me from danger. I continued her daughter's singing-master, and nothing more, but I lived peacefully, and was always welcome in Chambéri, which was far better than being considered a wit by her, and a serpent by everybody else.

Be that as it may, mamma saw that, in order to rescue me from the perils of my youth, she must treat me as a man, which she immediately proceeded to do, but in the most singular manner that ever occurred to a woman in similar circumstances. I found her manner more serious, and her utterances more moral than usual. The playful gaiety, which was usually mingled with her advice, was all at once succeeded by a sustained gravity, neither familiar nor severe, which seemed to pave the way for an explanation. After having in vain asked myself the reason of this change, I asked her, which was just what she expected. She proposed a walk in the little garden on the following day; the next morning found us there. She had taken precautions that we should be left undisturbed all day, and employed the time in preparing me for the kindness which she wished to show me, not, as another woman would have done, by artifices and coquetry, but by language full of feeling and good sense, better calculated to instruct than to seduce me, which appealed rather to my heart than to my senses. But, however admirable and useful the words she addressed to me may have been, although they were anything but cold and mournful, I did not listen to them

with all the attention they deserved, and did not impress them
on my memory, as I should have done at any other time. The
manner in which she began, the appearance of careful prep-
aration had disquieted me; while she was speaking, I was
dreamy and distracted, thinking less of what she was saying
than of what she wanted; and, as soon as I understood, which
was by no means easy, the novelty of the idea, which had
never once entered my head all the time I had been living
with her, it so completely took possession of me, that I was no
longer in a state to pay attention to what she said to me. I
only thought of her, and did not listen to her.

Most instructors are liable to the perverse idea, which I
have not avoided myself in my "Émile," of making young
people attentive to that which they desire to impress upon
them, by revealing to them the prospect of something in the
highest degree attractive. Struck by the object held before
him, a young man devotes his attention to that exclusively,
and, leaping lightly over your introductory discourses, makes
straight for the goal towards which you are leading him too
slowly for his liking. If it be desired to make him attentive,
he must not be allowed to go too far ahead; and it was just
in this particular that mamma showed her want of judgment.
With characteristic singularity, which accorded with her sys-
tematic mind, she took the superfluous precaution of attaching
conditions; but, as soon as I saw their reward, I no longer listened to them, and hastened to agree to everything. I even
doubt whether there is a man in the world sufficiently honest
and courageous to bargain in a similar case, or a woman
capable of pardoning him, if he ventured to do so. In consequence of the same singularity, she attached to the agreement
the most solemn formalities, and gave me eight days to think
over them, which, like a hypocrite, I assured her I did not
require; for, to crown the singularity of the whole affair, I was
really glad of the respite, so greatly had the novelty of these
ideas struck me, and so disordered did I feel the state of my
own to be, that I wanted time to set them in order.

It will be imagined that those eight days seemed eight centuries to me; on the contrary, I could have wished that they

had really lasted as long. I do not know how to describe my condition; it was a kind of fright mingled with impatience, during which I was so afraid of what I longed for, that I sometimes seriously endeavoured to think of some decent way of avoiding the promised happiness. Consider my ardent and lascivious temperament, my heated blood, my heart intoxicated with love, my vigorous health, my age. Remember that, in this condition, thirsting after women, I had never yet touched one; that imagination, need, vanity, and curiosity, all combined to devour me with the burning desire of being a man and showing myself one. Add to this, above all—for it must never be forgotten—that my tender and lively attachment to her, far from diminishing, had only become warmer every day, that I was never happy except with her; that I never left her except to think of her; that my heart was full, not only of her goodness and amiability, but of her sex, her form, her person; in a word, of her, under every aspect in which she could be dear to me. Do not imagine, that, because she was ten or twelve years older than myself, she had either grown old, or appeared so to me. During the five or six years since the first sight of her had so enchanted me, she had really altered very little, and, in my eyes, not at all. She had always appeared charming to me, and, at that time, everyone still considered her so. Her figure alone had become a little stouter. In other respects, it was the same eye, the same complexion, the same bosom, the same features, the same beautiful fair hair, the same cheerfulness, even the voice was the same, the silvery voice of youth, which always made so deep an impression upon me, that, even now, I cannot hear without emotion the tones of a pretty girlish voice.

What I had to fear in the expectation of possessing one who was so dear to me, was naturally the anticipation of it, and the inability to control my desires and imagination sufficiently to remain master of myself. It will be seen that, at an advanced age, the mere idea of certain trifling favours which awaited me in the company of the person I loved, heated my blood to such a degree that it was impossible for me to make with impunity the short journey which separated me from her.

How then was it that, in the flower of my youth, I felt so little eagerness for the first enjoyment? How was it that I could see the hour approach with more pain than pleasure? How was it that, instead of the rapture which should have intoxicated me, I almost felt repugnance and fear? There is no doubt that, if I had been able to escape my happiness with decency, I should have done so with all my heart. I have promised singularities in the history of my attachment to her; this is surely one which would never have been expected.

The reader, already disgusted, is doubtless of opinion that, being already possessed by another man, she degraded herself in my eyes by distributing her favours, and that a feeling of dis-esteem cooled those with which she had inspired me. He is mistaken. This distribution was certainly very painful to me, as much in consequence of a very natural feeling of delicacy as because I really considered it unworthy of her and myself; but it never altered my feelings towards her, and I can swear that I never loved her more tenderly than when I had so little desire to possess her. I knew too well her modest heart and her cold temperament to think for a moment that sensual pleasure had anything to do with this abandonment of herself; I was perfectly convinced that nothing but anxiety to save me from dangers that were otherwise almost inevitable and to preserve me entirely for myself and my duties, caused her to violate a duty which she did not regard in the same light as other women, as will be shown later. I pitied her and pitied myself. I should have liked to say to her: "No, mamma, it is not necessary; I will answer for myself without that." But I did not dare to do so—first, because it was not a thing to say, and, in the second place, because in the main I felt that it was not true, and that, in reality, there was only *one* woman who could protect me against other women and secure me against temptations. Without desiring to possess her, I was very glad that she prevented me from desiring the possession of other women, to such an extent did I look upon everything as a misfortune which would draw me away from her. Our long-continued and innocent intercourse, far from weakening my feelings for her, had strengthened them, but, at the same time, had given them a different turn, which made them more affectionate, more tender perhaps, but also less sensual. Having so long called her mamma, having enjoyed with her the intimacy of a son, I had become accustomed to look upon myself as one. I believe that this was really the cause of the little eagerness I felt to possess her, although she was so dear to me. I well remember that my early feelings, without being livelier, were more sensual. At Annecy, I was intoxicated; at Chambéri, I was no longer so. I still loved her as passionately as possible; but I loved her more for her own sake than for my own, or, at least, I sought happiness with her, rather than enjoyment; she was for me more than a sister, more than a mother, more than a friend, even more than a mistress; and for that very reason she was not a mistress for me. In short, I loved her too well to desire to possess her; that is most clearly prominent in my ideas.

The day, more dreaded than wished for, at length arrived. I promised everything, and kept my word. However, I obtained it. For the first time I found myself in the arms of a woman, a woman whom I adored. Was I happy? No; I tasted pleasure. A certain unconquerable feeling of melancholy poisoned its charm; I felt as if I had been guilty of incest. Two or three times, while pressing her in ecstasy to my arms, I wetted her bosom with my tears. She, on the other hand, was neither sad nor excited; she was tender and calm. As she was by no means sensual and had not looked for enjoyment, she felt no gratification, and never experienced remorse.

I repeat it: all her faults were due to her errors, none to her passions. She was well born, her heart was pure, she loved propriety; her inclinations were upright and virtuous, her taste was refined; she was formed for an elegance of manners which she always loved but never followed, because, instead of listening to her heart, which always guided her aright, she listened to her reason, which guided her wrongly. When she was led astray by false principles, these were always belied by her real feelings; but, unfortunately, she rather prided herself on her philosophy, and the morals which she drew from it corrupted those which her heart dictated.

M. de Tavel, her first lover, was her instructor in philosophy, and the principles which he taught her were those which he found necessary, in order to seduce her. Finding her attached to her husband, devoted to her duties, always cold, calculating, and inaccessible to sensual feelings, he endeavoured to reach her by sophistries, and succeeded in convincing her that the duties, to which she was so attached, were so much catechism-nonsense, intended solely for the amusement of children; that the union of the sexes was in itself a matter of the greatest indifference; that conjugal fidelity was merely an apparent obligation, the inner morality of which only had reference to public opinion; that the husband's repose was the only rule of duty which the wife need respect, so that secret acts of unfaithfulness, being nothing to him against whom they were committed, were equally nothing to the conscience; in short, he persuaded her that the thing was nothing in itself, that only scandal called it into existence, and that every woman who appeared virtuous owed it to that alone. In this manner the wretch attained his object, by corrupting the mind of a child whose heart he had been unable to corrupt. He was punished for it by an all-devouring jealousy, being convinced that she treated him as he had persuaded her to treat her husband. I do not know whether he was mistaken in this. The minister Perret was supposed to have been his successor. All I know is, that the cold temperament of this young woman, which ought to have protected her against this system, was just what subsequently prevented her from abandoning it. She could not conceive that anyone should attach such importance to that which possessed no importance for her. She never honoured by the name of virtue an abstinence which cost her so little.

She hardly ever misused these false principles for her own sake; but she misused them for the sake of others, and that in consequence of another maxim almost equally false, but more in harmony with the goodness of her heart. She always believed that nothing attached a man so strongly to a woman as possession; and, although her love for her friends was only friendship, it was a friendship so tender, that she employed all possible means at her disposal to attach them more strongly to her. The remarkable thing is, that she nearly always succeeded. She was so truly amiable, that, the greater the intimacy in which one lived with her, the more one found fresh reasons for loving her. Another thing worthy of notice is that, after her first weakness, she rarely bestowed her favours except upon the unfortunate; persons of distinction spent their labour upon her in vain; but, if she once began to feel sympathy for a man, he must have been little deserving of love if she did not end by loving him. If she sometimes chose those who were unworthy of her, the blame rested, not on any low inclinations, which were far removed from her noble heart, but only on her too generous, too kindly, too compassionate, and too feeling disposition, which she did not always control with sufficient judgment.

If some false principles led her astray, how many admirable ones did she possess, to which she always remained constant! By how many virtues did she make up for her weaknesses, if those errors can be so called, with which the senses had so little to do! The same man, who deceived her in one point, instructed her admirably in a thousand others; and, as her passions were not so unruly as to prevent her from following her reason, she took the right path when her sophisms did not mislead her. Her motives, even in her errors, were praiseworthy; owing to her mistaken ideas, she might do wrong, but she was incapable of doing so wilfully. She abhorred duplicity and lying; she was just, fair, humane, disinterested, faithful to her word, her friends, and the duties which she regarded as such, incapable of revenge or hatred, without the least idea that there was any merit in forgiveness. Finally, to return to those qualities which less admit of excuse, without knowing how to estimate the value of her favours, she never made a common trade of them; she was lavish of them, but she never sold them, although she was always at her wit's end how to live; and I venture to assert, that if Socrates could esteem Aspasia, he would have respected Madame de Warens. . . .

I do not know whether Claude Anet was aware of the intimacy of our relations. I have reason to believe that it did not

escape his notice. He was very quick-witted, but very discreet; he never said what he did not think, but he did not
always say what he thought. Without giving me the least hint
that he knew about it, he seemed to show by his conduct that
he did. This conduct was certainly not due to any lowness of
disposition, but to the fact that, having adopted his mistress's
principles, he could not disapprove if she acted in accordance
with them. Although no older than she was, he was so mature
and serious, that he looked upon us almost as two children,
who deserved to be indulged, and both of us regarded him as
a man worthy of respect, whose esteem we had to conciliate.
It was not until she had been unfaithful to him, that I understood the extent of the attachment that she felt for him. Since
she knew that I only felt, thought and breathed through her,
she showed me how much she loved him, in order that I might
feel the same affection for him, and she laid less stress upon
her friendship than upon her esteem for him, since this was
the feeling which I was capable of sharing most fully. How
often did she move our hearts, and make us embrace with
tears, at the same time telling us that we were both necessary
to her happiness in life! Let not those women who read this
laugh maliciously. With her peculiar temperament, there was
nothing suspicious about this necessity; it was solely the necessity of her heart.

Thus a companionship was established between us, of
which there is, perhaps, no other example upon earth. All our
wishes, cares, and inclinations were in common; none of them
went beyond our little circle. The habit of living together, to
the exclusion of the rest of the world, became so strong, that
if, during the course of our meals, one of the three was absent,
or a fourth came in, everything was upset, and, in spite of our
special bonds of attachments, our *tête-à-têtes* were not so
sweet as our party of three. What prevented all restraint between us was an extreme mutual confidence, and what prevented weariness was the fact that we were all constantly
employed. Mamma, always planning and always active, allowed neither of us to be idle; and, besides, we each of us had
enough to do on our own account, to keep our time fully occu-

pied. In my opinion, want of occupation is equally the scourge of society and solitude. Nothing narrows the mind more, nothing begets more nothings—gossips, tittle-tattle, bickering, and lies—than for people to be eternally shut up, opposite one another, in the same room, reduced, for the want of anything else to do, to the necessity of chattering incessantly. When everyone is busy, people only speak when they have something to say; but, when doing nothing, they are absolutely obliged to keep talking, which is the most wearisome and the most dangerous kind of constraint. I even venture to go further and maintain that, in order to make company really agreeable, not only must everybody be doing something, but something that requires a certain amount of attention. Knitting is as bad as doing nothing; and it takes as much trouble to amuse a woman who is knitting, as one who is sitting with her arms folded. Embroidering is different; she is sufficiently occupied to fill up the intervals of silence. What is disgusting and ridiculous, is to see, in the meantime, a dozen overgrown hobble-de-hoys get up, sit down again, walk backwards and forwards, turn round on their heels, move the porcelain chimney-ornaments about, and rack their brains in order to keep up an inexhaustible flow of words—a charming occupation truly! Such people, whatever they may do, will always be a burden to themselves and others. When I was at Motiers, I used to go to my neighbours' houses to make stay-laces; if I went back into the world, I should always carry a cup and ball in my pocket, and amuse myself with it all day, to avoid being obliged to speak when I have nothing to say. If everyone did the same, men would become less spiteful, their intercourse would become safer, and, in my opinion, more agreeable. In short, let wits laugh if they please, but I maintain that the only lesson of morality within the reach of the present generation is the morality of the cup and ball.

[Claude Anet dies, and Rousseau rejoices at inheriting his wardrobe. From now on, Madame de Warens, unable to manage her financial affairs, finds herself in ever greater trouble. To earn money, Rousseau decides to study harmony, goes to Besançon. But his trunk is confiscated by border guards, and he returns to Chambéri. He tells of two friends of this period, Gauffecourt and De Conzié.]

The germs of literature and philosophy, which were beginning to stir in my head and only waited for a little care and encouragement to develop themselves completely, found them in him. M. de Conzié had little talent for music, which was a good thing for me; for the lesson hours were devoted to everything else but singing scales. We breakfasted, talked, and read new publications, but never said a word about music. Voltaire's correspondence with the Crown Prince of Prussia was at that time causing some stir; we frequently conversed about these two celebrated men, one of whom, who had only lately ascended the throne, already gave promise of what he was soon to become, while the other, as vilified as he is now admired, caused us to lament sincerely the misfortune by which he seemed to be pursued, and which is so often the heritage of great minds. The prince had enjoyed little happiness in his youth; and Voltaire seemed born never to enjoy any. The interest which we took in both extended to everything connected with them. Nothing that Voltaire wrote escaped us. The pleasure which these readings afforded me inspired me with the desire of learning to write elegantly, and of attempting to imitate the beautiful colouring of this author, which enchanted me. Some time afterwards his "Philosophical Letters" appeared. Although certainly not his best work, it was that which most attracted me to study, and this growing taste was never extinguished from that time.

But the moment had not yet come for me to devote myself to it entirely. I still had a somewhat fickle disposition, a desire for rambling, which had been restrained rather than eradicated, and which was fostered by our manner of living at Madame de Warens', which was too noisy to suit my solitary disposition. The crowd of strangers who swarmed around her from all directions, and my conviction that they were only seeking, each in his own way, to deceive her, made my life at home a regular torture. Since I had taken the place of Claude Anet in his mistress's confidence, I attentively followed the condition of her affairs, and saw them going from bad to worse in a most alarming manner. A hundred times I had remonstrated, begged, pressed and entreated her, but always in vain. I had thrown myself at her feet, and represented to her, as forcibly as I was able, the catastrophe which threatened her; I had strongly advised her to curtail her expenses, and to begin with me; to undergo a little privation while she was still young, rather than, by continually increasing her debts and the number of her creditors, to expose herself to their annoyance and to poverty in her old age. Touched by the sincerity of my zeal, she became affected like myself, and made me the finest promises in the world. But, the moment some worthless fellow arrived, all was forgotten. After a thousand proofs of the uselessness of my remonstrances, what was left for me to do but to turn my eyes away from the mischief which I could not prevent? I withdrew from the house, the door of which I was unable to guard; I made little excursions to Nyon, Geneva and Lyons, which distracted my attention from my secret trouble, while at the same time they increased the cause of it owing to the expense. I can swear that I would joyfully have put up with any kind of retrenchment, if mamma would really have profited by such saving; but, feeling convinced that the money I denied myself would only find its way into the pockets of swindlers, I abused her generosity in order to share it with them, and, like a dog returning from the slaughter-house, carried off my bit from the piece which I had not been able to save. . . .

In this manner I passed two or three years, my attention divided between music, magisteries, schemes, and journeys; wandering incessantly from one thing to another; wanting to settle down to something, without knowing what, but gradually being drawn towards study, associating with men of letters, hearing literature discussed, even sometimes venturing to join in the discussion myself; rather adopting the terminology of books than understanding their contents. In my journeys to Geneva, I occasionally called upon my good old friend M. Simon, who encouraged my growing eagerness by entirely fresh news from the republic of letters, taken from

Baillet or Colomiés. At Chambéri I also frequently saw a Jacobin, a professor of physics, a good-natured friar, whose name I have forgotten, who often performed little experiments which amused me extremely. From his directions, and with the assistance of the "Mathematical Recreations" of Ozanam, I tried to make some sympathetic ink. With this object, having filled a bottle more than half full with quicklime, orpiment and water, I corked it tightly. Almost immediately it began to effervesce violently. I ran to uncork the bottle, but was too late; it burst in my face like a bomb. I swallowed so much chalk and orpiment that it nearly killed me. I could not see for more than six weeks, and this taught me not to dabble again in experimental physics, without any knowledge of the elements of science.

This event proved very detrimental to my health, which for some time had been sensibly deteriorating. I do not understand how it was that, although I had a good constitution, and did not indulge in any excesses, I visibly declined. I am pretty strongly built and broad-chested, and my lungs must have ample room to play; notwithstanding, I was short of breath, had a feeling of oppression, sighed involuntarily, had palpitation of the heart, and spat blood; a slow fever supervened, from which I have never been entirely free. How can one fall into such a state in the flower of one's age, without any internal injury, without having done anything to destroy health?

It is sometimes said that the sword wears out the scabbard. That is my history. My passions have made me live, and my passions have killed me. What passions? will be asked. Trifles, the most childish things in the world, which, however, excited me as much as if the possession of Helen or the throne of the universe had been at stake. In the first place—women. When I possessed one, my senses were calm; my heart, never. The needs of love devoured me in the midst of enjoyment; I had a tender mother, a dear friend; but I needed a mistress. I imagined one in her place; I represented her to myself in a thousand forms, in order to deceive myself. If I had thought that I held mamma in my arms when I embraced her, these embraces would have been no less lively, but all my desires would have been extinguished; I should have sobbed from affection, but I should never have felt satisfaction. Satisfaction! Does this ever fall to the lot of man? If I had ever, a single time in my life, tasted all the delights of love in their fulness, I do not believe that my frail existence could have endured it; I should have died on the spot.

Thus I was burning with love, without an object; and it is this state, perhaps, that is most exhausting. I was restless, tormented by the hopeless condition of poor mamma's affairs, and her imprudent conduct, which were bound to ruin her completely at no distant date. My cruel imagination, which always anticipates misfortunes, exhibited this particular one to me continually, in all its extent and in all its results. I already saw myself compelled by want to separate from her to whom I had devoted my life, and without whom I could not enjoy it. Thus my soul was ever in a state of agitation; I was devoured alternately by desires and fears.

Music was with me another passion, less fierce, but no less wasting, from the ardour with which I threw myself into it, from my persistent study of the obscure treatises of Rameau, from my invincible determination to load my rebellious memory with them, from my continual running about, from the enormous heap of compilations which I got together and often spent whole nights in copying. But why dwell upon permanent fancies, while all the follies which passed through my inconstant brain—the transient inclinations of a single day, a journey, a concert, a supper, a walk to take, a novel to read, a comedy to see, everything that was entirely unpremeditated in my pleasure or business, became for me so many violent passions, which, in their ridiculous impetuosity, caused me the most genuine torment? The imaginary sufferings of Cleveland, which I read of with avidity and constant interruption, have, I believe, afflicted me more than my own.

At Chambéri there was a Genevese, named M. Bagueret, who had been employed by Peter the Great at the Russian Court; he was one of the greatest rascals and greatest fools that I have ever seen, always full of schemes as mad as himself, who flung millions about like rain and thought nothing of an extra cipher. This man, who had come to Chambéri on account of some law-suit before the Senate, got hold of mamma, as was only to be expected, and in return for the ciphers which he generously lavished upon her, drew her few crowns, one by one, out of her purse. I disliked him; he saw it—never a difficult matter in my case—and left no kind of meanness untried, in order to gain my favour. He took it into his head to propose to teach me chess, which he himself played a little. I tried it, almost against my inclination; and, after I had learnt the moves indifferently, I made such rapid progress that, before the end of the first sitting, I was able to give him the rook which at first he had given me. That was enough; I was mad for chess from that moment. I bought a chess-board and a "Calabrois" manual; I shut myself up in my room, and spent days and nights in trying to learn all the openings by heart, in stuffing them into my head by force, and in playing by myself without rest or relaxation. After two or three months of this praiseworthy occupation and these incredible efforts, I went to the café, thin, sallow, and almost stupid. I tried my hand. I played again with M. Bagueret; he beat me once, twice, twenty times; all the different combinations had become mixed up in my head, and my imagination was so enfeebled, that I saw nothing but a cloud before my eyes. Whenever I wished, with the help of Philidor or Stamma, to practise myself in studying different games, the same thing happened to me; and, after exhausting myself with fatigue, I found myself weaker than before. For the rest, whether I gave up chess for a time, or endeavoured to improve myself by constant practice, I never made the slightest progress after the first sitting, and always found myself just where I was when it was over. I might practise for thousands of generations and not be able to do more than give Bagueret the rook, and nothing else. Time well employed! you will say; and I employed not a little of it in this way. I did not finish the first attempt, until I no longer had strength to continue it. When I left my room, I looked like a corpse, and, if I had continued to live in the same manner, I should certainly not have remained long above ground. It will be admitted that it is difficult, especially in the ardour of youth, for such a disposition to allow the body to enjoy continued good health.

The decline in my health affected my temper and moderated the ardour of my imagination. Feeling myself weaker, I became quieter, and lost, in some degree, my mania for travelling. I remained more at home, and was attacked, not by ennui, but by melancholy; my passions were succeeded by hysteria; my languor changed to sadness; I wept and I sighed about nothing; I felt life slipping away from me before I had enjoyed it. I sighed over the state in which I was leaving my poor mamma; over the state into which I saw her ready to fall. I can assert that my only regret was at leaving her, and leaving her in so lamentable a condition. At length, I became really ill. She nursed me more tenderly than any mother ever nursed her child; and this was beneficial to herself, since it diverted her from schemes, and kept away the promoters of them. How sweet would death have been if it had come then! If I had not enjoyed many of the good things of life, I had felt but few of its sorrows. My peaceful soul would have departed without that cruel feeling of the injustice of mankind, which poisons both life and death. I should have had the consolation that I was surviving myself in the better half of me; it could hardly have been called death. Had it not been for the uneasiness I felt concerning her lot, I could have died as easily as I could have fallen asleep; and my very uneasiness was connected with an affectionate and tender object, which softened its bitterness. I said to her: "My whole being is in your hands; make it happy." Two or three times, when I was worse than usual, I got up during the night and dragged myself to her room, to give her advice upon her conduct, which I may say was thoroughly correct and sensible, but in which my sympathy for her was more marked than anything else. As if tears had been food and medicine, those which I shed by her side, sitting on her bed, holding her hands in mine, seemed to give me strength. The hours slipped away in these nightly conversations, and I left her, feeling better than when

I entered; calm and content with the promises which she had made me, with the hopes with which she had inspired me, I went to sleep, peace in my heart, and resigned to Providence.

After I have had so many reasons to hate life, after all the storms which have shaken my existence, and only make it a burden to me, may God grant that the death which is to end it may not be more cruel than it would have been to me at that moment!

By her unremitting attention and watchfulness, and incredible exertions she saved me; and it is certain that she alone could have done so. I have little faith in the medicine of physicians, but a great deal in that of true friends; those things on which our happiness depends are always more salutary than anything else. If there is such a thing as a delightful sensation in life, it is that which we felt when we were restored to each other. Our mutual attachment was not increased, that was impossible; but it assumed a more intimate form which I cannot explain, more touching in its great simplicity. I became entirely her work, entirely her child, more so than if she had been really my mother. We began, without thinking of it, to be inseparable, to share, as it were, our existence in common; and feeling that we were not only necessary, but sufficient, for each other, we accustomed ourselves to think of nothing that was foreign to us, to limit our happiness and all our desires to that possession of each other, which was, perhaps, unique of its kind amongst human beings, which, as I have said, was not love, but a more real possession, which, without being dependent upon the senses, sex, age, or personal appearance, was concerned with all that which makes one what one is, and which one can only lose by ceasing to exist.

How came it that this delightful crisis did not bring happiness for the rest of her days and mine? It was not my fault; I can console myself with the conviction of that. Neither was it hers, at least, not wilfully. It was written that the ineradicable tendency of my disposition should soon reassert its sway. But this fatal recoil did not take place all at once. There was, thank Heaven, an interval—a short and precious interval—

which did not end through any fault of mine, and which I cannot reproach myself with having badly employed.

[Rousseau proposes to "mamma" that they settle down together in the country.]

She would have done so, and the resolution, which her good angel and mine suggested to me, would probably have assured us a happy and peaceful life, until death should have separated us. But we were not destined for such a lot. Mamma was fated to experience all the miseries of want and discomfort, after having passed her life in abundance, to enable her to quit it with less regret; while I, overwhelmed with misfortune of all kinds, was destined one day to serve as a warning to all who, inspired solely by love of justice and the public welfare, and trusting to the strength of their innocence alone, have the courage to tell the truth openly to the world, without the support of cabals, and without having formed a party to protect them.

An unfortunate apprehension kept her back. She did not dare to leave her uncomfortable house, for fear of displeasing the landlord. "Your plan of retirement," she said, "is charming, and I like it very much; but in such retirement we should have to live. If I leave my prison, I run the risk of losing my bread; and, when this fails us in the woods, we shall be obliged to return again to town to look for it. To lessen the chance of being obliged to do so, do not let us leave the town altogether. Let us pay this trifling annuity to the Comte de St. Laurent, that he may leave me mine. Let us look for some retreat, far enough from the town to allow us to live in peace, and near enough for us to return to it whenever it is necessary." This was what we did. After looking about a little, we settled upon Les Charmettes, an estate belonging to M. de Conzié, close to Chambéri, but as retired and solitary as if it had been a hundred leagues away. Between two rather high hills, there is a little valley extending from north to south, at the bottom of which a stream of water runs amongst the trees and pebbles. Along this valley, half-way up the hill, there are some scattered houses, a very pleasant retreat for anyone who is fond of a somewhat wild and retired asylum. Having looked at two or three of these houses, we at last chose the nicest, which belonged to a gentleman in the army, named Noiret. The house was very habitable. In front was a garden with a terrace, above that, a vineyard, and below, an orchard; facing it was a little forest of chestnut-trees, and a fountain close by; higher up on the mountain were pasture meadows; in short, everything requisite for the little country establishment we intended to set up. As far as I can remember times and dates, we took possession of it towards the end of the summer of 1736. I was delighted the first night we slept there. "Oh, mamma," said I to my dear friend, while I embraced her with tears of tenderness and joy, "this is the abode of happiness and innocence. If we do not find both here, it will be useless to look for them anywhere else."

BOOK SIX

[1736]

. . . AT THIS period commences the brief happiness of my life; here approach the peaceful, but rapid moments which have given me the right to say, *I have lived.* Precious and regretted moments! begin again for me your delightful course; and, if it be possible, pass more slowly in succession through my memory, than you did in your fugitive reality. What can I do, to prolong, as I should like, this touching and simple narrative, to repeat the same things over and over again, without wearying my readers by such repetition, any more than I was wearied of them myself, when I recommenced the life again and again? If all this consisted of facts, actions, and words, I could describe, and in a manner, give an idea of them; but how is it possible to describe what was neither said nor done, nor even thought, but enjoyed and felt, without being able to assign any other reason for my happiness than this simple feeling? I got up at sunrise, and was happy; I walked, and was happy; I saw mamma, and was happy; I left her, and was happy; I roamed the forests and hills, I wandered in the valleys, I read, I did nothing, I worked in the garden, I picked the fruit, I helped in the work of the house, and happiness followed me everywhere—happiness, which could not be referred to any definite object, but dwelt entirely within myself, and which never left me for a single instant.

[Jean-Jacques' health continues to decline.]

One morning, when I was no worse than usual, while lifting the top of a little table upon its stand, I became conscious of a sudden and almost incomprehensible disturbance in my whole body. I cannot compare it better than with a kind of storm, which arose in my blood, and in a moment gained the mastery over all my limbs. My veins began to beat so violently that I not only felt, but even heard it, especially the beating of the carotid arteries. This was accompanied by a loud noise in my ears, of three, or rather, four kinds; a dull and heavy buzzing, a more distinct murmur like that of running water, a sharp whistling sound, and the beating which I have just described, the pulsations of which I could easily count, without feeling my pulse or touching my body with my hands. This internal noise was so loud, that it deprived me of my hitherto keen faculties of hearing, and made me not altogether deaf, but hard of hearing, as I have continued to be from that day.

My surprise and affright may easily be imagined. I looked upon myself as dead; I took to my bed, and the physician was sent for; trembling with fear, I told him my case, which I considered hopeless. I believe he thought the same, but he acted as became his profession. He strung together a series of lengthy explanations of which I understood nothing; then, in consequence of his sublime theory, he commenced, *in anima vili*, the experimental cure which he was pleased to try. It was so painful, so disgusting, and produced so little effect, that I soon became tired of it; and, at the end of a few weeks, finding myself neither better nor worse, I left my bed and resumed my ordinary occupations, although the beating of my arteries and the buzzing in my ears still continued, and, in fact, have never left me for a moment from that day, that is to say, for thirty years.

Hitherto I had been a great sleeper. The total inability to sleep, by which all these symptoms have been accompanied, even to the present day, finally convinced me that I had not long to live. This conviction at first calmed my anxiety to recover.

[Rousseau says this accident "killed his passions" and turned him to thoughts of religion. He confides his feelings to "mamma."]

As she always reduced everything to a system, she had not failed to treat religion in the same manner. Her system of religion was made up of ideas of the most different kinds, some very sensible, others very foolish, of feelings connected with her character, and of prejudices arising from her education. As a rule, believers make God like themselves; the good represent him as good, the wicked, as wicked; malicious and bilious devotees see nothing but hell, because they would like to see the whole world damned; while loving and gentle souls do not believe in the existence of such a place. I have never been able to recover from my astonishment at finding the good Fénélon speak of it in his "Telemachus," as if he sincerely believed in it; but I hope that he lied then, for, after all, however truthful a man may be, he is obliged to lie sometimes—when he is a Bishop. Mamma did not lie to me; and her soul, free from gall and bitterness, which could not imagine a vindictive and ever-wrathful God, saw only mercy and compassion, where devotees see nothing but retributive justice and punishment. She often used to say that, if God were to be strictly just towards us, it would not be justice on His part, since He has not made us such as to require it, and would in such a case require from us more than He has given. The curious thing was that, while not believing in hell, she still believed in purgatory. The reason for this was that she did not know what to do with the souls of the wicked, feeling unable either to damn them or to put them with the good until they had become good themselves. In fact, it must be confessed that, both in this world and the next, the wicked are always a source of considerable embarrassment.

[Winter brings them back to town, and a dull season of study. They return to Les Charmettes with the first buds of spring.]

I got up every day before sunrise; I climbed through a neighbouring orchard to a very pretty path above the vineyard which ran along the slope as far as Chambéri. During my walk I offered a prayer, which did not consist merely of idle, stammering words, but of a sincere uplifting of the heart to the Creator of this delightful Nature, whose beauties were spread before my eyes. I never like to pray in a room: it has always seemed to me as if the walls and all the petty handiwork of man interposed between myself and God. I love to contemplate Him in His works, while my heart uplifts itself to Him. My prayers were pure, I venture to say, and for that reason deserved to be heard. I only asked for myself and for her, who was inseparably associated with my wishes, an innocent and peaceful life, free from vice, pain, and distressing needs; the death of the righteous, and their lot in the future. For the rest, this act of worship consisted rather of admiration and contemplation than of requests, for I knew that the best means of obtaining the blessings which are necessary for us from the giver of all true blessings, was to deserve, rather than to ask for them. My walk consisted of a tolerably long round, during which I contemplated with interest and pleasure the rustic scenery by which I was surrounded, the only thing of which heart and eye never tire. From a distance I looked to see if it was day with mamma. When I saw her shutters open, I trembled with joy and ran towards the house; if they were shut, I remained in the garden until she awoke, amusing myself by going over what I had learned the evening before, or by gardening. The shutters opened, I went to embrace her while she was still in bed, often still half asleep; and this embrace, as pure as it was tender, derived from its very innocence a charm which is never combined with sensual pleasure.

We usually took *café au lait* for breakfast. This was the period of the day when we were most undisturbed, and chatted most at our ease. We usually sat a considerable time over our breakfast, and from that time I have always had a great liking for this meal. I infinitely prefer the fashion of the Swiss and English, with whom breakfast is really a meal at which all the family assemble, to that of the French, who breakfast separately in their rooms, or, most commonly, take no breakfast at all. After an hour or two of conversation, I went to my books till dinner. I began with some philosophical treatise, such as the Logic of Port-Royal, Locke's Essay, Malebranche, Leibnitz, Descartes, etc. I soon observed that all these authors nearly always contradicted each other, and I conceived the fanciful idea of reconciling them, which fatigued me greatly, and made me lose considerable time. I muddled my head without making any progress. At last, abandoning this plan, I adopted one that was infinitely better, to which I attribute all the progress which, in spite of my want of talent, I may have made; for it is certain that I never had much capacity for study. As I read each author, I made a practice of adopting and following up all his ideas, without any admixture of my own or of those of anyone else, and without ever attempting to argue with him. I said to myself: "Let me begin by laying up a store of ideas, no matter whether they be true or false, provided only they are definite, until my head is sufficiently equipped with them to be able to select and compare them." I know that this method is not without its inconveniences; but it has answered my purpose of self-instruction. After I had spent some years in thinking exactly as others thought, without, so to speak, reflecting, and almost without reasoning, I found myself in possession of a fund of learning sufficient to satisfy myself, and to enable me to think without the assistance of another. Then, when travelling and business matters deprived me of the opportunity of consulting books, I amused myself by going over and comparing what I had read, by weighing everything in the scale of reason, and, sometimes, by passing judgment upon my masters. I did not find that my critical faculties had lost their vigour owing to my having begun to exercise them late; and, when I published my own ideas, I have never been accused of being a servile disciple, or of swearing *in verba magistri.**

From these studies I proceeded to elementary geometry, beyond which I never advanced, although I persistently attempted, in some degree, to overcome my weakness of memory by dint of retracing my steps hundreds of times, and by incessantly going over the same ground. I did not like Euclid, whose object is rather a chain of proofs than the connection of ideas. I preferred Father Lamy's "Geometry," which from that time became one of my favourite works, and which I am still able to read with pleasure. Next came algebra, in which I still took Father Lamy for my guide. When I was more advanced, I took Father Reynaud's "Science of Calculation"; then his "Analysis Demonstrated," which I merely skimmed. I have never got so far as to understand properly the application of algebra to geometry. I did not like this method of working without knowing what I was doing; and it appeared to me that solving a geometrical problem by means of equations was like playing a tune by simply turning the handle of a barrel-organ. The first time that I found by calculation, that the square of a binomial was composed of the square of each of its parts added to twice the product of those parts, in spite of the correctness of my multiplication, I would not believe it until I had drawn the figure. I had considerable liking for algebra, in so far as it dealt with abstract quantities; but, when it was applied to space and dimensions, I wanted to see the operation explained by lines; otherwise I was entirely unable to comprehend it.

After this came Latin. I found this my most difficult task, and I have never made much progress in it. At first I began with the Port-Royal method, but without result. Its barbarous verses disgusted me, and my ear could never retain them. The mass of rules confused me, and when learning the last, I forgot all that had preceded it. A man who has no memory does not want to study words; and it was just in order to strengthen my memory that I persisted in this study, which I was finally obliged to abandon. I was sufficiently acquainted with the

* "By the words of a teacher."

construction to be able to read an easy author with the help
of a dictionary. I kept to this plan with tolerable success. I
limited myself to translations, not written, but mental. By
dint of continual practice, I was able to read the Latin
authors with tolerable ease, but I have never been able to
speak or write in that language, which frequently caused me
embarrassment, when I found myself, I know not how, en-
rolled a member of the society of men of letters. . . .

Before noon I left my books, and, if dinner was not ready, I
paid a visit to my friends the pigeons, or worked in the garden
until it was. When I heard myself called, I was very glad to
run to table, provided with an excellent appetite; for it is a
remarkable thing that, however ill I may be, my appetite
never fails. We dined very pleasantly, talking of our affairs,
until mamma was able to eat. Two or three times a week,
when it was fine, we took our coffee in a cool and shady
arbour behind the house, which I had decorated with hops,
which made it very agreeable during the heat. We spent
some little time in looking at our vegetables and flowers, and
in talking about our mode of life, which heightened the enjoyment of it. I had another little family at the bottom of the
garden—some bees. I rarely failed to visit them, and mamma
often accompanied me. I took great interest in their work: it
amused me immensely to see them returning from their forag-
ing expeditions, their little legs often so loaded that they could
scarcely move. At first my curiosity made me too inquisitive,
and I was stung two or three times; but at last they got to
know me so well, that they let me go as close to them as I
pleased; and, however full their hives were, when they were
ready to swarm, I had them all round me, on my hands and
on my face, without ever getting stung. All animals rightly
distrust human beings; but when they once feel sure that they
do not mean to hurt them, their confidence becomes so great
that a man must be worse than a barbarian to abuse it.

I returned to my books, but my afternoon occupations deserved less to be called work and study than recreation and
amusement. I have never been able to endure close application in my room after dinner, and, generally speaking, any

effort during the heat of the day is painful to me. However, I occupied myself with reading without study, without restraint, and almost without any system. My most regular occupations were history and geography, and, as these did not require any great effort of mind, I made as much progress as was possible, considering my weak memory. . . .

[Jansenist writings instill in Jean-Jacques a great fear of being damned and going to Hell.]

According to my Jansenists, there was no doubt about the matter; but, according to my conscience, I thought differently. Always fearful, and a prey to cruel uncertainty, I had recourse to the most laughable expedients to escape from it, for which I would unhesitatingly have anyone locked up as a madman if I saw him doing as I did. One day, while musing upon this melancholy subject, I mechanically amused myself by throwing stones against the trunks of trees with my usual good aim, that is to say, hardly ever hitting one. While engaged in this useful exercise, it occurred to me to draw a prognostic from it to calm my anxiety. I said to myself: "I will throw this stone at the tree opposite; if I hit it, I am saved; if I miss it, I am damned." While speaking, I threw my stone with a trembling hand and a terrible palpitation of the heart, but with so successful an aim that it hit the tree right in the middle, which, to tell the truth, was no very difficult feat, for I had been careful to choose a tree with a thick trunk close at hand. From that time I have never had any doubt about my salvation! When I recall this characteristic incident, I do not know whether to laugh or cry at myself. You great men, who are most certainly laughing, may congratulate yourselves; but do not mock my wretchedness, for I swear to you that I feel it deeply.

[1737-1741. Rousseau makes a brief trip to Geneva, to claim an inheritance, returns to "mamma," to whom he gives his money.]

Meanwhile, my health was not completely re-established; on the contrary, I was visibly wasting away. I was as pale as a corpse and thin as a skeleton. The beating of my veins was terrible; the palpitations of my heart were more frequent. I continually suffered from shortness of breath, and my weakness at length became so great that I could scarcely move. I could not walk fast without a feeling of suffocation; I could not stoop without turning giddy; I could not lift the smallest weight; and I was forced to remain inactive, the greatest torment for a man as restless as I was. There is no doubt that my illness was, to a great extent, attributable to hysteria. This, which is the ailment of happy people, was mine. The tears which I often shed without any cause for weeping, my lively charm at the rustling of a leaf or the chirping of a bird, my changeable disposition amidst the calm of a most happy life—all these were indications of that weariness caused by happiness, which, so to speak, leads to an extravagant sensibility. We are so little formed for happiness in this world, that of necessity the soul or the body must suffer, when they do not suffer together, and a happy condition of the one nearly always injures the other. When I might have enjoyed life heartily, the decaying machinery of my body prevented me without anyone being able to localise the cause of the evil. Later, my body, in spite of my declining years and very real and painful sufferings, appears to have regained its strength, in order to feel my sufferings more keenly; and, while I am writing these words, weak and almost sixty years of age, overwhelmed by pains of every description, I feel that I possess more life and strength for suffering than I possessed for enjoyment in the flower of my age and in the bosom of the truest happiness.

[He sets out for Montpellier, to consult a famous physician. In his carriage he meets two interesting ladies.]

It was Madame de Larnage who undertook my conquest; and, from that time, it was good-bye to poor Jean-Jacques, or rather to my fever, hysteria, and polypus—good-bye to everything, when in her company, with the exception of certain palpitations of the heart, which remained, and of which she showed no inclination to cure me. The bad state of my health was our first subject of conversation. They saw that I was ill; they knew that I was going to Montpellier; and my appearance and manners must have made it clear that I was no profligate, for it was evident, from what followed, that they did not suspect that I was going there in order to be cured of the effects of debauchery. Although ill-health is no great recommendation amongst women, it made me interesting in the eyes of these ladies. In the morning they sent to know how I was, and invited me to take chocolate with them; and asked me how I had passed the night. On one occasion, in accordance with my praiseworthy habit of speaking without thinking, I answered that I did not know. This answer made them think that I was mad. They examined me more closely, and this examination did me no harm. I once heard Madame du Colombier say to her friend: "He has no manners, but he is likeable." This word greatly encouraged me, and caused me to act up to it.

As we became more intimate, I was obliged to speak about myself; to say who I was, and where I came from. This caused me some embarrassment, for I clearly saw that the word "convert" would ruin me in polite society and amongst ladies of fashion. I do not know what curious whim prompted me to pass myself off as an Englishman. I gave myself out as a Jacobite. I called myself Dudding, and they called me Mr. Dudding. A confounded Marquis de Torignan, who was with us, an invalid like myself, and old and ill-tempered into the bargain, took it into his head to enter into conversation with Mr. Dudding. He talked to me about King James, the Pretender, and the old Court of Saint-Germain. I was on thorns: I knew nothing about them, except the little I had read in Count Hamilton and the newspapers; but I made such good use of my scanty knowledge that I got out of it pretty well. Luckily, no one thought of asking me about the English language, of which I did not understand a single word.

[Jean-Jacques resists Madame de Larnage's persistent advances, fearing she is only making fun of him.]

Madame de Larnage stood her ground; tried to tempt me so often and spoke so tenderly to me, that a wiser man than myself would have found difficulty in taking it all seriously. The more she persisted, the more she confirmed me in my belief; and what tormented me still more was, that I became

seriously enamoured of her. I said, with a sigh, to myself and
to her: "Ah! if all you say were only true, I should be the
happiest of men." I believe that my raw simplicity only
piqued her fancy, and that she was unwilling to acknowledge
a defeat.

We had left Madame du Colombier and her suite at Romans. We continued our journey, slowly and most agreeably,—
Madame de Larnage, the Marquis de Torignan, and myself.
The Marquis, although an invalid and a grumbler, was a
decent fellow, but was not best pleased at seeing other people
enjoying themselves without being able to do so himself.
Madame de Larnage took so little trouble to conceal her fancy
for me, that he perceived it sooner than I did myself, and his
malicious sarcasms should at least have given me the confidence which I did not venture to draw from the lady's advances, had I not imagined, in a spirit of perversity, of which I
alone was capable, that they had come to an understanding
to amuse themselves at my expense. This foolish idea at last
completely turned my head, and made me play the utter sim-
pleton in a situation in which my heart being really smitten,
might have instructed me to act a far more distinguished part.
I cannot understand how it was that Madame de Larnage was
not disgusted with my sullenness, and did not dismiss me with
utter contempt. But she was a clever woman, who understood
the people she had to deal with, and saw clearly that there
was more silliness than lukewarmness in my behaviour.

She at last succeeded, with some difficulty, in making herself understood. We had reached Valence in time for dinner,
and, according to our praiseworthy custom, remained there for
the rest of the day. We put up outside the town, at Saint-
Jacques. I shall never forget this inn or the room which
Madame de Larnage occupied. After dinner she wanted to go
for a walk. She knew that the Marquis was not fond of walking. It was a plan to secure for herself a *tête-à-tête*, which she
had resolved to make the most of, for there was no more time
to be lost, if any was to be left to make use of. We walked
round the town, along the moats. I recommenced the long
story of my complaints, to which she replied so tenderly,

sometimes pressing my arm to her heart, that only stupidity like mine could have prevented me from being convinced that she spoke seriously. The unaccountable thing was, that I myself was greatly affected. I have said that she was attractive; love made her charming; it restored all the brightness of her early youth, and she managed her advances so cunningly, that she would have seduced a man of the greatest experience. I was very ill at ease, and frequently on the point of taking liberties; but the fear of offending or displeasing her, and the still greater dread of being derided, laughed at, mocked, of providing an anecdote for the table, and being complimented upon my courage by the merciless Marquis, kept me back and made me feel irritated at my foolish bashfulness, and at my inability to overcome it, while I reproached myself with it. I was on the rack. I had already abandoned my timid language, the absurdity of which I felt, now that I was so well on the road; but as I did not know how to act or what to say, I held my tongue and looked sulky. In a word, I did everything that was calculated to bring upon me the treatment which I feared. Happily, Madame de Larnage was more humane. She abruptly interrupted the silence by putting her arm round my neck, while, at the same time, her mouth, pressed upon my own, spoke too clearly for me to have any further doubt. The crisis could not have occured at a more happy moment. I became amiable. It was time. She had given me the confidence, the want of which has always prevented me from being natural. For once I was myself: never have my eyes, my senses, my heart and my mouth spoken so well; never have I repaired my errors so completely; and if this little conquest had cost Madame de Larnage some trouble, I had reason to believe that she did not regret it.

If I were to live a hundred years, I could never think of this charming woman without delight. I use the word charming, because, although she was neither young nor beautiful, and yet neither old nor ugly, there was nothing in her face to prevent her intellect and grace from exercising their full effect. In complete contrast to other women, her least freshness was in her face, and I believe that the use of rouge had

ruined it. She had reasons for her easy virtue: it was the best
way in which she could assert all her charms. It was possible
to look at her without loving her; it was impossible to possess
her without adoring her. This seems to me to prove that she
was not always so lavish of her favours as she was with me.
Her advances to me had been too sudden and lively to be
excusable; but her heart at least had as much to do with it as
her senses, and, during the brief and delicious period which I
spent with her, I had reason to believe, from the forced moderation which she imposed upon me, that although sensual
and voluptuous, she thought more of my health than her own
pleasure. . . .

We were in a country and a season of good cheer; and,
thanks to the Marquis, we enjoyed it to the full. I could have
dispensed with his extending his attentions even to our bed-
rooms; but he always sent his lackey to engage them in advance, and this rascal, either on his own responsibility or by
the Marquis's instructions, always took a room for him next
to Madame de Larnage, while I was poked away at the other
end of the house. But this caused me little embarrassment,
and only added piquancy to our rendezvous. This delightful
life lasted four or five days, during which I was intoxicated
with the sweetest pleasures. They were unadulterated and
lively, without the least alloy of pain, the first and only pleasures of the kind that I have enjoyed; and I can only say that I
owe it to Madame de Larnage that I shall not leave the world
without having known the meaning of pleasure.

If my feeling for her was not exactly love, it was at least
so tender a return for the love which she showed for me, it
was a sensuality so burning in its satisfaction, and an intimacy
so sweet in its intercourse, that it had all the charm of passion without that delirium which turns the brain and spoils
enjoyment. I have only felt true love once in my life, and it
was not with her. Nor did I love her as I had loved, and still
loved, Madame de Warens; but for that very reason the possession of her afforded me a hundred times greater enjoyment.
With mamma, my pleasure was always disturbed by a feeling of sadness, by a secret feeling of oppression at the heart,

which I found difficult to overcome. Instead of congratulating myself upon possessing her, I reproached myself with degrading her. With Madame de Larnage, on the contrary, I was proud of my manhood and my happiness, and abandoned myself with confident joy to the satisfaction of my desires. I shared the impression which I produced upon her. I was sufficiently master of myself to regard my triumph with as much self-complacency as pleasure, and to derive from it the means of redoubling it.

I do not remember where the Marquis, who belonged to the district, left us; but we were alone when we reached Montélimar, where Madame de Larnage made her maid get into my carriage, while I travelled in her own. I can assure you that in this manner we did not find the journey tedious, and I should have found it difficult to describe the country through which we passed. She was detained at Montélimar three days on business, during which, however, she only left me for a quarter of an hour to pay a visit, which brought her in return some importunate and pressing invitations, which she was by no means disposed to accept. She pleaded indisposition, which did not, however, prevent us from walking together alone every day in the most beautiful country and under the most beautiful sky in the world. Oh, those three days! I have had reason to regret them sometimes! I have never enjoyed their like again!

Travelling amours cannot last. We were obliged to separate, and I confess that it was time: not that I was surfeited, or anything like it; I became more attached to her every day; but, in spite of her discretion, I had little left except goodwill, and, before we separated, I wished to enjoy that little, which she submitted to, by way of precaution against the young ladies of Montpellier.

[They make plans to meet again, to spend the winter together.]

I had been told to go and see the Pont du Gard, and did not fail to do so. It was the first Roman work that I had seen. I expected to see a monument worthy of the hands which had erected it; for once, and for the only time in my life, the reality surpassed the expectation. Only the Romans could have produced such an effect.

The sight of this simple, yet noble, work produced the greater impression upon me, as it was situated in the midst of a desert, where silence and solitude bring the object into greater prominence, and arouse a livelier feeling of admiration; for this pretended bridge was nothing but an aqueduct. One naturally asks what strength has transported these enormous stones so far from any quarry, and united the arms of so many thousands of men in a spot where not one of them dwells. I went through the three storys of this superb building, within which a feeling of respect almost prevented me from setting foot. The echo of my footsteps under these immense vaults made me imagine that I heard the sturdy voices of those who had built them. I felt myself lost like an insect in this immensity. I felt, in spite of my sense of littleness, as if my soul was somehow or other elevated, and I said to myself with a sigh, "Why was I not born a Roman?" I remained there several hours in rapturous contemplation. I returned, distracted and dreamy, and this dreaminess was not favourable to Madame de Larnage. She had been careful to warn me against the girls of Montpellier, but not against the Pont du Gard. One never thinks of everything!

At Nîmes I went to see the amphitheatre. It is a far more magnificent work than the Pont du Gard, but it made far less impression upon me; either the latter had exhausted my powers of admiration, or the former, being situated in the midst of a town, was less calculated to arouse them. This vast and splendid circus is surrounded by ugly little houses, and the arena is filled with other houses, still smaller and uglier, so that the aspect of the whole produces a confused and incongruous effect, in which regret and indignation stifle pleasure and surprise.

[After some pleasant weeks at Montpellier, Rousseau decides to give up the adventure with Madame de Larnage, fearing, he says, to run the risk of seducing her sixteen-year-old daughter.]

One of the good results of virtuous actions is, that they elevate the soul and incline it to attempt something even better; for so great is human weakness, that we must reckon amongst virtuous actions abstention from the evil which we are tempted to commit. As soon as I had taken my resolution, I became another man, or rather, I became the man I had formerly been, whom the intoxication of the moment had caused to disappear. Full of good sentiments and good resolutions, I continued my journey with the intention of expiating my error, thinking only of regulating my future conduct by the laws of virtue, of devoting myself unreservedly to the service of the best of mothers, of vowing to her a loyalty equal to my attachment, and of listening to no other call but that of my duties. Alas! the sincerity of my return to virtue appeared to promise a different destiny; but my own was already written and begun, and at the moment when my heart, full of love for all that was good and honourable, saw nothing but innocence and happiness before it, I was approaching the fatal moment which was destined to drag behind it the long chain of my misfortunes. . . .

I arrived, then, punctual to the moment. When I was still some distance off, I looked ahead in the hope of seeing her on the road; my heart beat more violently, the nearer I approached. I arrived out of breath, for I had left my carriage in town; I saw no one in the court, at the door, or at the window. I began to feel uneasy and afraid that some accident had happened. I entered: everything was quiet: some workmen were eating in the kitchen: there were no signs that I was expected. The maid appeared surprised to see me: she knew nothing about my coming. I went upstairs; at last I saw her, my dear mamma, whom I loved so tenderly, so deeply and so purely; I ran up to her, and threw myself at her feet. "Ah!" said she, embracing me, "you are back again then, little one! have you had a pleasant journey? how are you?" This reception somewhat surprised me. I asked her whether she had received my letter. She answered, "Yes." "I should not have thought so," I said, and the explanation ended there. A young man was with her. I remembered having seen him in the house before I left, but now he seemed established there, as in fact he was. In a word, I found my place filled.

This young man belonged to the Vaud country; his father, named Vintzenried, was keeper, or, as he called himself, Captain of the Castle of Chillon. The son was a journeyman wig-maker, and was travelling the country in pursuit of his calling, when he first presented himself to Madame de Warens, who received him kindly, as she received all travellers, especially those from her own country. He was tall, fair-haired, insipid, tolerably well set up, with a face as dull as his intellect, and spoke like a *beau Léandre,* mingling all the airs and tastes of his calling with the long story of his conquests, and, according to his own account, mentioning only half the marchionesses with whom he had slept, and boasting that he had never dressed a pretty woman's head without decorating the husband as well. Vain, foolish, ignorant and insolent, he was in other respects the best fellow in the world. Such was the substitute who replaced me during my absence and the companion who was offered to me after my return.

If souls, when freed from their earthly bonds, still look down from the bosom of the eternal light upon that which takes place upon this earth, pardon me, dear and honoured shade, if I show no more favour to your faults than my own, but unveil both equally before the reader's eyes! I must and will be as true for you as for myself: you will always have much less to lose than I. Ah! how your amiable and gentle character, your inexhaustible goodness of heart, your frankness, and all your admirable qualities atone for your weaknesses, if simple errors of judgment deserve that name! You erred, but you were free from vice; your conduct was blameworthy, but your heart was always pure. . . .

The reader must have gained some knowledge of my heart, and of its truest and most constant feelings, especially those which brought me back to her at this moment. What a sudden and complete upset of my whole being! To judge of it, let the reader put himself in my place. I saw all the happy future which I had depicted to myself vanish in a moment. All the dreams of happiness which I had so fondly cherished disappeared, and I, who from my youth had never considered my existence except in connection with hers, for the first time found myself alone. This moment was frightful! those which followed were all gloomy. I was still young, but the pleasant feeling of enjoyment and hope which animates youth, deserted me for ever. From that time my sensible being was half dead. I saw nothing before me but the melancholy remains of an insipid life: and, if now and again an image of happiness floated lightly across my desires, this happiness was no longer that which was peculiarly my own: I felt that, even if I succeeded in obtaining it, I should still not be really happy.

I was so simple, and my confidence was so great that, in spite of the new-comer's familiar tone, which I looked upon as one of the results of mamma's easy-going disposition, which attracted everyone towards her, I should never have suspected the real reason for it, unless she had told me herself; but she hastened to make this avowal with a frankness which might well have increased my rage, if my heart had been capable of it. She herself considered it quite a simple matter, reproached me with my neglecting her when at home, and appealed to my frequent absences, as if her temperament had been such that it required the void to be filled as quickly as possible. "Ah, mamma," I said to her, with a heart wrung with grief, "what do you dare to tell me? What a reward for such devotion as mine! Have you so often saved my life, only in order to deprive me of that which made it dear to me? It will kill me, but you will regret my loss." She replied, with a calmness calculated to drive me mad, that I was a child, that people did not die of such things, that I should lose nothing, that we should be equally good friends, equally intimate in all respects, and that her tender attachment to me could neither diminish nor end except with her own life. In short, she gave me to understand that all my privileges would remain the same, and that, while sharing them with another, I should not find them in any way curtailed. Never did the purity, truth and strength of my attachment for her, never did the sincerity and uprightness of my soul make itself more plainly felt than at that moment. I threw myself at her feet, and, shedding floods of tears, clasped her knees. "No, mamma," I exclaimed, half distracted, "I love you too deeply to degrade you; the possession of you is too precious for me to be able to share it with another; the regrets which I felt when you first bestowed yourself upon me have increased with my affection; I cannot retain possession of you at the same price. I shall always worship you: remain worthy of it: I have still greater need to respect than to possess you. I resign you to yourself; to the union of our hearts I sacrifice all my pleasures. I would rather die a thousand times than seek an enjoyment which degrades one whom I love."

I remained true to this resolution, with a steadfastness worthy, I venture to say, of the feeling which had produced it. From that moment I only regarded this dear mamma with the eyes of a real son; and I must observe that, although my resolution did not meet with her private approbation, as I perceived only too clearly, she never attempted to make me abandon it, either by insinuating proposals, caresses, or any of those clever allurements which women so well know how to make use of without committing themselves, and which are rarely unsuccessful.

[Jean-Jacques' virtuous resolutions result only in a growing coldness in "mamma."]

The privation which I had imposed upon myself, and of which she had pretended to approve, is one of those things which women never pardon, however they pretend to take it; not so much for the sake of that of which they are themselves deprived, as by reason of the feeling of indifference which they consider it implies. Take the most sensible, the most philosophical, the least sensual woman: the most unpardonable crime that a man, for whom in other respects she cares nothing, can be guilty of towards her, is not to enjoy her favours when he has the chance of doing so. There can be no exception to this rule, since a sympathy, at once so natural and so deep, was impaired in her in consequence of an abstinence, the only motives of which were virtue, attachment, and esteem. From that moment, I no longer found in her that intimacy of hearts which had always afforded the sweetest enjoyment to my own. She no longer unbosomed herself to me, except when she had occasion to complain of the new-comer. When they were on good terms, I was rarely admitted to her confidence. At length, by degrees, she became entirely estranged from me. She still seemed pleased to see me, but no longer found my company indispensable; even had I passed whole days without seeing her, she would not have noticed it.

Insensibly I felt myself isolated and alone in that house of which I had formerly been the soul, and in which I led, so to speak, a double life. I gradually accustomed myself to disregard all that took place in it, and even kept aloof from those who dwelt in it. In order to spare myself continual torment, I shut myself up with my books, or wept and sighed to my heart's content in the midst of the woods. This life soon became unendurable. I felt that the personal presence of a woman who was so dear to me, while I was estranged from her heart, only aggravated my sorrow, and that I should feel the separation from her less cruelly if I no longer saw her. I therefore resolved to leave the house. I told her so, and, far from offering any opposition, she approved of it. She had a friend at Grenoble, named Madame Deybens, whose husband was a friend of M. de Mably, the *Grand-Prévôt* of Lyons. M. Deybens suggested to me that I should undertake the education of M. de Mably's children. I accepted the post, and set out for Lyons, without causing, almost without feeling, the slightest regret at a separation, the mere idea of which would formerly have caused us both the most deadly anguish.

I possessed almost sufficient knowledge for a tutor, and believed that I had the necessary qualifications. During the year which I spent at M. de Mably's, I had ample time to undeceive myself. My naturally gentle disposition would have made me well adapted for this profession, had not a violent temper been mingled with it. As long as all went well, and I saw that my trouble and attention, of which I was not sparing, were successful, I was an angel; but, when things went wrong, I was a devil. When my pupils did not understand me, I raved like a madman; when they showed signs of insubordination, I could have killed them, which was not the way to make them either learned or well-behaved. . . .

I was hardly more successful in regard to myself than my pupils. Madame Deybens had recommended me to Madame de Mably, and had requested her to form my manners and to give me the tone of society. She took some pains about it, and wanted to teach me how to do the honours of her house; but I showed myself so awkward, I was so bashful and so stupid, that she became discouraged, and gave me up. This, however, did not prevent me falling in love with her, after my usual manner. I managed to make her perceive it, but I never dared to declare my passion. She was never disposed to make advances, and all my ogling glances and sighs were in vain, so that I soon wearied of them, seeing that they led to nothing.

[Rousseau and his employer agree that he is ill-suited to the profession of tutor. Tempted by an overwhelming nostalgia for the old happy days, he returns to Annecy, hoping for "mamma's" caresses. But nothing has changed, and Jean-Jacques is condemned to his lonely room. Nonetheless, he conceives a plan to win a fortune for "mamma."]

Whilst reflecting upon the trouble I had found in learning to read notes, and the great difficulty I still felt in singing at sight, I began to think that this difficulty might be due to the nature of the case as much as to my own incapacity, especially as I knew that no one finds it an easy task to learn music. On examining the arrangement of the musical signs, I found them frequently very badly invented. I had long thought of denoting the scale by figures, to obviate the necessity of always drawing the lines and staves when the most trifling air had to be written. I had been hindered by the difficulties of the octaves, the time, and the values of the notes. This idea again occurred to me, and, on reconsidering it, I saw that these difficulties were not insurmountable. I carried it out successfully, and was at length able to note any music whatever by my figures with the greatest exactness, and also, I may say, with the greatest simplicity. From that moment, I considered my fortune made; and, in my eagerness to share it with her to whom I owed everything, I thought of nothing but setting out for Paris, feeling no doubt that, when I laid my scheme before the Academy, I should cause a revolution. I had brought a little money back from Lyons; I sold my books. In a fortnight my resolution was taken and carried out.

At last, full of the magnificent hopes which had inspired me, being ever and at all times the same, I started from Savoy with my system of music, as I had formerly started from Turin with my heron-fountain.

Such have been the errors and faults of my youth. I have related the history of them with a fidelity of which my heart approves. If, later, I have honoured my riper years with any virtues, I should have declared them with the same frankness, and such was my intention. But I must stop here. Time may lift many a veil. If my memory descends to posterity, perhaps it will one day learn what I had to say; then it will be understood why I am silent.

PART THE SECOND

BOOK SEVEN

[1741]

AFTER two years of silence and patience, in spite of my resolutions, I again take up my pen. Reader, suspend your judgment upon the reasons which force me to do so; you cannot judge of them until you have read the story of my life.

You have seen my peaceful youth pass away in a tolerably uniform and agreeable manner, without great disappointments or remarkable prosperity. This absence of extremes was in great part the result of my passionate but weak disposition, which, more easily discouraged than prompt to undertake, only quitted its state of repose when rudely shocked, but fell back into it again from weariness and natural inclination; and which, while keeping me away from great virtues, and still further from great vices, led me back steadily to the indolent and peaceful life for which I felt Nature intended me, and never permitted me to attain to greatness in anything, either good or bad. What a different picture I shall soon have to draw! Destiny, which for thirty years favoured my inclinations, during a second thirty thwarted them, and this continued opposition between my position and inclinations will be seen to have produced monstrous errors, unheard-of misfortunes, and all the virtues that can render adversity honourable, with the exception of strength of character.

The first part of my Confessions was written entirely from memory, and I must have made many mistakes in it. As I am obliged to write the second part also from memory, I shall probably make many more. The sweet remembrances of my best years, passed in equal innocence and tranquillity, have left me a thousand charming impressions, which I love to recall incessantly. It will soon be seen how different are the recollections of the remainder of my life. To recall them renews their bitterness. Far from increasing the painfulness of my situation by these melancholy retrospects, I put them away from me as much as possible, and frequently succeed so well, that I am unable to recall them even when it is necessary. This capacity for easily forgetting misfortunes is a consolation, which Heaven has bestowed upon me amidst those afflictions which destiny was one day fated to heap upon my head. My memory, which only revives the recollection of agreeable things, is the happy counterpoise of my fearful imagination, which causes me to foresee only a cruel future.

All the papers which I have collected to fill the gaps in my memory and to guide me in my undertaking, have passed into other hands, and will never return to mine. I have only one faithful guide upon which I can depend; the chain of the feelings which have marked the development of my being, and which will remind me of the succession of events, which have been either the cause or the effect of these feelings. I find it easy to forget my misfortunes, but I cannot forget my faults, still less my virtuous feelings, the recollection of which is too precious ever to be effaced from my heart. I may omit or transpose facts, I may make mistakes in dates, but I cannot be deceived in regard to what I have felt or what my feelings have prompted me to do; and this is the chief subject under discussion. The real object of my Confessions is, to contribute to an accurate knowledge of my inner being in all the different situations of my life. What I have promised to relate, is the history of my soul; I need no other memoirs in order to write it faithfully; it is sufficient for me to enter again into my inner self as I have hitherto done.

. . . I have no fear that the reader, forgetting that I am writing my Confessions, will ever imagine that I am writing my Apologia; but neither must he expect that I shall keep silence regarding the truth, when it speaks in my favour.

Besides, this truth is all that this second part has in common with the first, and the only advantage it can claim over it is, the greater importance of the facts related. With this exception, it cannot fail to be inferior to it in every respect. I wrote the first part with pleasure and gratification, and at my ease, at Wootton or in the Castle of Trye. All the memories which I had to recall were for me so many fresh enjoyments. I turned back to them incessantly with renewed pleasure, and I was able to revise my descriptions until I was satisfied with them, without feeling in the least bored. At the present time, my failing memory and enfeebled brain unfit me for almost every kind of work. I only undertake my present task under compulsion, with a heart oppressed by grief. It offers me nothing but misfortunes, treachery, perfidy, melancholy and heartrending recollections. I would give anything in the world to be able to bury in this darkness of time what I have to say; and, while constrained to speak in spite of myself, I am also obliged to hide myself, to employ cunning, to endeavour to deceive, and to lower myself to conduct utterly at variance with my nature. The roof under which I am has eyes, the walls around me have ears. Beset by spies and watchful and malevolent onlookers, uneasy and distracted, I hurriedly scribble a few disjointed sentences, which I have scarcely time to read over, still less to correct. I know that, in spite of the barriers set up around me in ever-increasing numbers, my enemies are still afraid that the truth may find some loophole through which to escape. How am I to set about bringing it to the light? I am making the attempt with little hope of success.

[Rousseau stays a brief time at Lyons, visiting old friends, including Bordes and the Abbé de Mably, and making a new friend, Roguin.]

I arrived at Paris in the autumn of 1741, with fifteen *louis d'or* in my pocket, my comedy of "Narcissus," and my musical scheme, as my sole resource. I had therefore little time to lose in trying to lay them out to the best advantage. I hastened to make use of my letters of introduction. A young man, who arrives in Paris with a pretty good appearance and advertises himself by his talents, is always sure of being well received, as I was. This procured me certain pleasures, but did not materially assist me.

[He meets Réaumur, who arranges for Rousseau to read his paper to the Academy of Sciences. It is now 1742. The

Academy appoints a committee of three incompetent people, who damn his invention with faint praise.]

After the great and fruitless exertions I had recently made, I needed a little rest. Instead of abandoning myself to despair, I quietly abandoned myself to my usual idleness and the care of Providence; and, in order to give the latter time to do its work, I proceeded to consume, in a leisurely manner, the few *louis* which I still had left. I regulated the expense of my careless pleasures, without entirely giving them up. I only went to the café every other day, and to the theatre twice a week. As for money spent on women, there was no need for retrenchment, for I have never in my life laid out a *sou* in this manner, except on one occasion, of which I shall have to speak presently.

The calmness, delight and confidence with which I abandoned myself to this indolent and solitary life, although I had not sufficient means to continue it for three months, is one of the peculiarities of my life and one of the oddities of my character. The great need of sympathy which I felt, was the very thing which deprived me of the courage to show myself; and the necessity of paying visits to people made them so unendurable, that I even gave up going to see the Academicians and other men of letters, with whom I was already on more or less intimate terms. Marivaux, the Abbé de Mably, and Fontenelle were almost the only persons whom I still continued to visit. I even showed my comedy of "Narcissus" to the first. He was pleased with it, and was kind enough to touch it up. Diderot, who was not so old, was about my own age. He was fond of music, and acquainted with the theory of it; we talked about it, and he also spoke to me of his own literary projects. This resulted in a most intimate connection between us, which lasted fifteen years, and would probably have still continued, if I had not, unfortunately, and by his own fault, been thrown into the same profession as himself.

[Rousseau studies Vergil in the Luxembourg and watches the chess masters at the cafés. Then he is recommended to Madame de Beuzenval and her daughter, Madame de Broglie.]

Seeing that it was nearly one o'clock, I wanted to retire, but Madame de Beuzenval said to me, "It is a long way to your quarter; stop and dine here." I needed no pressing. A quarter of an hour later I understood, from something she said, that the dinner to which she invited me was in the servants' hall. Although Madame de Beuzenval was undoubtedly a very good woman, she was of limited understanding, and, too full of her illustrious Polish nobility, had little idea of the respect due to talent. Even on this occasion, she judged me more by my manner than by dress, which, although simple, was very respectable, and by no means indicated a man who ought to be invited to dine at the servants' table. I had too long forgotten the way there, to desire to learn it again. Without showing all the annoyance I felt, I told Madame de Beuzenval that I remembered I was obliged to return to my quarter on business, and I again prepared to leave. Madame de Broglie went up to her mother and whispered a few words in her ear, which had their effect. Madame de Beuzenval rose to detain me, and said, "I hope you will do us the honour of dining *with us*." Believing that to show pride would be to play the fool, I stayed. Besides, Madame de Broglie's kindness had touched me, and rendered her attractive to me. I was very glad to dine with her, and I hoped that, when she knew me better, she would have no cause to regret having procured me this honour. The President of Lamoignon, a great friend of the family, dined there on the same occasion. Like Madame de Broglie, he was familiar with the small-talk jargon of Paris, which consisted of *petits mots* and delicate little allusions. In this poor Jean-Jacques had little chance of shining. I had the good sense not to try to play the wit, when Minerva was not agreeable, and I held my tongue. Would that I had always been as wise!—I should not be in the abyss in which I find myself to-day.

I was deeply grieved at my own dullness, and also because I was unable to justify, in the eyes of Madame de Broglie, what she had done in my behalf. After dinner, I bethought myself of my usual resource. I had in my pocket a letter in verse, which I had written to Parisot during my stay at Lyons. This fragment was not wanting in fire, to which I added by my manner of reciting, and I moved all three to tears. Whether my own vanity or the truth made me so interpret it, I thought I saw that Madame de Broglie's eyes said to her mother, Well, mamma, was I wrong in telling you, that this man was more fitted to dine with you than with your waiting-women? Until this moment my heart had been somewhat heavy, but after I had thus avenged myself, I was satisfied. Madame de Broglie pushed her favourable opinion of me a little too far, and believed that I should cause a sensation in Paris and become a favourite with the ladies. To guide my inexperience, she gave me the "Confessions of the Comte de ——." "This book," said she to me, "is a Mentor, of which you will have need in the world; you will do well to consult it sometimes." I have kept this copy for more than twenty years, out of a feeling of gratitude to the hand from which I received it, although I often laugh at the opinion which this lady appeared to entertain of my capacities for gallantry. Directly I had read the work, I desired to gain the friendship of the author. This inspiration was justified by the event. He is the only true friend I have had amongst men of letters.*

[Through his new friends, Jean-Jacques meets Madame Dupin. She receives him in a state of disarray. He immediately falls in love with her, but his advances are icily rebuffed. He dines with nobility, studies chemistry together with Madame Dupin's stepson. He decides to write an opera, "Les Muses Galantes." Before he gets very far in this work, Madame de Broglie arranges his appointment as secretary to M. de Montaigu, newly named ambassador to Venice. It is now 1743. Rousseau sets out on his journey, is quarantined in Genoa, finally reaches Venice. He soon masters his new duties, but finds M. de Montaigu incompetent, peculiar and obstinate, and is often compelled to act for him. This does not

* [This was Duclos. Rousseau, however, later added this footnote:] I was so long and so firmly convinced of this, that it was to him that I intrusted the manuscript of my Confessions after my return to Paris. The distrustful Jean-Jacques has never been able to believe in treachery and falsehood until he has been their victim.

earn him any goodwill. The ambassador's favorites intrigue against him, and conspire to ruin him. Covered with insults and humiliations, Rousseau resigns his post.

He describes the pleasures of Venice, particularly the different kinds of music.]

The music, which, according to my taste, is far superior to that of the opera, and which has not its like, either in Italy or the rest of the world, is that of the *scuole*. The *scuole* are charitable institutions, founded for the education of young girls without means, who are subsequently portioned by the Republic either for marriage or for the cloister. Amongst the accomplishments cultivated in these young girls music holds the first place. Every Sunday, in the church of each of these *scuole*, during Vespers, motets are performed with full chorus and full orchestra, composed and conducted by the most famous Italian masters, executed in the latticed galleries by young girls only, all under twenty years of age. I cannot imagine anything so voluptuous, so touching as this music. The abundant art, the exquisite taste of the singing, the beauty of the voices, the correctness of the execution—everything in these delightful concerts contributes to produce an impression which is certainly not "good style," but against which I doubt whether any man's heart is proof. Carrio and myself never missed going to Vespers in the Mendicanti, and we were not the only ones. The church was always full of amateurs; even operatic singers came to form their taste after these excellent models. What drove me to despair was the confounded gratings, which only allowed the sounds to pass through, and hid from sight the angels of beauty, of whom they were worthy. I could talk of nothing else. While speaking about it one day, at M. le Blond's, he said, "If you are so curious to see these young girls, it is easy to satisfy you. I am one of the directors of the institution. I will take you to a *goûter* * with them." I did not give him a moment's peace until he kept his word. When we entered the salon which confined these longed-for beauties I felt an amorous trembling, which I had never

* *Goûter:* a light meal between dinner and supper.

before experienced. M. le Blond presented these famous singers to me one after the other, whose names and voices were all that I knew about them. Come, Sophie . . . she was a horrible fright. Come, Cattina . . . she had only one eye. Come, Bettina . . . she was disfigured by small-pox. Hardly one of them was without some noticeable defect. The cruel wretch laughed at my painful surprise. Two or three, however, appeared passable; they only sang in the chorus. I was in despair. During the collation we teased them, and they became quite lively. Ugliness does not exclude certain graces, which I found they possessed. I said to myself, they could not sing so delightfully without soul; they must ·possess one. At last, the feeling with which I regarded them was so altered that I left the room almost in love with all these ugly creatures. I hardly dared to return to their Vespers. But I found cause for reassurance. I continued to find their singing delicious, and their voices lent such a fictitious charm to their faces that, as long as they were singing, I persisted in thinking them beautiful, in spite of my eyes. . . .

As for women, it is not in a city like Venice that a man abstains from them. Have you no confessions to make on this point? someone may ask. Yes, I have something to tell, and I will make this confession as frankly as the rest.

I have always disliked common prostitutes; however, at Venice there was nothing else within my reach, since my position excluded me from most of the distinguished houses in the city. M. le Blond's daughters were very amiable, but very reserved: besides, I had too much respect for their father and mother even to think of desiring them.

A young person named Mademoiselle de Catanéo, daughter of the agent of the King of Prussia, would have been more to my taste; but Carrio was in love with her—even marriage had been talked of. He was well-to-do, while I had nothing; his salary was a hundred *louis,* mine only a hundred *pistoles*: and, not to mention that I had no wish to poach on a friend's preserves, I knew that a man had no right to enter upon affairs of gallantry with a poorly-filled purse, wherever he was, especially in Venice. I had not lost the pernicious habit of cheating my desires, and, being too much occupied to feel keenly those which the climate causes, I lived nearly a year in Venice as chastely as I had lived in Paris, and I left it at the end of eighteen months, without having had anything to do with women, except twice, in consequence of special opportunities, which I will mention.

The first was provided for me by that honourable gentleman Vitali, some time after the formal apology which I forced him to make to me. At table, the conversation turned upon the amusements of Venice. The company reproached me for my indifference to the most piquant of all, and extolled the graceful manners of the Venetian women, declaring that they had not their equals in the world. Domenico said that I must make the acquaintance of the most amiable of all; he expressed himself ready to introduce me, and assured me that I should be delighted with her. I began to laugh at this obliging offer, and Count Peati, an old man of high character, said, with greater frankness than I should have expected from an Italian, that he considered me too sensible to allow myself to be taken to see a woman by my enemy. In fact, I had neither the intention nor the inclination; but, in spite of this, by one of those inconsistencies which I can hardly understand myself, I ended by allowing myself to be dragged there, against my inclination, heart and reason, and even against my will, simply from weakness and shame of exhibiting mistrust, and, in the language of the country, *per non parer troppo coglione.** The *padoana*, to whose house we went, was good-looking, even handsome, but her beauty was not of the kind that pleased me. Domenico left me with her. I sent for *sorbetti*, asked her to sing to me, and, at the end of half an hour, I put a ducat on the table, and prepared to go. But she was so singularly scrupulous, that she refused to take it without having earned it, and, with equally singular foolishness, I satisfied her scruples. I returned to the palace, feeling so convinced that I had caught the pox, that the first thing I did was to send for the physician and ask

* In order not to appear too great a blockhead.

him to give me some medicine. Nothing can equal the feeling of depression from which I suffered for three weeks, without any real suffering, or the appearance of any symptoms to justify it. I could not imagine that it was possible to get off unscathed from the embraces of the *padoana*. Even the physician had the greatest trouble imaginable to reassure me. He only succeeded by persuading me that I was formed in a peculiar manner, which lessened the chance of infection; and, although I have perhaps exposed myself to this risk less than any other man, the fact that I have never suffered in this respect seems to prove that the physician was right. However, this belief has never made me imprudent; and, if Nature has really bestowed this advantage upon me, I can declare that I have never abused it.

My other adventure, although with a woman also, was of a very different kind, both in its origin and consequences. I had mentioned that Captain Olivet invited me to dinner on board, and that I took with me the secretary of the Spanish embassy. I expected a salute of cannon. The crew received us, drawn up in line, but not a grain of priming was burnt. This mortified me greatly, on account of Carrio, who I saw was a little annoyed at it. Certainly, on merchant ships, people by no means as important as ourselves were received with a salute of cannon, and besides, I thought that I had deserved some mark of distinction from the captain. I was unable to conceal my feelings, a thing which I have never been able to do; and although the dinner was a very good one, and Olivet did the honours admirably, I began it in an ill-humour, eating little, and speaking still less.

When the first health was drunk, I expected at least a volley. Nothing of the kind! Carrio, who read my thoughts, laughed to see me sulking like a child. Before the dinner was half over, I saw a gondola approaching. "Faith!" said the captain to me, "take care of yourself; here comes the enemy." I asked him what he meant, and he answered with a jest. The gondola lay to, and I saw a dazzlingly beautiful young woman step out, coquettishly dressed and very nimble. In three bounds she was in the cabin and seated at my side, before I perceived that a place had been laid for her. She was a brunette of twenty years at the most, as charming as she was lively. She could only speak Italian. Her accent alone would have been enough to turn my head. While eating and chatting, she fixed her eyes upon me, and then, exclaiming, "O holy Virgin! O my dear Brémond, how long is it since I saw you!" she threw herself into my arms, pressed her lips close to mine, and squeezed me almost to suffocation. Her large, black, Oriental eyes darted shafts of fire into my heart, and although surprise at first caused me some disturbance, my amorous feelings so rapidly overcame me that, in spite of the spectators, the fair enchantress was herself obliged to restrain me. I was intoxicated, or rather delirious. When she saw me worked up to the pitch she desired, she moderated her caresses, but not her liveliness; and, when she thought fit to explain to us the true or pretended reason of her forwardness, she told us that I was the very image of one M. de Brémond, a director of the Tuscan custom-house; that she had been, and still was, madly in love with him; that she had left him, because she was a fool; that she took me in his place; that she wanted to love me, since it suited her; that, in like manner, I must love her as long as it suited her, and when she left me in the lurch, bear it patiently, as her dear Brémond had done. No sooner said than done. She took possession of me as if I had belonged to her, gave me her gloves to take care of, her fan, her shawl, and her headgear. She ordered me to go here and there, to do this and that, and I obeyed. She told me to send back her gondola, because she wanted to use mine, and I did so. She told me to change places with Carrio, because she had something to say to him, and I did so. They talked together for a long time in a low voice, and I did not disturb them. She called me: I went back to her. "Listen, Zanetto," she said to me; "I do not want to be loved in the French fashion; indeed, it would lead to no good. The moment you've had enough, leave me. But do not stop half-way, I warn you." After dinner we went to see the glass manufactory at Murano. She bought several little knickknacks, which without ceremony she left us to pay for; but she every-

where gave away in gratuities much more than we spent altogether. From the carelessness with which she threw away her
money and allowed us to throw away our own, it was easy to
see that she attached no value to it. When she demanded payment for herself, I believe it was more out of vanity than
greed. She was flattered by the price men put upon her
favours.

In the evening, we escorted her back to her apartments.
While we were talking, I noticed two pistols on her dressing-
table. "Ah!" said I, taking one up, "here is a beauty-spot box
of new manufacture; may I ask what it is used for? I know
you have other weapons, which fire better than these." After
some pleasantries of the same kind, she said, with an ingen-
uous pride which made her still more charming, "When I am
good-natured to those for whom I have no affection, I make
them pay for the weariness which they cause me; nothing can
be fairer; but, although I endure their caresses, I will not
endure their insults, and I shall not miss the first man who
shall show himself wanting in respect to me."

When I left her, I made an appointment for the next day. I
did not keep her waiting. I found her in a more than wanton
déshabillé, which is only known in southern countries, and
which I will not amuse myself with describing, although I
remember it only too well. I will only say that her ruffles and
tucker were edged with a silk border, ornamented with rose-
coloured bows, which appeared to me to set off a very beautiful skin. I discovered later that this was the fashion at Venice;
and the effect is so charming, that I am surprised that it has
never been introduced into France. I had no idea of the pleasures which awaited me. I have spoken of Madame de Larnage, in the transport which the recollection of her sometimes
still awakens in me; but how old, ugly, and cold she was
compared to my Zulietta! Do not attempt to imagine the
charms and graces of this bewitching girl; you would be far
from the truth. The young virgins of the cloister are not so
fresh, the beauties of the harem are not so lively, the houris of
paradise are not so piquant. Never was such sweet enjoyment
offered to the heart and senses of mortal man. Ah, if I had

only known how to taste of it in its full completeness, at least, for a single moment! I tasted it, it is true, but without charm; I dulled all its delights; I killed them, as it were, intentionally. No! Nature has not created me for pleasure. She has put into my wretched head the poison of that ineffable happiness, the desire for which she has planted in my heart.

If there is one circumstance in my life which well describes my character, it is that which I am about to relate. The vividness with which at this moment I recall the purpose of my book will, in this place, make me forget the false feeling of delicacy which would prevent me from fulfilling it. Whoever you may be, who desire to know the inmost heart of a man, have the courage to read the next two or three pages; you will become thoroughly acquainted with Jean-Jacques Rousseau.

I entered the room of a courtesan as if it had been the sanctuary of love and beauty; in her person I thought I beheld its divinity. I should never have believed that, without respect and esteem, I could have experienced the emotions with which she inspired me. No sooner had I recognised, in the preliminary familiarities, the value of her charms and caresses than, for fear of losing the fruit of them in advance, I was anxious to make haste to pluck it. Suddenly, in place of the flame which consumed me, I felt a deathly chill run through my veins; my legs trembled under me; and, feeling ready to faint, I sat down and cried like a child.

Who would guess the reason for my tears, and the thoughts that passed through my head at that moment? I said to myself: This object, which is at my disposal, is the masterpiece of nature and love; its mind and body, every part of it perfect; she is as good and generous as she is amiable and beautiful. The great ones of the world ought to be her slaves; sceptres ought to be laid at her feet. And yet she is a miserable street-walker, on sale to everybody; a merchant captain has the disposal of her; she comes and throws herself at my head, mine, although she knows that I am poor, while my real merits, being unknown to her, can have no value in her eyes. In this there is something incomprehensible. Either my heart deceives me, dazzles my senses, and makes me the dupe of a worthless slut, or some secret defect, with which I am unacquainted, must destroy the effect of her charms, and render her repulsive to those who would otherwise fight for the possession of her. I began to look for this defect with a singular intensity of mind, and it never occurred to me that the possible consequences of having anything to do with her might possibly have something to do with it. The freshness of her skin, her brilliant complexion, her dazzlingly white teeth, the sweetness of her breath, the general air of cleanliness about her whole person, so completely banished this idea from my mind, that, being still in doubt as to my condition since my visit to the *padoana,* I rather felt qualms of conscience as to whether I was in sufficiently good health for her, and I am quite convinced that I was not deceived in my confidence.

These well-timed reflections so agitated me that I shed tears. Zulietta, for whom this was certainly quite a novel sight under the circumstances, was astounded for a moment; but, after having walked round the room and looked in her glass, she understood, and my eyes convinced her, that dislike had nothing to do with this whimsical melancholy. It was an easy matter for her to drive it away, and to efface the slight feeling of shame; but, at the moment when I was ready to sink exhausted upon a bosom, which seemed to permit for the first time the contact of a man's hand and mouth, I perceived that she had only one nipple. I smote my forehead, looked attentively and thought I saw that this breast was not formed like the other. I immediately began to rack my brains for the reason of such a defect, and, feeling convinced that it was connected with some remarkable natural imperfection, by brooding so long over this idea, I saw, as clear as daylight, that, in the place of the most charming person that I could picture to myself, I only held in my arms a kind of monster, the outcast of nature, of mankind and of love. I pushed my stupidity so far as to speak to her about this defect. At first she took it as a joke, and said and did things in her frolicsome humour, which were enough to make me die of love; but as I was unable to conceal from her that I still felt a certain amount of uneasiness, she at last blushed, adjusted her dress, got up, and, without saying a word, went and seated herself at the window. I wanted to sit by her side, but she moved, sat down on a couch, got up immediately afterwards, and, walking about the room and fanning herself, said to me in a cold and disdainful tone, "Zanetto, lascia le donne, et studia la matematica."*

Before I left, I begged her to grant me another interview on the following day. She postponed it till the third day, adding, with an ironical smile, that I must want rest. I spent this interval very ill at ease, my heart full of her charms and graces, sensible of my folly, with which I reproached myself, regretting the moments which I had so ill employed, which it had only rested with myself to make the sweetest moments of my life, awaiting with the most lively impatience the time when I might repair their loss, but, nevertheless, still uneasy, in spite of myself, how I should reconcile the perfections of this adorable girl with her unworthy manner of life. I ran—I flew to her at the appointed hour. I do not know whether her ardent temperament would have been more satisfied with this visit. Her pride at least would have been flattered: and I enjoyed in anticipation the delight of proving to her, in every respect, that I knew how to repair my errors. She spared me the test. The gondolier, whom I sent to her apartments on landing, informed me that she had set out for Florence on the previous evening. If I had not felt my whole love for her when I had her in my arms, I felt it cruelly now, when I had lost her. My foolish regret has never left me. Amiable and enchanting as she was in my eyes, I could have consoled myself for the loss of her; but I confess that I have never been able to console myself for the thought that she only carried away a contemptuous recollection of me.

Such were my two adventures. The eighteen months which I spent at Venice have left me no more to tell, with the exception of a merely projected amour. Carrio, who was very fond of women, tired of always visiting those who belonged to

* Give up the ladies, and study mathematics.

others, took it into his head to keep one himself; and, as we were inseparable, he proposed to me an arrangement, common enough in Venice, that we should keep one between us. I agreed. The difficulty was to find one with whom we should run no risk. He was so industrious in his researches, that he unearthed a little girl between eleven and twelve years of age, whom her unworthy mother wanted to sell. We went together to see her. My compassion was stirred at the sight of this child. She was fair and gentle as a lamb; no one would have taken her for an Italian. Living costs little at Venice. We gave the mother some money, and made arrangements for the daughter's keep. She had a good voice, and, in order to provide her with a means of livelihood, we gave her a spinet and engaged a singing master for her. All this scarcely cost us two *sequins* a month, and saved more in other expenses; but, as we were obliged to wait until she was of a riper age, this was sowing a long time before we could reap. However, we were content to pass our evenings, to chat and play innocently with this child, and amused ourselves perhaps more agreeably than if we had possessed her, so true is it that what most attaches us to women is not so much sensuality, as a certain pleasure which is caused by living with them. My heart became insensibly attached to the little Anzoletta, but this attachment was paternal. My senses had so little to do with it that, in proportion as it increased, the possibility of allowing them to have any influence in like manner diminished. I felt that I should have dreaded connection with this child, after she had grown up, as an abominable incest. I saw that the worthy Carrio's feelings, unknown to himself, took the same direction. We procured for ourselves, without thinking of it, pleasures as delightful, though very different from those we had originally contemplated; and I am convinced that, however beautiful she might have grown, far from being the corrupters of her innocence, we should have been its protectors.

[Rousseau is unable to obtain redress for M. de Montaigu's injustices—such was the privilege of rank and position. He resolves to remain independent, resumes work on his opera, and moves to a small hotel near the Luxembourg Gardens.]

The justice and uselessness of my complaints left in my mind the seeds of indignation against our foolish civil institutions, whereby the real welfare of the public and true justice are always sacrificed to an apparent order, which is in reality subversive of all order, and of which the only effect is, to bestow the sanction of public authority upon the oppression of the weak and the injustice of the strong.

We had a new landlady, who came from Orléans. To help her with the linen, she had a young girl from her native place, about twenty-two or twenty-three years of age, who, like the landlady, took her meals with us. This girl, whose name was Thérèse le Vasseur, was of respectable family, her father being an official at the Orléans mint, and her mother engaged in business. The family was a large one, and, as the mint stopped working, the father found himself without resources, while the mother, who had become bankrupt, managed her affairs badly, gave up business, and came to Paris with her husband and daughter, who, by her own exertions, supported all three.

The first time I saw this girl appear at table, I was struck by her modest behaviour, and, still more, by her lively and gentle looks, which, in my eyes, at that time appeared incomparable. The company at table, besides M. de Bonnefond, consisted of several Irish priests, Gascons, and others of the same description. Our hostess herself had led an irregular life. I was the only person who spoke and behaved decently. They teased the girl, I took her part, and immediately their railleries were turned against me. Even if I had not felt naturally inclined towards this poor girl, a feeling of compassion, even of opposition, would have aroused my sympathy. I have always admired decency in words and manners, especially in the opposite sex. I openly avowed myself her champion. I saw that she was touched by my sympathy, and her looks, enlivened by gratitude which she dared not express, were thereby rendered more eloquent.

She was very bashful, and so was I. The intimacy, which this similarity of disposition seemed to keep at a distance, was, however, very speedily formed. The landlady, who perceived it, became furious, and her brutal behaviour gained me greater favour with the little one, who, having no one in the house except myself to help her, was grieved to see me go out, and sighed for her protector's return. The relation of our hearts, and the similarity of our dispositions soon exercised their usual effect. She thought that she saw in me an honourable man, and she was not mistaken. I thought that I saw in her a feeling, simple girl, free from coquetry, and I was not deceived either. I declared to her beforehand that I would never forsake her, but that I would never marry her. Love, esteem, and simple sincerity secured my triumph, and it was because her heart was tender and virtuous, that I was happy without being too audacious.

Her fear that it would annoy me not to find in her that which she believed I expected, delayed my happiness more than anything else. I saw that she was disturbed and confused before she gave herself up to me, anxious to make herself understood, and yet afraid to explain herself. Far from suspecting the real cause of her embarrassment, I quite wrongly attributed it to another, the idea of which was highly insulting to her character. Believing that she intended me to understand that my health might be endangered, I was greatly perplexed, and, although this did not restrain my feelings, for several days it poisoned my happiness. As neither of us understood the other, our conversations on the subject were so many riddles and ridiculous misunderstandings. She was inclined to believe that I was utterly mad, and I hardly knew what to think of her. At last we came to an explanation. She confessed to me with tears that she had once misconducted herself in the early years of her womanhood, when a skilful seducer had taken advantage of her ignorance. As soon as I understood her, I uttered a cry of joy. "Virginity!" I cried; "Paris is the right place, twenty is the right age to look for it! Ah, my Thérèse! I am only too happy to possess you, modest and healthy, and not to find what I never looked for."

At first I had only sought amusement; I now saw that I had found more and gained a companion. A little intimacy with this excellent girl, a little reflection upon my situation, made me feel that, while thinking only of my pleasures, I had done much to promote my happiness. To fill the place of my extinguished ambition, I needed a lively sentiment which should take complete possession of my heart. In a word, I needed a successor to mamma. As I should never live with her again, I needed someone to live with her pupil, in whom I might find the simplicity and docility of heart which she had found in me. I felt it necessary that the gentle tranquillity of private and domestic life should make up to me for the loss of the brilliant career which I was renouncing. When I was quite alone, I felt a void in my heart, which it only needed another heart to fill. Destiny had deprived me of, or, at least in part, alienated me from, that heart for which Nature had formed me. From that moment I was alone; for with me it has always been everything or nothing. I found in Thérèse the substitute that I needed. Thanks to her, I lived happily, as far as the course of events permitted. At first I tried to improve her mind, but my efforts were useless. Her mind is what Nature has made it; culture and teaching are without influence upon it. I am not ashamed to confess that she has never learnt how to read properly, although she can write fairly well. When I went to live in the Rue Neuve-des-Petits-Champs, opposite my windows, at the Hôtel de Pontchartrain there was a clock. For more than a month I did my utmost to teach her how to tell the time by it, but, even now, she can hardly do so. She has never been able to give the names of the twelve months of the year in correct order, and does not know a single figure, in spite of all the trouble I have taken to teach her. She can neither count money nor reckon the price of anything. The words which she uses in speaking are often the very opposite of those which she means. I once made a dictionary of the phrases she used, to amuse Madame de Luxembourg, and her absurd mistakes have become famous in the society in which I lived. But this person, so limited in understanding—so stupid, if you will—is a most excellent adviser in cases of difficulty. Frequently, in Switzerland, in England, and in France, at the time of the misfortunes which befell me, she saw what I did not see myself, gave me the best advice to follow, rescued me from dangers into which I was rushing blindly, and, in the presence of ladies of the highest rank, of princes and the great ones of the world, her opinions, her good sense, her answers, and her behaviour have gained for her the esteem of all, and for me, compliments upon her good qualities which I felt convinced were sincere.

When we are with those we love, sentiment nourishes the mind as well as the heart, and we have little need to search for ideas elsewhere. I lived with my Thérèse as pleasantly as with the most brilliant genius in the world.

[In this quiet, happy period, Rousseau completes his opera. Despite Rameau's jealous derision, it is played at Court. He revises another opera for the Court, but is cheated by Rameau of credit and compensation.

Jean-Jacques' father dies, and he receives a small inheritance.]

One evening, on entering my lodgings, I found the letter which was bound to contain it; I took it up, in order to open it, with an impatient trembling, of which I inwardly felt ashamed. "What!" said I contemptuously to myself, "shall Jean-Jacques suffer himself to be overcome by self-interest and curiosity?" I immediately put back the letter on the mantelpiece, undressed, went quietly to bed, slept better than usual, and got up rather late the next day, without thinking any more about my letter. While dressing, I caught sight of it, opened it leisurely, and found a bill of exchange inside. Many pleasant feelings entered my mind at once; but the liveliest of all was the consciousness of my victory over myself. I could mention a number of similar instances in the course of my life, but I am too pressed for time to relate everything. I sent a little of the money to poor mamma, regretting with tears the happy time when I should have laid the whole at her feet. All her letters showed signs of her distress. She sent me heaps of recipes and secret remedies, which she declared would make my fortune and her own. Already the thought of her wretchedness contracted her heart and narrowed her mind. The small sum which I was able to send he fell into the hands of the rascals by whom she was surrounded. She derived no benefit from anything. I was disgusted at the idea of sharing what I myself sorely needed with these wretches, especially after the fruitless attempts which I made to get her out of their hands, as will be afterwards related.

Time slipped away, and the money with it. We were two, even four in number, or, to speak more correctly, seven or eight; for, although Thérèse was disinterested to a degree almost unexampled, her mother was by no means the same. As soon as she found herself somewhat improved in circumstances—thanks to my attention—she sent for her whole family to share the fruits of it. Sisters, sons, daughters, grand-daughters—all came, with the exception of her eldest daughter, who was married to the manager of the carriage service at Angers. All that I did for Thérèse was turned by her mother to the benefit of these starvelings. As I had not to do with a covetous person, and was not under the influence of a foolish passion, I committed no follies. Content to keep Thérèse decently, but without luxury, protected against pressing needs, I consented to her handing over to her mother all that she was able to earn by her own exertions, nor did I limit myself to that; but, by a fatality which always pursued me, while mamma was plundered by the rascals who surrounded her, Thérèse was preyed upon by her family, and I could render no assistance in either case which benefited her for whom it was intended.

[Francueil succeeds in getting Rousseau's "Muses Galantes" performed at the Opera, but it is not a success. It is the year 1747. Rousseau is now doing secretarial work for Francueil and Madame Dupin. He and Francueil study chemistry with Rouelle, and spend the autumn at the Château de Chenonceaux.]

While I was growing fat at Chenonceaux, my poor Thérèse was increasing in size at Paris for another reason; and, on my return, I found the work which I had commenced in a more forward condition than I had expected. Considering my position, this would have thrown me into the greatest embarrassment, had not some table companions furnished me with the only means of getting out of the difficulty. This is one of those essential stories which I must relate with utmost simplicity, because, if I were to offer any explanation, I should be obliged either to excuse or to inculpate myself, and in this place I ought not to do either the one or the other.

During Altuna's stay at Paris, instead of going to an eating-house, we usually took our meals in our neighbourhood, nearly opposite the *cul-de-sac* of the Opera, at the house of one Madame la Selle, a tailor's wife, whose dinners were indifferent, but her table was always in request, on account of the good and reliable company which resorted there; no one was admitted unless he was known, and it was necessary to be introduced by one of the regular guests. Commandeur de Graville, an old rake, full of wit and politeness, but filthy in his language, lodged there, and attracted a jovial and brilliant company of young officers in the guards and musketeers; Commandeur de Nonant, protector of all the girls employed at the Opera, daily brought all the news from that haunt of vice. . . .

I there heard a number of amusing anecdotes, and also gradually adopted, thank Heaven! not the morals, but the principles which I found established. Honourable people injured, husbands deceived, women seduced, secret accouchements, these were the most ordinary topics; and he who contributed most to the population of the Foundling Hospital was always most applauded. I caught the infection; I formed my manner of thinking upon that which I saw prevalent amongst very amiable and, in the main, very honourable people. I said to myself, "Since it is the custom of the country, one who lives here may follow it." Here was the expedient for which I was looking. I cheerfully resolved to adopt it, without the least scruples on my own part; I only had to overcome those of Thérèse, with whom I had the greatest trouble in the world to persuade her to adopt the only means of saving her honour. Her mother, who, in addition, was afraid of this new embarrassment in the shape of a number of brats, supported me, and Thérèse at last yielded. We chose a discreet and safe midwife, one Mademoiselle Gouin, who lived at the

Point Saint-Eustache, to take care of this precious charge; and when the time came, Thérèse was taken to her house by her mother for her accouchement. I went to see her several times, and took her a monogram, which I had written on two cards, one of which was placed in the child's swaddling clothes, after which it was deposited by the midwife in the office of the hospital in the usual manner. The following year the same inconvenience was remedied by the same expedient, with the exception of the monogram, which was forgotten. On my side there was no more reflection, no greater approval on the mother's; she obeyed with a sigh. Later, all the vicissitudes which this fatal conduct produced in my manner of thinking, as well as in my destiny, will become apparent; for the present, let us keep to this first period. Its consequences, as cruel as they were unforeseen, will force me to return to it only too frequently.

Here I will mention my first acquaintance with Madame d'Epinay, whose name will frequently recur in these Memoirs. Her maiden name was Mademoiselle d'Esclavelles, and she had just married M. d'Epinay, son of M. de Lalive de Belle-garde, farmer-general. Her husband, like M. de Francueil, was musical. She also was musical, and devotion to the art led to a great intimacy between the three. M. de Francueil introduced me to Madame d'Epinay, who sometimes invited me to supper. She was amiable, witty, and talented, and certainly a very desirable acquaintance. But she had a friend, Mademoiselle d'Ette, who was supposed to be very spiteful, and lived with the Chevalier de Valory, who did not enjoy a good reputation either. I believe that the society of these two people did harm to Madame d'Epinay, to whom Nature had given, together with a very libidinous disposition, qualities admirably adapted to regulate or counterbalance its extravagances. M. de Francueil partly inspired her with the friendship he himself entertained for me, and confessed his relations with her, which, for this reason, I would not speak of here, had they not become public property, and even reached the ears of M. d'Epinay himself. M. de Francueil made singular revelations to me concerning this lady, which she never mentioned to me herself, and of which she never thought I had been informed. I never opened, and never will open, my lips on the subject, to her or anyone else. All the confidential communications from one quarter and another rendered my situation very embarrassing, especially with Madame de Francueil, who knew me sufficiently well not to distrust me, although I was intimate with her rival. As well as I was able, I consoled this poor lady, whose husband certainly did not return the love which she felt for him. I listened to these three persons separately, and kept their secrets so faithfully, that not one of the three extracted from me any of the secrets of the other two, while at the same time I did not conceal from either of the women my attachment to her rival. Madame de Francueil, who wanted to make use of me in several ways, had to put up with a formal refusal, and Madame d'Epinay, who on one occasion wanted to intrust me with a letter for Francueil, not only met with a similar denial, but I plainly declared that, if she wanted to drive me from her house forever, she had only to propose the same thing to me again. I must, however, do justice to Madame d'Epinay. Far from showing herself displeased with my conduct, she spoke in the highest terms of it to Francueil, and made me as welcome as ever. In this manner, amidst the stormy relations between these three persons, whom I had to manage most carefully, upon whom I in a manner depended, and to whom I was sincerely attached, I retained to the end their friendship, their esteem, and their confidence, while I behaved with gentleness and complaisance, but always with uprightness and firmness. In spite of my awkwardness and stupidity, Madame d'Epinay insisted on my taking part in the entertainment at La Chevrette, a château near Saint-Denis belonging to M. de Bellegarde. There was a stage there, on which performances were frequently given. A part was given to me, which I studied for six months without intermission, but when the piece was performed, I had to be prompted in it from beginning to end. After this trial, no more parts were offered to me.

The acquaintance of Madame d'Epinay also procured me that of her step-sister, Mademoiselle de Bellegarde, who soon afterwards became Comtesse de Houdetot. When I first saw her, it was just before her marriage, and she conversed with me for a long time with that charming familiarity which is natural to her. I found her very amiable; but I was far from foreseeing that this young person would one day decide the destiny of my life, and was fated to drag me down, although innocently, into the abyss in which I find myself to-day.

Although, since my return from Venice, I have not spoken of Diderot, or my friend Roguin, I had not neglected either, and with the former especially I had daily grown more and more intimate. He had a Nanette, just as I had a Thérèse: this was a further point of agreement between us. But the difference was, that my Thérèse, who was at least as good-looking as his Nanette, was of a gentle disposition and an amiable character, calculated to gain the attachment of an honourable man, while his Nanette, who was a regular shrew and a fish-wife, exhibited no redeeming qualities which could compensate, in the eyes of others, for her defective education. However, he married her, which was very praiseworthy, if he had promised to do so. As for myself, having made no promise of the kind, I was in no hurry to imitate him.

I had also become connected with the Abbé de Condillac, who, like myself, was unknown in the literary world, but was destined to become what he is at the present day. I was, perhaps, the first who discovered his abilities, and estimated him at his proper value. He also seemed to enjoy my company; and while, shut up in my room in the Rue Jean-Saint-Denis, near the Opera, I was composing my act of "Hésiode," he sometimes dined with me *tête-à-tête*, and we shared the expenses. He was at that time engaged upon his "Essai sur l'origine des connaissances humaines," his first work. When it was finished, the difficulty was to find a bookseller to take it. The booksellers of Paris are always arrogant and hard towards a new author, and metaphysics, which was not much in fashion at the time, did not offer a very attractive subject. I spoke of Condillac and his work to Diderot, and introduced them to each other. They were made to like each other, and did so. Diderot induced Durant the bookseller to accept the Abbé's manuscript, and this great metaphysician received for his first book—and that almost as a favour—one hundred crowns, and even that he would perhaps not have received but for me. As we lived at a great distance from one another, we all three met once a week at the Palais-Royal, and dined together at the Hôtel du Panier Fleuri. These little weekly dinners must have been exceedingly agreeable to Diderot, for he, who nearly always failed to keep his other appointments, never missed one of them. On these occasions I drew up the plan of a periodical, to be called *Le Persifleur*, to be written by Diderot and myself alternately. I sketched the outlines of the first number, and in this manner became acquainted with D'Alembert, to whom Diderot had spoken of it. However, unforeseen events blocked our plans, and the project fell through.

These two authors had just undertaken the "Dictionnaire Encyclopédique," which at first was only intended to be a kind of translation of Chambers's, almost like that of James's "Dictionary of Medicine," which Diderot had just finished. The latter wanted to secure my assistance in this second enterprise, and proposed that I should undertake the musical part of it. I consented, and completed it very hastily and indifferently, in the three months which were allowed me and all the other collaborators in the work. But I was the only one who was ready at the time appointed. I handed him my manuscript, which I had had copied by one of M. de Francueil's lackeys, named Dupont, who wrote a very good hand, paying him ten crowns out of my own pocket, for which I have never been reimbursed. Diderot, on the part of the booksellers, promised me some remuneration, which neither of us ever mentioned again to the other.

The undertaking was interrupted by his imprisonment. His "Pensées philosophiques" had brought upon him a certain amount of annoyance, which led to no further consequences. It was different with his "Lettre sur les aveugles," which contained nothing that deserved censure except a few personal allusions, at which Madame Dupré de Saint-Maur and M. de Réaumur took offense, and for which he was confined in the donjon of Vincennes. It is impossible to describe the anguish which my friend's misfortune caused me. My melancholy imagination, which always exaggerates misfortune, became alarmed. I thought that he would be imprisoned for the rest of his life; I nearly went mad at the idea. I wrote to Madame de Pompadour, entreating her to procure his release, or to get me imprisoned with him. I received no answer to my letter; it was too unreasonable to produce any effect, and I cannot flatter myself that it contributed to the subsequent alleviation of the hardships of poor Diderot's confinement. Had its severity continued without relaxation, I believe that I should have died of despair at the foot of this accursed donjon. Besides, even if my letter produced but little effect, neither did I myself claim much merit for it, for I only mentioned it to one or two people, and never to Diderot himself.

BOOK EIGHT

[1749]

I HAVE been obliged to pause at the end of the preceding book. With the present book commences, in its first origin, the long chain of my misfortunes.

Having lived in two of the most brilliant houses in Paris, I had made some acquaintances, in spite of my want of tact; amongst others, at Madame Dupin's, the young hereditary prince of Saxe-Gotha and Baron de Thun, his tutor; at M. de la Popelinière's, M. Séguy, a friend of Baron de Thun, who was known in the literary world by his beautiful edition of Rousseau.* The Baron invited M. Séguy and myself to spend a day or two at Fontenay-sous-Bois, where the Prince had a country house. We accepted the invitation. While passing Vincennes, I felt so distressed at the sight of the donjon, that

---

* Jean-Baptiste Rousseau, the poet.

the Baron perceived the effects of my emotion on my countenance. At supper the Prince spoke of Diderot's confinement.
The Baron, in order to make me speak, accused the prisoner
of impudence, which I myself displayed by the impetuosity
with which I defended him. This excess of zeal was excused
in a man who was inspired by attachment to an unfortunate
friend, and the conversation took another turn. Two Germans,
belonging to the Prince's suite, were present: M. Klüpfel, a
man of great ability, his chaplain, who afterwards supplanted
the Baron, and became his tutor; and a young man named
Grimm, who held the post of reader until he could find
some other place, and whose modest equipment showed how
urgent was his need for finding something of the kind. From
that same evening, Klüpfel and myself formed an acquaintance which soon ripened into friendship. My acquaintance
with M. Grimm did not advance so rapidly; he kept himself
in the background, and gave no signs of the boastfulness
which he afterwards displayed when he became prosperous.
At dinner the next day the conversation turned upon music;
he spoke well upon the subject. I was delighted when I heard
that he was able to accompany on the piano. After dinner,
some music was sent for, and we amused ourselves for the
rest of the day on the Prince's piano. In this manner began
that friendship, at first so pleasant to me, and in the end so
fatal, of which, from this time forth, I shall have so much
to say.

On my return to Paris, I received the agreeable news that
Diderot had been released from the donjon, and confined to
the château and park of Vincennes on parole, with permission
to see his friends. How painful it was to me not to be able to
run to him on the spot! But I was detained for two or three
days at Madame Dupin's by duties which I could not neglect
and, after what seemed three or four centuries of impatience,
I flew into my friend's arms. O indescribable moment! He
was not alone; D'Alembert and the treasurer of the Sainte
Chapelle were with him. When I entered, I saw no one
except him. I made a single bound, I uttered a single cry; I
pressed my face to his; I embraced him closely without a

utterance, except that of my tears and sighs; I was choked
with tenderness and joy. The first thing he did, after leaving
my arms, was to turn towards the ecclesiastic and say to
him: "You see, sir, how my friends love me!" Completely
overcome by my emotion, I did not at that time think of this
manner of turning it to advantage; but, when occasionally
reflecting upon it afterwards, I have always thought that this
would not have been the first idea that would have occurred
to me had I been in Diderot's place.

I found him greatly affected by his imprisonment. The
donjon had made a terrible impression upon him, and, although he was comfortable at the castle and allowed to walk
where he pleased in a park that was not even surrounded
by walls, he needed the society of his friends, to avoid giving
way to melancholy. As I was certainly the one who had most
sympathy with his sufferings, I believed that I should also
be the one whose presence would be most consoling to
him, and, in spite of very pressing engagements, I went at
least every other day, alone or with his wife, to spend the
afternoon with him.

The summer of 1749 was excessively hot. Vincennes is
reckoned to be two leagues distant from Paris. Being unable to afford a conveyance, I set out at two o'clock in the
afternoon on foot, when I was alone, and walked fast, in
order to get there sooner. The trees on the road—always
lopped after the fashion of the country—hardly afforded any
shade, and often, exhausted by heat and fatigue, I threw
myself on the ground, being unable to walk any further. In
order to moderate my pace, I bethought myself of taking a
book with me. One day I took the *Mercure de France*, and,
while reading as I walked, I came upon the subject proposed
by the Academy of Dijon as a prize essay for the following
year: "Has the progress of the arts and sciences contributed
more to the corruption or purification of morals?"

From the moment I read these words, I beheld another
world and became another man. Although I have a lively
recollection of the impression which they produced upon me,
the details have escaped me since I committed them to paper

in one of my four letters to M. de Malesherbes. This is one of the peculiarities of my memory which deserves to be mentioned. It only serves me so long as I am dependent upon it. As soon as I commit its contents to paper it forsakes me, and when I have once written a thing down, I completely forget it. . . .

What I distinctly remember on this occasion is, that on my arrival at Vincennes I was in a state of agitation bordering upon madness. Diderot perceived it. I told him the reason, and read to him the Prosopopoea of Fabricius,* written in pencil, under an oak-tree. He encouraged me to allow my ideas to have full play, and to compete for the prize. I did so, and from that moment I was lost. The misfortunes of the remainder of my life were the inevitable result of this moment of madness.

With inconceivable rapidity, my feelings became elevated to the tone of my ideas. All my petty passions were stifled by the enthusiasm of truth, liberty and virtue; and the most astonishing thing is, that this fervour continued in my heart for more than four or five years, in a higher degree, perhaps, than has ever been the case with the heart of any other man.

I worked at this Essay in a very curious manner, which I have adopted in almost all my other works. I devoted to it the hours of the night when I was unable to sleep. I meditated in bed with my eyes shut, and turned and returned my periods in my head with incredible labour. Then, when I was finally satisfied with them, I stored them up in my memory until I was able to commit them to paper; but the time spent in getting up and dressing myself made me forget everything, and when I sat down in front of my paper I could recall scarcely anything of what I had composed. I conceived the idea of making Madame le Vasseur my secretary. I had taken lodgings for her, her husband and her daughter, nearer to my own; and she, in order to save me the expense of a servant, came every morning to light my fire and attend to my

---

* *Prosopopée de Fabricius:* soliloquy of the famous Roman general, invented by Rousseau in his essay.

little wants. When she came, I dictated to her from my bed the result of my labours of the preceding night; and this plan, to which I have long adhered, has saved me from forgetting much.

When the Essay was finished I showed it to Diderot, who was pleased with it, and suggested a few corrections. This production, however, although full of warmth and vigour, is altogether destitute of logic and arrangement. Of all the works that have proceeded from my pen, it is the weakest in argument and the poorest in harmony and proportion; but, however great a man's natural talents may be, the art of writing cannot be learnt all at once.

I sent off the work without mentioning it to anyone, with the exception, I fancy, of Grimm, with whom I began to be on most intimate terms after he went to live with the Comte de Frièse. He had a piano, which formed our meeting-place, and at which I spent in his company all my spare moments, singing Italian airs and *barcarolles,* without break or intermission from morning till evening, or rather, from evening till morning; and whenever I was not to be found at Madame Dupin's I was sure to be found at Grimm's, or, at least, in his company, either on the promenade or at the theatre. I gave up going to the Comédie Italienne, where I had a free pass, but which he did not care for, and paid to go to the Comédie Française, of which he was passionately fond. At length I became so powerfully attracted to this young man, and so inseparable from him, that even poor "aunt" was neglected— that is to say, I saw less of her, for my attachment to her has never once wavered during the whole course of my life.

[Jean-Jacques experiences increasing trouble with his deceitful, interfering "mother-in-law."]

This woman, whom I loaded with care, attention, and little presents, and whose affection I was exceedingly anxious to gain, by reason of my utter inability to succeed, was the only cause of trouble in my little establishment; for the rest, I can say that, during these six or seven years, I enjoyed the most perfect domestic happiness that human weakness can permit. My Thérèse's heart was that of an angel; intimacy increased our attachment, and we daily felt more and more how perfectly we were made for each other. If our pleasures could be described, their simplicity would appear ridiculous; our walks, *tête-à-tête*, outside the city, where I spent my eight or ten *sous* magnificently in some beer-house; our little suppers at the open window, at which we sat opposite each other on two low chairs placed upon a trunk which filled up the breadth of the window-niche. In this position, the window served us as a table, we breathed the fresh air, we could see the surrounding country and the passers-by, and, although we were on the fourth story, we could look down upon the street while we ate. Who could describe, who could feel the charm of these meals, at which the dishes consisted of nothing more than a quartern loaf of coarse bread, a few cherries, a morsel of cheese, and half a pint of wine, which we shared between us? Friendship, confidence, intimacy, tranquillity of mind, how delicious are your seasonings! Sometimes we remained there till midnight, without thinking of it or suspecting how late it was, until the old lady informed us. But let us leave these details, which must appear insipid or ridiculous. I have always felt and declared, that it is impossible to describe true enjoyment.

At the same time I indulged in a somewhat coarser enjoyment, the last of the kind with which I have to reproach myself. I have mentioned that Klüpfel, the minister, was of an amiable disposition; my relations with him were nearly as intimate as with Grimm, and became equally confidential. They sometimes shared my table. These meals, somewhat more than simple, were enlivened by the witty and broad jokes of Klüpfel and the humorous Germanisms of Grimm, who had not yet become a purist.

Sensuality did not preside at our little orgies; its place was supplied by gaiety, and we were so well satisfied with each other that we were unable to separate. Klüpfel had furnished a room for a little girl, who, notwithstanding, was at everybody's disposal, since he was unable to keep her by himself. One evening, as we were entering the *café*, we met him coming out to go and sup with her. We made fun of him; he revenged himself gallantly by taking us to share the supper, and then turning the tables on us. The poor creature appeared to me to be of a fairly good disposition, very gentle, and little adapted for her profession, for which an old hag, whom she had with her, dressed her as well as she was able. The conversation and the wine enlivened us to such a degree that we forgot ourselves. The worthy Klüpfel did not desire to do the honours of his table by halves, and all three of us, in turn, went into the adjoining room with the little one, who did not know whether she ought to laugh or cry. Grimm has always declared that he never touched her, and that he remained so long with her simply in order to amuse himself at our impatience. If he really did not touch her, it is not likely that he was prevented by any scruples, since, before going to live with the Comte de Frièse, he lived with some girl in the same quarter of Saint-Roch.

I left the Rue des Moineaux, where this girl lived, feeling as ashamed as Saint-Preux, when he left the house where he had been made drunk, and I had a vivid remembrance of my own story when writing his. Thérèse perceived, from certain indications, and, above all, from my confused air, that I had something to reproach myself with; I relieved my conscience of the burden by making a prompt and frank confession. In this I did well; for, the next morning, Grimm came in triumph to her, to give her an exaggerated account of my offence, and since that time he has never failed spitefully to remind her of it. This was the more inexcusable in him, since I had freely and voluntarily taken him into my confidence and had the right to expect from him that he would not give me cause to repent it. I never felt so much as on this occasion the goodness of my Thérèse's heart, for she was more indignant at Grimm's conduct than offended at my unfaithfulness, and I only had to submit to tender and touching reproaches on her part, in which I did not detect the slightest trace of anger.

This excellent girl's good-heartedness was equalled by her simplicity of mind. Nothing more need be said; however, I may be permitted to mention an example of it, which I rec-

ollect. I had told her that Klüpfel was preacher and chaplain
to the Prince of Saxe-Gotha. In her estimation a preacher was
so extraordinary a person that, oddly confounding two most
dissimilar ideas, she got it into her head to take Klüpfel for
the Pope. I thought she was mad when she told me, for the
first time, on my return home, that the Pope had called to
see me. I made her explain herself, and made all haste to go
and tell the story to Grimm and Klüpfel, whom we ever afterwards called Pope, and gave the name of Pope Joan to the
girl in the Rue des Moineaux. Our laughter was inextinguishable, and almost choked us. Those who have made me say,
in a letter which they have been pleased to attribute to me,
that I have only laughed twice in my life, were not acquainted with me at that time or in my youthful days; otherwise, this idea would certainly never have occurred to them.

[1750-1752.]—In the following year (1750) I heard that
my Essay, of which I had not thought any more, had gained
the prize at Dijon. This news awoke again all the ideas
which had suggested it to me, animated them with fresh
vigour, and stirred up in my heart the first leavening of virtue
and heroism, which my father, my country, and Plutarch had
deposited there in my infancy. I considered that nothing
could be grander or finer than to be free and virtuous, above
considerations of fortune and the opinion of mankind, and
completely independent. Although false shame and fear of
public disapproval at first prevented me from living in accordance with my principles, and from openly insulting the
maxims of my age, from that moment my mind was made
up, and I delayed carrying out my intention no longer than
was necessary for contradiction to irritate it and render it
victorious.

While philosophising upon the duties of man, an event
occurred which made me reflect more seriously upon my own.
Thérèse became pregnant for the third time. Too honest
towards myself, too proud in my heart to desire to belie my
principles by my actions, I began to consider the destination
of my children and my connection with their mother, in the
light of the laws of nature, justice, and reason, and of that

religion—pure, holy and eternal, like its author—which men have polluted, while pretending to be anxious to purify it, and which they have converted, by their formulas, into a mere religion of words, seeing that it costs men little to prescribe what is impossible, when they dispense with carrying it out in practice.

If I was wrong in my conclusions, nothing can be more remarkable than the calmness with which I abandoned myself to them. If I had been one of those low-born men, who are deaf to the gentle voice of Nature, in whose heart no real sentiment of justice or humanity ever springs up, this hardening of my heart would have been quite easy to understand. But is it possible that my warm-heartedness, lively sensibility, readiness to form attachments, the powerful hold which they exercise over me, the cruel heartbreakings I experience when forced to break them off, my natural goodwill towards all my fellow-creatures, my ardent love of the great, the true, the beautiful, and the just; my horror of evil of every kind, my utter inability to hate or injure, or even to think of it; the sweet and lively emotion which I feel at the sight of all that is virtuous, generous, and amiable; is it possible, I ask, that all these can ever agree in the same heart with the depravity which, without the least scruple, tramples underfoot the sweetest of obligations? No! I feel and loudly assert—it is impossible. Never, for a single moment in his life, could Jean-Jacques have been a man without feeling, without compassion, or an unnatural father. I may have been mistaken, never hardened. If I were to state my reasons, I should say too much. Since they were strong enough to mislead me, they might mislead many others, and I do not desire to expose young people, who may read my works, to the danger of allowing themselves to be misled by the same error. I will content myself with observing, that my error was such that, in handing over my children to the State to educate, for want of means to bring them up myself, in deciding to fit them for becoming workmen and peasants rather than adventurers and fortune-hunters, I thought that I was behaving like a citizen and a father, and considered myself a member of

Plato's Republic. More than once since then, the regrets of my heart have told me that I was wrong; but, far from my reason having given me the same information, I have often blessed Heaven for having preserved them from their father's lot, and from the lot which threatened them as soon as I should have been obliged to abandon them. If I had left them with Madame d'Epinay or Madame de Luxembourg, who, from friendship, generosity, or some other motive, expressed themselves willing to take charge of them, would they have been happier, would they have been brought up at least as honest men? I do not know; but I do know that they would have been brought up to hate, perhaps to betray, their parents; it is a hundred times better that they have never known them.

My third child was accordingly taken to the Foundling Hospital, like the other two. The two next were disposed of in the same manner, for I had five altogether. This arrangement appeared to me so admirable, so rational, and so legitimate, that, if I did not openly boast of it, this was solely out of regard for the mother; but I told all who were acquainted with our relations. I told Grimm and Diderot. I afterwards informed Madame d'Epinay, and, later, Madame de Luxembourg, freely and voluntarily, without being in any way obliged to do so, and when I might easily have kept it a secret from everybody; for Gouin was an honourable woman, very discreet, and a person upon whom I could implicitly rely. The only one of my friends in whom I had any interest in unbosoming myself was M. Thierry, the physician who attended my poor "aunt" in a dangerous confinement. In a word, I made no mystery of what I did, not only because I have never known how to keep a secret from my friends, but because I really saw no harm in it. All things considered, I chose for my children what was best, or, at least, what I believed to be best for them. I could have wished, and still wish, that I had been reared and brought up as they have been.

[Rousseau censures those who later broadcast his secret.]
It could only have been disclosed by those very people to

whom I had confided it, and, in fact, it was not until after I had broken with them, that it was so disclosed. By this single fact they are judged. Without desiring to acquit myself of the blame which I deserve, I would rather have it upon my shoulders than that which their malice deserves. My fault is great, but it was due to error; I have neglected my duties, but the desire of doing an injury never entered my heart, and the feelings of a father cannot speak very eloquently on behalf of children whom he has never seen; but, to betray the confidence of friendship, to violate the most sacred of all agreements, to disclose secrets poured into our bosoms, deliberately to dishonour the friend whom one has deceived, and who still respects us while leaving us—these are not faults; they are acts of meanness and infamy.

I have promised my confession, not my justification; therefore I say no more on this point. It is my duty to be true; the reader's to be just. I shall never ask more from him than that. . . .

[Francueil promotes Rousseau to the post of cashier, and worry over his responsibilities makes him ill.]

I have already mentioned, in the first part of this work, that I was almost dead when I was born. A defective formation of the bladder caused, during my childhood, an almost continual retention of urine; and my aunt Suzon, who took care of me, had the greatest difficulty in keeping me alive. However, she at length succeeded: my robust constitution at length gained the upper hand, and my health improved so much during my youth that, with the exception of the attack of languor which I have described, and the frequent necessity of making water, which the least heating of the blood always rendered a matter of difficulty, I reached the age of thirty without feeling my early infirmity at all. The first touch of it which I had was on my arrival at Venice. The fatigue of the journey, and the fearful heat which I had suffered, brought on a constant desire to make water and an infection of the kidneys, which lasted till the beginning of the winter. After my visit to the *padoana,* I looked upon myself as a dead man, and yet I never suffered the slightest inconvenience from it.

After having exhausted myself more in imagination than in reality for my Zulietta, I was in better health than ever. It was only after Diderot's confinement that the overheating, caused by my journeys to Vincennes during the fearful heat, brought on a violent pain in the kidneys, and since that time I have never recovered my health completely.

At the time of which I am speaking, having perhaps overtired myself with my distasteful work at the confounded office, I became worse than before, and was confined to my bed for five or six weeks in the most melancholy condition that can be imagined. Madame Dupin sent the celebrated Morand to see me, who, in spite of his cleverness and delicacy of touch, caused me incredible suffering, and could never get to probe me. He advised me to consult Daran, who managed to introduce his bougies, which were more flexible, and afforded me some relief; but, when giving Madame Dupin an account of my condition, he declared that I had less than six months to live.

This verdict, which I afterwards heard, caused me to reflect seriously upon my condition, and upon the folly of sacrificing the repose and comfort of my few remaining days to the slavery of an employment for which I felt nothing but aversion. Besides, how could I reconcile the strict principles which I had just adopted with a situation which harmonised so ill with them? Would it not have been very bad taste in me, cashier of a Receiver-General of Finance, to preach disinterestedness and poverty? These ideas fermented so strongly in my head together with the fever, and combined so powerfully, that from that time nothing could uproot them, and, during the period of my recovery, I quietly determined to carry out the resolutions which I had made during my delirium. I renounced forever all plans of fortune and promotion. Resolved to pass my few remaining days in poverty and independence, I employed all my strength of mind in breaking away from the bonds of the opinion of the world, and in courageously carrying out everything which appeared to me to be right, without troubling myself about what the world might think of it. The obstacles which I had to overcome, the efforts which I made to triumph over them, are incredible. I succeeded as much as was possible, and more than I had myself hoped. If I had been as successful in shaking off the yoke of friendship as that of public opinion, I should have accomplished my purpose, perhaps the greatest, or, at any rate, the most conducive to virtue, that a mortal has ever conceived; but, while I trampled underfoot the senseless judgments of the common herd of the so-called great and wise, I suffered myself to be subjugated and led like a child by so-called friends, who, jealous of seeing me strike out a new path by myself, while pretending to try to make me happy, were really engaged only in making me appear ridiculous; they began by doing their best to degrade me, in order to succeed later in calumniating me. It was the change in my way of life, dating from this period, rather than my literary celebrity, that drew their jealousy upon me; they would perhaps have forgiven me for distinguishing myself in the art of writing; but they could not forgive me for setting an example in my change of conduct, which seemed likely to cause them inconvenience. I was born for friendship; my easy and gentle disposition found no difficulty in cherishing it. As long as I was unknown to the world, I was loved by all who knew me, and had not a single enemy; but, as soon as I became known, I had not a single friend. This was a great misfortune; it was a still greater one that I was surrounded by people who called themselves my friends, and who only made use of the privileges which this name allowed them to drag me to my ruin. The sequel of these memoirs will reveal this odious intrigue; at present I only point out its origin; my readers will soon see the first link forged.

[He decides to earn his living copying music.]

The success of my first Essay made it easier for me to carry out this resolution. After it had gained the prize, Diderot undertook to get it printed. While I was in bed he wrote me a note, informing me of its publication and the effect it had produced. "It has gone up like a rocket," he told me; "such a success has never been seen before." This voluntary approval of the public, in the case of an unknown author, gave me the first real assurance of my ability, as to which, in spite of my inner feelings, I had until then always been doubtful. I saw the great advantage I might derive from it in view of the resolution which I was on the point of carrying out, and I judged that a copyist of some literary celebrity would not be likely to suffer from want of work.

As soon as my resolution was taken and confirmed, I wrote a note to M. de Francueil to inform him of it, thanking him and Madame Dupin for all their kindness, and asking for their custom. Francueil, quite unable to understand the note, and believing that I was still delirious, came to me in all haste, but he found my mind so firmly made up that he was unable to shake my resolution. He went and told Madame Dupin and everyone else that I had gone mad. I let him do so, and went my way. I commenced my reformation with my dress. I gave up my gold lace and white stockings, and put on a round wig. I took off my sword and sold my watch, saying to myself with incredible delight, "Thank Heaven, I shall not want to know the time again!" M. de Francueil was kind enough to wait some time before he found a successor to me. At last, when he saw that my mind was made up, he gave my post to M. d'Alibard, formerly tutor to young Chenonceaux, known in the botanical world for his "Flora Parisiensis." * . . .

The success of my first writings had made me the fashion. The position which I had taken up aroused curiosity; people were anxious to make the acquaintance of the singular man, who sought no one's society, and whose only anxiety was to live free and happy after his own fashion; this was sufficient to make this an impossibility for him. My room was never free from people who, under different pretexts, came to rob me of my time. Ladies employed a thousand artifices to get me to dine with them. The more I offended people, the more

---

* I have no doubt that Francueil and his associates now give a totally different account of all this, but I appeal to what he said about it at the time, and for a long time afterwards, to all his acquaintances, until the conspiracy was formed. Men of good sense and honour cannot have forgotten his words [Rousseau].

obstinate they became. I could not refuse everybody. While I made a thousand enemies by my refusals, I was incessantly a slave to my desire to oblige; and, however I managed, I never had an hour to myself during the day.

I then discovered that it is by no means so easy as one imagines to be poor and independent. I wanted to live by my profession; the public would not have it. They invented a thousand ways of indemnifying me for the time which they made me lose. Presents of all kinds were always being sent to me. Soon I should have been obliged to show myself like Punch, at so much a head. I know no slavery more cruel and degrading than that. I saw no remedy for it, except to refuse all presents, great and small, and to make no exception in favour of anyone. The only effect of this was to increase the number of the donors, who desired to have the honour of overcoming my resistance, and of compelling me to be under an obligation to them, in spite of myself. Many, who would not have given me a crown if I had asked for it, never ceased to importune me with their offers, and to avenge themselves when they found them rejected, charged me with arrogance and ostentation, in consequence of my refusal. . . .

I used to go for a solitary walk, during which, dreaming of my grand system, I jotted down some ideas on paper with the aid of a pocket-book and pencil, which I always carried about with me. In this manner the unforeseen unpleasantnesses of a condition which I had chosen for myself threw me entirely into a literary career, by way of escaping from them; and this is the reason why, in all my early works, I introduced the bitterness and ill-humour which caused me to write them.

Another circumstance contributed to this. Thrown, in spite of myself, into the great world, without possessing its manners, and unable to acquire or conform to them, I took it into my head to adopt manners of my own, which might enable me to dispense with them. Being unable to overcome my foolish and disagreeable shyness, which proceeded from the fear of offending against the rules of polite society, I resolved, in order to give myself courage, to trample them underfoot.

Shame made me cynical and sarcastic. I affected to despise
the politeness which I did not know how to practise. It is true
that this rudeness, in harmony with my new principles, became ennobled in my mind and assumed the form of daunt-
less virtue; and on this lofty basis, I venture to assert, it supported itself longer and more successfully than would naturally have been expected from an effort so contrary to my disposition. However, in spite of the reputation for misanthropy,
which my outward appearance and some happy remarks
gained for me in the world, it is certain that, in private, I
always sustained my part badly. My friends and acquaintances led this unsociable bear like a lamb, and, limiting my
sarcasms to unpalatable but general truths, I was never
capable of saying a single discourteous word to anyone whatsoever.

[Grimm, socially successful, turns away from Rousseau,
who is distressed by this reward for his friendship.]

I said to him one day, "Grimm, you are neglecting me; I
forgive you. When the first intoxication of noisy success has
produced its effect, and you begin to perceive its emptiness,
I hope that you will come back to me: you will always find
me the same. For the present, do not put yourself out; I
leave you to do as you please, and will wait for you." He
told me that I was right, made his arrangements accordingly,
and went his own way so completely, that I only saw him in
the company of our mutual friends.

Our chief meeting-place, before he became so closely connected with Madame d'Epinay, was the Baron d'Holbach's
house. This Baron was the son of a self-made man, who possessed an ample fortune, which he used nobly. He received at
his house men of letters and learning, and, by his own knowledge and accomplishments, was well able to hold his own
amongst them. Having been long intimate with Diderot, he
had sought my acquaintance through him, even before my
name became known. A natural repugnance for a long time
prevented me from meeting his advances. One day he asked
me the reason, and I said to him, "You are too wealthy." He
persisted, and finally prevailed. My greatest misfortune has

ever been inability to resist flattery, and I have always regretted yielding to it.

[In 1752, Rousseau composes another opera, "Le Devin du village." It is played at Court.]

I now come to one of the critical moments of my life, in which it is difficult to confine myself to simple narrative, because it is almost impossible to prevent even the narrative bearing the stamp of censure or apology. However, I will attempt to relate how, and from what motives I acted, without adding an expression of praise or blame.

On that day I was dressed in my usual careless style, with a beard of some days' growth and a badly combed wig. Considering this want of good manners as a proof of courage, I entered the hall where the King, the Queen, the Royal Family, and the whole Court were presently to arrive. I proceeded to take my seat in the box to which M. de Cury conducted me; it was his own—a large stage box, opposite a smaller and higher one, where the King sat with Madame de Pompadour. Surrounded by ladies, and the only man in front of the box, I had no doubt that I had been put there on purpose to be seen. When the theatre was lighted up, and I found myself, dressed in the manner I was, in the midst of people all most elegantly attired, I began to feel ill at ease. I asked myself whether I was in my right place, and whether I was suitably dressed. After a few moments of uneasiness, I answered "Yes," with a boldness which perhaps was due rather to the impossibility of drawing back than to the force of my arguments. I said to myself: I am in my place, since I am going to see my own piece performed; because I have been invited; because I composed it solely for that purpose; because, after all, no one has more right than myself to enjoy the fruit of my labour and talents. I am dressed as usual, neither better nor worse. If I again begin to yield to public opinion in any single thing, I shall soon become its slave again in everything. To be consistent, I must not be ashamed, wherever I may be, to be dressed in accordance with the condition of life which I have chosen for myself. My outward appearance is simple and careless, but not dirty or slovenly. A beard in itself is not so, since it is bestowed upon us by Nature, and, according to times and fashions, is sometimes even an ornament. People will consider me ridiculous, impertinent. Well, what does it matter to me? I must learn how to put up with ridicule and censure, provided they are not deserved. After this little soliloquy, I felt so encouraged that I should have behaved with intrepidity, if it had been necessary. But, whether it was the effect of the presence of the ruler, or the natural disposition of those near me, I saw nothing in the curiosity, of which I was the object, except civility and politeness. This so affected me, that I began to be uneasy again about myself and the fate of my piece, and to fear that I might destroy the favourable impressions which showed only an inclination to applaud me. I was armed against their raillery; but their kindly attitude, which I had not expected, so completely overcame me, that I trembled like a child when the performance began.

I soon found I had no reason for uneasiness. The piece was very badly acted, but the singing was good, and the music well executed. From the first scene, which is really touching in its simplicity, I heard in the boxes a murmur of surprise and applause hitherto unheard of at similar performances. The growing excitement soon reached such a height, that it communicated itself to the whole audience, and, in the words of Montesquieu, "the very effect increased the effect." In the scene between the two good little people, this effect reached its highest point. There is never any clapping when the King is present: this allowed everything to be heard, and the piece and the author were thereby benefited. I heard around me women, who seemed to me as beautiful as angels, whispering and saying to each other in a low tone, "Charming! delightful! every note speaks to the heart!" The pleasure of affecting so many amiable persons moved me to tears, which I was unable to restrain during the first duet, when I observed that I was not the only one who wept. . . .

And yet I am sure that at this moment I was much more affected by sensual impulse than by the vanity I felt as an author. If none but men had been present, I am convinced that I should not have been consumed, as I was, by the incessant desire of catching with my lips the delightful tears which I caused to flow. I have seen pieces excite more lively transports of admiration, but never so complete, so delightful and so moving an intoxication, which completely overcame the audience, especially at a first performance before the Court. Those who saw it on this occasion can never have forgotten it, for the effect was unique.

The same evening, M. le Duc d'Aumont sent word to me to present myself at the château on the following day at eleven o'clock, when he would present me to the King. M. de Cury, who brought me the message, added that he believed that it was a question of a pension, the bestowal of which the King desired to announce to me in person.

Will it be believed, that the night which succeeded so brilliant a day was for me a night of anguish and perplexity? My first thought, after that of this presentation, was a certain necessity, which had greatly troubled me on the evening of the performance, and had frequently obliged me to retire, and might trouble me again on the next day, in the gallery or the King's apartments, amongst all the great people, while waiting for His Majesty to pass. This infirmity was the chief cause which prevented me from going into society, or from staying in a room with ladies when the doors were closed. The mere idea of the situation in which this necessity might place me, was enough to affect me to such an extent that it made me feel ready to faint, unless I should be willing to create a scandal, to which I should have preferred death. Only those who know what this condition is, can imagine the horror of running the risk of it.

I next pictured myself in the King's presence and presented to His Majesty, who condescended to stop and speak to me. On such an occasion, tact and presence of mind were indispensable in answering. Would my accursed timidity, which embarrasses me in the presence of the most ordinary stranger, leave me when I found myself in the presence of the King of France? would it suffer me to select, on the spur of the moment, the proper answer? It was my desire, without abandoning the austerity of tone and manner which I had assumed, to show that I was sensible of the honour which so great a monarch bestowed upon me. It was necessary that I should convey some great and useful truth in words of well-selected and well-deserved eulogy. To be able to prepare a happy answer beforehand, it would have been necessary to know exactly what he might say to me; and, even had this been possible, I felt perfectly certain that I should not be able to recollect in his presence a single word of all that I had previously thought over. What would become of me at this moment, before the eyes of all the Court, if, in my embarrassment, some of my usual silly utterances were to escape my lips? This danger alarmed, frightened, and made me tremble so violently, that I resolved, at all hazards, not to expose myself to it.

I lost, it is true, the pension, which was in a manner offered to me; but, at the same time, I escaped the yoke which it would have imposed upon me. Adieu truth, liberty, and courage! How could I, from that time forth, have dared to speak of independence and disinterestedness? I could only flatter or keep my mouth closed if I accepted this pension; and besides, who would guarantee the payment of it? What steps should I have had to take, how many people I should have been obliged to solicit! It would have cost me more trouble and far more unpleasantness to keep it, than to do without it. Consequently, in renouncing all thoughts of it, I believed that I was acting in a manner quite consistent with my principles, and sacrificing the appearance to the reality. I communicated my resolution to Grimm, who had nothing to say against it. To others I alleged my ill-health as an excuse, and I left the same morning.

My departure caused some stir, and was generally censured. My reasons could not be appreciated by everybody; it was much easier to accuse me of a foolish pride, and this more readily allayed the jealousy of all who felt they would not have acted like myself. The following day, Jelyotte wrote me a note, in which he gave me an account of the success of my piece and of the great fancy which the King himself had conceived for it. "All day long," he informed me, "his Majesty is continually singing, with the most execrable voice in his kingdom, and utterly out of tune, *J'ai perdu mon serviteur; j'ai perdu tout mon bonheur.*" He added that, in a fortnight, a second performance of the "Devin" was to be given, which would establish in the eyes of all the public the complete success of the first.

Two days later, as I was going to supper at Madame d'Epinay's, about nine o'clock in the evening, a coach passed me at the door. Someone inside made a sign to me to get in. I did so; the person was Diderot. He spoke to me about the pension more warmly than I should have expected a philosopher to speak on such a subject. He did not regard my unwillingness to be presented to the King as an offence; but he considered my indifference about the pension as a terrible crime. He said to me that, even if I was disinterested on my own account, I had no right to be so in regard to Madame le Vasseur and her daughter; that I owed it to them to neglect no honourable means, within my reach, of providing for their support; and as, after all, it could not be said that I had refused this pension, he insisted that, since there appeared a disposition to bestow it upon me, I ought to ask for it and obtain it, at any cost. Although I felt touched by his zeal, I was unable to approve of his principles, and we had a lively discussion on the subject, the first which had ever occurred between us. All our subsequent disputes were of the same kind, he dictating to me what he maintained I ought to do, while I as firmly refused, because I did not believe it was my duty.

It was late when we separated. I wanted to take him with me to supper at Madame d'Epinay's, but he would not go; and, in spite of the efforts which the desire of bringing together those whom I regard with affection caused me to make from time to time, to induce him to visit her—I even went so far as to take her to his door, which he refused to open to us—he always declined to see her, and never spoke of her except with great contempt. It was only after my disagreement with both that they became intimate, and that he began to speak of her with respect.

From that time Diderot and Grimm seemed to make it their object to set the women-folk against me, by giving them to understand that, if they were not better off, it was entirely my fault, and that they would never do any good with me. They tried to induce them to leave me, and promised them, through Madame d'Epinay's interest, a license to sell salt, or a tobacconist's shop, and I know not what besides. They even tried to drag Duclos and D'Holbach into their alliance, but the former persistently refused to join them. At the time I had some notion of their intrigues, but I only learned them clearly a long time afterwards, and I often had reason to lament the blind and indiscreet zeal of my friends, who, in endeavouring to reduce me, in my ill-health, to a state of most melancholy isolation, imagined that they were doing their utmost to make me happy by the very means which, beyond all others, were most adapted to make me utterly miserable.

[The "Devin" is a success in Paris. D'Holbach persuades him to insert a modified version of a song written for himself, saying no one would ever see the original. Later, Grimm shows it to his friends, and Rousseau is accused of not having written the "Devin."]

The comedians gained some very ardent support for Italian music. Paris was divided into two parties, more violently opposed than if it had been a matter of religion or of an affair of State. One, the more numerous and influential, composed of the great, the wealthy and the ladies, supported the French music; the other, more lively, more proud, and more enthusiastic, was composed of real connoisseurs, persons of talent, and men of genius. This little group assembled at the Opera, under the Queen's box. The other party filled the rest of the pit and house; but its chief meeting-place was under the King's box. This was the origin of these celebrated party names, "King's corner" and "Queen's corner." The dispute, as it became more animated, gave rise to several brochures. If the "King's corner" attempted to be witty, it was ridiculed by the "Petit Prophète"; if it attempted to argue, it was crushed by the "Lettre sur la musique Française." These two little pamphlets, by Grimm and myself respectively, are all that have survived the quarrel; all the rest are already forgotten.

But the "Petit Prophète," which, in spite of my denial, was for a long time attributed to me, was taken as a joke, and did not bring the least annoyance upon its author, whereas the "Lettre sur la musique" was taken seriously and roused against me the whole nation, which considered itself insulted in its music. A description of the incredible effect of this bro-chure would be worthy of the pen of Tacitus. It was the time of the great quarrel between Parliament and clergy. The Parliament had just been banished; the ferment was at its height; everything pointed to an approaching outburst. From the moment the brochure appeared, all other quarrels were at once forgotten; nothing was thought of, except the perilous condition of French music, and the only outburst was against myself. It was such that the nation has never quite re-covered from it. At Court, the only doubt was whether the Bastille or exile should be the punishment; and the Royal warrant of arrest would have been drawn up, had not M. de Voyer shown the ridiculous aspect of the affair. Anyone who sees it stated that this brochure possibly prevented a revolu-tion in the State will believe that he is dreaming. It is, how-ever, an actual truth, which all Paris can still attest, since it is at the present day no more than fifteen years since this singular incident took place.

Although my liberty was not attacked, I was unsparingly insulted, and even my life was in danger. The Opera orchestra entered into an honourable conspiracy to assassinate me when I left the theatre. Being informed of this, I only attended the Opera more frequently than before, and it was not until a long time afterwards that I learned that M. Ancelet, an officer in the Musketeers, who was kindly disposed towards me, had prevented the plot from being carried out, by causing me to be protected, unknown to myself, when I left the theatre. . . .

But I paid dearly for the pecuniary ease which this piece

procured me by the endless annoyance which it brought upon me. It was the germ of the secret jealousies, which did not break out until long afterwards. From the time of its success, I no longer found in Grimm, Diderot, or, with few exceptions, in any of the men of letters with whom I was acquainted, the cordiality, the frankness, or pleasure in my society, which I believed I had hitherto found in them. As soon as I appeared at the Baron's, the conversation ceased to be general. Those present collected in small groups and whispered together, so that I was left alone, without knowing whom to speak to. For a long time I endured this mortifying neglect, and, finding that Madame d'Holbach, who was gentle and amiable, always received me kindly, I put up with her husband's rudeness as long as it was possible. One day, however, he attacked me without reason or excuse, and with such brutality—in the presence of Diderot, who never said a word, and of Margency, who has often told me since then, that he admired the gentleness and moderation of my answers—that at last, driven away by this unworthy treatment, I left his house, resolved never to enter it again. However, this did not prevent me from always speaking respectfully of himself and his house; while he never expressed himself in regard to me in other than most insulting and contemptuous terms. He never spoke of me except as the little *cuistre,** without, however, being able to point to a single wrong of any kind which I had ever done to him or anyone in whom he took an interest. This was the manner in which he fulfilled my predictions and my fears. As for myself, I believe that my friends would have forgiven me for writing books—even excellent books—because such a reputation was attainable by themselves; but they were unable to forgive me for having composed an opera, or for its brilliant success, because not one of them was capable of following the same career, or aspiring to the same honour. Duclos alone, superior to such jealousy, seemed to become even more attached to me. He introduced me to Mademoiselle Quinault, by whom I was treated with as

* Ill-bred pedant.

much attention, politeness, and friendliness as I had found wanting at the Baron's house.

It was, I think, in this year (1753) that the "Origin of Inequality amongst Mankind" appeared as the subject proposed for discussion by the Academy of Dijon. Struck by this great question, I felt surprised that this Academy had ventured to propose it; but since it had had the courage to do so, I thought I might have the courage to discuss it, and undertook the task.

[He goes to Saint-Germain, to meditate in silence.]

The remainder of the day, I buried myself in the forest, where I sought and found the picture of those primitive times, of which I boldly sketched the history. I demolished the pitiful lies of mankind; I dared to expose their nature in all its nakedness, to follow the progress of time and of the things which have disfigured this nature; and, comparing man, as man has made him, with the natural man, I showed him, in his pretended perfection, the true source of his misery. My soul, uplifted by these sublime considerations, ascended to the Divinity; and, seeing my fellow creatures following blindly the path of their prejudices, their errors, their misfortunes, and their crimes, I cried aloud to them with a feeble voice which they could not hear, "Fools, who continually complain of Nature, learn that you bring all your misfortunes upon yourselves."

The result of these meditations was the "Essay on Inequality," a work which was more to Diderot's taste than any of my other writings. He gave most useful advice concerning it,* but it only found few readers in Europe who understood it,

---

* At the time when I wrote these words, I had no suspicion of Diderot's and Grimm's great conspiracy; otherwise I should easily have seen how the former abused my confidence, in order to give my writings the harsh tone and air of gloominess which ceased to be found in them when he no longer guided me. The description of the philosopher who, in the course of an argument, stops up his ears, in order to harden himself against the complaints of a man in distress, is in his style; and he had supplied me with several others, even stronger still, which I could never bring myself to use. But, as I attributed to his confinement in the donjon of Vincennes this melancholy tinge, which may be found again, in considerable proportions in his "Clairval," it never occurred to me to suspect any evil intention [Rousseau].

and none of the latter ever chose to speak of it. It was written as a prize competition: I sent it, feeling certain beforehand that it would be unsuccessful, as I knew well that the prizes of Academies were not intended for works of the kind.

This excursion and occupation were beneficial to my health and temper. Several years before, tortured by my retention of urine, I had put myself unreservedly into the physicians' hands, and they, without alleviating my sufferings, had exhausted my strength and undermined my constitution. After my return from Saint-Germain, I found myself stronger and better. I took the hint, and determined to recover or die without the assistance of physicians or drugs. I said good-bye to them for ever, and began to live without any fixed rules, remaining quiet when I could not walk, and walking as soon as I was strong enough to do so. Life in Paris, amongst pretentious people, was little to my taste; the cabals of men of letters, their shameful quarrels, their lack of candour as exhibited in their books, the haughty airs they gave themselves in society, were all so hateful to me and so antipathetic, I found so little gentleness, open-heartedness, and frankness, even in the society of my friends, that, disgusted with this tumultuous life, I came to long earnestly for residence in the country; and, as I saw no prospect of my profession allowing me to settle there, I hastened to spend in it at least the few hours which I had to spare. For several months, at first after dinner, I used to go for a walk by myself in the Bois de Boulogne, to think over subjects for future works, and did not return till nightfall.

[1754-1756. Rousseau and Thérèse journey to Geneva, and start out in the company of their good friend Gauffecourt.]

I must mention this journey as the period of the first experience which, in the course of a life of forty-two years, gave a shock to the confidence of my naturally unsuspicious disposition, to which I had always abandoned myself without reserve and without inconvenience. We had a hired carriage, which conveyed us by very short daily stages without changing horses. I often got down and walked. We had scarcely performed half the journey, when Thérèse showed the greatest repugnance to remaining alone in the carriage with Gauffecourt, and when, in spite of her entreaties, I wanted to get down, she did the same, and walked with me. For some time I scolded her for this whim, and even opposed it so strongly, that she felt obliged to declare the reason for her conduct. I thought that I was dreaming, I fell from the clouds, when I heard that my friend De Gauffecourt, more than sixty years old, gouty, impotent, and worn out by a life of pleasure and dissipation, had been doing his utmost, since we had started, to corrupt a person who was no longer young or beautiful, and who belonged to his friend, and that by the lowest and most disgraceful means, even going so far as to offer her money, and attempting to excite her passions by reading a disgusting book to her and showing her the disgraceful pictures of which it was full. Thérèse, in a fit of indignation, once threw his villainous book out of the carriage; and she told me that, the very first day, when I had gone to bed before supper with a very violent headache, he had employed all the time, during which he was alone with her, in attempts and actions more worthy of a satyr or he-goat than of an honourable man, to whom I had confided myself and my companion. What a surprise! what an entirely new cause of grief for me! I, who had until then believed that friendship was inseparable from all the amiable and noble sentiments which constitute all its charm, for the first time in my life found myself compelled to couple it with contempt, and to withdraw my confidence and esteem from a man whom I loved, and by whom I believed myself to be loved! The wretch concealed his disgraceful conduct from me; and, to avoid exposing Thérèse, I found myself compelled to conceal my contempt from him, and to keep hidden, in the bottom of my heart, feelings which he was never to know. Sweet and holy illusion of friendship! Gauffecourt was the first to lift thy veil before my eyes. How many cruel hands since then have prevented it from covering thy face again!

At Lyons I left Gauffecourt, to take the road through Savoy, as I could not bring myself to be so near mamma again, without seeing her once more. I saw her again—my

God! in what a condition! How low had she fallen! What was left of her former virtue? Could it be the same Madame de Warens, once so brilliant, to whom M. Pontverre, the *curé*, had sent me? How my heart was torn! The only resource I could see for her was, that she should leave the country. I reiterated, earnestly but in vain, the entreaties which I had several times addressed to her in my letters, begging her to come and live quietly with me, and let me devote my life and Thérèse's to make her own happy. Clinging to her pension, from which, although it was regularly paid, she had for a long time drawn nothing, she refused to listen to me. I gave her a small portion of my money, much less than I ought to have given, much less than I should have given her, if I had not felt certain, that she would not have spent a *sou* upon herself. During my stay in Geneva, she took a journey to Chablais, and came to see me at Grange-Canal. She had no money to continue her journey. I had not as much with me as she wanted, and sent it to her by Thérèse an hour later. Poor mamma! Let me mention one more proof of her goodness of heart. Her sole remaining jewel was a little ring; she took it from her finger and placed it upon that of Thérèse, who immediately replaced it, at the same time kissing and bathing in her tears that noble hand. Ah! then would have been the moment to pay my debt! I ought to have left all and followed her, to have never left her until her last hour, to have shared her lot, whatever it might have been. I did nothing of the kind. Occupied with another attachment, I felt the tie which bound us loosened, for want of any hope of being able to make it of any use to her. I wept over her, but did not follow her. Of all the stings of conscience that I have ever felt, this was the sharpest and most lasting. My conduct deserved the terrible punishment which since then has never ceased to overwhelm me; I hope it may have atoned for my ingratitude, which, indeed, showed itself in my conduct, but has wounded my heart too deeply for it ever to have been the heart of an ungrateful man.

Before I left Paris, I had sketched the dedication of my "Essay on Inequality." I finished it at Chambéri, and dated it

from that place, thinking it better, in order to avoid all unpleasantness, not to date it either from France or Geneva. On
my arrival in this city, I gave myself up to the republican
enthusiasm which had led me there. This enthusiasm was increased by the reception I met with. Fêted and made much
of by all classes, I abandoned myself entirely to patriotic zeal,
and, ashamed of being excluded from my rights as a citizen
by the profession of a religion different from that of my
fathers, I resolved publicly to return to the latter. As the
Gospel was the same for every Christian, and as the essential
part of the doctrine only differed in the attempts of different
people to explain what they were unable to understand, I said
to myself that, in each country, it was the right of the Sovereign alone to define the manner of worship and to settle this
unintelligible dogma, and that it was consequently the duty
of every good citizen to accept the dogma and to follow the
manner of worship prescribed by the law. Constant associ-
ation with the encyclopaedists, far from shaking my faith,
had strengthened it, in consequence of my natural aversion
to disputes and parties. The study of man and the universe
had everywhere shown me the final causes and the intelligence which directed them. The reading of the Bible, especially the Gospels, to which I had for several years devoted
myself, had taught me to despise the low and foolish interpretations given to the teaching of Jesus Christ by persons
utterly unworthy of understanding it. In a word, philosophy,
while firmly attaching me to what was essential in religion,
had released me from the petty and rubbishy forms with
which it has been obscured. Believing that, for an intelligent
man, there could not be two ways of being a Christian, I also
believed that all religious form and discipline, in each country, came under the jurisdiction of the law. From this reasonable, social, and pacific principle, which has brought upon
me such cruel persecutions, it followed that, if I desired to
become a citizen, I ought to be a Protestant, and to return
to the religion of my country. I accordingly determined to
do so.

[Rousseau decides to settle with Thérèse at Geneva, and

returns to Paris planning to break up his establishment. But the "Essay on Inequality" arouses resentment in Geneva.]

However, this ill-success would not have kept me from carrying out my intention of retiring to Geneva, had not motives, which had greater influence over my heart, contributed to this result. M. d'Epinay, being desirous of adding a wing which was wanting to the château of La Chevrette, went to extraordinary expense to finish it. One day, having gone, in the company of Madame d'Epinay, to see the work, we continued our walk a quarter of a league further, as far as the reservoir of the waters of the park, which adjoined the forest of Montmorency, where there was a pretty kitchen-garden, attached to which was a small and very dilapidated cottage, called the Hermitage. This solitary and agreeable spot had struck my attention when I saw it for the first time before my journey to Geneva. In my transport, I let fall the exclamation, "Ah, madam, what a delightful place to live in! Here is a refuge ready made for me." Madame d'Epinay did not take much notice of my words at the time; but, on this second visit, I was quite surprised to find, in place of the old ruins, a little house almost entirely new, very nicely arranged, and very habitable for a small establishment of three persons. Madame d'Epinay had had the work carried out quietly and at very trifling expense, by taking some materials and some of the workmen from the château. When she saw my surprise, she said, "There, Mr. Bear, there is your asylum; you chose it; friendship offers it to you. I hope that it will put an end to your cruel idea of separating from me." I do not believe that I have ever felt more deeply or more delightfully touched; I bathed with my tears the beneficent hand of my friend; and, if I was not vanquished from that moment, I was sorely shaken in my resolution. Madame d'Epinay, who was unwilling to be beaten, became so pressing, employed so many different means, and so many persons, in order to get over me—even enlisting Madame le Vasseur and her daughter in her service—that she finally triumphed over my resolutions. Abandoning the idea of settling in my native country, I decided, and promised, to live in the Hermitage; and, while the building was getting dry, she undertook to see after the furniture, so that all was ready for occupation the following spring.

One thing which greatly contributed to confirm my resolution, was the fact that Voltaire had settled in the neighbourhood of Geneva. I knew that this man would cause a revolution there; that I should find again in my own country the tone, the airs, and the manners which drove me from Paris; that I should have to maintain a perpetual struggle; and that no other choice would be left to me, except to behave either as an insufferable pedant, or as a coward and a bad citizen. The letter which Voltaire wrote to me about my last work caused me to hint at my apprehensions in my reply; the effect which it produced confirmed them. From that moment I looked upon Geneva as lost, and I was not mistaken. I ought perhaps to have defied the storm, if I had felt that I was capable of doing so. But what could I, timid, and a poor speaker, have done unaided against one who was arrogant, wealthy, supported by the credit of the great, brilliantly eloquent, and already the idol of the women and young men? I was afraid of exposing my courage uselessly to danger; I only listened to the voice of my naturally peaceable disposition, and my love of tranquillity which, if it deceived me then, still deceives me at the present day in this particular. By retiring to Geneva, I should have spared myself great misfortunes; but I doubt whether, with all my ardent and patriotic zeal, I should have done anything great or serviceable to my country.

Tronchin, who, nearly about the same time, settled at Geneva, came to Paris some time afterwards to play the quack, and brought away some of its treasures. On his arrival, he came to see me with the Chevalier de Jaucourt. Madame d'Epinay was very anxious to consult him privately, but it was difficult to get through the crowd. She had recourse to me, and I induced him to go and see her. Thus, under my auspices, they commenced a connection, which, later, they strengthened at my expense. Such has ever been my lot; no sooner have I brought together separate friends of my own,

than they infallibly combined against me. Although, in the
conspiracy, which the Tronchins from that time entered into,
to reduce their country to a state of servitude, they must all
have felt a mortal hatred towards me, the doctor for a long
time continued to show me proofs of his goodwill. He even
wrote to me after his return to Geneva, offering me the post
of honorary librarian. But my mind was made up, and this
offer did not shake my resolution.

[He receives a surprise visit from his old friend Venture.]

But, after he had left, the remembrance of our former intimacy so vividly recalled the recollections of my own youth,
so delightfully and so completely devoted to the angelic
woman who was now no less changed than himself, the little
incidents of that happy time, the romantic day's journey to
Toune, spent so innocently and delightfully in the company
of the two charming girls whose only favour had been a kiss
on the hand, which, nevertheless, had left behind such lively,
touching and lasting regret; all the delightful transports of a
young heart, which I had then felt in all their force, and
which I thought were gone for ever; all these tender reminiscences made me weep for my past youth and its delights,
henceforth lost for me. Ah! how I should have wept over
their tardy and melancholy return, if I had foreseen the
sorrow they were to cost me! . . .

In my singular and unique situation, I owe too much to
truth to owe anything further to anyone else. In order to know
me well, one must know me in all my aspects, both good and
bad. My Confessions are necessarily connected with those of
many others. I make both with equal frankness in all that
relates to myself, as I do not think that I am bound to treat
anyone else with greater consideration than myself, although
I should certainly like to do so. I desire to be always just and
truthful, to say as much good of others as I can, only to
speak evil when it concerns myself, and when I am compelled
to do so. Who, in the position in which I have been placed
by the world, has the right to demand more from me? My
Confessions are not written to appear during my lifetime, or
that of the persons concerned in them. If I were the master

of my own destiny and of that of this work, it should not see the light until long after my death and their own. But the efforts, which the dread of truth causes my powerful oppressors to make, in order to efface all traces of it, force me to do all that the most scrupulous fairness and the strictest sense of justice allow me, in order to preserve these traces. If the remembrance of me were destined to die with me, rather than compromise anyone, I would, without a murmur, endure an unjust and momentary ignominy; but, since my name is destined to live, it is incumbent upon me to endeavour to hand down with it the remembrance of the unfortunate man who bore it—such as he really was, not such as his unjust enemies incessantly endeavour to represent him.

BOOK NINE

[1756]

I WAS so impatient to take up my abode in the Hermitage, that I could not wait for the return of fine weather; and, as soon as my new home was ready, I hastened to betake myself thither, amidst the loud ridicule of the Holbachian clique, who openly predicted that I should not be able to endure three months' solitude, and that they would soon see me returning to confess my failure and live in Paris as they did. I myself, who had been for fifteen years out of my element, and now saw that I was on the point of returning to it, took no notice of their raillery. Ever since I had been thrown into the world against my will, I had not ceased to regret my dear Charmettes, and the blissful life which I had led there. I felt that I was born for the country and retirement; it was impossible for me to live happily anywhere else. In Venice, amidst the bustle of public business, in the position of a kind of diplomatic representative, in my proud hopes and schemes of promotion; in Paris—in the whirl of high society, in the sensual enjoyment of suppers, in the brilliant spectacles of the theatre, in the cloud of vain-glory which surrounded me—the recollection of my groves, brooks, and solitary walks was ever present to distract and sadden me, to draw from me sighs of longing and regret. All the toil to which I had been able to subject myself, all the ambitious schemes which, by fits and starts, had roused my zeal, had no other end in view but that of one day enjoying the happy country ease, to which at that moment I flattered myself I had attained. Without having acquired the respectable independence which I considered could alone lead me to it, I judged that, owing to my peculiar position, I was able to dispense with it, and to reach the same end by quite a different road. I had no income whatever; but I had a name, I possessed ability. I was temperate and had freed myself from the most expensive wants, which are satisfied in obedience to popular opinion. Besides, although indolent, I could work hard when I chose; and my indolence was not so much that of a confirmed idler as of an independent person, who only cares to work when he is in the humour for it. My copying was neither a brilliant nor a lucrative employment, but it was certain. The world approved of my courage in having chosen it. I could always feel sure of work, and, if I worked hard, of earning sufficient to live upon. Two thousand *francs*, the remains of the profits of the "Devin du Village" and my other writings, was a sufficient capital to keep me from being pushed for money for some time, and several works which I had in hand promised me, without being obliged to draw upon the booksellers, a sufficient addition to my funds to enable me to work comfortably without over-exerting myself and even to employ to advantage the leisure of my walks. My little household, consisting of three people, who were all usefully employed, was not very expensive to keep up. In short, my resources, which corresponded to my wants and desires, bade fair to promise me lasting happiness in the life which my inclination had chosen for me. . . .

Of the different works which I had on the stocks, the one which I had long had in my head, at which I worked with the greatest inclination, to which I wished to devote myself all my life, and which, in my own opinion, was to set the seal upon my reputation—was my "Institutions Politiques." Thirteen or fourteen years ago, I had conceived the idea of it, when, during my stay at Venice, I had had occasion to observe the faults of its much-vaunted system of government. Since then, my views had become greatly enlarged by the historical study of morals. I had come to see that everything was radically connected with politics, and that, however one proceeded, no people would be other than the nature of its government made it; thus this great question of the best government possible appeared to me to reduce itself to the following: What kind of government is best adapted to produce the most virtuous, the most enlightened, the wisest, and, in short, the best people, taking the word "best" in its widest signification? I thought that I perceived that this question was very closely connected with another, very nearly, although not quite the same. What is the government which, from its nature, always keeps closest to the law? This leads to the question. What is the law? and to a series of questions equally important. I saw that all this led me on to great truths conducive to the happiness of the human race, above all, to that of my country, in which I had not found, in the journey I had just made thither, sufficiently clear or correct notions of liberty and the laws to satisfy me; and I believed that this indirect method of communicating them was the best suited to spare the pride of those whom it concerned, and to secure my own forgiveness for having been able to see a little further than themselves. . . .

Those who judge, from the result, that my confidence deceived me, may be deceived themselves. In the storm which has overwhelmed me, my books have served as an excuse, but it was against myself personally that the attack was directed. They cared little about the author, but were eager to ruin Jean-Jacques. . . .

[Rousseau also plans a work—never written—"La Morale Sensitive," based on the materialistic principle that conduct can be modified by modifying the impressions objects make upon our organs.]

All these various projects afforded me material for meditation during my walks, for, as I believe I have already said, I can only think while walking: as soon as I stop, I can think no longer; my brain can only move with my feet. However, I had taken the precaution of providing myself with an indoor task for rainy days. This was my "Dictionary of Music"; the scattered, mutilated, and raw materials of which made it necessary to rewrite the work almost entirely. I bought some books which I required for the purpose. I had spent two months in making extracts from a number of others which I borrowed from the King's library, and some of which I was even allowed to take with me to the Hermitage. These were my materials for compiling indoors, when the weather did not allow me to go out, or when I was tired of my copying. This arrangement suited me so well, that I adhered to it both at the Hermitage and at Montmorency, and even, subsequently, at Motiers, where I finished this work while continuing others; and I always found a real relaxation in a change of occupation.

I followed for some time, with tolerable exactness, the distribution of time that I had marked out for myself, and was very well satisfied with it; but, when the fine weather brought back Madame d'Epinay more frequently to Épinay or La Chevrette, I found that attentions, which at first did not cost me much, but which I had not reckoned upon, greatly upset my other arrangements. I have already said that Madame d'Epinay had some very amiable qualities; she was very devoted to her friends and served them most zealously; and, as she spared neither time nor trouble, she certainly deserved that they should show her some attentions in return. Hitherto I had fulfilled this duty without feeling that it was one; but at last I discovered that I had loaded myself with a chain, the weight of which only friendship prevented me from feeling: I had made the burden heavier by my dislike of crowded rooms. Madame d'Epinay availed herself of this to make a proposal, which seemed to suit me well, and suited her even better; this was that she should let me know when she would be alone, or nearly so. I consented, without foreseeing to what I was binding myself. The consequence was, that I no longer visited her when it was convenient to me, but when it suited her, so that I was never sure of having a whole day at my disposal. This tie considerably spoiled the pleasure which my visits to her had formerly afforded me. I found that the freedom which she had so often promised me, was only granted to me on condition that I never made use of it; and, when once or twice I attempted to do so, it gave occasion to so many messages, so many notes and such apprehensions concerning my health, that I plainly saw that nothing but being completely confined to my bed could excuse me from running to her at the first intimation of her wishes. I was obliged to submit to this yoke. I submitted, and with tolerably good grace for so bitter an enemy of dependence as I was, since my sincere attachment to her prevented me in great measure from feeling the chain which accompanied it.

[In the society of Madame d'Epinay, D'Holbach and Grimm, Rousseau was always treated as an insignificant person. This, he says, suited him perfectly, except when alone with her.]

. . . I did not know what attitude to assume, as I did not venture to talk about literature, of which I was not competent to judge, nor about gallantry, since I was too bashful, and I feared, more than death itself, the ridiculous appearance of an old beau. Besides, this idea never occurred to me when with Madame d'Epinay, and would perhaps never have occurred to me once in my life, even had I spent it altogether in her society; not that I had any personal repugnance to her— on the contrary, I perhaps loved her too much as a friend, to be able to love her as a lover. It gave me pleasure to see her and to talk with her. Her conversation, although agreeable enough in society, was dull in private; my own, which was by no means fluent, was not much assistance to her. Ashamed of a too lengthy silence, I strained every nerve to enliven the interview; and, although it often tired me, it never wearied me. I was very glad to show her trifling attentions, to give her little brotherly kisses, which did not appear to excite her sensuality any more than my own, and that was all. She was very thin, very pale, her breast was as flat as my hand. This defect alone would have been sufficient to chill me; my heart and senses have never been able to see a woman in one who has no breasts; and other reasons, which it would be useless to mention, always caused me to forget her sex. . . .

I was so weary of salons, waterfalls, groves, flower-gardens, and their still more wearisome exhibitors; I was tired of stitching, pianos, sorting wool, making bows, foolish witticisms, insipid affectations, trifling story-tellers, and big suppers that, when I caught a glimpse of a simple thornbush, a hedge, a barn, or a meadow; when I inhaled, while passing through a hamlet, the fragrance of a savoury chervil omelette; when I heard from a distance the rustic refrain of the *bisquières*,° I wished all rouge, furbelows, and ambergris at the devil; and, regretting the good-wife's homely dinner and the native wine, I should have been delighted to slap the face of M. le chef and M. le maître, who forced me to dine at my usual supper-hour, and to sup at a time when I am usually asleep. . . .

I have always considered the day which united me to my Thérèse as that which determined my moral being. I needed an attachment, since that which should have sufficed me had been so cruelly broken. The thirst for happiness is never quenched in man's heart. Mamma was growing old and degraded. It was clear to me that she could never again be happy in this world. Thus, the only thing left for me was to seek for a happiness which should be my own, since I had for ever lost all hope of sharing hers. I drifted for some time from one idea, from one plan, to another. My voyage to Venice would have plunged me into public affairs, if the man with whom I was to be connected had been possessed of common sense. I am easily discouraged, especially in difficult and long-winded undertakings. My ill-success in this disgusted me with all others; and since, in accordance with my old maxim, I looked upon distant objects as decoys for fools, I determined

---

° Female goatherds.

to live henceforth without any fixed plan, as I no longer saw anything in life which might have tempted me to exert myself.

It was just at that time that we became acquainted. The gentle character of this good girl appeared to me so well suited to my own, that I united myself to her by means of an attachment which neither time nor wrongs have been able to lessen, and everything which ought to have broken it has only increased it. The strength of this attachment will be seen in the sequel, when I lay bare the wounds and pangs with which she has rent my heart during the height of my misery, without a word of complaint to anyone ever escaping me, until the moment when I am writing these lines.

When it becomes known that, after having done all and braved everything, to avoid being separated from her, after having lived with her for twenty-five years, in spite of destiny and mankind, I finally married her in my old age, without any expectation or solicitation on her part, without any engagement or promise on my own, it will be believed that a mad love, which turned my head from the first day, gradually led me on to the last extravagance; and it will be the more readily believed, when the special and weighty reasons, which should have prevented me from ever doing such a thing, also become known. What then will the reader think, when I declare to him, in all the sincerity which he must now recognise as part of my character, that, from the first moment when I saw her up to this day, I never felt the least spark of love for her; that I no more desired her possession than that of Madame de Warens, and that the sensual needs, which I satisfied in her person, were only for me those of sexual impulse, without being in any way connected with the individual? He will perhaps believe that, being constituted differently from other men, I was incapable of feeling love, since it did not enter into the feelings which attached me to those women who have been most dear to me. Patience, reader! the fatal moment is approaching, when you will be only too rudely undeceived.

I repeat myself; I know it; but it is unavoidable. The first, the greatest, the most powerful, the most irrepressible of all my needs was entirely in my heart; it was the need of a companionship as intimate as was possible; it was for that purpose especially that I needed a woman rather than a man, a female rather than a male friend. This singular want was such, that the most intimate corporal union had been unable to satisfy it; I should have wanted two souls in the same body; without that, I was always conscious of a void. I thought that the moment had come, when I should feel it no longer. This young person, amiable by reason of a thousand excellent qualities, and, at that time, even by her personal appearance, which was without a trace of unnaturalness or coquetry, would have confined my whole existence in herself, if I had been able to confine hers to me, as I had hoped. I had nothing to fear from men; I am certain that I am the only man she ever truly loved, and her passions were so cool, that she rarely felt the want of other men, even when I had ceased to be one to her in this respect. I had no family; she had one; and this family, the members of which were all of a far different character from herself, was not such that I could ever have regarded it as my own. This was the first cause of my unhappiness. What would I not have given to have been able to make myself her mother's child! I tried all I could to do so, but never succeeded. It was useless for me to attempt to unite all our interests; it was impossible. She always created interests different from mine, set them in opposition to mine, and even to those of her daughter, which were already identical with them. She and her other children and grandchildren became so many leeches, and the least injury they did to Thérèse was that of robbing her. The poor girl, who was accustomed to give in, even to her nieces, allowed herself to be robbed and ruled without saying a word; and it pained me to see that, while I exhausted my money and good advice in vain, I could do nothing to assist her. I tried to get her away from her mother; but she always opposed it. I respected her opposition, and esteemed her the more for it; but this refusal was none the less prejudicial to her interests and my own. Devoted to her mother and the rest of her family, she belonged more to them than to me, even more than to herself. Their greed was not so ruinous to her as their advice was pernicious; in short, if, thanks to her love for me and her naturally good disposition, she was not completely their slave, she was sufficiently so to prevent, in great part, the effect of the good principles which I endeavoured to instill into her, and to cause us always to remain two, in spite of all my efforts to the contrary. . . .

Being unable to enjoy to the full this intimate intercourse of which I felt the need, I sought to supplement it in a manner which, although it did not completely fill the void, caused me to feel it less. For want of a friend, who should be entirely devoted to me, I needed friends whose impulse might overcome my indolence. For this reason I cultivated and strengthened my relations with Diderot and the Abbé de Condillac, entered into fresh and still closer relations with Grimm, and, in the end, owing to the unlucky Essay, the history of which I have related, I found myself thrown back, without any idea of it, upon literature, which I thought I had abandoned for ever.

My first writings led me by a new path into another intellectual world, the simple and lofty economy of which I was unable to look upon without enthusiasm. My continued attention to it soon convinced me, that there was nothing but error and folly in the doctrine of our philosophers, and misery and oppression in our social arrangements. Deluded by my foolish pride, I thought that I was born to destroy all these illusions, and, believing that, in order to gain a hearing, it was necessary for my manner of life to harmonize with my principles, I adopted the singular course which I have not been permitted to continue, in which I set an example for which my pretended friends have never forgiven me, which at first made me ridiculous, and would have ended by making me respectable, if it had been possible for me to persevere in it.

Hitherto I had been good; from that moment I became virtuous, or, at least, intoxicated with virtue. This intoxication had commenced in my head, but had passed on into my heart. The noblest pride sprang up therein on the ruins of uprooted vanity. I pretended nothing; I became really what I seemed; and, for the four years at least, during which this state of effervescence lasted in all its force, there was nothing great or beautiful, which a man's heart could contain, of which I was not capable between heaven and myself. This was the origin of my sudden eloquence, of the truly celestial fire which inflamed me and spread over my first writings, and which for forty years had not emitted the least spark, since it was not yet kindled.

I was truly transformed; my friends and acquaintances no longer recognised me. I was no longer the shy, bashful rather than modest man, who did not venture to show himself or utter a word, whom a playful remark disconcerted, whom a woman's glance caused to blush. Audacious, proud, undaunted, I carried with me everywhere a confidence, which was firmer in proportion to its simplicity, and had its abode rather in my soul than in my outward demeanour. The contempt for the manners, principles, and prejudices of my age, with which my deep meditations had inspired me, rendered me insensible to the raillery of those who possessed them, and I pulverised their trifling witticisms with my maxims, as I should have crushed an insect between my fingers. What a change! All Paris repeated the penetrating and biting sarcasms of the man who, two years before and ten years afterwards, never knew how to find the thing he ought to say, nor the expression he ought to use. Anyone who endeavours to find the condition of all others most contrary to my nature will find it in this. If he desires to recall one of those brief moments in my life during which I ceased to be myself, and became another, he will find it again in the time of which I speak; but, instead of lasting six days or six weeks, it lasted nearly six years, and would, perhaps, have lasted until now, had it not been for the special circumstances which put an end to it, and restored me to Nature, above which I had attempted to elevate myself.

This change began as soon as I had left Paris and the sight of the vices of the great city ceased to keep up the indignation with which it had inspired me. As soon as I lost sight of men, I ceased to despise them; as soon as I lost sight of the wicked, I ceased to hate them. My heart, little adapted for hatred, only caused me to deplore their wretchedness, from which it did not distinguish their wickedness. This gentler, but far less lofty, frame of mind soon dulled the burning enthusiasm which had so long carried me away, and, without anyone perceiving it, even without perceiving it myself, I became again shy, courteous, and timid; in a word, the same Jean-Jacques as I had been before.

If this revolution had merely restored me to myself, and had gone no further, all would have been well; but, unfortunately, it went much further, and carried me away rapidly to the other extreme. From that time my soul, in a state of agitation, no longer kept its centre of gravity, and its oscillations, ever renewed, always went beyond it. I must describe at some length this second revolution—the terrible and fatal epoch of a destiny without example among mankind.

[Grimm, Diderot and Madame d'Epinay attempt to estrange Thérèse and her family from Jean-Jacques. Madame le Vasseur joins in the plot, but Thérèse remains loyal.]

If I had been more observant, I should have seen, from that moment, that I was nourishing a serpent in my bosom; but my blind confidence, which nothing had as yet diminished, was such that it never even occurred to me, that anyone could wish to injure a person who deserved to be loved. While I saw a thousand conspiracies formed around me, all I could complain of was the tyranny of those whom I called my friends, and whose only object, as I imagined, was to force me to be happy in their own fashion rather than in my own.

. . . Thérèse, by dividing her attentions, sometimes caused me to feel that I was alone, for I could no longer regard as a society the relations between us three. Then it was that I felt keenly the mistake which I had committed, at the beginning of our connection, in not having taken advantage of the pliability which was the result of her affection, to improve her mind and furnish her with a store of knowledge, which by drawing us closer together in our retirement, would have filled up her time and my own agreeably, and prevented us from ever noticing the length of a *tête-à-tête*. Not that our conversation ever flagged, or that she showed any signs of weariness during our walks; but we had not a sufficient number of ideas in common to make a great stock. We could no longer speak incessantly of our plans, which henceforth were limited to plans of enjoyment. The objects around us inspired me with reflections which were beyond her comprehension. An attachment of twelve years had no longer need of words; we knew each other too well to be able to find anything fresh. The only resource left was gossip, scandal, and feeble jokes. It is in solitude especially that one feels the advantage of living with someone who knows how to think. I had no need of this resource to amuse myself in her society; but she would have needed it, in order to be able always to amuse herself in mine. The worst thing was, that we were obliged to hold our interviews secretly; her mother, who had become a nuisance to me, forced me to look out for opportunities. I felt under restraint in my own house—this is saying everything. The atmosphere of love ruined simple friendship. We enjoyed an intimate intercourse without living in intimacy. . . .

Thus it happened that, half deceived in my expectation, leading a life after my own inclination, in a spot which I had chosen for myself, with a person who was dear to me, I nevertheless at length found myself almost isolated. What I still lacked prevented me from enjoying what I possessed. In the matter of happiness and enjoyment, I must have all or nothing. . . .

I lived with her without restraint, and, so to say, as I pleased. Nevertheless, a secret feeling of oppression never left me, whether I was with her or away from her. While possessing her, I felt that she was still not mine; and the mere idea that I was not all in all to her, caused her to seem hardly anything to me.

I had friends of both sexes, to whom I was attached by the purest friendship and the most perfect esteem. I counted upon the truest return of these feelings on their part, and it never even occurred to me ever once to doubt their sincerity; yet this friendship was more painful to me than agreeable, owing to their obstinacy, even their affectation, in opposing all my inclinations, tastes, and manner of life. It was enough for me to seem to desire anything which concerned myself alone, and which did not depend upon them, in order to see them all immediately combine to force me to renounce it. This obstinate desire to control me absolutely in all my fancies—which was the more unjust as, far from attempting to control theirs, I did not even take the trouble to make myself acquainted with them—became so cruelly burdensome to me, that at last I never received a letter from them without feeling, when I opened it, a certain alarm, which was only too well justified by the perusal of it. I thought that, in the case of people who were all younger than myself, and who all stood in sore need themselves of the good advice which they lavished upon me, it was treating me too much like a child. "Love me," said I to them, "as I love you; as for the rest, do not interfere with my affairs, any more than I interfere with yours. That is all I ask of you." If they have granted me one of these two requests, it has certainly not been the latter.

I had a retired abode in a charming solitude. Master within my own four walls, I could live there in my own fashion, without being subjected to anyone's control. But this abode imposed upon me certain duties which were pleasant to fulfill, but indispensable. My liberty was altogether precarious. In a position of greater subjection than if I had been under orders, I was supposed to be so by inclination. When I got up, I could never once say to myself: I will spend this day as I please. Besides being dependent upon Madame d'Epinay's arrangements, I had still a more importunate claim upon me—that of the public and chance visitors. The distance of my residence from Paris did not prevent the daily arrival of crowds of idlers, who, not knowing what to do with their own time, wasted mine without the slightest scruple. When I least expected it, I was mercilessly assailed, and I rarely made agreeable plans for spending the day without finding them upset by the arrival of some unexpected visitor.

In short, amidst the blessings which I had most eagerly longed for, finding no pure enjoyment, I returned by fits and starts to the unclouded days of my youth, and I sometimes cried, with a sigh, to myself, "Ah! this is not Les Charmettes!"

The recollections of the different periods of my life led me to reflect upon the point which I had reached, and I saw myself, already in my declining years, a prey to painful evils, and believed that I was approaching the end of my career, without having enjoyed in its fullness scarcely one single pleasure of those for which my heart yearned, without having given scope to the lively feelings which I felt it had in reserve, without having tasted or even sipped that intoxicating pleasure which I felt was in my soul in all its force, and which, for want of an object, always found itself kept in check, and unable to give itself vent in any other way but through my sighs.

How came it to pass that I, a man of naturally expansive soul, for whom to live was to love, had never yet been able to find a friend entirely devoted to myself, a true friend—I, who felt admirably adapted to be one myself? How came it to pass that, with feelings so easily set on fire, with a heart full of affection, I had never once been inflamed with the love of a definite object? Consumed by the desire of loving, without ever having been able to satisfy it completely, I saw myself approaching the portals of old age, and dying without having lived.

These melancholy but touching reflections caused me to turn my thoughts towards myself with a regret which was not without its pleasure. It seemed to me that destiny owed me something which it had not yet granted me. Why had I been born with delicate faculties, if they were to remain unemployed to the end? The consciousness of my inner value, while calling forth the feeling of having been unfairly depreciated, in some degree compensated for it, and caused me to shed tears which it was a pleasure to me to allow to flow.

I pursued these reflections in the most beautiful season of the year, in the month of June, in cool groves, amidst the song of the nightingale and the purling of brooks. Everything combined to plunge me again into that too seductive indolence, to which I was naturally inclined, but from which the hard and austere frame of mind, to which a long period of inner ferment had brought me, should have delivered me once and for all. Unhappily, I went on to recall the dinner at the Château of Toune, and my meeting with those two charming girls at the same season of the year, and in a spot almost like that where I was at the moment. This recollection, rendered still more charming by the breath of innocence which pervaded it, brought back others of the same kind. Presently, I saw gathered round me all the objects which had touched my heart with emotion during my youth—Mademoiselle Galley, Mademoiselle de Graffenried, Mademoiselle de Breil, Madame Basile, Madame de Larnage, my young pupils, even the piquant Zulietta, whom my heart can never forget. I saw myself surrounded by a seraglio of houris and by my old acquaintances, the liveliest desire for whom was no new sensation for me. My blood became heated and inflamed, my head swam, in spite of my hairs already growing grey: and the serious citizen of Geneva, the austere Jean-Jacques, close upon his forty-fifth year, suddenly became again the love-sick shepherd. The intoxication which seized me, although so sudden and extravagant, was, notwithstanding, so strong and lasting, that nothing less than the unforeseen and terrible crisis of the unhappiness into which it plunged me would have been able to cure me of it.

However, this intoxication, to whatever point it was carried, did not go so far as to make me forget my age and my position, flatter me with the idea that I could still inspire love, or make me attempt to communicate this devouring, but barren fire, by which, from childhood, I felt my heart in vain consumed. I did not hope, I did not even desire it; I knew that the time for love was over; I was too keenly conscious of the ridicule heaped upon elderly beaux, to expose myself to it, and I was not the man to become presumptuous and self-confident in my declining years, after having so rarely displayed such qualities during my best days. Besides, as a friend of peace, I should have dreaded domestic storms, and I loved

Thérèse too sincerely, to expose her to the annoyance of seeing me entertain livelier feelings for others than those with which she herself inspired me.

What did I do on this occasion? The reader must have already guessed, if he has hitherto followed me with the least attention. The impossibility of grasping realities threw me into the land of chimeras, and, seeing nothing in existence which was worthy of my enthusiasm, I sought nourishment for it in an ideal world, which my fertile imagination soon peopled with beings after my own heart. This resource was never so welcome to me or so fruitful. In my continued ecstasies, I intoxicated myself with full draughts of the most delightful sensations that have ever entered the heart of man. I entirely forgot the human race, and created for myself societies of perfect beings, heavenly alike in their beauties and virtues; trusty, tender, and loyal friends such as I never found in this world below. I found such pleasure in soaring into the empyrean, in the midst of the charming objects by which I was surrounded, that I passed the hours and days in it without taking count of them, and, forgetting everything else, no sooner had I hastily eaten a morsel of food, than I burned to escape, in order to run to my groves again. When ready to set out for my world of enchantment, if I saw some wretched mortals arrive who came to keep me back upon earth, I was unable to conceal or restrain my annoyance, and, losing control over myself, I gave them so rude a reception, that it might almost have been called brutal. This only increased my reputation as a misanthrope, whereas it would have gained for me a very different one, if the world had read my heart better.

At the height of my greatest exaltation, I was suddenly pulled back like a kite by the string, and restored to my place by Nature, assisted by a smart attack of my complaint. I employed the only remedy which afforded me relief, that is to say, the bougies, which put a stop to my celestial amours; for, besides that a man is seldom amorous when he is suffering, my imagination, which is animated in the open air and under the trees, languishes and dies in a room and under the rafters of a ceiling. I have often regretted that Dryads did not exist; it would most assuredly have been amongst them that I should have found the object of my attachment.

Other domestic disturbances occurred at the same time to increase my annoyance. Madame le Vasseur, while paying me the most effusive compliments, was doing her utmost to alienate her daughter from me. I received letters from my old neighbourhood, in which I was informed that the worthy old woman, without my knowledge, had contracted debts in the name of Thérèse, who knew it, but said nothing to me about it. That I had to pay them annoyed me much less than their having been kept a secret from me. How could she, from whom I had never kept a secret, keep one from me? Can one conceal anything from those whom one loves? The Holbachian clique, finding that I never went to Paris, began to be seriously afraid that I was comfortable in the country, and that I should be foolish enough to remain there. Then began those intrigues, the object of which was to get me back, indirectly, to the city. Diderot, who did not want to show himself so soon, began by detaching Deleyre from me, whom I had made acquainted with him, and who received and handed on to me the impressions which Diderot desired to give him, without perceiving their real purpose.

Everything seemed in league to tear me from my delightful and foolish reveries. Before I had recovered from my attack of illness, I received a copy of the poem on the destruction of Lisbon, which I supposed was sent to me by the author.* This put me under the obligation of writing to him, and saying something about his composition. This I did in a letter which was printed a long time afterwards without my consent, as will be mentioned later.

Surprised to hear this poor man, overwhelmed, so to speak, by fame and prosperity, declaim bitterly against the miseries of this life, and declare everything to be bad, I formed the senseless plan of bringing him to himself again, and proving to him that everything was good. Voltaire, while always

* Voltaire.

appearing to believe in God, has never really believed in anything but the Devil, since his pretended God is nothing but a malicious being, who, according to him, finds no pleasure except in doing injury. The absurdity of this doctrine, which is obvious, is particularly revolting in a man loaded with blessings of every kind, who, from the bosom of happiness, endeavours to reduce his fellows to despair by the fearful and cruel picture of all the calamities from which he is himself exempt. I, who had a better right to count and weigh the evils of human life, examined them impartially, and proved to him that Providence is acquitted of responsibility in regard to every single one, and that they all have their origin in man's abuse of his faculties, rather than in the nature of things themselves. I treated him in this letter with all possible regard, consideration, delicacy, and I venture to say, respect. But, as I knew how easily his self-love was irritated, I did not send the letter to himself, but to Dr. Tronchin, his physician and friend, with full authority to deliver or suppress it, whichever he thought best. Tronchin gave him the letter. Voltaire, in reply, wrote me a few lines to the effect that, as he was ill and also nurse to someone else, he would defer his answer to another occasion, and said not a word about the subject. Tronchin, who sent this letter to me, enclosed it in one from himself, in which he expressed little esteem for the person who had handed it to him.

I have never published, or even shown, these two letters, since I am not fond of making a show of such petty triumphs; the originals will be found in my collection (Bundle A, Nos. 20 and 21). Since then, Voltaire has published the answer which he promised me, but never sent. It is no other than the romance of "Candide," of which I cannot speak, because I have not read it.

All these distractions ought to have cured me completely of my fantastic amours, and they were perhaps a means offered me by Heaven to prevent their fatal consequences; but my unlucky star was in the ascendant, and I had scarcely begun to go out again, when my heart, my head, and my feet again took the same paths. I say the same, in certain respects; for my ideas, a little less exalted, this time remained upon earth, but made so dainty a selection of everything amiable that could be found, that this selection was hardly less chimerical than the imaginary world, which I had abandoned.

I represented to myself love and friendship, the two idols of my heart, under the most enchanting forms. I took delight in adorning them with all the charms of the sex which I had always adored. I imagined two female friends, rather than two of my own sex, because if an instance of such friendship is rarer, it is at the same time more amiable. I bestowed upon them two analogous, but different, characters; two faces, not perfect, but after my taste, lighted up by kindliness and sensibility. I made one dark, the other fair; one lively, the other gentle; one prudent, the other weak, but with so touching a weakness, that virtue seemed to gain by it. I gave to one a lover, whose tender friend the other was, and even something more; but I admitted no rivalry, no quarreling, no jealousy, because it is difficult for me to imagine painful feelings, and I did not wish to mar this charming picture by anything which degraded Nature. Smitten by my two charming models, I identified myself with the lover and the friend as far as it was possible for me; but I made him young and amiable, bestowing upon him, in addition, the virtues and defects which I was conscious of in myself.

In order to place my characters in the midst of suitable surroundings, I successively passed in review the most beautiful spots that I had seen in the course of my travels. But I found no woodland sufficiently delightful, no landscape sufficiently moving, to satisfy my taste. The valleys of Thessaly might have satisfied me, if I had seen them; but my imagination, tired of inventing, wanted some actual spot which might serve as a foundation, and create for me an illusion as to the reality of the inhabitants whom I intended to place there. For a long time I thought of the Borromean Islands,* the charming aspect of which had delighted me; but I found too much ornament and artificiality there. However, a lake

* In the Lago Maggiore.

was absolutely necessary, and I ended by choosing that one, on the shores of which my heart has never ceased to wander. I fixed upon that part of the shore, where my wishes had long placed my residence, in the imaginary happiness to which my destiny has limited me. The birthplace of my poor mamma still possessed a special charm for me. The contrast of natural situations, the richness and variety of the landscape, the magnificence, the majesty of the whole, which enchants the senses, moves the heart, and elevates the soul, finally decided me, and I established my young *protégés* at Vevay. This was all I imagined at the moment; the remainder was not added until later.

For a long time I confined myself to this indefinite plan, because it was sufficient to fill my fancy with agreeable objects, and my heart with feelings, upon which it loves to feed itself. These fictions, by their constant recurrence, at length assumed greater consistency, and fixed themselves in my brain under a definite shape. It was then that it occurred to me to give expression upon paper to some of the situations which they offered me, and, recalling all the feelings of my youth, to give play, to a certain extent, to the desire of loving, which I had never been able to satisfy, and by which I felt myself devoured.

At first, I scribbled upon paper a few scattered letters, without sequence or connection; and when I wanted to put them together, I was often greatly embarrassed. What seems almost incredible, but is nevertheless perfectly true, is that the first two parts were written almost entirely in this manner, without my having formed any definite plan, and without my foreseeing that I should one day be tempted to make a regular work of it. Thus it will be seen, that these two parts, composed later of materials which were not shaped for the place which they occupy, are full of wordy padding, which is not found in the others.

In the height of my reveries, I received a visit from Madame d'Houdetot, the first she had ever paid me in her life, but which, unfortunately, was not the last, as will be seen later. The Comtesse d'Houdetot was the daughter of the late

M. de Bellegarde, farmer-general, and sister of M. d'Epinay and MM. de Lalive and de la Briche, both of whom were afterwards introducers of ambassadors.° I have mentioned how I became acquainted with her before she was married. Since then, I never saw her except at the festivities at La Chevrette, at Madame d'Epinay's, her sister-in-law. Having frequently spent several days with her, both at Épinay and at La Chevrette, I not only found her always very amiable, but I fancied that I perceived that she was favourably disposed towards myself. She was fond of walking with me; we were both of us good walkers, and our conversation never flagged. However, I never visited her in Paris, although she asked, and even pressed me to do so. Her connection with M. de Saint-Lambert, with whom I was becoming intimate, rendered her still more interesting to me; and it was in order to bring me news of this friend, who at the time was, I believe, at Manon, that she came to the Hermitage.

This visit somewhat resembled the commencement of a romance. She lost her way. Her coachman had left the road at a place where it turned off, and tried to cross straight from the mill at Clairvaux to the Hermitage; her carriage stuck in the mud at the bottom of the valley; she decided to get out and finish the journey on foot. Her thin shoes were soon wet through; she sank in the mire; her servants had the greatest trouble imaginable to extricate her, and at last she reached the Hermitage in a pair of boots, making the air ring with shouts of laughter, in which I joined when I saw her arrive. She was obliged to change all her clothes; Thérèse provided for her wants, and I persuaded her to put aside her dignity, and join us in a rustic collation, at which she greatly enjoyed herself. It was late, and she remained only a short time; but the meeting was so cheerful that she was delighted, and seemed disposed to come again. However, she did not carry out her intention until the following year; but alas! this delay was not of the least avail to protect me.

[1757.]—When the bad weather began again, and I was

* Persons whose duty it was to conduct ambassadors to an audience with the Sovereign.

confined to the house, I tried to resume my stay-at-home occupations, but found it impossible. I saw everywhere nothing but my two charming friends, their friend, their surroundings, the country in which they lived, the objects which my fancy created or embellished for them. I no longer belonged to myself for a single moment. My delirium never left me. After several fruitless attempts to banish all these imaginary creations from my mind, I became at last completely seduced by them, and all my efforts were thenceforth devoted to reducing them to some sort of order and coherence, in order to work them up into a kind of romance.

I was chiefly embarrassed by the shame which I felt at contradicting myself so openly and so boldly. After the strict principles which I had just laid down with so much noise, after the austere maxims which I had preached so strongly, after the biting invectives which I had launched against the effeminate books which breathed nothing but love and tenderness, could anything more unexpected or more shocking be imagined, than to see me, all at once, enroll myself with my own hand amongst the authors of those books which I had so strongly censured? I felt this inconsistency in all its force. I reproached myself with it, I blushed for it, I was vexed with myself for it; but all this was unable to bring me back to reason. Completely enthralled, I was forced to submit to the yoke at all risks, and to make up my mind to brave public opinion, except in regard to considering later, whether I should decide to show my work or not: for I did not as yet suppose that I should ever determine to publish it.

Having taken this resolution, I threw myself heartily into my reveries, and, after repeatedly turning them over and over in my head, I at last sketched the kind of plan, with the execution of which the public is acquainted. This was certainly the best advantage that could be derived from my follies: the love of the good, which has never left my heart, turned them naturally towards useful objects, which might have been productive of moral advantage. My voluptuous pictures would have lost all their grace, if the gentle colouring of innocence had been wanting in them. A weak girl is an object of pity, which may be rendered interesting by love, and which is frequently not less amiable; but who can endure without indignation the sight of fashionable manners? What can be more revolting than the pride of an unfaithful wife, who, openly trampling underfoot all her duties, nevertheless claims that her husband should be deeply grateful for the favour which she grants him—of being kind enough not to allow herself to be caught in the act? Perfect beings do not exist; the lessons which they give are too far remote from us. But—that a young person, born with a heart equally tender and virtuous, while still unwedded, should allow herself to be overcome by love, and when wedded, should find strength to overcome it in her turn and become virtuous again—if anyone should tell you that this picture is, on the whole, scandalous and unprofitable, he is a liar and a hypocrite: do not listen to him.

Besides morality and conjugal fidelity, which are radically connected with all social order, I had another and deeper object in view—harmony and public peace, an object greater and perhaps more important in itself, and certainly so at the moment. The storm aroused by the "Encyclopédie," far from subsiding, was at that time at its height. The two parties, let loose against each other with desperate frenzy, were more like mad wolves ready to tear each other to pieces in their rage, than Christians and philosophers desirous of mutually enlightening, convincing, and leading each other back into the way of truth. It may almost be said that nothing was wanting on either side but active leaders of sufficient importance, for the quarrel to degenerate into civil war; and God only knows what would have been the result of a civil war waged on behalf of religion, in which the most cruel intolerance was in the main the same on both sides. A born enemy of all party spirit, I had frankly told some hard truths to both parties, to which they had paid no attention. I bethought myself of another expedient, which, in my simplicity, I considered admirable: this was to soften their mutual hatred by destroying their prejudices, and to point out to each party the merits and virtues of the other as worthy of public esteem and the respect of all mankind. This by no means sensible scheme, which assumed good faith amongst men, and which led me into the mistake with which I reproached the Abbé de Saint-Pierre, met with the success which it deserved: it entirely failed to reconcile the two parties, and only brought them together again in order to overwhelm me. Meanwhile, until experience had shown me my folly, I devoted myself to it, I venture to say, with a zeal worthy of the motive which inspired me, and I sketched the two characters of Wolmar and Julie in a state of rapture, which made me hope that I should succeed in making both amiable, and, what is more, by means of each other.

Satisfied with having roughly sketched my plan, I returned to the situations of detail which I had marked out. The result of the form in which I arranged them was the two first parts of "Julie," which I wrote and made a fair copy of during the winter months with indescribable pleasure, using the finest gilt-edged paper, blue and silver writing-sand to dry the ink, and blue ribbon to fasten my manuscript; in short, nothing was sufficiently elegant or refined for the charming girls, with whom, like another Pygmalion, I was infatuated. Every evening, by the fireside, I read and read again these two parts to the women-folk. The daughter, without saying a word, and moved to tenderness, joined her sobs to mine; the mother, finding no compliments in it, understood nothing of it, remained quiet, and contented herself with repeating to me, during the intervals of silence, "That is very fine, sir." . . .

I think, however, that I remember that, during this interval of peace, and even in the depths of my solitude, I did not remain altogether undisturbed by the Holbachians. Diderot stirred up some annoyances against me, and, unless I am very much mistaken, it was during this winter that the "Fils Naturel" appeared, of which I shall have to speak presently. Not to mention that, for reasons which will subsequently appear, very few trustworthy records of that period have been preserved, even those which I have been permitted to keep are very inaccurate in regard to dates. Diderot never dated his letters. Madame d'Epinay and Madame d'Houdetot only put the day of the week, and Deleyre usually did the same. When I wanted to arrange these letters in order, I was obliged to grope in the dark and to supply the omissions by uncertain dates, upon which I cannot rely. Therefore, as I am unable to fix with certainty the date of the commencement of these quarrels, I prefer to relate afterwards, in a single section, all that I can recollect about them.

The return of spring had redoubled my tender frenzies, and in my erotic transports I had composed for the last parts of "Julie" several letters which have a flavour of the rapturous frame of mind in which I wrote them. I may mention, amongst others, that which deals with the Elysium and the walk along the shores of the lake, which, if I rightly recollect, are at the end of the fourth part. If anyone can read these two letters, without feeling his heart softened and melted by the same emotion which dictated them to me, he had better shut the book; he is incapable of judging of matters of sentiment.

Exactly at the same time, I had a second unexpected visit from Madame d'Houdetot. In the absence of her husband, who was a captain in the *Gendarmerie,* and of her lover, who was also in the service, she had come to Eaubonne, in the midst of the valley of Montmorency, where she had taken a very nice house. It was from there that she made a second excursion to the Hermitage. On this occasion, she came on horseback, dressed in men's clothes. Although I am not fond of such masquerades, I was charmed with the air of romance in this particular case, and this time—it was love. As it was the first and only time in my life, and its consequences have stamped it indelibly upon my recollection with terrible force, I must be permitted to enter with some detail into the matter.

Madame la Comtesse d'Houdetot was approaching her thirtieth year, and was by no means handsome. Her face was pitted with small-pox, her complexion was coarse, she was short-sighted, and her eyes were rather too round, but, notwithstanding, she looked young, and her features, at once lively and gentle, were attractive. She had an abundance of luxuriant black hair, which curled naturally, and reached down to her knees. Her figure was neat, and all her movements were marked by awkwardness and grace combined. Her wit was both natural and agreeable; gaiety, lightheartedness, and simplicity were happily united in it. She overflowed with delightful sallies of wit, which were perfectly spontaneous, and which often fell from her lips involuntarily. She possessed several agreeable accomplishments, played the piano, danced well, and composed very pretty verses. As for her character, it was angelic; gentleness of soul was the foundation of it; and, with the exception of prudence and strength, all the virtues were combined in it. . . .

She had been married very young and against her inclinations to the Comte d'Houdetot, a man of position and a gallant soldier, but a gambler and a quarreller, and a person of but few amiable qualities, whom she had never loved. She found in M. de Saint-Lambert all the good qualities of her husband, together with others that were more agreeable—intellect, virtue, and talent. If one can excuse anything in the manners of the age, it is undoubtedly an attachment, which is refined by its duration, honoured by its effects, and only cemented by mutual esteem.

As far as I have been able to judge, she came to see me a little from her own inclination, but more from a desire to please Saint-Lambert, who had exhorted her to do so, and was right in believing that the friendship, which was beginning to be formed between us, would make this society agreeable to all three. She knew that I was aware of their relations, and, being able to speak of him to me without restraint, it was natural that she should find my society agreeable. She came; I saw her. I was intoxicated with love without an object. This intoxication enchanted my eyes; this object became centred in her. I saw my Julie in Madame d'Houdetot, and soon I saw only Madame d'Houdetot, but invested with all the perfections with which I had just adorned the idol of my heart. To complete my intoxication, she spoke to me of Saint-Lambert in the language of passionate love. O contagious power of love! When I listened to her, when I found myself near her, I was seized with a delightful shivering, which I have never felt when with anyone else. When she spoke, I felt myself overcome by emotion. I imagined that I was interesting myself only in *her* feelings, when my own were similar. I swallowed in deep draughts the contents of the poisoned cup, of which as yet I only tasted the sweetness. At last, without either of us perceiving it, she inspired me with all those feelings for herself which she expressed for her lover. Alas! it was very late, it was very hard for me, to be consumed by a passion, as violent as it was unfortunate, for a woman whose heart was full of love for another!

In spite of the extraordinary emotions which I had felt in her presence, I did not at first understand what had happened to me. It was not until she had left me that, when I attempted to think of Julie, I was surprised to find that I could think of nothing but Madame d'Houdetot. Then the scales fell from my eyes; I understood my misfortune, I groaned over it, but I did not foresee its results. I hesitated for a long time how I should behave towards her, as if real love left anyone sufficiently rational to be able to act in accordance with the result of such deliberations. I had not made up my mind, when she came again and took me by surprise. On this occasion, I understood the state of things. Shame, the companion of evil, made me speechless. I trembled before her, not venturing to open my mouth or lift my eyes. I was inexpressibly troubled, and she must have seen it. I resolved to confess it, and to leave her to guess the reason. This would be telling her the truth plainly enough.

If I had been young and attractive, and Madame d'Houdetot had shown herself weak, I should here blame her conduct. Nothing of the kind; I can only applaud and admire it. The course she took was equally generous and prudent. She could not suddenly give up my acquaintance without telling Saint-Lambert the reason, for he had himself persuaded her to visit me. This would have exposed two friends to the risk of a rupture, and, perhaps, of a public scandal, which she desired to avoid. She esteemed me and wished me well. She pitied my folly, and, without flattering, lamented it, and endeavoured to cure me of it. She was very glad to be able to keep for herself and her lover a friend whom she valued. Nothing gave her more pleasure than to speak of the close and happy intimacy which we might form between us, as soon as I should have recovered my senses. She did not, however, altogether confine herself to these friendly exhortations, and, when necessary, did not spare the harsher reproaches which I had so well deserved.

I spared myself even less. As soon as I was alone, I came to myself again. I was calmer for having spoken. Love, when it is known to her who inspires it, becomes more endurable. The energy with which I reproached myself for the love which I felt, must have cured me of it, if it had been possible. I summoned to my aid all the most powerful arguments I could think of, to stifle it. My moral sense, my feelings, my principles, the shame, the disloyalty, the crime, the abuse of a trust confided to me by friendship and, lastly, the absurdity, at my age, of being inflamed with a most extravagant passion for one whose heart, already engaged, could neither make me any return, nor permit me to entertain the least hope—a passion, besides, which, far from having anything to gain by constancy, became more unbearable from day to day: I thought of all these.

Who would believe that the last consideration, which should have added weight to all the rest, was the one which weakened their force? What scruples, said I to myself, need I entertain in regard to a folly by which I am the only sufferer? Am I a young gallant of whom Madame d'Houdetot should feel alarmed? Would it not be said, to judge from my conceited remorse, that my gallantry, my manner, and my personal appearance were on the way to lead her astray? O poor Jean-Jacques! love on to your heart's content, with a perfectly safe conscience, and have no fear that your sighs will ever injure Saint-Lambert.

My readers have seen that I was never presuming, even in my youth. This way of thinking was in keeping with the bent of my mind; it flattered my passion; it was sufficient to make me abandon myself to it unreservedly, and even laugh at the irrelevant scruples, which I thought I had created rather out of vanity than in accordance with the dictates of reason. What a lesson for honest souls, whom vice never attacks openly, but whom it finds the means to surprise, ever hiding itself under the mask of some sophism—frequently, of some virtue!

Guilty without remorse, I soon became so without measure: and I beg the reader to observe how my passion followed the track of my disposition, to drag me finally into the abyss. At first, it assumed a humble attitude, to reassure me; and then, in order to encourage me, pushed this humility to mistrust. Madame d'Houdetot, without relaxing her efforts to recall me to my duty and reason, without ever flattering my folly for a moment, treated me in other respects with the greatest gentleness, and assumed towards me a tone of the tenderest friendship. This friendship would have been enough for me, I declare, if I had believed it to be sincere; but, as I found it too pronounced to be true, I proceeded to get the idea into my head that love, which was from this time forth so ill-suited to my age and general appearance, had degraded me in the eyes of Madame d'Houdetot; that, in the extravagance of her youth, she only desired to amuse herself with me and my superannuated passions; that she had taken Saint-Lambert into her confidence, and that, indignation at my disloyalty having brought him over to her views, there was an understanding between them to turn my head completely, and then to laugh at me. This folly, which had caused me, at twenty-six years of age, to make a fool of myself with Madame de Larnage, whom I did not know, would have been excusable in me, at the age of forty-five, in the case of Madame d'Houdetot, if I had not known that she and her lover were both too honourable to indulge in so cruel an amusement.

Madame d'Houdetot continued to pay me visits, which I was not slow to return. Like myself, she was fond of walking: we took long walks in an enchanted country. Content to love her, and to venture to declare it, my situation would have been most delightful, had not my extravagant folly completely destroyed its charm. At first, she utterly failed to understand the silly petulance with which I received her tenderness; but my heart, which has ever been incapable of concealing any of its emotions, did not long leave her in ignorance of my suspicions. She tried to treat them as a joke; but this expedient was unsuccessful. Violent attacks of rage would have been the result: she accordingly altered her tone. Her compassionate gentleness remained unshaken. She reproached me in a manner which cut me to the heart; she exhibited, in regard to my unjust apprehensions, an uneasiness which I abused. I demanded proof that she was not laughing at me. She saw that there was no other way of reassuring me. I became pressing; the matter was a delicate one. It is surprising—it is, perhaps, unique—that a woman, who had ventured to go so far as to hesitate should have got out of the affair so well. She refused me nothing that the most tender friendship could grant. She granted nothing that could expose her to the charge of infidelity, and I had the humiliation of seeing that the flames, which the slightest favours on her part kindled in my heart, never threw the slightest spark into her own. . . .

But I am wrong in speaking of an unrequited love; to some extent mine was returned; it was equal on both sides, although it was not mutual. We were both intoxicated with love; she for her lover, I for her. Our sighs, our delightful tears mingled together. Tender confidants, our feelings were so closely connected, that it was impossible that they should not unite in something; and yet, amidst this dangerous intoxication, she never forgot herself for a moment; as for myself, I protest, I swear that if, sometimes carried away by my senses, I attempted to make her unfaithful, I never truly desired it. The vehemence of my passion by itself kept it within bounds. The duty of self-denial had exalted my soul. The splendour of all the virtues adorned in my eyes the idol of my heart; to have soiled its divine image would have been its annihilation. I might have committed the crime; it has been committed a hundred times in my heart; but—to degrade my Sophie! could that ever have been possible? No, no! I told her so myself a hundred times. Had it been in my power to satisfy myself, had she abandoned herself to me of her own accord, I should, except in a few brief moments of delirium, have refused to be happy at such a cost. I loved her too dearly to desire to possess her.

It is nearly a league from the Hermitage to Eaubonne; on my frequent visits, I sometimes passed the night there. One bright moonlight evening, after having supped together, we went for a walk in the garden. At the bottom of this garden there was a rather large copse, through which we made our way to a pretty grove, adorned with a cascade, the idea of which she had carried out at my suggestion. Immortal souvenir of innocence and bliss! It was in this grove that, seated by her side on a grassy bank, under an acacia in full bloom, I found, to express the feelings of my heart, language that was really worthy of them. For the first and only time in my life I was sublime, if one may so call all the amiability and seductive charm that the tenderest and most ardent love can inspire in a man's heart. What intoxicating tears I shed upon her knees! What tears I caused her to shed in spite of herself! At last, in an involuntary transport, she exclaimed, "Never, no, never was a man so amiable; never did a lover love like you! But your friend Saint-Lambert is listening to us. My heart cannot love twice." I sighed; and was silent; I embraced her—what an embrace! But that was all. For six months she had lived alone, that is to say, far from her lover and her husband; during three of these months I saw her nearly every day, and Love was always with us. We had supped alone; we were alone, in a grove, beneath the light of the moon; and, after two hours of the liveliest and tenderest conversation, she left, in the middle of the night, this grove and the arms of her friend, as free from guilt, as pure in heart and person as she had entered it. Reader, weigh all these circumstances: I will add no more.

At the same time, let no one imagine that, on this occasion, my feelings left me as undisturbed as in the presence of Thérèse or mamma. I have already said that this time it was love—love in all its force and in all its frenzy. I will not describe the agitation, the shivering, the palpitation, the convulsive movements, or the faintness of the heart, which I felt continually. The reader can judge of it from the impression which her image alone produced upon me. I have said that it was a considerable distance from the Hermitage to Eaubonne. I went past the hills of Andilly, which are delightful. As I walked, I dreamed of her whom I was going to see, of the tender reception, of the kiss which awaited me on my arrival. This kiss alone, this fatal kiss, even before I received it, inflamed my blood to such a degree that I felt dizzy, my eyes swam, I was blinded; my trembling knees could no longer support me; I was obliged to stop and sit down; my whole bodily machinery was utterly out of gear; I felt ready to faint. Aware of the danger, I tried, when I set out again, to distract my attention and to think of something else. I had scarcely gone twenty yards, when the same recollections and their incidental results returned to the attack, and I found it impossible to shake them off. In spite of all my efforts, I do not believe that I have ever succeeded in accomplishing this journey alone, without paying the penalty. I arrived at Eaubonne, weak, exhausted, and worn out, scarcely able to stand upright. The moment I saw her, I was completely reinvigorated. By her side, I felt nothing but the importunity of an inexhaustible and ever useless vigour. On the road, within sight of Eaubonne, there was a pleasant terrace called Mont Olympe, where we sometimes met. If I arrived first, I had to wait for her. How painful was this waiting! In order to divert my attention, I attempted to write notes with my pencil, which I might have written with my purest blood. I was never able to finish a single one that was legible. When she found one in the niche which we had agreed upon, all she could read in it was the truly deplorable state I was in when I wrote it. This state, and, above all, its continuance during three months of excitement and self-restraint, so exhausted me that I did not recover for several years, and, finally, brought on a rupture, which I shall carry with me, or which will carry me with it, into the grave. Such was the only amorous enjoyment of the man of the most inflammable temperament, but, at the same time, of the most retiring disposition that Nature has perhaps ever produced. Such were the last happy days that have been permitted to me upon earth. I now commence the long series of the misfortunes of my life, which was seldom, if ever, interrupted.

Throughout the course of my life, as has been seen, my heart, transparent as crystal, has never been able to conceal, even for a moment, any feelings at all lively which may have taken refuge in it. The reader can judge whether I found it possible to conceal for long my affection for Madame d'Houdetot. Our intimacy was patent to everybody; we made no secret or mystery of it: it was not of a kind to require it; and, as Madame d'Houdetot had the tenderest friendship for me, of which she made no reproach, while I felt for her an esteem, the full justice of which no one knew better than myself, we afforded—she, by her frankness, absence of mind, and thoughtlessness; I, by my truthfulness, awkwardness, pride, impatience, and impetuosity—in our delusive security, more opportunity for attack than we should have done if we had been guilty. We went together to La Chevrette, we frequently met there, sometimes even by appointment. We lived there as usual, walking alone every day while talking of our love, our duties, our friend, our innocent schemes, in the park, opposite Madame d'Epinay's apartments, beneath her windows, from which she continually watched us, and, thinking herself defied, glutted her heart, by means of her eyes, with rage and indignation.

All women possess the art of concealing their anger, especially when it is strong. Madame d'Epinay, who was violent but deliberate, possesses this art in an eminent degree. She pretended to see nothing, to suspect nothing; and, while she redoubled her care and attention to me, and almost flirted with me, she at the same time pretended to overwhelm her sister-in-law with rudeness and marks of contempt, with which she appeared to wish to inspire me as well. It may be imagined that she did not succeed; but I was on the rack. Torn by contradictory feelings, while at the same time I felt touched by her tenderness, I had difficulty in restraining my anger, when I saw her wanting in respect to Madame d'Houdetot. The angelic gentleness of the latter enabled her to endure everything without complaining, even without resenting it. Besides, she was frequently so absent-minded, and always so little sensitive to such things, that half the time she did not even notice it.

I was so taken up with my passion, that, seeing nothing but Sophie—this was one of Madame d'Houdetot's names—I did not even notice that I had become the talk of the whole household and of the visitors. Baron d'Holbach, who, as far as I know, had never before been to La Chevrette, was one of the latter. If I had been as mistrustful as I afterwards became, I should have strongly suspected Madame d'Epinay of arranging this visit, in order to afford him the gratification of the amusing spectacle of the amorous citizen. But at that time I was so stupid, that I did not even see what was glaringly obvious to everyone. However, all my stupidity did not prevent me from finding the Baron more contented and jovial than usual. Instead of scowling at me, he discharged at me a volley of witticisms, of which I understood nothing. I opened my eyes wide without answering; Madame d'Epinay was obliged to hold her sides to restrain her laughter; I could not make out what was the matter with them. As the limits of jest were not yet exceeded, the best thing I could have done, if I had understood, would have been to join in it. But it is true that, amidst all the Baron's mocking joviality, it was easy to perceive the light of a spiteful joy in his eyes, which would perhaps have made me uneasy, if I had noticed it as much at the time, as I afterwards did when I recalled it to mind.

One day, when I went to see Madame d'Houdetot at Eaubonne, on her return from one of her journeys to Paris, I found her sad, and saw that she had been crying. I was obliged to restrain myself, since Madame de Blainville, her husband's sister, was present; but, as soon as I had a moment to myself, I told her of my uneasiness. "Ah!" she said, with a sigh, "I am much afraid that your follies will deprive me of all peace for the rest of my life. Saint-Lambert has been informed, and wrongly informed. He does me justice, but he is annoyed, and, what is worse, he does not tell me all. Happily, I have made no secret of our friendship, which was formed under his auspices. My letters, like my heart, were full of you; I have concealed nothing from him except your insensate love, of which I hoped to cure you, and which, although he does not mention it, I can see that he considers a crime on my part. Someone has done us an ill turn, and wronged me; but never mind. Let us either break off our acquaintance, or do you behave yourself as you ought. I do not wish to have anything more to conceal from my lover."

Thérèse had the discretion to say nothing to me for a long time about all these attempts; but at last, seeing my embarrassment, she felt bound to tell me all, so that, knowing with whom I had to deal I might take steps to protect myself against the treachery which was intended against me. My indignation and fury were indescribable. Instead of dissembling with Madame d'Epinay, as she had done with me, and employing counterplots, I abandoned myself without restraint to my natural impetuosity, and, with my usual thoughtlessness, broke out openly. My imprudence may be gauged by the following letters, which sufficiently show how each of us proceeded on this occasion:

LETTER FROM MADAME D'EPINAY (PACKET A, No. 44).

"What is the reason that I do not see you, my dear friend? I am uneasy about you. You promised me faithfully that you would confine yourself to going backwards and forwards from the Hermitage. Upon that, I left you to do as you pleased; but no, you have let a week go by. Unless I had been told that you were well, I should think that you were ill. I expected you yesterday or the day before, but I see no signs of you. My goodness! what can be the matter with you? You have no business, you can have nothing to annoy you either: for I flatter myself that you would have come at once to confide in me. You must be ill, then. Relieve my anxiety immediately, I beg you. Adieu, my dear friend. May this 'Adieu' bring a 'Good morning' from you."

ANSWER.

"*Wednesday Morning.*

"I cannot yet say anything to you. I am waiting until I am better informed, as I shall be, sooner or later. Meanwhile, rest assured that accused innocence will find a defender sufficiently zealous to give the slanderers, whoever they may be, some cause for repentance."

Second Letter from Madame d'Epinay
(Packet A, No. 45).

"Do you know that your letter alarms me? What does it mean? I have read it more than five-and-twenty times. In truth, I do not understand it. I can only learn from it that you are uneasy and tormented, and that you are waiting until you are so no longer, before speaking to me about it. My dear friend, is this what we agreed? What has become of our friendship, our confidence? and how have I lost it? Are you angry with me or because of me? In any case, come this evening, I entreat you. Remember that you promised, not a week ago, to keep nothing on your mind, but to let me know of it at once. My dear friend, I rely upon that confidence. . . . Stay! I have just read your letter again. I do not understand it any better, but it makes me tremble. You seem to me painfully agitated. I wish I could calm you; but as I do not know the reason of your uneasiness, I do not know what to say to you, except that I shall be as unhappy as yourself until I have seen you. If you are not here by six o'clock this evening, I shall start to-morrow for the Hermitage, whatever kind of weather it is, and whatever my state of health, for I can no longer endure this uneasiness. Good day, my dear, good friend. At all risks, I venture to tell you, without knowing whether I need do so or not, to try and take care of yourself and arrest the progress which solitude allows uneasiness to make. A fly becomes a monster. I have often experienced it."

Answer.

"*Wednesday Evening.*

"I can neither come to see you nor receive your visit, as

long as my present uneasiness continues. The confidence of which you speak no longer exists, and it will not be easy for you to regain it. At present, I see in your eagerness nothing but the desire of extracting from the confession of another some advantage which may promote your views. My heart, so ready to unbosom itself to another which opens to receive it, shuts its doors in the face of slyness and cunning. I recognise your usual adroitness in the difficulty which you find in understanding my letter. Do you believe me simple enough to think that you have not understood it? No; but I shall know how to overcome your cunning by frankness. I am going to explain myself more clearly, in order that you may comprehend me still less.

"Two lovers, firmly united and worthy of each other's love, are dear to me; I expect that you will not understand whom I mean unless I tell you their names. I assume that attempts have been made to part them, and that I have been made use of to inspire one of them with jealousy. The choice is not very clever, but it appeared convenient for malicious purposes; and it is you whom I suspect of these designs. I hope that this makes matters clearer.

"So then the woman, whom I esteem above all others, would knowingly have the infamy of dividing her heart and her person between two lovers, and I the disgrace of being one of these two wretches? If I knew that, for a single moment in your life, you could have entertained such thoughts of her and me, I should hate you to my dying day; but I only accuse you of having said, not of having thought it. I do not understand, in such a case, which of the three you have desired to injure; but, if you love tranquillity, you should dread being so unfortunate as to succeed. I have neither concealed from you, nor from her, how much evil I see in certain connections; but I desire that they should be put an end to by means as honourable as the feelings which originally formed them, and that an illicit love should be changed into an eternal friendship. Should I, who never injured anyone, be made the innocent means of doing harm to my friends? No; I would never forgive you; I should become your irreconcilable enemy. Your secrets alone should be respected; for I will never be disloyal.

"I do not imagine that my present embarrassment can last long. I shall soon know whether I am mistaken. Then I shall perhaps have a great injury to repair, and I shall never have done anything in my life with greater goodwill. But, do you know how I shall repair my errors during the short time which I have still to spend near you? By doing what no one but myself will do; by telling you frankly what the world thinks of you, and the breaches in your reputation which you have to repair. In spite of all the pretended friends by whom you are surrounded, when you see me depart, you may say farewell to truth; you will never find anyone else to tell it to you."

THIRD LETTER FROM MADAME D'EPINAY (PACKET A, No. 46).

"I did not understand your letter of this morning; I told you so, because it was the truth. I understand that of this evening. Do not be afraid that I shall ever answer it; I am only too anxious to forget it; and although you excite my pity, I have been unable to resist the bitterness with which it fills my soul. I employ slyness and cunning against you! I accused of the blackest of infamies! Good-bye; I regret that you have—good-bye; I do not know what I am saying—good-bye. I should be only too glad to forgive you. Come when you like; you will meet with a better reception than your suspicions would entitle you to. You can spare yourself the trouble of thinking about my reputation. It matters little to me what it is. My conduct is good; that is enough for me. I may add, that I am absolutely ignorant of what has happened to the two persons who are as dear to me as to you."

[In order to remain at the Hermitage, Rousseau decides to visit Madame d'Epinay, and try to extricate himself without compromising Madame d'Houdetot or Thérèse. But Madame d'Epinay asks nothing; they embrace and weep. He foolishly thinks all is forgotten.]

As will presently be seen, this was not the only trouble

which my own weakness brought upon me; but I also suffered others, equally annoying, which I had certainly not brought upon myself, and which were caused solely by the desire of others to tear me away from my solitude, by dint of tormenting me in it.* These troubles came upon me from Diderot and the Holbachian clique. Since my establishment at the Hermitage, Diderot had never ceased to harass me, either himself or through Deleyre; and I soon saw, from the jests of the latter upon my walks in the forest, with what delight they had travestied the hermit as an amorous shepherd. But it was not a question of this in my encounter with Diderot, the cause of which was more serious. After the publication of the "Fils Naturel," he had sent me a copy of it, which I had read with the interest and attention which one naturally bestows on the works of a friend. On reading the kind of poetical prose dialogue which he had added to it, I was surprised, and even somewhat saddened, to find in it, amongst several discourteous but endurable remarks directed against those who live a solitary life, the following harsh and bitter sentence, without anything to tone it down: "Only the wicked are alone." This sentence is, it appears to me, ambiguous, and capable of two interpretations, one quite true, the other equally false; since it is impossible for a man who is and who desires to be alone, to be able or desirous to injure anyone, and therefore he cannot be wicked. The sentence in itself therefore required an explanation; it required it still more on the part of an author who, when he wrote the sentence, had a friend who was living in retirement and solitude. It appeared to me shocking and dishonourable that, when publishing it, he should either have forgotten this solitary friend, or that, if he had remembered him, he should not have made, at least in the general statement, the honourable and just exception which he owed not only to this friend, but to the

* That is to say, the desire of tearing away the old woman from it, whose services were necessary in arranging the conspiracy. It is astonishing that, during the whole of this long storm, my stupid confidence in others prevented me from understanding that it was not I, but she, whom they wanted to see in Paris again [Rousseau].

many respected philosophers, who, in all ages, have sought peace and tranquillity in retirement, and of whom, for the first time since the existence of the world, an author permits himself, by a single stroke of the pen, to make so many villains without distinction.

I was tenderly attached to Diderot, I esteemed him sincerely, and I reckoned upon the same feelings on his part with perfect confidence. But, worn out by his unwearying obstinacy in eternally opposing me in my tastes, inclinations, manner of living, in fact, in everything which concerned myself alone; disgusted at seeing a man younger than myself attempting to control me absolutely like a child; sick of his readiness in making promises, and his carelessness in fulfilling them; weary of so many appointments made and broken on his part, and of his fancy for continually making fresh ones, only to be broken again; tired of waiting for him in vain three or four times a month, on days fixed by himself, and of dining alone in the evening, after having gone as far as Saint-Denis to meet him, after waiting for him the whole day, my heart was already full of his continued want of consideration. The last instance appeared to me more serious, and wounded me still more deeply. I wrote to him to complain of it, but with a gentleness and emotion which caused me to drench the paper with my tears; and my letter was touching enough to have drawn tears from him. No one would guess how he replied upon the matter; here is his answer word for word (Packet A, No. 33):

"I am very glad that my work has pleased you, that it has affected you. You are not of my opinion concerning hermits; say as much good of them as you please, you will be the only one in the world of whom I shall think it; and yet I should be able to say a good deal on the matter, if I could say it to you without offending you. A woman of eighty years of age! etc. . . ."

At the beginning of my stay at the Hermitage, Madame le Vasseur did not seem comfortable, and appeared to find it too lonely. Her remarks on the subject were repeated to me, and I offered to send her back to Paris if she preferred it, to pay for her lodging there, and to look after her just as if she were still with me. She refused my offer, declared that she was very well satisfied with the Hermitage, and that the country air did her good, which it was easy to see was true, for she seemed to grow younger, and was in far better health than at Paris. Her daughter even assured me that she would have been, on the whole, very sorry if we had left the Hermitage, which really was a charming residence; that she was very fond of pottering about in the garden and in the orchard, of which she had the management, and that she had only said what she had been told to say, to try and induce me to return to Paris.

This attempt having proved unsuccessful, they endeavoured to obtain, by appealing to my scruples, the result which my readiness to oblige had not produced; they declared that it was a crime on my part to keep the old woman there, far from the assistance which she might need at her age, without considering that she and many other old people, whose life is prolonged by the healthy air of the country, might procure this assistance from Montmorency, which was close to my doors—as if Paris had been the only place in which there were old people, and it was impossible for them to live anywhere else. Madame le Vasseur, who was a large and very ravenous eater, was subject to overflows of bile and violent attacks of diarrhœa, which lasted several days, and acted as a remedy. At Paris she took nothing for them, and let Nature take its course. She did the same at the Hermitage, since she knew well that she could do nothing better. Never mind; because there were no physicians and apothecaries in the country, to leave her there showed a wish for her death, although she was in very good health there. Diderot ought to have fixed the age at which it is no longer permitted, under penalty of being charged with manslaughter, to allow old people to live out of Paris.

This was one of the two monstrous accusations, in regard to which he made no exception in my case, in his statement

that "Only the wicked are alone"; and this was the meaning
of his pathetic exclamation and the etcetera which he so
kindly added, "A woman of eighty years of age! etc."

[Rousseau explains this last allusion. There is more squab-
bling with Diderot. Of course, everyone sides with the
latter, and Rousseau, knowing his friend to be plagued with
troubles, journeys to Paris to visit him.]

Diderot received me cordially. How many wrongs can a
friend's embrace wipe out! What resentment, after that, can
still remain in the heart? We entered into few explanations.
There is no need of it in a case of mutual abuse. There is
only one thing to be done—to forget it. There had been no
underhand proceedings, at least as far as I knew; it was not
the same as with Madame d'Epinay. He showed me the outline of the "Père de Famille." "That," said I to him, "is the
best defence of the 'Fils Naturel.' Remain silent, work this
piece out carefully, and then suddenly fling it at your enemies' head as your only reply." He did so, and found the plan
successful. I had sent him the first two parts of "Julie" nearly
six months before, asking for his opinion of them. He had
not yet read them. We read a portion of them together. He
found it all *feuillet;* that was the word he used, meaning
that it was overloaded with words and full of padding. I had
already felt this myself; but it was the babbling of delirium;
I have never been able to correct it. The last parts are different. The fourth especially, and the sixth, are masterpieces of
diction.

On the second day after my arrival, he insisted upon taking
me to supper at M. d'Holbach's. We were far from agreeing.
I even wanted to break the agreement concerning the manuscript on Chemistry, as I was indignant at being under an
obligation for it to such a man. Diderot was completely victorious. He swore that M. d'Holbach had a most sincere affection for me; that I must excuse his manner, which was the
same to everybody, and from which his friends had to suffer
more than anyone. He represented to me that to refuse the
production of this manuscript, after having accepted it two
years before, would be an insult to the donor, which he had

not deserved; that this refusal might even be misinterpreted, as a secret reproach to him for having been so long in fulfilling the agreement. "I see D'Holbach every day," he added; "I know his inner self better than you do. If you had not reason to be satisfied with it, do you think your friend capable of advising you to act meanly?" In short, with my usual weakness, I allowed myself to be overcome, and we went to supper with the Baron, who received me in his usual manner; but his wife received me coldly, and almost rudely. I no longer recognised the amiable Caroline who, before she was married, showed me so many marks of goodwill. Long before, I had fancied that I perceived that, since Grimm had been a constant visitor at the house of Aine, I was no longer regarded with so favourable an eye.

While I was in Paris, Saint-Lambert arrived on leave. As I knew nothing of it, I did not see him until after my return to the country, at first at La Chevrette, and afterwards at the Hermitage, where he came with Madame d'Houdetot to ask me to invite him to dinner. It may be imagined how pleased I was to receive them; but I was still more pleased to see the good understanding between them. Rejoiced that I had not disturbed their happiness, I felt happy in it myself; and I can swear that, during the whole course of my mad passion, but especially at this moment, even if I had been able to take Madame d'Houdetot from him, I should not have wished, and I should not even have felt tempted to do so. I found her so amiable, so devoted to Saint-Lambert, that I could hardly imagine that she might have been equally devoted in her love for myself; and, without desiring to disturb their union, all that I had most truly desired from her in my delirium, was that she should allow herself to be loved. In short, however violent the passion with which I had been inflamed for her, I felt it as delightful to be the confidant as the object of her affections, and I have never for a moment regarded her lover as my rival, but always as my friend. It will be said that this was not yet actual love. So be it; but then, it was more.

As for Saint-Lambert, he behaved honourably and judiciously. As I was the only guilty party, I alone was punished, and that even mercifully. He treated me severely, but amicably; and I saw that I had lost something of his esteem, but nothing of his friendship. I consoled myself, since I knew that it would be easier for me to regain the former than the latter, and that he was too sensible to confound an involuntary and momentary weakness with a radical vice. If, in all that had taken place, there had been errors on my part, they were trifling ones. Was it I who sought his mistress? Was it not he who had sent her to me? Was it not she who had sought me? Could I have avoided seeing her? What could I do? They alone had done the mischief, and I had been the one to suffer from it. In my place, he would have done just as I did, perhaps worse; for, in short, however faithful, however estimable Madame d'Houdetot may have been, she was a woman. He was very often absent; the opportunities were frequent, the temptations were great, and it would have been very difficult for her always to defend herself with equal success against a more enterprising lover. It was certainly a great thing for her and for me, in such a situation, that we had been able to fix the limits, which we never permitted ourselves to overstep.

Although, in the bottom of my heart, I could produce sufficiently honourable testimony in my favour, appearances were so much against me, that the unconquerable feeling of shame, by which I was always dominated, gave me, in his presence, the appearance of a guilty person, and he often abused it in order to humiliate me. A single incident will make our mutual relations clear. After dinner I read to him the letter which I had written to Voltaire the year before, and which he had heard spoken of. He went to sleep while I was reading it; and I, formerly so proud, now so foolish, did not venture to discontinue reading, and read on while he snored. Thus did I humble myself; thus did he avenge himself; but his generosity never permitted him to do so except when we three were alone.

After he went away again, I found Madame d'Houdetot greatly altered in her behaviour towards me. I was as surprised as if I ought not to have expected it. I was more affected by it than I ought to have been, and this caused me much suffering. It seemed that everything by which I expected to be cured only plunged deeper into my heart the arrow which I had at length rather broken off than pulled out.

I was resolved to conquer myself completely, and to leave nothing undone to change my foolish passion into a pure and lasting friendship. With this object, I had formed the most admirable plans in the world, which I needed Madame d'Houdetot's assistance in carrying out. When I attempted to speak to her, I found her absent and embarrassed. I felt that she had ceased to feel any pleasure in my society, and I saw clearly that something had taken place which she did not want to tell me, and which I have never learnt. This change, of which I was unable to obtain an explanation, tortured me cruelly. She asked me to return her letters: I returned them all, with a fidelity which, to my great mortification, she for a moment doubted. This doubt was another unexpected pang for me, as she must have well known. She did me justice, but not immediately. I understood that the examination of the packet which I had returned to her had made her conscious of her injustice. I even saw that she reproached herself, and this gave me a certain advantage again. She could not take back her own letters without returning mine. She told me that she had burnt them; in my turn, I ventured to doubt it, and I confess that I doubt it still. No; one does not throw such letters into the fire. The letters in "Julie" have been called passionate. Good heavens! what would have been thought of mine? No, no; a woman capable of inspiring such a passion will never have the courage to burn the proofs of it.

No sooner was Grimm at La Chevrette, where already I was not very comfortable, than he made my stay completely unendurable by putting on airs, which I had never seen exhibited by anyone before, and of which I had not even an idea. The day before his arrival, I was turned out of the best visitor's-room, which I was occupying, next to Madame d'Epinay's; it was got ready for Grimm, and another, in a more remote part of the house, was given to me. "See," said I to Madame d'Epinay with a laugh, "see how the newcomers turn out the old." She appeared embarrassed; and I understood the reason for this better in the evening, when I learned that, between her room and that which I was leaving, there was a secret door of communication, which she had not thought it worth while to show me. Her relations with Grimm were no secret to anybody, neither in her own house nor in public, nor even to her husband; however, far from admitting it to me, her confidant in secrets of far greater importance, and which she knew were perfectly safe with me, she stoutly denied it. I understood that this reserve was due to Grimm, who, although he was the depositary of all my secrets, was unwilling that I should have any of his own in my keeping.

However much my former feelings, which were not yet extinguished, and the man's real merits, prejudiced me in his favour, these feelings were not proof against the efforts he took to destroy them. He received me in the style of the Comte de Tuffière;* he hardly condescended to return my greeting; he never addressed a single word to me, and soon cured me of addressing any to him, by never answering me at all. He took precedence everywhere, and held first place, without ever paying any attention to me. I could have let that pass, if he had not displayed an offensive affectation. A single incident out of a thousand will explain what I mean. One evening, Madame d'Epinay, feeling slightly unwell, told the servants to bring her something to eat upstairs to her room, where she intended to have her supper by the side of the fire. She asked me to go upstairs with her, which I did. Grimm came up afterwards. The little table was already laid, but only for two. Supper was brought in; Madame d'Epinay took her seat on one side of the fire. M. Grimm took an easy chair, settled himself in the other corner, drew up the little table between them, unfolded his napkin, and proceeded to eat, without saying a single word to me. Madame d'Epinay blushed, and, to induce him to apologise for his rudeness, offered me her own place. He said nothing, and did not even

* Character in "Le Glorieux," a comedy by Destouches (1732).

look at me. As I was unable to get near the fire, I decided to
walk up and down the room, until they brought me a plate.
At last, he allowed me to sup at the end of the table, away
from the fire, without making the slightest apology to me, his
senior, in ill-health, an older acquaintance of the family, who
had introduced him to the house, the honours of which he
ought even to have shown to me, as the favourite of the lady
of the house. All his behaviour to me was very much after the
same pattern. He did not treat me exactly as his inferior; he
looked upon me as a perfect nonentity. I found it hard to
recognise the former *cuistre* who, in the Prince of Saxe-
Gotha's establishment, felt himself honoured by a look from
me. I found it still harder to reconcile this profound silence,
and this insulting haughtiness, with the tender friendship
which he boasted he entertained for me, in the presence of
these who he knew entertained it for me themselves. It is
true that he rarely gave any signs of it, except to sympathise
with my pecuniary position, of which I never complained, or
to compassionate my melancholy lot, with which I was quite
content, or to lament that I so harshly rejected the beneficent
attentions which he declared he was eager to show me. It was
by artifices like this that he caused his tender generosity to
be admired, my ungrateful misanthropy to be censured, and
imperceptibly accustomed everyone to imagine, that the relations between a protector like himself and an unfortunate
creature like me could only be, on the one side, benefits, and,
on the other, obligations, without supposing, even as a remote
possibility, a friendship between two equals. As for myself, I
have vainly tried to discover in what respect I could be under
an obligation to this new patron. I had lent him money, he
had never lent me any; I had nursed him during his illness, he
hardly ever came to see me during mine; I had introduced
him to all my friends, he had never introduced me to one of
his; I had sung his praises with all my might, he . . . if he
sang my praises, it was less publicly, and in quite a different
manner. He has never rendered or even offered to render me
any service of any kind. How then was he my Mycaenas?

how was I his *protégé*? This was beyond my powers of comprehension, and it still remains so.

It is true that, more or less, he was arrogant with everybody, but with no one so brutally as with myself. I remember that, on one occasion, Saint-Lambert was on the point of throwing his plate at his head, when he ventured to give him the lie publicly at table, by saying rudely, "That is not true." To his naturally sarcastic tone, he united the conceit of an upstart, and his continual impertinence even made him ridiculous. Intercourse with great people had led him to assume airs which one only sees in the least sensible amongst them. He never summoned his lackey except with an "Eh!"—as if my fine gentleman did not know which of his numerous attendants was on duty. When he gave him a commission to execute, he threw the money on the ground, instead of putting it into his hand. At last, forgetting altogether that he was a man, he treated him with such disgusting contempt and cruel disdain on every occasion that the poor lad, who was a very good fellow, whom Madame d'Epinay had given him, left his service, without any other cause of complaint than the impossibility of enduring such treatment. He was the La Fleur of this new "Glorieux." As foppish as he was vain, with his large, dull eyes and his flabby face, he pretended to have great success with the ladies; and, after his farce with Mademoiselle Fel, he was considered by numbers of the fair sex to be a man of deep feeling. This had made him the fashion and had given him a taste for feminine neatness. He began to play the dandy: his toilet became a serious matter. Everybody knew that he made up, and I, who at first refused to believe it, began to be convinced, not only by his beautiful complexion and by the fact of finding some pots of cosmetic on his dressing-table, but because one morning, on entering his rooms, I found him brushing his nails with a little brush made for the purpose, an occupation which he proudly continued in my presence. I argued that a man who could spend two hours every morning in brushing his nails might very well employ a few minutes in filling up the wrinkles in his skin with cosmetic. The worthy Gauffecourt, who was no fool, had humorously nicknamed him "Tiran le Blanc."

All this was merely ridiculous, but very antipathetic to my character, and at last made me suspicious of his. I could scarcely believe that a man, whose head was so turned, could have his heart in the right place. He prided himself, more than anything else, upon his sensibility of soul and vigorous energy of feeling. How did that agree with those defects, which are peculiar to little minds only? How could the lively and continuous flights, which a feeling heart takes in pursuit of things outside it, allow him time to busy himself with such petty cares for his little person? Why, good heavens! one who feels his heart inflamed by this heavenly fire seeks to pour it forth, and to display his inner self. He would be eager to show his heart upon his face; he will never think of any other cosmetics.

I remembered the compendium of his morality, which Madame d'Epinay had told me of, and which she had adopted. This consisted of one single article, namely, that the sole duty of man is, to follow in everything the inclinations of his heart. This code of morality when I heard of it, afforded me terrible material for thought, although at that time I only looked upon it as a witticism. But I soon saw that this principle was really his rule of conduct, and, in the sequel, I had only too convincing proof of it at my own expense. It is the inner doctrine, of which Diderot has so often spoken to me, but of which he has never given me any explanation. . . .

More than this: my own friends, whom I made his own, and who had all been devotedly attached to me before they made his acquaintance, showed a sensible alteration in their feelings and behaviour towards me, after they had made it. He never introduced one of his friends to me. I introduced him to all mine, and he ended by depriving me of them all. If such are the results of friendship, what will be the results of hatred?

Diderot himself, at the outset, warned me several times that Grimm, upon whom I bestowed such confidence, was not my friend. Subsequently, he altered his tone, when he himself had ceased to be a friend.

It was not until later that I learned from him all that had taken place between them in the matter; but I learned enough at the time from Thérèse to see that, in the whole affair, there was some secret design, and that they were anxious to dispose of me, if not against my will, at least without my knowledge; or that they certainly wished to make use of these two persons as their tools in some secret design. In all this there was certainly something very dishonourable. The opposition of Duclos proves it beyond contradiction. Let him who pleases believe that it was friendship.

One would have said that his object was to make me dependent upon him and his interest for my subsistence, and to exhaust my resources until I should be reduced to such a condition.

In short, as I had several times already done in the case of Diderot and the Baron d'Holbach, partly of my own accord and partly through weakness, I made all those advances which I had a right to demand: I went to see Grimm, like a second Georges Dandin,* to apologise for offences of which he had been guilty against myself; always under the mistaken conviction, which all my life long has caused me to abase myself before my pretended friends, that there is no hatred so strong that it cannot be disarmed by gentleness and good behaviour; whereas, on the contrary, the hatred of the wicked is only strengthened by the impossibility of finding anything to justify it, and the consciousness of their own injustice is only an additional grievance against him who is the victim of it. Without going further than my own history, I have a strong proof of this axiom in the conduct of Grimm and Tronchin, who became my two most implacable enemies, of their own inclination, for their own pleasure, out of sheer caprice, without being able to quote a single instance of any kind in which I had done either of them wrong, and whose

* In Molière's play, the deceived husband who is made to apologise to his wife.

rage increases daily, like that of the tiger, from the ease with which they are able to glut it.

I expected that Grimm, confused by my condescension and advances, would receive me with open arms and the tenderest affection. As a fact, he received me like a Roman Emperor, with an unparalleled haughtiness. I was utterly unprepared for this reception. Embarrassed at having to play a part so ill-suited to me, in a few words I timidly explained the object of my visit. Before taking me back into favour, he delivered, with great dignity, a long harangue which he had prepared, containing a list of his numerous and rare virtues, especially in matters of friendship. He dwelt for some time upon a circumstance, which at first struck me considerably—that he always kept the same friends. While he was speaking, I said to myself that it would be cruel on my part to make myself the only exception to this rule. He returned to this so frequently and with such affectation, that he at last made me think that, if in this he only listened to the feelings of his heart, he would show himself less struck by this sentiment which he so freely expressed, and that he was making use of it as a trick which might serve his purpose of self-advancement. Hitherto I had been in the same case: I had always kept all my friends; since my earliest childhood I had not lost a single one, except by death, and yet I had never made it a subject of reflection; it was not a principle which I had laid down for myself. Since we both had this advantage in common, what right had he to boast of it as peculiar to himself, unless he already designed to deprive me of it? He devoted himself to the task of humiliating me by proving that our mutual friends preferred him to me. I was as well aware as he was of this preference; the question was, how he had obtained it. By superior merits or address, by exalting himself, or by endeavouring to humiliate me? At last, when he had put between us, to his heart's content, all the distance which could attach value to the favour which he intended to grant me, he bestowed upon me the kiss of peace in a slight embrace, which resembled the *accolade* which the King bestows upon newly-created knights. I fell from the clouds; I was amazed; I did not know what to say; I could not utter a single word. The whole scene had the appearance of a reprimand given by a master to a pupil, when he lets him off a flogging. I never think of it without feeling how deceptive are judgments founded upon appearances, to which the vulgar attach such weight, and how frequently audacity and pride are on the side of the guilty, shame and embarrassment on the side of the innocent.

We were reconciled; this was at least a relief to my heart, which is always mortally distressed by a quarrel. It may be imagined that such a reconciliation produced no alteration in his manners; it simply deprived me of the right of complaining of them. Accordingly, I resolved to endure everything, and to say nothing.

So many annoyances, one after another, threw me into a state of depression, which scarcely left me strength to regain command of myself. Without any reply from Saint-Lambert, neglected by Madame d'Houdetot, no longer venturing to open my heart to anyone, I began to fear that, in making friendship the idol of my heart, I had wasted my life in sacrificing to chimeras. In proof of this, out of all my friendships, there only remained two men, who had retained my full esteem, and whom my heart could trust: Duclos, whom I had lost sight of since my retirement to the Hermitage, and Saint-Lambert. I believed that I could only repair my injustice towards the latter by opening my heart to him unreservedly; and I resolved to make a full and complete confession to him, in everything which did not compromise his mistress. I have no doubt that this resolution was another snare set by my passion, in order to keep me closer to it; but it is certain that I should have thrown myself unreservedly into her lover's arms, that I should have submitted myself completely to his guidance, and that I should have pushed my frankness as far as it could go.

[Rousseau does not write this letter, when he hears that Saint-Lambert has not replied because he has suffered a stroke.]

But it is time to proceed to the great and sudden change

in my destiny, the catastrophe which has divided my life into two parts, so different from each other, and which, from a very trifling cause, has drawn such terrible effects.

One day, when I least expected it, Madame d'Epinay sent for me. When I entered the room, I observed, in her eyes and manner, an appearance of embarrassment, which was the more striking to me as it was unusual, since no one in the world knew better than she how to control her features and movements. "My friend," said she, "I am leaving for Geneva; my chest is in a bad state, my health is breaking up so rapidly that I must go and consult Tronchin, even if I have to neglect everything else." This resolution, so abruptly taken, at the commencement of bad weather, astonished me the more, as, when I left her thirty-six hours before, not a word had been said about it. I asked her whom she intended to take with her. She told me that she meant to take her son and M. de Linant, and then added, in an indifferent tone, "And won't you come too, my dear bear?" As I did not believe that she spoke seriously, since she knew that, in the time of year upon which we were just entering, I was hardly in a fit state to leave my room, I spoke jestingly of the advantage of one sick person being accompanied by another. She herself did not seem to have meant the proposition seriously, and nothing more was said about it. During the rest of my visit, we spoke of nothing but the preparations for her journey, into which she threw herself with great energy, as she had made up her mind to start in a fortnight.

I did not need much penetration to understand that there was some secret reason for this journey which was concealed from me. This secret, which was a secret to me alone in the house, was discovered the very next day by Thérèse, to whom Teissier, the *maître d'hôtel*, who had heard it from the lady's-maid, revealed it. Although I am under no obligation to Madame d'Epinay to keep the secret, since I did not learn it from her, it is too closely connected with those which she did confide to me, for me to be able to make any distinction. On this point, therefore, I will say nothing. But these same secrets, which never have been, and never will be revealed by

me, either by word of mouth or the pen, have become known
to too many, for it to be possible that they can have remained
unknown to any of Madame d'Epinay's associates.

When I was informed of the true motive of this journey, I
should have recognised the secret instigation of the hand of
an enemy, in the attempt to make me the chaperon of Madame d'Epinay; but, as she had not pressed me at all to
accompany her, I persisted in regarding the attempt as not
seriously intended, and I merely laughed at the fine figure that
I should have cut, if I had been foolish enough to undertake
the charge. Besides, she gained considerably by my refusal,
for she succeeded in persuading her husband himself to
accompany her.

A few days afterwards I received the following letter from
Diderot. This letter, merely folded in two, so that anyone
could easily read its contents, was addressed to me, "Care of
Madame d'Epinay," and intrusted to M. de Linant, the tutor
of the son and the confidant of the mother.

Letter from Diderot (Packet A, No. 52).

"I am born to love you and to cause you annoyance. I hear
that Madame d'Epinay is going to Geneva, and I do not hear
it said that you accompany her. My friend, if you are satisfied with Madame d'Epinay, you must go with her; if you
are dissatisfied, you must go all the more readily. Are you
over-burdened with the weight of the obligations under
which she has laid you? here is an opportunity of partly dis-
charging them and of lightening your burden. Will you find
another opportunity in your life of showing your gratitude to
her? She is going into a country where she will be as if she
had fallen from the clouds. She is ill; she will need amusement and distraction. Winter, too! Consider, my friend. The
objection on the score of your health may be far stronger
than I think it is; but, are you worse to-day than you were a
month ago, and than you will be at the beginning of spring?
Will you make the journey, three months hence, more comfortably than now? For myself, I declare to you that, if I
could not endure the carriage, I would take a stick and follow

her. Then, are you not afraid that your behaviour may be misinterpreted? You will be suspected either of ingratitude or of some other secret motive. I am well aware that, whatever you do, you will always have the testimony of your conscience on your side; but is this testimony sufficient by itself, and is it allowed to neglect, up to a certain point, that of other men? Besides, my friend, I write this letter in order to discharge an obligation to you as well as to myself. If it displeases you, throw it in the fire, and think no more of it than if it had never been written. I salute, love, and embrace you."

I trembled with rage, and felt so utterly astounded while reading this letter, that I could scarcely finish it; but this did not prevent me from observing how cleverly Diderot affected a gentler, more flattering, and more polite tone than in any of his other letters, in which he at most addressed me as "my dear," without condescending to call me "friend." I easily perceived the indirect means by which this letter had reached me: the address, style, and the way in which it arrived, betrayed the roundabout manner of proceeding clumsily enough; for we usually corresponded through the post or the Montmorency messenger, and this was the first and only time that he made use of the present method of communication.

When my first transports of indignation permitted me to write, I hastily threw off the following reply, which I immediately took from the Hermitage, where I was at the time, to La Chevrette, to show it to Madame d'Epinay, to whom, in my blind passion, I intended to read it, as well as Diderot's letter.

"My dear friend, you cannot know either the extent of my obligations to Madame d'Epinay, or how far they are binding, or whether she has really need of me on her journey, or wishes me to accompany her, or whether it is possible for me to do so, or the reasons I may have for refusing. I do not object to discuss all these points with you; but, in the meantime, you must admit that to dictate to me so positively what I ought to do, without being in a position to judge, is, my dear philosopher, to talk nonsense. The worst thing about it is, that I see that the opinion is not your own. Not to mention that I am little disposed to allow myself to be led by a third or fourth person under your name, I find in these indirect acts a certain amount of underhandedness, which ill suits your frankness, which, for both our sakes, you will do well to avoid for the future.

"You express yourself afraid that my conduct may be mis-interpreted; but I defy a heart like yours to venture to think ill of mine. Others would perhaps speak better of me, if I were more like them. Heaven preserve me from gaining their approval! Let the wicked spy upon me and interpret my conduct as they please. Rousseau is not a man to fear them, or Diderot a man to listen to them.

"You wish me to throw your letter in the fire if it displeases me and to think no more about it. Do you think that what comes from you can be so easily forgotten? My dear friend, you hold my tears in the pain which you cause me, as cheap as my life and health, in the care which you exhort me to take. If you could correct yourself of this, your friendship would be so much sweeter to me, and I should be so much the less to be pitied."

On entering Madame d'Epinay's room, I found Grimm with her, which delighted me. I read to them, in a loud and clear voice, my two letters, with an intrepidity of which I should not have believed myself capable, and, when I had finished, I added a few remarks which did not belie it. I saw that this unexpected audacity on the part of a man usually so timid, astonished and astounded them both. They did not answer a word. Above all, I saw that arrogant man cast down his eyes, not venturing to meet the angry flashes from my own; but, at the same instant, in the bottom of his heart, he was vowing my destruction, and I am positive that they agreed upon it before they parted.

It was about this time that I at last received, through Madame d'Houdetot, Saint-Lambert's letter (Packet A, No. 57), dated from Wolfenbuttel, a few days after his accident, written in answer to mine, which had been greatly delayed on the road. This reply afforded me some consolation, which I greatly needed at that moment, in the proofs of esteem and friendship of which it was full, and which gave me the courage and strength to deserve them. From that moment I did my duty; but it is certain that, if Saint-Lambert had shown himself less sensible, less generous, less a man of honour, I should have been lost beyond recall.

[He says au revoir to Madame d'Epinay, and then to Madame d'Houdetot, as the two women leave for the winter.]

We formed the charming plan of an intimate companionship among us three, and we had reason to hope that the execution of this plan would be lasting in its results, seeing that all the feelings which can unite upright and feeling hearts were the foundation of it, and we combined, in our three selves, sufficient talents and knowledge to render any foreign elements unnecessary. Alas! while abandoning myself to the prospect of so charming a life, I little thought of that which awaited me.

We afterwards spoke of my relations with Madame d'Epinay. I showed her Diderot's letter, together with my answer; I told her all the circumstances connected with it, and informed her of my resolution to leave the Hermitage. She vigorously opposed it, and with arguments which were all-powerful with my heart. She declared that she would have much liked me to go with her to Geneva, as she foresaw that she would inevitably be compromised by my refusal; indeed, Diderot's letter seemed to announce it beforehand. However, as she knew my reasons as well as myself, she did not insist upon this point; but she begged me at any price to avoid scandal, and to palliate my refusal by reasons sufficiently plausible to remove the unjust suspicion that she had anything to do with it. I told her that it was no easy task that she was imposing upon me; but that, being resolved to atone for my offences, even at the cost of my reputation, I desired to give the preference to hers, as far as honour would allow me to go. It will soon be seen whether I knew how to keep my promise.

I can swear that, far from my unfortunate passion having lost any of its force, I never loved my Sophie so fondly, so tenderly, as on that day. But Saint-Lambert's letter, my sense of duty, and horror of treachery, made such an impression upon me that, during the whole of the interview, my senses left me completely at peace in her company, and I was not even tempted to kiss her hand. At parting, she kissed me before her servants. This kiss, so different from those which I had sometimes stolen from her beneath the trees, was a guarantee to me that I had regained command over myself. I am nearly certain that, if my heart had had time to strengthen itself without interruption, three months would have been more than enough to cure me completely.

Here end my personal relations with Madame d'Houdetot: relations, of which every man has been able to judge by appearances according to the nature of his own heart, but in which the passion with which this amiable woman inspired me, the liveliest passion that a man has perhaps ever felt, will always be honoured in Heaven's sight and our own, by the rare and painful sacrifices which we both made to duty, honour, love and friendship. We had too high an opinion of each other to be able to degrade ourselves easily. We must have been utterly unworthy of esteem to make up our minds to lose a mutual regard of such great value; and the energy of our feelings, which might have made us guilty, was the very thing which prevented us from becoming so.

Thus, after a long friendship for the one of these two women, and a deep affection for the other, I took farewell of both on the same day: of one, never to see her again in my life; of the other, only to see her twice more, upon occasions of which I shall afterwards speak.

[He has promised Madame d'Houdetot to help her by remaining at the Hermitage, and by explaining his refusal to accompany Madame d'Epinay. He decides generously to sacrifice himself rather than compromise either woman.]

This sacrifice, which my enemies perhaps expected, and by which they have known how to profit, has caused the ruin of my reputation, and, thanks to their efforts, has robbed me of the esteem of the public; but it has restored to me my own, and has consoled me in my misfortunes. This is not the last time, as will be seen, that I have made similar sacrifices, nor the last time that they have been taken advantage of to overwhelm me.

Grimm was the only one who appeared to have taken no part in this affair; and it was to him that I resolved to address myself. I wrote a long letter to him, in which I exposed the absurdity of wishing me to look upon it as my duty to take the journey to Geneva, the uselessness of it, even the embarrassment I should have been to Madame d'Epinay, and the inconveniences which would have resulted to myself. In this letter, I could not resist the temptation of letting him see that I was well informed, and that it seemed to me singular that anyone should expect me to undertake the journey, while he himself was considered exempt, and his name was not even mentioned. . . .

This letter concluded with an exhibition of confidence by which any other man would have been touched. While I exhorted Grimm to consider my reasons well, and afterwards to inform me of his opinion, I gave him to understand that his advice, whatever it might be, would be followed. Such was really my intention, even if he had declared himself in favour of my going. As M. d'Epinay had undertaken to be his wife's escort on the journey, my company would have assumed quite a different aspect: whereas, at first, it was I who was asked to undertake this duty, and there was no question of M. d'Epinay until I had refused.

Grimm did not reply for some time. His answer was curious. I will here give a copy of it (See Packet A, No. 59):

"Madame d'Epinay's departure is put off; her son is ill, and she is obliged to wait until he has recovered. I will think over your letter. Stay quietly at your Hermitage. I will let you know my opinion in time. As she will certainly not leave for some days, there is no hurry. Meanwhile, if you think fit, you can make your offers to her, although that appears to me a matter of indifference. For, as I know your position as well as you know it yourself, I have no doubt that she will reply to them as she ought. It seems to me that the only thing to be gained by it is, that you will be able to say to those who urge

you, that, if you do not go, it will not be for want of having
offered your services. Besides, I do not see why you think it
absolutely necessary that the philosopher° should be the
speaking-trumpet of all the world; and why do you imagine,
because his advice is that you should go, that all your friends
are of the same opinion? If you write to Madame d'Epinay,
her answer may serve as a reply to all those friends, since
you set such great store upon replying to them. Adieu. I
salute Madame le Vasseur and the 'Criminal.' "†

[But Rousseau only writes to Madame d'Epinay about her
son's illness.]

After long waiting, in a state of cruel anxiety, into which
this barbarous man had plunged me, I heard, eight or ten
days later, that Madame d'Epinay had set out, and I received a second letter from him. It contained only seven or
eight lines, which I did not read through. . . . It proclaimed
a rupture, but in terms such as only the most infernal hate
can dictate, and which, from his eagerness to make them
offensive, seemed almost silly. He forbade me to enter his
presence as he might have warned me off his estates. His
letter, to make it appear ridiculous, only needed to be read
with greater calmness. Without copying it, without even
reading it to the end, I sent it back to him immediately with
the following note:

"I refused to listen to my just suspicions. Too late I understand your character.

"This, then, is the letter which you wanted time to think
over. I send it back to you; it is not for me. You can show
mine to all the world, and hate me without concealment:
that will be one falsehood less on your part."

. . . This was exactly what he wanted, and everything

---

* Diderot.

† M. le Vasseur was in the habit of calling his wife, who ruled him rather
strictly, the "Criminal-Lieutenant." Grimm, in jest, gave the same name to
the daughter, and, for shortness, afterwards omitted the second word.

turned out as he had planned. He sent my letter all around Paris, together with remarks of his own, which, however, did not prove so successful as he had expected. It was not considered that the permission to show my letter, which he had known how to extort from me, exempted him from reproach, for having so lightly taken me at my word in order to injure me. People kept asking what personal wrong I had done to him that could justify so violent a hatred. . . .

This was the way in which this man, after having so long deceived me, at last threw off the mask, convinced that, in the state to which he had brought matters, he no longer needed it. Relieved from all apprehension of being unjust towards this wretch, I left him to his own reflections, and ceased to think of him. Eight days after the receipt of his letter, I received from Geneva an answer from Madame d'Epinay to my former letter (Packet B, No. 10). I saw, from the tone which she assumed for the first time in her life, that both, reckoning upon the success of their plans, were acting in concert, and that, looking upon me as a man lost beyond all hope of safety, they intended to devote themselves from that time forth, without any risk, to the pleasure of completely crushing me.

In fact, my condition was most deplorable. I saw all my friends leaving me, without my knowing how or why. Diderot, who boasted of alone remaining faithful to me, and who had, for three months past, promised to pay me a visit, never came at all. The winter now began to make itself felt, and, with it, attacks of my usual complaints. My constitution, although vigorous, had been unable to sustain the conflicts of so many contradictory passions. I was in a state of exhaustion, which left me neither strength nor courage to resist anything. Even if my promises, even if the continued remonstrances of Diderot and Madame d'Houdetot had allowed me to leave the Hermitage at this moment, I did not know either where to go or how to drag myself there. I remained stupid and motionless, without power to think or act. The mere idea of taking a step, of writing a letter, of saying a word, made me shudder. However, I could not leave Madame d'Epinay's letter unanswered, without confessing that I deserved the treatment with which she and her friend overwhelmed me. I decided to communicate my feelings and resolutions to her, not doubting for a moment that the feelings of humanity, generosity, propriety, and the good qualities which I believed I had recognised in her, in spite of those that were bad, would make her hasten to agree with me. My letter was as follows:

"THE HERMITAGE, *November 23rd,* 1757.

"If one could die of grief, I should not be alive now. But at last I have made up my mind. All friendship between us is over, madam; but that which no longer exists still preserves its rights, which I know how to respect. I have by no means forgotten your kindness towards me, and you can reckon upon all the gratitude which a man can feel for one whom he can no longer love. All further explanation would be useless: I keep my own conscience, and refer you to your own.

"I wanted to leave the Hermitage, and I ought to have done so. But it is declared that I must remain here until spring; and since my friends desire it, I will remain until then, if you consent to it."

After this letter had been written and despatched, my only thought was to remain quiet at the Hermitage, take care of my health, endeavour to recover my strength, and make arrangements to leave in the spring, without creating any disturbance or openly proclaiming the rupture. But this was not what M. Grimm and Madame d'Epinay reckoned upon, as will be seen directly.

A few days later, I at last had the pleasure of receiving from Diderot the visit which he had so often promised, and as often failed to keep his word. It could not have occurred at a more opportune moment; he was my oldest friend; he was almost the only friend I had left; under these circumstances, my delight at seeing him may be imagined. My heart was full; I poured its contents into his. I enlightened him upon many facts which had been kept from him, or had been disguised or invented. I told him what I felt justified in telling him of all that had taken place. I made no pretence of concealing from him what he knew only too well—that a love, as unfortunate as it was foolish, had been the instrument of my destruction; but I never admitted that Madame d'Houdetot knew of it, or, at least, that I had declared it to her. I told him of Madame d'Epinay's unworthy artifices to intercept the very innocent letters written to me by her sister-in-law. I desired that he should learn these details from the lips of the persons whom she had attempted to seduce. Thérèse gave him an exact account of everything; but my feelings may be imagined, when it came to the mother's turn, and I heard her declare and maintain that she knew nothing at all about it! This was her statement, in which she never wavered. Not four days since, she had repeated all the details to me, and then, in my friend's presence, she flatly contradicted me. This attitude appeared to me decisive; and I then keenly felt my imprudence in having so long kept such a woman near me. I did not break out into invectives; I hardly condescended to say a few contemptuous words to her. I felt how much I owed to the daughter, whose unassailable uprightness contrasted strongly with her mother's contemptible cowardice. But, from that moment, my mind was made up in regard to the old woman, and I only waited for a suitable opportunity to carry out my determination.

This opportunity came sooner than I had expected. On the 10th of December I received an answer from Madame d'Epinay. Its contents were as follows (Packet B, No. 11):

"GENEVA, *December 1st,* 1757.

"After having given you, for several years, every possible proof of friendship and sympathy, I can now only pity you. You are very unhappy. I wish your conscience may be as clear as mine. That may be necessary for your future tranquillity.

"Since you wanted to leave the Hermitage, and ought to have done so, I am astonished that your friends have prevented you. As for myself, I do not consult my friends as to my duties, and I have nothing more to say to you concerning yours."

A dismissal so unexpected, but so clearly expressed, did not leave me a moment to hesitate. I was bound to leave the Hermitage at once, whatever the weather or the state of my health might be, even if I had to sleep in the woods or on the snow, with which the ground was covered, and in spite of anything Madame d'Houdetot might say or do; for, although I was ready to humour her in everything, I was not prepared to disgrace myself.

I found myself in the most terrible embarrassment of my life; but my mind was made up: I swore that, whatever might happen, I would not sleep in the Hermitage after a week. I set about removing my effects, having determined to leave them in the open field rather than keep the key longer than the week; for I was anxious, above all, that everything should be settled before anyone could write to Geneva and receive an answer. I was filled with a courage which I had never felt before: all my vigour had returned to me. Honour and indignation, upon which Madame d'Epinay had not reckoned, restored it to me. Fortune assisted my boldness. M. Mathas, *procureur fiscal* of M. le Prince de Condé, heard of my difficulties. He offered me a little house which stood in his garden at Mont-Louis, in Montmorency. I accepted his offer with eagerness and gratitude. The bargain was soon concluded. I hastily bought some furniture, in addition to what I had already, that Thérèse and myself might have a bed to sleep on. With great trouble, and at great expense, I managed to get my goods removed in a cart. In spite of the ice and snow, my removal was effected in two days, and, on the 15th of December, I gave up the keys of the Hermitage, after having paid the gardener's wages, as I could not pay my rent.

I told Madame le Vasseur that we must separate; her daughter tried to shake my resolution, but I was inflexible. I saw her off to Paris in the messenger's cart, with all the furniture and effects belonging to her and her daughter in common. I gave her some money, and undertook to pay for her lodging with her children or elsewhere, to provide for her as long as it was in my power, and never to let her want for bread as long as I had any myself. Lastly, the day after my arrival at Mont-Louis, I wrote the following letter to Madame d'Epinay:

"MONTMORENCY, *December 17th*, 1757.

"Madame,—Nothing is so simple or so necessary as to leave your house, since you do not approve of my remaining there. As you refused to allow me to spend the rest of the winter at the Hermitage, I left it on the 15th of December. I was fated to enter and to leave it in spite of myself. I thank you for the stay which you invited me to make there, and I would thank you still more if I had paid less dearly for it. You are right in thinking that I am unhappy: no one in the world knows better than yourself the extent of that unhappiness. If it is a misfortune to be deceived in the choice of one's friends, it is equally cruel to be disabused of so pleasant a mistake."

Such is the true story of my stay at the Hermitage, and of the reasons which caused me to leave it. I have been unable to interrupt this narrative, and it was important to give the most exact details, since this period of my life has exercised an influence upon the future, the effects of which will last to my dying day.

BOOK TEN

[1758]

[ROUSSEAU is afflicted with illness. Doubtless disappointed at seeing him escape from her clutches, instead of degrading himself and crying for mercy, Madame d'Epinay writes him in a mild tone.]

After all that passed, being no longer able to trust Madame d'Epinay, I did not desire to renew my connection with her. I did not answer the letter at all, and our correspondence ended with it. Seeing that I had made up my mind, she did the same; and entering into all the plans of Grimm and the Holbachian clique, she united her efforts with theirs in order to ruin me. While they were working at Paris, she was working at Geneva. Grimm, who afterwards went to join her, finished what she had begun. Tronchin, whom they easily gained over, vigorously assisted them, and became my most violent persecutor, without having the least cause of complaint against me, any more than Grimm. All three, acting together, secretly sowed in Geneva the seed which, four years later, was seen to spring up.

[They spread false rumors about him in Paris. Grimm is the master plotter, the others are his willing tools. Rousseau is upright, but alone, never flattering, never compromising with truth. They have powerful connections and are unscrupulous. Grimm has determined to ruin him.]

This undertaking was difficult, seeing that it was necessary for him to palliate its injustice in the eyes of those who were to assist in it. It was necessary to deceive those who were honourable; it was necessary to keep everyone away from me, and not to leave me a single friend, either great or small. What do I say? it was necessary for him not to allow a single word of truth to penetrate to me. If a single generous man had come and said to me, "You are playing the virtuous man;

270

and yet, look how you are treated, and how you are judged—
what have you to say?" Truth would have triumphed, and
Grimm would have been lost. He knew it; but he had
sounded his own heart, and estimated men at their true
value. I regret, for the honour of humanity, that he calculated
so accurately.

In these underground paths, his steps, to be sure, were
obliged to be slow. He has for twelve years pursued his
plans, and the most difficult thing still remains for him to do—
to deceive the entire public. There are eyes which have
watched him more closely than he thinks. He is afraid of
this, and does not yet venture to expose his plot to the light
of day.* . . . His great cleverness consists in appearing to
treat me indulgently, while in reality defaming me, and in
giving his perfidity the appearance of generosity.

[The torment is the greater, as Rousseau is unable to determine the nature of these mysterious accusations. But he finds
an outlet in writing his "Letter to D'Alembert on the Theatre,"
against the latter's corrupting proposal for establishing a
theatre at Geneva. He also continues his novel, the "New
Héloïse"—both in the bitter cold of an open "turret" in his
garden.]

Full of all that had just happened to me, still shaken by
so many violent emotions, my heart mingled the feelings of
its sufferings with the ideas with which meditation upon my
subject had inspired me: my work showed evident traces of
this mingling. Without perceiving it, I described my situation
at that time: I portrayed Grimm, Madame d'Epinay, Madame
d'Houdetot, Saint-Lambert and myself. While writing, what
delightful tears I shed! Alas! in what I wrote it is only too
evident that love, the fatal love of which I was doing my
utmost to cure myself, was not yet banished from my
heart. . . .

I revised and made a fair copy of this letter, and was about
to get it printed, when, after a long silence, I received a letter

* Since these words were written, he has taken the plunge with the most
complete and inconceivable success. I believe that it is Tronchin who has
supplied him with the courage and the means [Rousseau].

from Madame d'Houdetot, which overwhelmed me with a fresh affliction, the most painful that I had as yet suffered. She told me in this letter (Packet B, No. 34), that my passion for her was known throughout Paris; that I had spoken of it to persons who had made it public; that these rumours had reached the ears of her lover, and had nearly cost him his life; that at last he did her justice, and that they had become reconciled; but that she owed it to him, as well as to herself and her reputation, to break off all intercourse with me; that, in the meanwhile, she assured me that they would never cease to take an interest in me, that they would defend me before the public, and that she would send from time to time to inquire after me.

"And you too, Diderot!" I exclaimed. Unworthy friend! Nevertheless, I could not make up my mind to condemn him yet. My weakness was known by other persons who might have caused it to be talked about. I wanted to doubt; but soon I was unable to do so any longer.

[Saint-Lambert generously comes to visit him, speaks to Thérèse in his absence.]

As for Madame d'Houdetot, he gave Thérèse a detailed account of many circumstances with which neither she nor even Madame d'Houdetot were acquainted—things which I alone knew, which I had mentioned to Diderot alone under the seal of friendship; and it was Saint-Lambert himself to whom he had chosen to confide them. This finally decided me. Resolved to break with Diderot once and for all, I had nothing further to think about, except the manner of doing it; for I had perceived that secret ruptures always proved prejudicial to me, since they left a mask of friendship to my most cruel enemies. . . .

I decided to insert in my work, in the form of a note, a passage from Ecclesiasticus, which announced it and even the attendant circumstances, in terms sufficiently clear to anyone who was well informed, while it had no meaning for others. I further took care only to allude to the friend whom I was renouncing in the respectful terms which are always due to friendship even when it no longer exists. All this may be seen in the work itself.

[Rousseau, overwhelmed with indignation when Saint-Lambert condemns him for breaking with Diderot and adding to the latter's troubles, renounces his friendship. But Madame d'Epinay invites him to dinner with Madame Dupin, Francueil, Saint-Lambert and Madame d'Houdetot. Rousseau's arrival creates a sensation. Saint-Lambert and Madame d'Houdetot speak to him in friendly fashion, although the nearness of the latter almost makes him faint. Only later was he to "realize" that Grimm had already won them to his side.

In 1759, Rousseau finishes the "New Héloïse." Malesherbes, director of censorship, helps him with the publication.]

I have always considered M. de Malesherbes as a man of unassailable uprightness. Nothing that has ever occurred has made me doubt his honesty for a moment; but since his weakness is as great as his honour, he sometimes injures those, in whom he takes an interest, by his efforts to protect them. He not only ordered more than a hundred pages of the Paris edition to be cut out, but he mutilated the copy of the good edition which he sent to Madame de Pompadour, in a manner which deserved to be called a breach of faith. I have said somewhere in this work, that a coal-heaver's wife is more worthy of respect than the mistress of a Prince. This phrase had occurred to me in the fervour of composition, and I swear that no personal allusion was intended. On reading the work over again, I saw that others would certainly see one. However, I would not strike out the phrase, in accordance with my very injudicious principle of leaving nothing out, because it might be considered to contain some personal allusion, provided my conscience assured me that nothing of the kind had been intended when I wrote it; and I contented myself with substituting the word "Prince" for "King," which I had at first written. This alteration did not satisfy M. de Malesherbes; he suppressed the whole sentence in a fresh sheet, which he had printed on purpose and glued in as neatly as possible in Madame de Pompadour's copy. She did not remain in ignorance of this piece of jugglery: some worthy souls were kind enough to inform her of it. I myself did not hear of it until some time afterwards, when I began to feel the consequences.

[Rousseau refuses an offer—arranged by Malesherbes—to join the staff of the *Journal des Savants*.]

But, at length, the insupportable restraint of not being able to work when I pleased, and of being tied to time, and, still more, the certainty of inefficiently performing the duties which I should have been obliged to undertake, prevailed over all, and made me decide to refuse a post for which I was not adapted. I knew that my talent consisted entirely in a certain lively interest in the subjects which I had to treat, and that nothing but the love of the great, the true, and the beautiful, could enliven my genius. What would the contents of the different books, from which I should have had to make extracts, or even the books themselves, have mattered to me? My indifference to the whole thing would have frozen my pen and deadened my mind. It was thought that I could write according to the rules of a trade, like all other literary men, whereas I have never been able to write except from inspiration.

[He is disgusted both with the literary and the aristocratic world.]

. . . I determined to make it lasting, to renounce fashionable and literary society altogether, to give up writing books, and to confine myself for the remainder of my days to the limited and peaceful sphere for which I felt that I was born.

The profits of the "Letter to D'Alembert" and the "New Héloïse" had somewhat improved the state of my finances, which had been almost exhausted at the Hermitage. I saw about 1,000 crowns in prospect. "Émile," to which I seriously began to devote my attention after I had finished "Héloïse," was well advanced, and I expected that its profits would at least double that sum. I formed the resolution of investing this fund in such a manner as to bring me in a small annuity, which, together with my copying, would be sufficient to keep me without writing any more. I still had two works in hand. The first was my "Institutions politiques." I examined the state of this work, and found that it would still require several years of labour. I had not the courage to continue it and to wait until it was finished, before carrying out my resolution. I accordingly abandoned it, and decided to extract what was possible, and to burn the rest; and, pushing on this work vigorously, without discontinuing "Émile," in less than two years I put the finishing touch to the "Contrat Social."

There still remained the "Dictionnaire de Musique." This was a purely mechanical work which could be taken up at any time, and which I had undertaken merely for the sake of the money. I reserved to myself the right of abandoning it, or finishing it at my leisure, according as my other combined resources might render it necessary or superfluous. In regard to the "Morale Sensitive," of which I had only made an outline, I abandoned it altogether.

As my last intention, if I could dispense with copying altogether, was to remove to a distance from Paris, where the constant stream of visitors made it expensive for me to live, and deprived me of the time to make provision for myself, I kept in reserve, in order to prevent in my retirement the feeling of weariness which is said to come upon an author when he has laid down his pen, an occupation which might fill up the void in my solitude, without leading me into the temptation of publishing anything more during my lifetime. I do not know what whim had prompted Rey, for a long time past, to urge me to write the Memoirs of my life. Although, as far as incidents were concerned, they were not at that time particularly interesting, I felt that they might be made so by the candour with which I was capable of treating the subject; and I was determined to make it a work unique of its kind, by an unexampled veracity, which, for once at least, would enable the outside world to behold a man as he really was in his inmost self. I had always ridiculed the false ingenuousness of Montaigne, who, while pretending to confess his defects, is most careful to attribute to himself only such as are amiable; whereas I, who have always believed, and still believe, myself to be, all things considered, the best of men, felt that there is no human heart, however pure it may be, which does not conceal some odious vice. I knew that I was represented in the world under features so utterly different from my own, and sometimes so distorted, that in spite of my defects, none of which I had the least desire to conceal, I could not help being the gainer by showing myself in my true character. Besides, this was impossible without also showing others as they were, and consequently this work could not be published until after my own death and that of several others. This further emboldened me to write my Confessions, for which I shall never have to blush before anybody. I accordingly determined to devote my leisure to carrying out this undertaking, and I commenced to collect the letters and papers which might guide or assist my memory, greatly regretting all that I had torn up, burned, or lost, up to this time.

This project of complete retirement, one of the most sensible that I had ever formed, made a very strong impression on my mind, and I had already commenced to carry it out, when Heaven, which was preparing a different destiny for me, flung me into a fresh whirl of excitement.

[Rousseau enters into close friendship with his distinguished neighbors, the Maréchal de Luxembourg, his wife, and the Comtesse de Boufflers. He spends part of his time in a small house on their estate, working on his "Émile." Each day, he reads part of the "New Héloïse" to his entranced hostess, at her bedside.]

How eagerly I ran every morning at sunrise to breathe the perfumed air of the peristyle! What delicious *café au lait* I took there with my Thérèse! My cat and dog kept us company. This retinue alone would have been enough for my whole life; I should never have experienced a moment's weariness. I was in an earthly paradise; I lived there in the same state of innocence, and enjoyed the same happiness.

The success of this expedient surpassed my expectations. Madame de Luxembourg took a violent fancy to "Julie" and its author; she spoke of nothing but me, thought of nothing but me, flattered me the whole of the day, and embraced me ten times a day. She insisted that I should always sit by her at table, and when any great noblemen wanted to take this place, she told them that it belonged to me, and made them sit somewhere else. It is easy to imagine the impression which these charming manners produced upon me, who am subjugated by the slightest marks of affection. I became sincerely attached to her, in proportion to the attachment which she showed for me. My only fear, when I perceived this infatuation, was that, as I felt I was not sufficiently agreeable to keep it alive, it might change to disgust, and, unfortunately for me, this fear was only too well founded.

There must have been a natural opposition between her turn of mind and my own, since, independently of the many stupid and injudicious remarks which every moment escaped me in the course of conversation, and even in my letters, and when I was on the best of terms with her, there were certain things which displeased her, without my being able to imagine the reason. I will only mention one instance out of twenty. She knew that I was making a copy of "Héloïse" for Madame d'Houdetot, at so much a page; she wanted me to make one for her on the same terms. I promised to do so; and, consequently, entering her name as one of my customers, I wrote her a few line of polite thanks, or, at least, I had intended them as such. I received the following answer, which utterly astonished me (Packet C, No. 43):

"VERSAILLES, *Tuesday*.

"I am delighted, I am satisfied; your letter has given me infinite pleasure; I hasten to inform you and to thank you for it.

"Here are the exact words of your letter: 'Although you are certainly a very good customer, I feel some difficulty about taking your money; properly speaking, I ought to pay for the pleasure of being permitted to work for you.' I will not mention the subject again. I regret that you do not tell me more about the state of your health. Nothing interests me more. I love you with all my heart; and, I assure you, it is with great sorrow that I write this to you for it would be a great pleasure to me to tell it to you by word of mouth. M. de Luxembourg loves you and embraces you in all sincerity."

On receiving this letter, I hastened to reply to it before examining it more fully, in order to protest against any impolite interpretation; and, after having devoted several days to this examination with a feeling of uneasiness which may be imagined, without being able to understand what was the matter, I wrote the following note as a final answer on the subject:

"Montmorency, *December* 8th, 1759.

"Since writing my letter, I have examined the passage in question hundreds and hundreds of times. I have considered it in its own natural meaning, I have considered it in every meaning that could be put upon it, and I confess, Madame la Maréchale, that I am at a loss to know whether it is I who owe you excuses or whether it is not rather yourself who owe them to me."

It is now ten years since these letters were written. I have often thought of them since: and, even to this day, I am so stupid on this point, that I have not been able to understand what she could find in the passage in question that was, I will not say offensive, but even calculated to cause her displeasure.

In reference to this manuscript of "Héloïse," which Madame de Luxembourg wanted to have, I ought to mention here what I had intended to do, in order to give it some special distinction above all the rest. I had written the adventures of Lord Edward separately, and I had long been undecided whether I should insert them, either wholly or in extracts, in this work, in which they seemed to me to be out of place. I finally decided to cut them out altogether, because, not being in keeping with the tone of the remainder, they would have spoiled its touching simplicity. I had a weightier reason, when I made the acquaintance of Madame de Luxembourg. In these adventures there was a Roman Marchioness of very odious character, some features of which, without being applicable to her, might perhaps have been applied to her by those who only knew her by reputation. I therefore congratulated myself upon the resolution I had taken, and determined to keep to it. But, being extremely desirous of enriching her copy with something which was not contained in any others, I was misguided enough to think of these unfortunate adventures, and I formed the plan of making a selection of them and adding it to the work—a mad project, the extravagance of which can only be explained by the blind fatality which was dragging me to my destruction. *Quos vult perdere Jupiter dementat.*

I was foolish enough to make this extract with great care and labour, and to send it to her as if it had been the most beautiful thing in the world, at the same time informing her, as was true, that I had burnt the original, that the extract was intended for her alone, and would never be seen by anybody, unless she herself showed it; and this action on my part, far from proving to her my prudence and discretion, as I expected, only gave her an idea of the opinion which I myself held as to the application of the features of the work, by which she might have felt offended. My imbecility was so great, that I entertained no doubt that she would be enchanted by what I had done. She did not compliment me upon it as heartily as I expected, and, to my very great surprise, never spoke to me of the manuscript which I had sent her. I myself, delighted with my conduct in the matter, did not suspect till long afterwards, in consequence of other indications, the effect which it had produced.

[Rousseau asserts that living with the great never went to his head, that he retained his simple ways of life.

He is teased by the Marquise de Verdelin.]

However, from continually seeing her, I at last became attached to her. She, like myself, had her sorrows; our mutual confidences made our *tête-à-têtes* interesting. Nothing unites hearts so much as the pleasure of shedding tears together. We sought each other's society in order to console ourselves, and the need for this made me overlook much. I had shown such roughness in my outspokenness to her, and had sometimes shown so little respect for her character, that I really must have felt a great deal, to believe that she could sincerely pardon me. The following is a sample of the letters which I sometimes wrote to her, in regard to which it is worthy of notice that she never, in any of her answers, showed the least sign of annoyance:

"MONTMORENCY, *November 5th*, 1760.

"You inform me, madame, that you have not expressed yourself very well, in order to give me to understand that I have expressed myself very badly. You speak of your pretended stupidity, in order to make me sensible of my own. You boast of being nothing more than a 'good woman,' as if you were afraid of being taken at your word, and you make excuses to me in order to make me feel that I owe you some in return. Yes, madame, I know it well; it is I who am a fool, a 'good man,' and worse still, if it is possible. It is I who do not choose my terms sufficiently well to please a fine French lady, who pays as much attention to phrases and speaks as well as you do. But you must consider that I take them in the ordinary meaning of the language, without being familiar with the polite acceptations which are sometimes attached to them in the virtuous society of Paris. If my expressions are sometimes ambiguous, I endeavour, by my conduct, to give them a definite meaning," etc.

About the same time, I was guilty of an act of folly which did not help to keep me in her good graces. Although I had no acquaintance with M. de Silhouette,* and was little inclined to like him, I had a great opinion of his administrative powers. When he began to lay a heavy hand upon the financiers, I saw that he was not commencing the operation at a favourable moment. Nevertheless, I wished him all success; and, when I heard that he had been removed from office, I

---

* Controller-general of Finance in 1757.

was so thoughtless as to write the following letter to him, which assuredly I do not attempt to justify:

"Montmorency, *December 2nd, 1759.*

"Condescend, sir, to accept the homage of a recluse who is unknown to you, but who esteems you for your talents, who respects you for your administration, and who has done you the honour of believing that it would not long remain in your hands. Unable to save the State, except at the expense of the capital which has destroyed it, you have dared to brave the outcries of the money-grubbers. When I saw how you crushed these wretches, I envied you your office. Now that I see how you have abandoned it without belying yourself, I admire you. Be satisfied with yourself, sir; you take with you from it an honour which you will long enjoy without a rival. The execrations of rascals are the glory of an upright man."

[1760.]—Madame de Luxembourg, who knew that I had written this letter, spoke to me about it when she came out at Easter; I showed it to her; she wished for a copy, and I gave her one; but I did not know, when I did so, that she herself was one of those money-grubbers who had an interest in sub-leases and had caused the removal of Silhouette. To judge from my numerous follies, it seemed as if I purposely wanted to arouse the hatred of an amiable and influential woman, to whom I was becoming more sincerely attached every day, and whose displeasure I was far from wishing to bring upon myself, although by my repeated acts of stupidity, I was doing everything that was wanted to produce such a result. . . .

For my own part, I tried to reassure myself as to the effect of my follies by the evidence which I produced to myself, that none of them had been committed with the intention of offending her; as if a woman could ever pardon such follies, even though she is perfectly certain that they were not the result of deliberate intention.

However, although she seemed to see and feel nothing, although I found no abatement in her warmth, and no alteration in her manner towards me, a continually growing presentiment, which was only too well founded, made me tremble incessantly, for fear her infatuation for me might be succeeded by disgust. Could I expect, on the part of so great a lady, a constancy which would be proof against my lack of skill in supporting it? I did not even know how to conceal from her this dim presentiment, which disquieted me and only made me more sullen and awkward. This may be seen from the following letter, which contains a very singular prediction.

N.B.—This letter, which is undated in my rough copy, was written in October, 1760, at the latest.

"How cruel your kindness is! Why disturb the tranquillity of a recluse, who renounced the pleasures of life, in order to feel their annoyances no longer? I have spent my life in the vain endeavour to find lasting attachments: I have been unable to form any in the ranks which were accessible to me. Am I to look for them in yours? Neither interest nor ambition has any temptations for me; I have little vanity: I am rather timid; I can resist everything except affection. Why do you both attack me in a weakness which I must overcome, since, considering the distance which separates us, the overflowings of tender hearts cannot bring mine near to you. Will gratitude be sufficient for a heart which knows not two ways of giving itself and only feels capable of friendship? Friendship, Madame la Maréchale! Ah! therein lies my misfortune. It is very handsome of you and Monsieur le Maréchal to use this term; but I am a fool to take you at your word. You are amusing yourselves: I am forming an attachment for you, and the end of the game has fresh sorrows in store for me! How I hate all your titles, and how I pity you for having them! You seem to me so worthy to taste the charms of private life. Why do you not live at Clarens? I would go there in search of the happiness of my life; but—the château of Montmorency, the Hôtel de Luxembourg! Is that where one ought to see Jean-Jacques? Is that where a friend of equality, who, in thus paying for the esteem which is shown for him, believes that he is returning as much as he receives, ought to carry the affections of a tender heart? You are good, and also feeling: I know it: I have seen it. I regret that I have not been able to believe it sooner; but, considering the position which you hold, and the manner in which you live, nothing can make a lasting impression upon you; and so many new interests efface each other, that not one is permanent. You will forget me, madame, after you have made it impossible for me to imitate you. You will have done much to make me unhappy and unable to justify myself."

I coupled M. de Luxembourg's name with hers, in order to make the compliment less harsh for her; besides, I was so sure of him, that I had never for a moment felt any anxiety as to the duration of his friendship. None of my apprehensions in regard to his wife ever extended to him. I have never felt the least mistrust of his character, which I knew was weak, but trustworthy. I had no more fear of a coldness on his part than expectation of a heroic attachment. The simplicity and familiarity of our intercourse showed how each of us depended upon the other. We were both right: as long as I live I shall honour and cherish the memory of this worthy gentleman; and, whatever attempts may have been made to part him from me, I am as certain that he died my friend, as if I had received his last sigh.

[During their next stay at Montmorency, Madame de Luxembourg brings her grand-daughter with her.]

Her name was Amélie. She was a charming person. Her face, gentleness, and timidity were truly maidenly. Nothing could have been more amiable or more interesting than her features, nothing tenderer or more chaste than the feelings which they inspired. Besides, she was a mere child, not yet eleven years of age. Madame la Maréchale, finding her too shy, did her best to rouse her. She several times allowed me to kiss her, which I did with my usual awkwardness. Instead of the pretty things which anyone else in my place would have said, I stood mute and utterly confused. I do not know which of us was the more bashful, the poor little one or myself. One day I met her alone on the staircase of the little château; she was coming to see Thérèse, with whom her governess still

was. Not knowing what to say to her, I asked her to give me
a kiss, which, in the innocence of her heart, she did not refuse, as she had already given me one that very morning, by
her grandmamma's orders, and in her presence. The next day,
while reading "Émile" at Madame la Maréchale's bedside, I
came upon a passage, in which I have justly censured the
very thing that I had myself done the day before. She found
the observation very just, and made some sensible remark
upon it, which caused me to blush. How I curse my incredible
stupidity, which has often caused me to appear vile and
guilty, when I have only been foolish and embarrassed—a
foolishness which is regarded as only a false excuse in the case
of a man who is known to be not wanting in intelligence! I
can swear that in this kiss, which was so blameable, as in all
the rest, Mademoiselle Amélie's heart and feelings were no
purer than my own. I can even swear that, if at that moment I
could have avoided meeting her, I would have done so; for,
although I was very pleased to see her, I was greatly at a loss
to find something agreeable to say to her in passing. How is it
that a child can intimidate a man whom the power of kings
fails to alarm? What is a man to do? How is he to behave, if
he is utterly destitute of presence of mind? If I force myself
to speak to people whom I meet, I infallibly utter some foolish
remark; if I say nothing, then I am a misanthrope, a wild
animal, a bear. Complete imbecility would have been far more
favourable to me; but the talents which I lacked in society
have made those which I possessed the instruments of my
ruin.

At the end of her stay on this occasion, Madame de Luxembourg carried out a good work, in which I had some share.
Diderot had very rashly offended Madame la Princesse de
Robeck, a daughter of M. de Luxembourg. Her *protégé* Palissot avenged her by the comedy of the *Philosophes,* in which I
was held up to ridicule, and Diderot was very severely handled. The author was more merciful to me, not so much, I
believe, on account of the obligations under which he was to
me, as for fear of displeasing his patroness' father, who he
knew entertained an affection for me. Duchesne, the book-

seller, with whom I was not acquainted at the time, sent me the piece when it was printed, I suspect by Palissot's instructions, who perhaps thought that I should be glad to see a man pulled to pieces, with whom I had broken off relations. He was greatly mistaken. When I broke with Diderot, whom I believed to be weak and indiscreet rather than absolutely wicked, I still preserved in my heart a feeling of attachment, even of esteem, for him, and of respect for our old friendship, which I am convinced was for a long time as sincere on his part as on my own. The case is quite different with Grimm, a man whose character is false, who never loved me, who is not even capable of loving, and who, with a light heart, without any reason for complaint, simply in order to satisfy his spiteful jealousy, has secretly become my bitterest calumniator. He is no longer anything to me. Diderot will always be my old friend. My tenderest feelings were moved at the sight of this hateful piece; I could not bear to read it, and, without finishing it, I sent it back to Duchesne, together with the following letter:

"Montmorency, *May* 21st, 1760.

"Sir,—On looking through the piece which you have sent me, I have shuddered at finding myself praised. I refuse to accept this horrible present. I am convinced that, in sending it to me, you did not intend to insult me; but you either do not know, or you have forgotten, that I have had the honour of being the friend of a man deserving of respect, who is unworthily traduced and calumniated in this libellous production."

Duchesne handed this letter round. Diderot, who ought to have been touched by it, was annoyed. His *amour-propre* could not pardon me the superiority of a generous action, and I heard that his wife attacked me on every possible occasion, with a rage which affected me but little, since I knew that everybody looked upon her as a regular fish-wife.

Diderot, in his turn, found an avenger in the Abbé Morellet, who wrote a little *brochure* against Palissot, after the manner of the "Petit Prophète," called "La Vision." In this pamphlet he very imprudently insulted Madame de Robeck, whose friends caused him to be imprisoned in the Bastille; she herself was not of a sufficiently revengeful disposition—not to mention that at that time she was a dying woman—to have had anything to do with it.

At the same time I had another affair on hand, which was the occasion of the last letter I ever wrote to Voltaire—a letter which he exclaimed loudly against as an abominable insult, but which he never showed to anyone. I will here supply the omission. . . .

"Montmorency, *June 17th*, 1760.

"Sir,—I never thought to find myself writing to you again. But, having learnt that the letter which I wrote to you in 1756 has been printed at Berlin, I feel it my duty to give you an account of my conduct in regard to it, and I will fulfil this duty in all truthfulness and sincerity.

"This letter, having been really addressed to yourself, was never meant to be printed. I communicated its contents, conditionally, to three persons to whom the rights of friendship did not permit me to refuse anything of the kind, and whom these same rights of friendship still less permitted to abuse their trust by violating their promise. These three persons are: Madame de Chenonceaux, Madame Dupin's step-daughter; Madame la Comtesse d'Houdetot; and a German named Grimm. Madame de Chenonceaux was anxious for the letter to be printed, and asked my consent. I told her that it depended upon you. Your consent was asked; you refused it, and nothing more was said about the matter.

"Nevertheless, M. l'Abbé Trublet, with whom I have no sort of connection, has just written, with a most friendly mark of attention, to inform me, that he has received the sheets of a journal belonging to M. Formey, in which he has read this identical letter, accompanied by a note, in which the editor, under date of the 23rd October, 1759, says that he found it some weeks ago in the Berlin booksellers' shops, and that, since it is one of those pamphlets which soon disappear beyond hope of return, he thought it his duty to allot it a place in his journal.

"This, sir, is all that I know about the matter. It is quite certain that hitherto this letter has never even been heard of in Paris. It is quite certain that the copy, whether in manuscript or print, which has fallen into M. Formey's hands, can only have come to him either through you, which is not likely, or through one of the three persons whom I have just mentioned. Lastly, it is quite certain that the two ladies are incapable of such a breach of confidence. From my retreat, I cannot gain any further information about the matter. You have correspondents, by whose assistance it would be easy for you, if it were worth the trouble, to trace it back to its source, and learn the truth about the facts.

"In the same letter, M. l'Abbé Trublet informs me that he is keeping back the number of the journal, and will not lend it without my consent, which I certainly will never give. But this copy may not be the only one in Paris. My wish is that the letter may not be printed there, and I will do my best to prevent it; but, in case I am unable to succeed, and, being informed in time, may be able to secure the prior right, then I will not hesitate to have it printed myself. This appears to me to be only fair and natural.

"As for your reply to the same letter, it has not been communicated to anyone, and you may feel assured that it will never be printed without your consent,* which I shall never be so indiscreet as to ask for, for I know well, that what one man writes to another, is not meant for the public. But if you like to write an answer for publication, addressed to me, I promise you that I will faithfully add it to my letter, without a single word of reply on my part.

"I do not like you, sir: you have done me injuries, which I could not but feel most deeply—me, your disciple and most enthusiastic admirer. You have ruined Geneva in return for the shelter you have found there: you have alienated my fellow-citizens from me, in return for the eulogies which I

---

* That is to say, during his life-time and mine: and surely, the most scrupulous behaviour, especially in dealing with a man who tramples it ruthlessly under foot, cannot require more [Rousseau].

have lavished upon you in their midst: it is you who have made life in my native country unendurable for me: it is you who will cause me to die in a foreign land, deprived of all the consolations of a dying man, and to be thrown into a gutter, as the last token of respect: while you will be followed to the grave with all the honours that a man can expect. In fact, I hate you, since you have so willed it; but I hate you as a man still more worthy of loving you, if you had so chosen. Of all the sentiments towards you, with which my heart was filled, the only one that survives is the admiration which one cannot refuse to your splendid genius, and admiration for your writings. If I can honour nothing but your talents, the fault is not mine. I shall never fail in the respect that is due to them, or in the behaviour which such respect demands. Farewell, sir!" °

In the midst of all these petty literary squabbles, which only confirmed me more and more in my resolution, I was the recipient of the greatest honour which the profession of letters has ever conferred upon me, and of which I felt most proud: M. le Prince de Conti condescended to visit me twice, once at the little château, and once at Mont-Louis. On both occasions, he selected the time when Madame de Luxembourg was not at Montmorency, in order to make it clearer that he only came to see me. I have never had any doubt that I owed his kindness originally to Madame de Luxembourg and Madame de Boufflers; but neither have I any doubt that I owe the kindness with which he has never ceased to honour me since then, to his own feelings and myself.†

* It will be observed that, although this letter has been written nearly seven years, I have neither mentioned it nor shown it to a living soul. This has also been the case with the two letters which M. Hume forced me to write to him last summer, until he made the uproar about them, which everybody knows of. The evil that I have to say about my enemies, I say to themselves privately; as for the good, when there is any, I say it openly and with a good heart [Rousseau].

† Notice the persistency of this blind and stupid confidence, in the midst of all the ill-treatment, which ought to have disabused me of it. It never disappeared until after my return to Paris in 1770 [Rousseau].

As my apartment at Mont-Louis was very small, and the situation of the turret was delightful, I took the Prince there; and he, to crown his favours, desired that I would have the honour of playing a game of chess with him. I knew that he could beat the Chevalier de Lorenzi, who was a much better player than myself. However, in spite of the signs and grimaces of the Chevalier and those who were present, which I pretended not to see, I won the two games which we played. When they were finished, I said to him in a respectful, but serious tone, "My Lord, I have too much respect for your most serene Highness, not to beat you always at chess." This great Prince, so witty and learned, who deserved to be spared from flattery, felt—at least, I think so—that I was the only person present who treated him as a man, and I have every reason to believe that he felt really grateful to me for it.

Even if he had been displeased, I could not reproach myself with wishing to deceive him in anything, and I certainly have not to reproach myself with having ill-requited his goodness in my heart, although I certainly sometimes requited it with a bad grace, whereas he himself displayed infinite delicacy in the manner in which he showed it. A few days afterwards, he sent me a hamper of game, which I accepted in a proper manner, Some time after that, he sent me a second hamper, accompanied by a note from one of his officers of the hunt, written by his instructions, informing me that the contents had been shot by His Highness himself. I accepted it; but I wrote to Madame de Boufflers that I would accept no more. This letter was generally blamed, and deservedly. To refuse presents of game from a Prince of the blood, who, besides, displays such delicacy in sending them, shows rather the boorishness of an ill-bred person who forgets himself, than the delicate feeling of a proud man, who desires to preserve his independence. I have never read over this letter without blushing for it, or without reproaching myself for having written it. However, I have not undertaken to write my Confessions in order to be silent upon my follies, and the present instance disgusts me with myself too much for me to allow myself to conceal it.

If I did not commit the additional folly of becoming his rival, I very nearly did so; for, at the time, Madame de Boufflers was still his mistress, and I knew nothing about it. She came to see me pretty often with the Chevalier de Lorenzi. She was handsome and still young. She affected the old Roman spirit, while I was always romantic; this was a sufficient similarity. I was nearly caught; I believe she saw it. The Chevalier saw it also; at least, he spoke to me about it, and in a manner not calculated to discourage me. But this time I was prudent—and it was time to be so, at fifty years of age. Full of the good advice which I had just given to the grey-beards in my letter to D'Alembert, I was ashamed to profit so little by it myself. Besides, after learning what I did not know before, I must have lost my head entirely, if I had dared to carry my rivalry so high! Lastly, being perhaps not yet thoroughly cured of my passion for Madame d'Houdetot, I felt that nothing could henceforth take her place in my heart, and I bade adieu to love for the remainder of my life. At the moment of writing these lines, a young woman, who had her designs upon me, has just made dangerous advances to me, and that with very significant glances; but, if she had pretended to forget my fifty years, I have remembered them. After having extricated myself from this snare, I have no longer any fear of falling, and I feel that I can answer for myself for the rest of my days.

Madame de Boufflers had observed the emotion which her presence caused me, and could also see that I had triumphed over it. I am neither foolish nor vain enough to believe that, at my age, I can have inspired her with any fancy for me; but, from certain expressions which she made use of to Thérèse, I believe that I aroused a certain feeling of curiosity in her mind. If this is the case, and if she has not forgiven me for not having satisfied this curiosity, it must be admitted that I was born to be the victim of my weaknesses, since victorious love was so fatal to me, and vanquished love even more fatal still.

Here ends the collection of letters which has served me as a guide in these two books. Henceforth, I can only follow in the footsteps of my recollections; which, however, in reference to this cruel period of my life, are so vivid, and have left so strong an impression upon me that, lost in the vast ocean of my misfortunes, I am unable to forget the details of my first shipwreck, although its results only afford me confused recollections. Accordingly, in the following book, I can still proceed with tolerable certainty. If I go further, I shall have to grope in the dark.

BOOK ELEVEN

[1761]

ALTHOUGH "Julie," which had been in the press for a long time, was not yet published at the end of 1760, it was beginning to make a great stir. Madame de Luxembourg had spoken of it at Court, Madame d'Houdetot in Paris. The latter had even obtained permission from me for Saint-Lambert to have it read in manuscript to the King of Poland, who was delighted with it. Duclos, to whom I had also had it read, had spoken of it to the Academy. All Paris was impatient to see this romance; the booksellers' shops in the Rue Saint-Jacques and the Palais-Royal were besieged by persons making inquiries about it. At last it appeared, and its success, contrary to what is usually the case, corresponded to the eagerness with which it had been expected. Madame la Dauphine, who was one of the first who read it, spoke of it to M. de Luxembourg as a delightful work. Opinions were divided amongst men of letters; but amongst the general public the verdict was unanimous; the ladies, especially, became infatuated with the book and the author to such an extent, that there were few, even amongst the highest circles, whose conquest I could not have made if I had been so disposed. . . .

Amidst so many prejudices and factitious passions, one must know how to analyse properly the human heart, in order to disentangle the true feelings of nature. A delicacy of tact is necessary, which can only be acquired by intercourse with the great world, in order to feel, if I may so venture to say, the delicacies of heart of which this work is full. I unhesitatingly place the fourth part of it by the side of the "Princesse de Clèves," and I assert that, if these two works had been read only in the provinces, their true value would never have been recognised. It is, therefore, not surprising that the book met with the greatest success at Court. . . .

The feature which has been least observed, and which will always make it a work unique of its kind, is the simplicity of the subject and the sustained interest which, confined to three persons, is kept up through six volumes, without the aid of incidents, romantic adventures, or improprieties of any kind, either in the characters or in their actions. Diderot has paid great compliments to Richardson upon the enormous variety of his situations and the number of characters introduced by him. Richardson certainly has the merit of having given them all distinctive characteristics; but, in regard to their number, he has the fault common to most insipid writers of romance, who make up for the barrenness of their ideas by the aid of characters and incidents. It is easy to excite interest by incessantly presenting unheard-of incidents and new faces, who pass like the figures in a magic-lantern; but it is far more difficult to sustain this interest continually by means of the same objects, without the aid of wonderful adventures. And if, other things being equal, the simplicity of the subject adds to the beauty of the work, the romances of Richardson, though superior in so many other things, cannot, in this respect, be compared to mine. However, it is dead—I know it, and I know the reason; but it will come to life again.

My only fear was that, owing to its extreme simplicity, the development of the story might prove wearisome, and that I had not been able to keep up a sufficiently lively interest to the end. I was reassured by an incident which, of itself alone, flattered me more than all the compliments which this work has procured me.

It appeared at the beginning of the Carnival. A book-hawker took it to Madame la Princesse de Talmont * one day when there was a ball at the Opera. After supper she dressed herself to go, and, while waiting, began to read the new romance. At midnight she ordered her horses to be put in, and went on reading. She was informed that her carriage was waiting; she made no reply. Her servants, seeing that she had forgotten herself, went to tell her that it was two o'clock. "There is no hurry yet," she answered, and still went on reading. Some time afterwards, her watch having stopped, she rang the bell to know what time it was. When she heard that it was four o'clock, she said, "Then it is too late to go to the ball; take out the horses," undressed herself, and spent the rest of the night in reading.

Since hearing of this incident, I have always wanted to see Madame de Talmont, not only to learn from her own lips if it is strictly true, but also because I have never thought it possible that anyone could feel so lively an interest in "Julie" without possessing the sixth sense, that moral sense, with which so few hearts are endowed, and without which it is impossible for anyone to understand my own.

What made the women so favourably disposed towards me was their conviction that I had written my own history, and that I myself was the hero of this romance. This belief was so firmly established, that Madame de Polignac wrote to Madame de Verdelin, begging her to persuade me to let her see the portrait of Julie. Everyone was convinced that it was impossible to express sentiments so vividly without having felt them, or to describe the transports of love so glowingly, unless they came straight from the heart. In this they were right. It is quite true that I wrote this romance in a state of most feverish ecstasy, but they were wrong in thinking that it had needed real objects to produce this condition; they were far from understanding to what an extent I am capable of being inflamed by beings of the imagination. Had it not been for a few reminiscences of my youth and Madame d'Houdetot, the love which I felt and described would have had only the

* It was not she, but another lady whose name I do not know; but I have been assured of the fact [Rousseau].

nymphs of the air for its object. I did not desire either to confirm or refute an error which was to my advantage. It may
be seen in the preface, in the form of a dialogue, which I had
printed separately, how I left the public in suspense on that
point. Rigid moralists may say that I ought to have declared
the truth without reserve. For my own part, I do not see what
obligation there was for me to do so; and I think that I
should have shown far more stupidity than frankness in making such a declaration, when there was no necessity for it.

[Various incidents produce a growing coldness in Madame
de Luxembourg, including his *faux pas* in praising a bad portrait of her.]

My ability lay in telling useful but hard truths to mankind
with a certain amount of energy and courage; and I ought to
have stopped at that. I was not born, I will not say to flatter,
but to praise. The awkwardness of the praises which I attempted to bestow has done me more harm than all the severity of my reproaches. I will here quote a terrible example
of this. . . .

[He fears his praise of the Choiseul ministry, in the "Contrat
Social," will not turn out to his advantage,* nor his informing
Madame de Boufflers that her tragedy resembled closely a
little-known English play. He mentions other contacts.]

I may mention M. le Président Hénault, who, as a member
of the society of authors, was not free from their faults; Madame du Deffand and Mademoiselle de Lespinasse, both of
them on intimate terms with Voltaire and D'Alembert, with
the latter of whom Mademoiselle de Lespinasse finally lived—
of course, in a most respectable manner: let no one imagine
that I mean anything else. I had begun by feeling a lively interest in Madame du Deffand, whom I pitied on account of
the loss of her eyesight; but her manner of living, so entirely
contrary to mine, that she got up about the time that I went
to bed; her extravagant passion for trifling displays of wit;
the importance which she attached to the most contemptible
rags which appeared whether complimentary or abusive; the

---

* Rousseau was mistaken; the passage caused no offense.

despotic violence of her oracular utterances; her exaggerated prepossessions in favour of or against everything, which prevented her from speaking of any subject except hysterically; her incredible prejudices, her unconquerable obstinacy, her unreasoning enthusiasm to which she was carried away by the stubbornness of her impassioned judgments—all this soon discouraged me from the attentions which I was ready to pay her. I neglected her; she noticed it. This was sufficient to put her in a rage; and, although I felt how greatly a woman of this character was to be feared, I preferred to expose myself to the scourge of her hatred than to that of her friendship. . . .

[Even the name of Rousseau's dog, "Duke," is used by enemies to cause him trouble. He finishes the "Contrat Social," works on the "Dictionary of Music."]

The "Contrat Social" was printed with little delay. It was different with "Emile," for the publication of which I was obliged to wait, before I could carry out my project of retirement. From time to time, Duchesne sent me specimens of type to choose from; and after I had made a choice, instead of putting the work in hand, he sent me fresh ones. When we had at last settled upon the size and type, and several sheets had already been struck off, in consequence of a slight alteration which I made in a proof he began all over again, and, at the end of six months, we were not so far advanced as on the first day. While these experiments were going on, I discovered that the book was being printed in France as well as in Holland, and in two separate editions. What could I do? The manuscript was no longer under my control. Far from having had anything to do with the French edition, I had always opposed it; but, at length, since it was being brought out, whether I liked it or not, and served as a model for the other, I was obliged to glance over it and look at the proofs, to prevent my work being mutilated and disfigured. Besides, the work was being printed with such definite approval on the part of the magistrate, that the undertaking was in some sort under his direction; he frequently wrote to me, and even came to see me on the subject, on a certain occasion of which I will speak presently. . . .

Feeling sure that everything connected with the work was in order, firmly convinced that it enjoyed not only the approval and protection of the magistrate, but even deserved and had obtained the favour of the ministry, I congratulated myself upon my courage in acting rightly, and laughed at the faint-heartedness of my friends, who seemed anxious about me. Duclos was amongst the number, and I confess that my confidence in his uprightness and shrewdness might have alarmed me if I had felt less confidence in the usefulness of the work and the honour of its patrons. He came to see me on the part of M. Baille, while "Émile" was in the press, and spoke to me about it. I read to him the "Savoyard Vicar's Profession of Faith"; he listened to it quietly, and, as it seemed to me, with great pleasure. When I had finished, he said to me: "What, citizen! is this part of a book which is being printed in Paris?" "Yes," I answered; "and it was to be painted at the Louvre, by order of the King." "I admit it," said he; "but be kind enough not to tell anyone that you have read me this extract." This singular way of expressing himself surprised, but did not alarm me. I knew that Duclos saw a good deal of M. de Malesherbes; and I found it difficult to understand how he could hold so different an opinion in regard to the same thing.

I had lived at Montmorency for more than four years, without having enjoyed one single day of good health. Although the air was excellent, the water is bad; and this may very well have been one of the causes which aggravated my usual complaints. About the end of the autumn of 1761 I fell seriously ill, and spent the whole winter in almost constant suffering. My physical ailments, increased by numerous uneasinesses, made them still more painful to me. For some time secret and gloomy forebodings had been disturbing me, although I did not know to what they referred. I received several curious anonymous letters, and even signed ones which were equally curious; one from a councillor of the Parliament of Paris, who, dissatisfied with the present constitution of affairs, and prognosticating no good from its results, wished to consult me as to the choice of an asylum in Geneva or Switzerland, to which he and his family might retire; another from M. de ——, *président à mortier* in the Parliament of——, who proposed to me to draw up a memorandum and remonstrances for this Parliament, which at that time was out of favour with the Court, at the same time offering to supply me with all the materials and documents which I might require.

When I am suffering, I am easily irritated. This was what happened when I received these letters, and I showed it by my answers, in which I flatly refused to do what I was asked. I certainly do not reproach myself for refusing, since these letters might have been snares set for me by my enemies,* and what I was asked to do was opposed to the principles from which I was still less than ever inclined to depart; but, when I might have refused politely, I refused rudely; and therefore in that I was wrong.

The two letters of which I have just spoken will be found amongst my papers. The letter from the councillor did not altogether surprise me, because, in common with him and many others, I thought that the break up of the constitution threatened France with speedy destruction. The disasters of an unfortunate war,† which were all the fault of the Government; the incredible financial disorders; the continued disagreements in the administration, which had hitherto been conducted by two or three ministers openly opposed, and who, in order to injure each other, were ruining the kingdom; the general discontent of the people and of all classes in the State; the stubbornness of an obstinate woman,‡ who, ever sacrificing her intellectual powers, if she possessed any, to her inclinations, almost invariably kept the most capable men out of office, in order to fill them with those who were her favourites; all these things contributed to justify the forebod-

* For instance, I knew that the President ——— was intimately connected with the Encyclopaedists and the Holbachians.

† The Seven Years' War.

‡ Madame de Pompadour.

ings of the councillor, the public, and myself. These forebodings several times made me consider whether I should
not act wisely in seeking a refuge for myself outside the
kingdom, before the troubles, which seemed to threaten it,
broke out; but, reassured by my insignificance and peaceful
disposition, I believed that, in the retirement in which I intended to live, no storm could reach me. . . .

While my condition grew worse, the printing of "Émile"
proceeded more slowly, and was at last entirely suspended. I
was unable to learn the reason. Guy did not condescend either
to write to me again or to answer my letters. I could not procure information from anyone, and knew nothing of what was
going on, M. de Malesherbes being in the country at the time.
No misfortune, whatever it may be, ever troubles or over-
whelms me, provided that I know in what it consists; but I
am naturally afraid of darkness; I dread and hate its gloomy
appearance; mystery always makes me uneasy; it is too much
opposed to my disposition, which is frank to the verge of
imprudence. During the daytime, the sight of the most
hideous monster would, I believe, alarm me but little; but if
I were to see by night a figure in a white sheet, I should be
afraid. Thus my fancy, kindled by this prolonged silence,
busied itself in conjuring up for me a number of phantoms.
The more I had at heart the publication of my last and best
work, the more I tormented myself to find out what could be
delaying it; and, as I always went to extremes in everything,
I saw in the suspension of the printing the suppression of the
book. Meanwhile, as I was unable to imagine the reason or
the manner of this interruption, I remained a prey to the
most cruel uncertainty. I wrote letter after letter to Guy, M.
de Malesherbes, and Madame de Luxembourg; and as no
answers came at all, or did not come when I expected them,
I was utterly confused and almost beside myself. Unfortunately I heard, at the same time, that Father Griffet, a Jesuit,
had spoken of "Émile," and had even quoted passages from
it. In a moment my imagination, like a flash of lightning, disclosed the whole iniquitous mystery; I saw its progress as
clearly and as surely as if it had been revealed to me. I imag-

ined that the Jesuits, furious at the tone of contempt in which I had spoken of their colleges, had got possession of my work; that it was they who were delaying its publication; that, having been informed by their friend Guérin of my present condition, and foreseeing my speedy death, of which I myself entertained no doubt, their object was to delay the printing until that event occurred, with the intention of mutilating and altering the work, and, in order to serve their own ends, of attributing to me opinions totally different from my own. It is astonishing what a crowd of facts and circumstances entered my head to accommodate themselves to this mad idea, and to give it an air of probability—nay, to prove and demonstrate its truth. I knew that Guérin was completely devoted to the Jesuits. I attributed to them all the friendly advances which he had made to me. I persuaded myself that it was at their instigation that he had urged me to enter into negotiations with Néaulme; that it was through the latter that they had got hold of the first sheets of my work; and that they had subsequently found means to make Duchesne stop printing, and perhaps to get possession of my manuscript, in order to work upon it at their leisure, until my death should leave them free to publish their travesty of it. I had always felt, in spite of Father Berthier's show of affection, that the Jesuits had no love for me, not only as being an Encyclopaedist, but also because my views were even more hostile to their principles and influence than the unbelief of my colleagues, since atheistic and religious fanaticism, which approach closely in their common intolerance, are even capable of uniting, as they have done in China, and as they do now against myself; whereas rational and moral religion, which takes away all human control over the conscience, deprives of further resource those who claim that power. . . .

I saw nothing but Jesuits everywhere, without reflecting that they, on the eve of their annihilation, and fully occupied with their own defence, had something else to do than to intrigue against the printing of a book in which they were not concerned. I am wrong, however, in saying "without reflection"; I certainly did think of it. M. de Malesherbes himself

even took care to make the objection, as soon as he heard of
my fantastic idea; but, owing to another of these caprices, to
which a man is subject who attempts, in the bosom of obscurity, to judge of secret and important affairs of which he
knows nothing, I refused to believe that the Jesuits were in
danger, and I regarded such rumours as a ruse on their part
to lull their adversaries to sleep. Their past and ever consistent successes gave me so terrible an idea of their power,
that I already lamented the degradation of the Parliament. I
knew that M. de Choiseul had studied amongst the Jesuits,
that Madame de Pompadour was not on bad terms with them,
and that their league with the favourites and ministers had
always been considered of great service to both parties against
their common enemies. The Court appeared to be neutral; and
feeling convinced that, if the society one day met with a
severe check, the Parliament would never be strong enough to
give it, I drew from this inaction on the part of the Court the
justification of their confidence and the augury of their
triumph. In short, seeing in all the rumours of the day nothing
but a feint and snares on their part, and believing that, in
their position of security, they had time to attend to everything, I had no doubt that they would soon crush Jansenism,
the Parliament, the Encyclopaedists, and all who had not
submitted to their yoke; and that, if they permitted my book
to appear, it would not be until they had transformed it into
a weapon for themselves, by making use of my name in order
to deceive my readers.

I felt that I was dying. I can scarcely understand how it
was that my extravagant notions did not prove my death-
blow, so terribly was I alarmed at the idea that my memory
would be dishonoured in a work which was my best and most
worthy of me. I never felt such dread of death; and I believe
that, if I had died then, I should have died in a state of utter
despair. . . .

. . . At last the printing was resumed and proceeded more
rapidly; and I have never known why it had been suspended.
M. de Malesherbes took the trouble to come to Montmorency
to calm my agitation, and he succeeded. My perfect confidence

in his uprightness, having overcome the derangement of my
poor head, rendered effectual every effort on his part to restore its equilibrium. After what he had seen of my distress
and frenzy, it was natural that he should consider that I
greatly deserved to be pitied. The talk of the philosophical
cabal, by which he was surrounded, repeated over and over
again, came back to his mind. When I went to live at the
Hermitage, they publicly declared, as I have already said,
that I should not be able to stand it long. When they saw
that I persevered, they said that it was due to obstinacy,
pride, and shame at the idea of giving in, but that I was
really wearied to death, and was very unhappy. M. de
Malesherbes believed it and wrote to me. Feeling deeply this
mistake on the part of a man whom I so highly esteemed, I
wrote to him four letters one after the other, in which I explained the true reasons for my conduct, and at the same time
faithfully described my tastes, my character, and all the
feelings of my inmost heart. These four letters, written off-
hand, hurriedly, with a single stroke of the pen, and which I
never even read over, are perhaps the only compositions
which I have ever written with perfect ease during the whole
of my life, and, what is even more astonishing, at a time
when I was suffering deeply and was in a state of the utmost
depression. Feeling my strength giving way, I sighed at
the thought that I was leaving behind, in the minds of honourable men, so unjust an opinion of myself; and, by means of
the sketch hastily thrown off in these four letters, I attempted,
in some degree, to supply the place of the Memoirs which I
had proposed to write.

[The "Contrat Social" appears a few weeks before
"Émile."]

At that time, I certainly had as much reason as ever to
reckon upon the kindness of M. de Luxembourg, and his
support in case of necessity; for he never gave me more
frequent or more touching proofs of his friendship. During
his Easter visit, my melancholy state of health did not allow
me to go to the château; but he never let a day pass without
paying me a visit, and, seeing that my sufferings were inces-

sant, he at last persuaded me to let him send for Brother
Côme. He brought him to me himself, and had the courage,
certainly rare and meritorious in a great nobleman, to remain
with me during the operation, which was a long and painful
one. However, it was only a question of being probed; but
I had never been able to submit to it, even at the hands of
Morand, who made the attempt several times, but always
unsuccessfully. Brother Côme, whose skill and lightness of
hand was unequalled, at last succeeded in introducing a
very small probe, after having caused me great suffering for
more than two hours, during which I did my utmost to restrain my cries, to avoid distressing the tender-hearted Marquis. On the first examination, Brother Côme thought he had
discovered a large stone, and told me so; on the second, he
could not find it. After having made a second and third
examination, with a care and exactitude which made the time
seem very long, he declared that there was no stone at all,
but that the prostate gland was scirrhous and abnormally
swollen. He found the bladder large and in good condition,
and he ended by expressing his opinion that I should suffer greatly, and that I should live for a long time. If the second prediction is fulfilled as completely as the first, my sufferings are not nearly at an end.

Thus, after having been successively treated for so many
years for complaints which I never had, I ended by learning
that my malady, incurable without being fatal, would last
as long as myself. . . .

Freed from imaginary evils, more cruel than those which
were real, I endured the latter more patiently. There is no
doubt that, since that time, I have suffered much less from
my malady than I had ever done before, and I never remember that I owe this relief to M. de Luxembourg, without
being stirred to fresh emotion when I think of him. . . .

"Émile" at last appeared, without my having heard any
more about fresh proofs or other difficulties. Before its publication, M. de Luxembourg asked me to return all the letters
from M. de Malesherbes, which had reference to the work.
My great confidence in both, my feeling of perfect security,

prevented me from considering the extraordinary, and even alarming, aspect of this request. I gave up the letters, with the exception of one or two which had inadvertently been left in some books. . . .

The publication of this book did not take place with the outburst of approval which had followed that of all my other writings. Never did a work meet with such praise from private individuals, and so little approbation from the public. What those who were most capable of judging said and wrote to me about it, confirmed me in the opinion that it was the best, as well as the most important, of my writings. But all this was told me with the most curious circumspection, as if it had been a matter of importance to keep all favourable opinion of it secret. Madame de Boufflers, who declared to me that the author of such a work deserved statues and the homage of all mankind, without any ceremony begged me, at the end of her note, to send it back to her. D'Alembert, who wrote to me to the effect that the work decided my superiority, and was bound to place me at the head of all men of letters, did not sign his note, although he had signed all those which he had previously written to me. Duclos, a friend on whom I could depend, an upright but cautious man, and who thought highly of the work, avoided expressing any opinion of it in writing. La Condamine fell upon the "Profession of Faith," and beat about the bush. Clairaut, in his letter, confined himself to the same part of the book, but was not afraid to declare how greatly he had been touched by reading it: he told me, in so many words, that the perusal of it had warmed his old soul. Of all those to whom I sent my book, he was the only one who told the world, openly and unreservedly, how highly he thought of it.

Mathas, to whom I had also given a copy before it was on sale, lent it to M. Blaire, Parliamentary Councillor, and father of the Intendant of Strasbourg. M. de Blaire had a country house at Saint-Gratien, and Mathas, who was an old acquaintance, sometimes went to see him when he was able. He made him read "Émile" before it came out. M. de Blaire, on giving it back to him, made the following remark, which was re-

peated to me on the same day: "M. Mathas, this is a very
fine book; but it will soon be spoken of more than is desirable
for the author." When he repeated this to me, I merely
laughed, and saw nothing more in it than the self-importance
of a magistrate, who makes a mystery of everything. All the
disturbing expressions, which were repeated to me, made
equally little impression upon me; and, far from foreseeing
in the least the catastrophe which was close at hand, convinced of the beauty and usefulness of my work, certain that
I was in order in all respects, sure, as I believed I had a right
to be, of all the influence of Madame de Luxembourg, and
even of the favour of Ministers, I congratulated myself upon
the resolution which I had taken—to retire in the midst of my
triumphs, and when I had just crushed all those who were
jealous of me.

One thing alone alarmed me in regard to the publication
of the work, not so much out of consideration of my own
safety as from a desire to quiet my conscience. At the Hermitage and at Montmorency, close to my doors, I had seen with
indignation the vexatious annoyances inflicted, owing to the
jealous care with which the pleasures of princes are guarded,
upon the unfortunate peasants, who are obliged to put up
with the damage caused to their fields by the game, not
venturing to protect themselves further than by making a
noise, and compelled to spend the nights amidst their beans
and peas, beating kettles, drums, and bells, to keep off the
wild boars. A witness of the barbarous severity with which M.
le Comte de Charolois caused these poor people to be treated,
I had made an attack upon this cruel behaviour, towards
the end of "Émile." This was another violation of my principles, which has not remained unpunished. I heard that the
officers of M. le Prince de Conti treated the peasants upon his
estates with hardly less cruelty. I trembled for fear that this
Prince, towards whom I entertained the deepest feelings of
respect and gratitude, might apply to himself the attack which
a feeling of revolted humanity had caused me to make upon
his uncle, and be offended at it. However, as my conscience
completely justified me on this point, I quieted myself by its

testimony, and I was right. At least, I have never heard that this great Prince paid the slightest attention to this passage, which was written long before I had the honour of his acquaintance. . . .

The dull murmur which precedes the storm began to make itself heard. All keen-witted persons saw clearly that, in regard to my book and myself, some plot was brewing, which would soon explode. As for me, my feeling of security and stupidity were so great, that, far from having any idea of my misfortune, I did not even suspect the cause, after I had felt the effects of it. My opponents began by cleverly spreading the idea that, while the Jesuits were severely treated, no favouritism could be shown towards books and authors who attacked religion. I was reproached for having put my name to "Émile," as if I had not put it to all my other writings, against which nothing had been said. . . .

I remained calm. The rumours increased and soon assumed a different character. The public, and, above all, the Parliament, appeared irritated by my calmness. At the end of a few days the excitement became terrible; the threats changed their object, and were addressed directly to myself. Members of Parliament might be heard saying quite openly, that it was no good to burn the books; that the authors ought to be burnt as well. As for the booksellers, not a word was said about them. The first time that these expressions of opinion, more worthy of an inquisitor of Goa than of a senator, were repeated to me, I had no doubt that they were an invention of the Holbachians intended to frighten me and drive me out of of the country. I laughed at this childish trick, and said to myself that if they had known the real state of things, they would have sought some other means of frightening me; but at length the rumour became so pronounced, that it was clear that it was serious. M. and Madame de Luxembourg had made their second visit to Montmorency somewhat earlier than usual this year, and were there at the beginning of June. I heard very little said about my new books, in spite of the stir which they created in Paris; and neither M. nor Madame de Luxembourg said a word to me on the matter.

One morning, however, when I was alone with M. de Luxembourg, he asked me, "Have you said anything against M. de Choiseul in the 'Contrat Social'?" Starting back with surprise, I replied, "I? No, certainly not; that I swear to you; on the contrary, I have pronounced upon him, with a pen which is not given to flattery, the most splendid eulogy that a minister has ever received." With that, I quoted the whole passage to him. "And in 'Émile'?" he went on to ask. "Not a word," I answered; "there is not even a single word in it which refers to him." "Ah!" said he, with more vivacity than usual, "you ought to have done the same thing in the other book, or to have made yourself clearer." "I thought that I had done so," I answered; "I esteemed him highly enough for that." He was on the point of speaking again; I saw that he was ready to unbosom himself; but he checked himself and remained silent. Oh! the misery of a courtier's diplomacy, which, even in the best of hearts, overpowers friendship itself!

This conversation, although brief, enlightened me upon my situation, at least, in regard to certain things, and made me understand that it was certainly I who was attacked. I deplored this unheard-of fatality, which turned to my disadvantage all the good that I said and did. However, believing that I had Madame de Luxembourg and M. de Malesherbes to protect me in this matter, I did not see how it would be possible for my enemies to thrust them aside and reach me; for, in addition, I felt from that moment that it would no longer be a question of equity and justice, and that no one would trouble himself to examine whether I was really right or wrong. However, the storm roared louder and louder. Even Néaulme himself, in his wearisome chatter, showed me how greatly he regretted having had anything to do with this work, and the certainty which he seemed to entertain of the fate which threatened both the book and its author. One thing, however, still comforted me. I found Madame de Luxembourg so calm, so contented, so cheerful even, that she must have known what she was about, since she did not show the least anxiety on my account, did not utter a word of sympathy or apology, and regarded the turn the affair was taking with as much coolness as if she had nothing to do with it, and had never taken the least interest in myself. The only thing that surprised me was, that she said nothing at all to me. It appeared to me that she ought to have said something. Madame de Boufflers seemed more uneasy. She came to and fro in an agitated manner, showed great activity, assured me that M. le Prince de Conti was also exerting himself to ward off the blow which was being prepared for me, and which she attributed simply to the present state of affairs, in which it was of importance to the Parliament not to give the Jesuits an opportunity of accusing it of indifference in religious matters. She seemed, however, to have little confidence in the success of the Prince's efforts or her own. The drift of all her conversations, which were more alarming than reassuring, was the same: to induce me to leave the country and retire to England, where she offered to find me several friends, amongst others the celebrated Hume, with whom she had long been acquainted. . . .

Seeing that, although this observation had made a certain impression upon me, I could not yet bring myself to decide upon flight, she spoke to me of a few weeks at the Bastille as a means of escaping from the jurisdiction of the Parliament, which does not interfere with State prisoners. I made no objection to this singular favour, provided that it was not solicited in my name. As she said no more about it, I afterwards assumed that she had only proposed the idea in order to try me, and that an expedient, which would have put an end to everything, was not desired.

A few days afterwards, M. le Maréchal received from the *curé* of Deuil, a friend of Grimm and Madame d'Epinay, a letter, containing the information, which he declared came from a trustworthy source, that the Parliament intended to proceed against me with extreme severity, and that, on a certain day, which he mentioned, a warrant would be issued for my apprehension. I regarded this as an invention on the part of the Holbachians; I knew that the Parliament paid great attention to forms, and that it would be an infringement of them all, to commence on this occasion with a warrant of arrest, before it had been judicially established whether I acknowledged the book and was really its author. I said to Madame de Boufflers: "It is only in the case of those crimes which disturb the public safety, that a warrant is issued, upon a simple information, for the arrest of the accused, for fear they may escape punishment. But, when it is desired to punish an offence like mine, which deserves honours and rewards, the custom is, to proceed against the book, and to avoid attacking the author as much as possible." Upon this, she pointed out to me a very subtle distinction, which I had forgotten, in order to prove to me that it was a favour to me to issue a warrant, instead of summoning me to be heard. On the following day, I received a letter from Guy, in which he informed me that, having been with M. le Procureur-général the same day, he had seen upon his desk the rough draft of an indictment against "Émile" and its author. Observe that the said Guy was a partner of Duchesne, who had printed the work, and also, having no anxiety on his own account, gave this information to the author out of charity. One may imagine how likely it all appeared to me! It was so simple, so natural, that a bookseller, when admitted to an audience of the *procureur-général*, should quietly read the manuscripts and rough drafts scattered over his desk! Madame de Boufflers and others assured me that it was true. In consequence of the absurdities which were being continually dinned into my ears, I was inclined to believe that everybody had gone mad.

Feeling sure that, under all this, there was some secret which was being withheld from me, I quietly awaited the issue of events, having full confidence in my upright behaviour and innocence throughout the affair, and being only too happy, whatever persecution might await me, to be summoned to the honour of suffering for the truth's sake. Far from being afraid, and keeping myself concealed, I went every day to the château, and took my usual walk in the afternoon. On the 8th of June, the day before the issue of the decree, I took it in company with two professors belonging to the Oratory, Father Alamanni and Father Mandard. We took some provisions with us to Champeaux, where we enjoyed a hearty meal. We had forgotten to take glasses, and supplied their place with stalks of rye, through which we sucked the wine from the bottles, eagerly picking out the thickest stalks, in order to see which could suck the hardest. I have never been so gay in my life.

I have mentioned how I suffered from sleeplessness in my youth. Since then, I had accustomed myself to read in bed every night, until I found my eyes getting heavy. Then I put out my candle, and tried to doze for a few minutes, which did not last long. My usual evening reading was the Bible, and in this manner I have read the whole of it through at least five or six times. On this particular evening, finding myself more wakeful than usual, I continued my reading for a longer time, and read the whole book, which ends with the history of the Levite of Ephraim—the Book of Judges, if I am not mistaken, for I have never looked at it since then. This history greatly affected me, and I was pondering over it in a half-dreamy state, from which I was suddenly roused by a noise and a light. The latter was carried by Thérèse, who was showing the way to M. la Roche, who, seeing me start up abruptly, said to me, "Do not be alarmed: I come from Madame la Maréchale, who has written to you herself, and also sends you a letter from M. le Prince de Conti." Inside Madame de Luxembourg's letter I found another, which had been brought to her by a special messenger from the Prince, containing the information that, in spite of all his efforts, it had been decided to proceed against me with the utmost rigour of the law. "The excitement," so he wrote, "is very great: nothing can avert the blow: the Court demands it, the Parliament wills it: at seven o'clock to-morrow morning the warrant of arrest will be issued, and executed immediately. I have obtained an assurance that, if he makes his escape, he will not be pursued; but, if he persists in his wish to allow himself to be taken, then he will be arrested." La Roche besought me, in Madame de Luxembourg's name, to get up and go and consult with her. It was two o'clock: she had just gone to bed. "She is waiting for you," he added, "and will not go to sleep until she has seen you." I hurriedly dressed myself, and hastened to her.

For the first time in her life she appeared to me agitated. Her anxiety touched me. In this moment of surprise, in the middle of the night, I myself was not free from excitement, but when I saw her I forgot myself, and thought only of her and the melancholy part which she would play if I allowed myself to be taken; for, while I felt that I had courage enough never to speak anything but the truth, even though it was bound to injure and ruin me, I did not feel that I had sufficient presence of mind or cleverness, or even, perhaps, sufficient firmness, to avoid compromising her, if I was hard pressed. This decided me to sacrifice my reputation for the sake of her peace of mind, and, on this occasion, to do for her, that which nothing would have induced me to do for myself. The moment my mind was made up, I told her, as I did not wish to depreciate the value of my sacrifice, by allowing it to be purchased from me. I am convinced that she could not have been mistaken as to my motives, but she did not say a single word to me which showed that she appreciated them. I was so shocked at this indifference that I even hesitated whether I should not draw back, but M. de Luxembourg appeared upon the scene, and Madame de Boufflers arrived from Paris a few moments afterwards. They did what Madame de Luxembourg ought to have done. I allowed myself to be flattered, I was ashamed to go back on my word, and the only question remaining was, where I should go, and when I should start. M. de Luxembourg proposed that I should stay a few days at his house, *incognito,* which would give me more time to consider and decide upon my course of action. I would not agree to this, any more than to the suggestion that I should go secretly to the Temple. I persisted in my intention of setting out the same day, rather than remain in concealment anywhere.

Feeling that I had secret and powerful enemies in the kingdom, I decided that, in spite of my attachment for France, I had to leave it to ensure my being let alone. My first impulse was to retire to Geneva, but a moment's reflection was sufficient to dissuade me from committing so great an act of folly. I knew that the French Ministry, which had even greater power in Geneva than in Paris, would not leave me in peace in one of these two cities any more than in the other, if it was determined to persecute me. I knew that the "Discours sur l'Inégalité" had aroused against me, in the Council, a feeling of hatred, which was the more dangerous, as that body did not venture to show it openly.

[He knows, too, that Dr. Tronchin is lying in wait in Geneva and that all its inhabitants are gnawed with jealousy of him. He decides on Berne.]

Madame de Boufflers strongly disapproved of this resolution, and made fresh efforts to persuade me to cross over to England. She did not shake my determination. I have never liked England or the English, and all the eloquence of Madame de Boufflers, far from overcoming my dislike, only seemed to increase it, without my knowing why.

[M. de Luxembourg offers to keep his papers, and to burn some. Rousseau trustingly accepts, then bids Thérèse adieu.]

La Roche brought her to the château, without telling her anything; she believed that I was already far away; when she saw me, she uttered a piercing cry, and flung herself into my arms. Oh, friendship, union of hearts, intercourse, and intimacy! During this sweet and cruel moment all the happy, tender, and peaceful days which we had spent in company, crowding together, made me feel the more keenly the anguish of our first separation, after we had rarely lost sight of each other for a single day, during a period of nearly seventeen years. M. de Luxembourg, who witnessed our embrace, was unable to restrain his tears, and left us alone. . . .

When I embraced her at the moment of separation, I was conscious of a most singular emotion, and I said to her, with a fervour, which was, alas! only too prophetic: "My child, you must arm yourself with courage. You have shared the prosperity of my happy days; it now remains for you, since you desire it, to share my misery. You must expect nothing but insults and affliction if you follow me. The lot, which begins for me on this melancholy day, will attend me until my last hour."

Nothing further remained for me to do, except to think about my departure. The officers of justice were to have arrived at ten o'clock. It was four o'clock in the afternoon when I started, and they had not yet arrived. It had been settled that I should travel by the post; I had no conveyance. M. le Maréchal made me a present of a cabriolet, and lent me horses and a postillion as far as the first post, where, thanks to the arrangements he had made, no difficulty was made about providing me with horses.

As I had not dined at table, and had not shown myself in the château, the ladies came to say good-bye to me in the *entresol*, where I had spent the day. Madame la Maréchale embraced me several times, with every appearance of melancholy; but I no longer perceived in her embraces the heartiness of those which she had lavished upon me two or three years before. Madame de Boufflers also embraced me and spoke very kindly to me. . . .

M. le Maréchal did not open his mouth; he was as pale as death. He persisted in accompanying me as far as the conveyance, which was waiting for me at the watering-place. We crossed the garden without uttering a word. I had a key to the park, with which I opened the gate; after which, instead of putting it back into my pocket, I gave it to him without a word. He took it with surprising eagerness, of which I have been unable to avoid thinking frequently since then. I have rarely in my life experienced a more bitter moment than that of this separation. Our embrace was long and silent; we both felt that it was a last farewell.

Between La Barre and Montmorency I met, in a hired coach, four men dressed in black, who saluted me with a smile. From what Thérèse afterwards told me concerning the appearance of the officers, the hour of their arrival, and the manner in which they behaved, I have always been convinced that it was they whom I met; especially as I subsequently heard that, instead of the warrant having been issued against me at seven o'clock, as I had been informed, it had

not been put in force until midday. I had to pass right through
Paris. There is not much facility for concealment in an open
carriage. In the streets, I saw several persons who saluted me
as if they knew me, but I did not recognise one of them. . . .

In abandoning myself to the reflections upon all that had
recently happened to me, which presented themselves to my
mind, I had ample resources against weariness during my
journey; but this suited neither the bent of my mind nor the
inclinations of my heart. It is astonishing how easily I forget
misfortunes, when once they are past, however recent they
may be. The recollection of them grows weaker and finally
disappears without difficulty as soon as they have happened,
to the same extent as the thought of them, as long as they are
in the future, alarms and troubles me. My cruel imagination,
which tortures itself incessantly in anticipating misfortunes
which do not yet exist, distracts my memory, and prevents me
from recalling to mind those which are past. No further precautions are possible against what has happened, and it is
useless to trouble oneself about it. In a manner I exhaust my
misfortunes in advance. The greater my suffering in foreseeing them, the more easily I forget them; while, on the
contrary, incessantly occupied with the thought of my past
happiness, I recall it and, so to speak, chew the cud of it to
such an extent that, when I desire it, I am able to enjoy it
over again. . . .

I do not know whether my heart can conquer its hatred, for
it has never felt any; and I think too little about my enemies
to have the merit of forgiving them. I will not say to what
extent they torment themselves, in order to torment me. I am
at their mercy, they have absolute power, they make use of it.
There is only one thing beyond their power, which I defy
them to do. Although they torment themselves about me, they
cannot compel me to torment myself about them.

The day after my departure, I had so completely forgotten
all that had recently happened—the Parliament, Madame de
Pompadour, M. de Choiseul, Grimm, D'Alembert, their plots,
and their accomplices—that I should never have thought of it

again, had it not been for the precautions which I was obliged to take. . . .

On entering the territory of Berne I ordered a halt. I got out of the carriage, flung myself upon the ground, kissed and embraced it, and, in my delight, cried out: "O Heaven, protector of virtue, I offer my praise to thee! I set foot in a land of liberty." Thus it is that, in the blind confidence of my hopes, I have always been seized with passionate fondness for that which was destined to bring misfortune upon me. The surprised postillion thought I was mad. I got into the carriage again, and, a few hours afterwards, I had the pure and lively satisfaction of being pressed in the arms of the worthy Roguin. Ah! let us take breath for a few moments with this worthy host! I must recover my courage and strength; I shall soon have need of both.

It is not without reason that, in this narrative, I have described in detail all the circumstances which I have been able to recollect. Although they may not seem very clear in themselves, they may throw light upon the course of events, when the reader once holds the thread of the plot; for instance, although they do not give the first idea of the problem which I have to propose, they afford considerable assistance in solving it.

If we assume that, in order to carry out the plot which was directed against me, my removal was absolutely necessary, then, in order to bring it about, everything was bound to happen almost exactly as it did. But if, instead of allowing myself to be terrified by Madame de Luxembourg's nocturnal embassy and disturbed by her anxiety, I had continued to hold out as I had begun; and if, instead of remaining at the château, I had returned from it to my bed and slept quietly until morning, would the warrant have been put into execution just the same? This is an important question, upon the answer to which depends the answer to many others; and, in order to investigate it, it is important to observe the hour of the decree of arrest that was threatened and the hour of its actual issue. This is a homely but expressive example of the importance of the most trifling details in the exposition of facts whose secret causes are being sought, in order to discover them by a process of induction.

BOOK TWELVE

HERE commences the work of darkness, in which, for eight years past, I have been entombed, without ever having been able, in spite of all my efforts, to penetrate its frightful obscurity. In the abyss of misfortune in which I am submerged, I feel the strokes of the blows which are directed against me. I perceive their immediate instrument, but I cannot see either the hand which guides them or the means which it employs. Shame and misfortune fall upon me as if of themselves, and unawares. When my heart, torn with grief, gives vent to lamentation, I seem like a man who complains without reason, and the authors of my ruin have discovered the incomprehensible art of making the public the accomplice of their plot, without their suspecting it or perceiving its effect. Therefore, while narrating the events which concern me, the treatment which I have suffered, and all that has happened to me, I am not in a position to trace them back to the moving spirit, or to assign the causes, while stating the facts. These first causes are all indicated in the three preceding books. All the interests that concern me and all the secret motives are there set forth. But it is impossible for me to explain, even conjecturally, how these various causes are combined in order to bring about the strange events of my life. If, amongst my readers, there are any sufficiently generous to desire to fathom these mysteries and discover the truth, let them carefully read again the three preceding books, let them make use of the information within their reach in dealing with each fact they read of in what follows, let them go back from intrigue to intrigue, from agent to agent, until they come to the prime movers of all. I know well what will be the result of their inquiries, but I myself am lost in the dark and tortuous windings of the subterranean paths which will lead them to it.

I did not long remain in doubt as to the reception which awaited me at Geneva, in case I felt inclined to return there. My book was burned there, and a warrant was issued against me on the 18th of June, that is to say, nine days after it had been issued in Paris. In this second decree, so many incredible absurdities were heaped together, and the ecclesiastical edict was so distinctly violated, that at first I refused to believe the news when it reached me, and, when it was actually confirmed, I trembled lest so manifest and crying an infringement of every law, commencing with that of common sense, should turn Geneva upside down. But I need not have disturbed myself; everything remained quiet. If there was any disturbance amongst the people, it was only directed against me, and I was publicly treated by all the town-gossips and pedants like a pupil threatened with a flogging for having said his catechism badly.

These two decrees gave the signal for the cry of execration which went up against me throughout Europe with unexampled fury. All the newspapers, journals, and pamphlets sounded a most terrible note of alarm. The French especially— that gentle, polite, and generous people, who so pride themselves on their good-breeding and respect for the unfortunate—suddenly forgetting their favourite virtues, distinguished themselves by the number and violence of the insults with which they vied with one another in overwhelming me. I was called an infidel, an atheist, a lunatic, a madman, a wild beast, a wolf. The next manager of the *Journal de Trévoux** made a side attack upon my pretended wolfishness, which was a fairly convincing proof of his own. In short, it almost seemed as if people in Paris were afraid of coming into collision with the police, if, when publishing a book upon any subject whatever, they omitted to interlard it with insults against myself. Seeking in vain for the cause of this universal animosity, I was ready to believe that all the world had gone mad. What!

* A Jesuit newspaper.

the compiler of the "Paix Perpetuelle" the promoter of discord! the editor of the "Vicaire Savoyard" an infidel! the author of the "New Héloïse" a wolf! the author of "Émile" a madman! Good heavens! what then should I have been if I had published the work upon "L'Esprit," or something of the same kind? And yet, in the storm which burst upon the head of the author * of this book, the public, instead of uniting its voice to that of his persecutors, avenged him by its eulogies. Compare his book and mine, the different reception which they have met with, the manner in which the two authors have been treated in the different countries of Europe, and then find, if possible, reasons for these differences which can satisfy a sensible man. That is all I ask, then I will say no more.

[He takes his own lodging, sends for Thérèse, but is forced to flee from the canton.]

My difficulty was, to know where to go. Geneva and France were closed to me, and I clearly foresaw that, in this matter, everyone would be eager to imitate his neighbour's example.

Madame Boy de la Tour proposed to me to take up my quarters in an empty furnished house, belonging to her son, in the village of Motiers, in Val-de-Travers, in the county of Neufchâtel. I only had to cross a mountain to get there. The offer was the more opportune, since, in the territory of the King of Prussia, I should naturally be sheltered from persecution; at least, religion could not be alleged as an excuse for it. But a secret objection, which it did not become me to express, was calculated to make me hesitate. The innate love of justice, by which my heart was always consumed, united to my secret liking for France, had inspired me with aversion for the King of Prussia, who, in his principles and conduct, appeared to me to trample underfoot all respect for natural law and human obligations. Amongst the framed engravings, with which I had decorated the walls of my turret at Montmorency, was a portrait of this Prince, underneath which I had written a distich, which concluded as follows:

* Helvétius.

"Il pense en philosophe, et se conduit en roi." *

This line, which, proceeding from any other pen, would have been high praise, contained, coming from mine, a meaning which was by no means ambiguous, and which, besides, was only too clearly explained by the line which preceded it.† My numerous visitors had all seen this distich. The Chevalier de Lorenzi had even copied it for D'Alembert, and I had no doubt that the latter had taken care to make use of it to present me in a favourable light to the King. I had further aggravated my first offence by a passage in "Émile," in which, under the name of Adrastus, King of the Daunians, I had sufficiently indicated whom I had in view. I knew that the remark had not escaped the critics, since Madame de Boufflers had on several occasions mentioned the subject. I therefore felt sure of being inscribed in red ink on the registers of the King of Prussia; and supposing, besides, that his principles were such as I had ventured to attribute to him, my writings and their author could not fail to meet with his disapproval; for it is well known that the wicked and tyrants have always conceived a deadly hatred towards me, even without knowing me, on a simple perusal of my works.

However, I ventured to throw myself upon his mercy, and I believed that I was running but little risk. I knew that the baser passions only overmaster the weak, and have but little hold upon minds of a strong stamp, such as I had always recognised in his. I argued that it was part of his plan of government to show himself magnanimous on such an occasion, and that it was not beyond the reach of his character to be so in reality. I argued that the desire of a mean and easy vengeance would never for a moment counterbalance in him the love of glory; and, putting myself in his place, I thought it not impossible that he might take advantage of circum-

---

* He thinks as a philosopher, and acts as a king.

† "La gloire, l'intérêt, voilà son Dieu, sa loi." From a note in the Firmin-Didot edition we learn that this line did not really precede the one quoted above. The latter was underneath the portrait, the other verse was written at the back.

stances to overwhelm with the weight of his generosity the man who had ventured to think ill of him. I accordingly went to settle at Motiers, with a confidence, the value of which I considered him capable of appreciating. I said to myself, "When Jean-Jacques raises himself to the level of Coriolanus, will Frederic show himself lower than the Volscian general?"

[He hesitates about Thérèse's joining him, for fear of incurring an obligation towards her.]

I must speak without reserve. I have never concealed either my poor mamma's faults or my own. I must not show greater favour to Thérèse either; and, pleased as I am to render honour to one who is so dear to me, neither do I wish to conceal her faults, if so be that an involuntary change in the heart's affections is really a fault. I had long since observed that her affection for me had cooled. I felt that she no longer was towards me what she had been in our best days; and I felt it the more, as I was still the same towards her. I was conscious again of an unpleasantness, the effects of which I had formerly felt with mamma; and the effect was the same with Thérèse. Let us not look for perfections which are not to be found in nature; it would be the same with any other woman whatsoever. The course of action I had taken in regard to my children, however rational it had appeared to me, had not always left my heart in peace. While thinking over my "Traité de l'Education," I felt that I had neglected duties from which nothing could excuse me. My remorse at length became so keen, that it almost extorted from me a public confession of my error at the beginning of "Émile"; and the allusion itself is so obvious in a certain passage, that it is surprising to me how anyone, after having read it, can have had the courage to reproach me. My situation, however, was at that time the same, and even aggravated by the animosity of my enemies, who only sought to find me at fault. I was afraid of a repetition; and, not desiring to run the risk of it, I preferred to condemn myself to strict continence, than to expose Thérèse to the risk of finding herself in the same condition again. Besides, I had observed that intercourse with women distinctly aggravated my ill-health; the corresponding vice, of which I have never been able to cure myself completely, appeared to me to produce less injurious results. These two reasons combined caused me to form resolutions which I had sometimes been very inconsistent in keeping, but in which I had persevered with greater firmness for the last three or four years. Since then I had observed a coldness on the part of Thérèse; she had the same attachment for me from a feeling of duty, no longer from love. This naturally made our relationship less pleasant, and I thought that, feeling sure that I should continue to look after her wherever she might be, she would perhaps prefer to remain in Paris than to wander through the world with me. However, she had exhibited such grief at our separation, she had exacted from me such positive promises that we should come together again, she had so strongly expressed a desire to that effect since my departure, both to the Prince de Conti and M. de Luxembourg, that, far from having the courage to speak to her of separation, I could scarcely bear to think of it myself; and, when I once felt how utterly impossible it was for me to do without her, my **only** thought was to call her back to me immediately. I accordingly wrote to her to set out; she came. It was hardly two months since I had left her; but it was our first separation, after the many years we had been together. We had both felt it cruelly. What a shock, when we embraced each other! How sweet are tears of tenderness and joy! How my heart revels in them! Why have I been permitted to shed so few!

On my arrival at Motiers, I had written to Lord Keith, Marshal of Scotland, Governor of Neufchâtel, to inform him that I had taken refuge in His Majesty's territory, and to ask him for his protection. He replied with the well-known generosity which I expected from him. He invited me to go and see him. I went with M. Martinet, lord of the manor of Val-de-Travers, who stood high in his Excellency's esteem. The venerable appearance of this illustrious and virtuous Scotsman made a powerful impression upon my heart, and that very moment was the commencement of that strong attachment between us, which on my part has always remained the same, and would still be the same on his, had not the traitors, who have robbed me of all the consolations of life, profited by my absence to deceive him, weakened as he is by old age, and to misrepresent me in his eyes.

[Keith, in exile because of his support of the Stuart pretender, was gruff but sincere. They become close friends.]

What tears of tenderness I have often shed on my way, while thinking of the paternal kindness, the amiable virtues, and the gentle philosophy of this worthy old man! I called him my father, and he called me his child. These sweet names give a partial idea of the attachment which united us, but they do not give an idea of the need of each other which we felt, and of our continued desire to be together. He insisted upon putting me up at the château of Colombier, and for a long time pressed me to take up my quarters permanently in the apartment which I occupied. At last, I told him that I was freer at my own house, and that I preferred to spend my time in going to see him. He approved of my frankness, and said no more about the matter. O my good lord! O my worthy father! how my heart is still stirred by emotion when I think of you! Oh! the barbarians! What a blow have they dealt me in separating you from me! But, no, no, great man: you are, and always will be, the same for me, who am ever the same! They have deceived you, but they have not altered you.

[Rousseau writes to Frederic the Great, urging him bluntly to turn to peaceful glories.]

Shortly after my establishment at Motiers-Travers, having received every possible assurance that I should be left in peace, I assumed the Armenian costume. This was not a new idea of mine; it had often occurred to me in the course of my life, and it often occurred to me again at Montmorency, where the constant use of bougies, which frequently compelled me to keep my room, made me sensible of the advantages of a long garment. The chance afforded by an Armenian tailor, who frequently came on a visit to a relation at Montmorency, tempted me to take advantage of it, in order to assume this new costume, in spite of what people might say, to which I paid but little heed. However, before adopting this new outfit, I desired to have the advice of Madame de Luxembourg, who strongly advised me to do so. I accordingly procured a little Armenian wardrobe; but the storm, which was roused against me, made me put off wearing it until the times were calmer, and it was not until several months later that, being obliged by fresh attacks of my complaint to have recourse to bougies, I thought that I might, without risk, assume this dress at Motiers, especially after having consulted the pastor of the place, who told me that I could wear it even in church without giving offence. I accordingly put on the jacket, caftan, fur cap, and girdle; and, after having been present at divine service in it, I saw no impropriety in wearing it in the presence of my Lord Marshal. His Excellency, when he saw me thus attired, said, by way of compliment, "*Salaam alek*"; this ended the matter, and I never afterwards wore any other dress.

Having entirely abandoned literature, I only thought of leading a quiet and peaceful life, as far as it depended upon myself. When alone, I have never known what it is to feel weary, even when I am entirely unemployed; my imagination fills up every void, and is alone sufficient to occupy me. It is only the idle gossip of a room, when people sit opposite each other, moving nothing but their tongues, that I have never been able to endure. When walking or moving, I can put up with it; the feet and eyes are at least employed; but, to remain with folded arms, talking about the weather and the flies buzzing round, or, what is worse, exchanging compliments, that is to me unendurable torture. That I might not live quite like a savage, I took it into my head to learn to make laces. I took my cushion with me on my visits, or, like the women, I worked at my door, and talked with the passers-by.

[The clergy stirs up the municipal authorities and the people against him. He asks permission to partake of Holy Communion.]

At the moment when I least expected it, M. de Montmoulin came to tell me, not only that he was willing to admit me to the Communion, under the condition for which I had stipu-

lated, but, more than this, that he and his elders considered it
a great honour to have me as one of the members of their
flock. I was never so surprised in my life, and nothing has
ever afforded me greater consolation. It appeared to me a
most gloomy fate, to live always isolated in the world, especially in time of adversity. In the midst of so many proscrip-
tions and persecutions, I found the greatest consolation in
being able to say to myself, At least I am amongst my
brethren; and I went to Communion with a heart greatly
moved and affected to tears, which was perhaps the prepa-
ration most acceptable to God that one could take to His
table.

[Attacks continue against him in the French press, and he
is censured by the Sorbonne. In 1763, the Archbishop of
Paris writes an episcopal letter against him, to which he pub-
lishes a reply. Desiring to stay at Motiers, he takes up his
"Dictionary of Music" again.]

My books, which had recently been sent on to me, furnished me with the means of finishing this work: my papers,
which were sent at the same time, enabled me to start upon
my Memoirs, to which I intended henceforth to devote my
sole attention. I began by copying some letters in a collection,
to serve as a guide to my memory in the order of events and
dates. I had already picked out those which I intended to
keep for this purpose, and they were arranged in an almost
unbroken series for the last ten years. However, while arranging them for copying, I found a gap which surprised me.
This embraced a period of nearly six months, from October,
1756, to the following March. I perfectly remembered having
included in my collection a number of letters from Diderot,
Deleyre, Madame d'Epinay, Madame Chenonceaux, and
others, which bridged over this gap and could no longer be
found. What had become of them? Had anyone touched my
papers during the few months they had remained at the
Hôtel de Luxembourg? This was inconceivable: for I had seen
M. de Luxembourg himself take the key of the room in which
I had deposited them. As several letters from ladies, and all
those from Diderot, were undated, and as I had been obliged

to fill in these dates from memory and, as it were, groping in the dark, in order to arrange these letters in order, I at first thought that I had made some mistakes in dates, and I went over all the letters which were undated, or in which I had myself inserted the dates, to see if I could not find those which were needed to fill up the gap. This attempt was unsuccessful: I found that the gap was a real one, and that the letters had certainly been abstracted. By whom and for what reason? This was beyond my powers of comprehension.

[He attributes the theft to D'Alembert, who wished either to stir up trouble against him, or to use his ideas. Not until seven years later did he suspect the frightful purpose of the theft. In 1764, Rousseau strikes against his foes with his "Lettres écrites de la Montagne." Madame de Luxembourg stops writing to him. M. de Luxembourg dies, and this he calls his first great loss. Then Madame de Warens dies.]

My second loss, more painful and irreparable, was that of the best of women and mothers, who, already burdened with years, and overburdened with misery and infirmities, left this valley of tears for the abode of the blessed, where the pleasing recollection of the good we have done in this world below is its everlasting reward. Go, gentle and kindly soul, to join Fénélon, Bernex, Catinat, and those who, like them, have opened their hearts to genuine charity. Go, taste the fruit of your own, and prepare for your pupil the place which he one day hopes to occupy by your side! Happy, amidst all your misfortunes, since Heaven, by putting an end to them, has spared you the cruel spectacle of his! Afraid of saddening her heart by the narrative of my early disasters, I had not written to her at all after my arrival in Switzerland; but I wrote to M. de Conzié for news of her, and it was from him that I learned that she had ceased to alleviate the sufferings of others, and that her own were over. I, also, shall soon cease to suffer; but, if I did not believe that I should see her again in the next world, my feeble imagination would refuse to entertain the idea of the perfect happiness to which I look forward.

My third and last loss—for I had then no more friends to lose—was that of my Lord Marshal. I did not lose him by death; but, tired of serving ungrateful masters, he left Neuf-châtel, and I have never seen him again. He still lives, and will, I hope, survive me; he still lives, and, thanks to him, all my ties upon earth are not broken; there is still left a man worthy of my friendship, the real value of which consists even more in that friendship which one feels than in that which one inspires; but I have lost the delight with which his friendship filled me, and I can now do no more than reckon him amongst those whom I still love, but with whom I have no further connection. . . .

Before his departure, foreseeing the storm which was about to be raised against me, he sent me, of his own accord, letters of naturalisation, which seemed to be a very safe precaution-ary measure, to make it impossible for me to be driven out of the country. The Corporation of Couvet in Val-de-Travers imitated the Governor's example, and granted me the rights of a native, free of charge, like the first. Thus, being a full citizen in every respect, I was protected against legal expul-sion, even by the Prince; but my enemies have never been able to use legal means in persecuting a man who, more than any other, has always shown the greatest respect for the laws.

[The Abbé de Mably also turns against Jean-Jacques, at-tacks him as a seditious demagogue. Rousseau condemns this sudden blow against a friend in a time of misfortune.]

Some time afterwards appeared the "Dialogues de Pho-cion," which appeared to me a barefaced and shameless com-pilation from my works. When I read the book, I felt that the author had made up his mind in regard to me, and that, from that time forth, I should have no bitterer enemy. I believe that he was never able to forgive me for having written the "Con-trat Social," which was far above his powers, or for the "Paix Perpetuelle," and that he only wanted me to make a selection from the Abbé de Saint-Pierre's writings, because he thought that I should not be so successful in it.

The further I advance in my narrative, the less I am able to preserve its proper order and sequence. The unsettled con-dition of the rest of my life has not left events time to ar-range themselves in succession in my head. They have been too numerous, too mixed up, too disagreeable to be able to be related without confusion. The only strong impression which they have left upon my mind is that of the horrible mystery in which their causes are enveloped, and of the deplorable condition to which they have reduced me. My narrative can only proceed at haphazard, as the ideas come back to me. I remember that, during the time of which I am speaking, being absorbed in my Confessions, I was so imprudent as to talk about them to everybody, never once imagining that anyone had any interest or desire, and, still less, the power, to throw obstacles in the way of this undertaking; and, even had I thought so, I should not have shown any greater discretion, since my disposition renders it absolutely impossible for me to conceal any of my thoughts or feelings. As far as I can judge, the fact of this undertaking becoming known was the real cause of the storm which was raised with the object of driving me out of Switzerland, and delivering me into the hands of those who might prevent me from carrying it out.

I had another work in view, which was regarded with little less disfavour by those who were afraid of the first: this was a general edition of my works. Such an edition appeared to me necessary, in order to establish the authenticity of the books bearing my name, which were really by me, and to put the public in a position to be able to distinguish them from the pseudonymous writings, which my enemies attributed to me, in order to discredit and degrade me. In addition to that, this edition would be a simple and honourable way of insuring a means of subsistence; in fact, it was the only one, for I had abandoned bookmaking, my Memoirs could not be published during my lifetime, I did not earn a penny in any other manner, and was always spending money; so that I saw that I should be at the end of my resources as soon as the profits of my last writings were exhausted. These considerations had strongly inclined me to bring out my "Dictionnaire de Musique," which was as yet incomplete. It had brought me in 100 *louis* in ready money and an annuity of 100 crowns; but it was easy to see that 100 *louis* would not long last a man, who spent more than sixty every year; and an income of 100 crowns was nothing for one, upon whom beggars and others swooped down incessantly like a flock of starlings.

A company of Neufchâtel business-men offered to undertake the collected edition, and a printer or bookseller of Lyons, named Reguillat, somehow or other managed to thrust himself among them in the capacity of manager. An agreement was concluded on reasonable and satisfactory terms, considering the object I had in view. My printed works and others still in manuscript were enough to fill six volumes quarto. I further agreed to exercise a general supervision over the edition, in return for which I was to receive an annuity of 1,600 French *livres*, and 1,000 crowns down.

[1765.]—The agreement was concluded, but not signed, when the "Lettres écrites de la Montagne" appeared. The terrible outburst against this infernal work and its abominable author alarmed the company, and the enterprise fell through. I should compare the effect of this last work to that of the "Lettre sur la Musique Française," only that this letter, while bringing hatred upon me and exposing me to danger, at least left me in possession of esteem and respect. But, after this last work, the inhabitants of Geneva and Versailles seemed to be astonished that a monster like myself was permitted to live. The Little Council, egged on by the French Resident, and instructed by the *Procureur-général*, issued a declaration concerning my work, in which, after stigmatising it in most outrageous terms, that body declared that it was not even worthy of being burned by the hands of the executioner, and added, with a cleverness bordering on burlesque, that it would be impossible for anyone to answer it without disgracing himself, or even to mention it. I wish I could give a copy of this curious document, but, unfortunately, I have not got it, and I do not remember a single word of it. I sincerely wish that some one of my readers, animated by a desire for truth and justice, would read the whole of the "Lettres écrites de la Montagne" over again. I venture to assert that he will recognise the stoical moderation which characterises this work, after the violent and cruel insults which people had just vied with one another in heaping upon the author. But, being unable to reply to the abuse, because it contained none, or to the arguments, because they were unanswerable, my enemies had recourse to the expedient of pretending to be too indignant to answer; and it is certainly true that, if they took irrefutable arguments for insults, they must have felt themselves greatly insulted! . . .

However, the excitement was beginning. The book was publicly burnt—I do not know where.* From Geneva, from Berne, and, perhaps, from Versailles, the focus of disturbance soon shifted to Neufchâtel, especially Val-de-Travers, where, even before the clerical party had given any signs of movement, they had begun to hound the people by underhand means. I venture to say that I ought to have been loved by the people of that country, as I have been by all those amongst whom I have lived. I bestowed alms freely, left none of the needy in my neighbourhood without assistance, never refused to render any service within my power which was consistent with justice, perhaps even making myself too familiar with everybody, and, as far as I was able, I refused every distinction which might have aroused jealousy. All this, however, did not prevent the people, secretly stirred up by someone unknown to me, from gradually becoming infuriated against me, and publicly insulting me in broad daylight, not only in the country and on the roads, but in the open street. Those to whom I had rendered the greatest services were the most virulent; and even people to whom I continued to render them, although they did not venture to show themselves, urged on the rest, and seemed anxious to avenge themselves in this manner for the humiliation of being under an obligation to me. Montmoulin seemed to see nothing and did not as yet show himself; but, as a celebration of the Communion was close at hand, he paid me a visit to advise me not to present myself, at the same time assuring me that he was not at all angry with me, and that he would leave me undisturbed. I thought this a curious kind of compliment. It reminded me of Madame de Boufflers' letter, and I could not imagine to

* In Paris, together with Voltaire's "Dictionnaire Philosophique."

whom it could be a matter of such importance whether I communicated or not. As I considered it would be an act of cowardice to give way to him, and, besides, did not desire to give the people a fresh excuse to raise the cry of "infidel" against me, I bluntly refused to do what he asked, and he went home highly displeased, at the same time giving me to understand that I should be sorry for it.

[Montmoulin summons him to the Consistory to account for his religious beliefs, under pain of excommunication.]

What a lucky circumstance, and what a triumph would it have been for me, if I had been able to speak, and, so to say, had carried my pen in my mouth! With what overwhelming superiority, with what ease should I have overthrown the poor minister in the midst of his six peasants! Greed of authority had caused the Protestant clergy to forget all the principles of the Reformation: all that I needed, in order to remind him of this, and to reduce him to silence, was to explain my first "Lettres de la Montagne," for which they had been foolish enough to censure me. My text was ready, I had only to expand it, and my enemy was reduced to silence. I should not have been so silly as to confine myself to the defensive: it was easy enough for me to take the offensive without his even perceiving it, or being able to protect himself against it. The wretched persons who composed the clerical caste, as thoughtless as they were ignorant, had themselves placed me in the most favorable position I could have desired, for crushing them as I pleased. But—I should have been obliged to speak, and to speak on the spot, to find ideas, turns of expression, and suitable words on the spur of the moment, never to lose my presence of mind or coolness, never to be flustered for a moment. What could I hope from myself—I who felt so strongly my inability to express myself impromptu? I had been most humiliatingly reduced to silence at Geneva, in the presence of an assembly which was entirely favourable to me, and had made up its mind beforehand to approve of everything that I said. Here, it was quite the contrary: I had to do with a person who was prepared to cavil, who substituted cunning for knowledge, who would lay a hundred traps for me before I perceived one, and was fully determined to put me in the wrong, at whatever cost. The more I considered my position, the more perilous it seemed to me; and, convinced that it would be impossible for me to extricate myself with success, I bethought myself of another expedient. I pondered over a speech which I proposed to deliver before the Consistory, in order to challenge its authority and to relieve myself of the necessity of replying. The matter was very simple: I wrote the speech, and proceeded to learn it by heart with unequalled enthusiasm. Thérèse, hearing me muttering and incessantly repeating the same phrases, in the endeavour to cram them into my head, laughed at me. I hoped in the end to know my speech by heart. I knew that the lord of the manor, as the Prince's official, would be present at the meeting of the Consistory, and that, in spite of the bottles of wine distributed by Montmollin, and his intrigues, most of the Elders were well disposed towards me. I had on my side reason, truth, justice, the King's protection, the authority of the Council of State, and the wishes of all good patriots who were affected by the establishment of this inquisition; in fact, everything contributed to my encouragement.

The day before the time appointed, I knew my speech by heart; I recited it without a mistake. I went over it again all night in my head: in the morning I had forgotten it: I hesitated at each word, I fancied myself already in the presence of the illustrious assembly; I was confused, I stammered, I lost my head; at last, almost at the moment of starting, my courage failed me entirely. I remained at home, I determined to write to the Consistory, hastily giving my reasons for not appearing, and alleging as an excuse my ill-health, which, considering the state I was in, would really have made it almost impossible for me to go through the whole sitting.

[The excommunication is not voted, and Montmoulin now tries to stir up the people.]

I was preached at from the pulpit, called the Antichrist, and chased in the country like a were-wolf. My Armenian costume was sufficient description for the people: I felt the disadvantage of it cruelly, but to abandon it under the circumstances appeared to me an act of cowardice. I could not make up my mind to do this, and I calmly walked about the country in my caftan and fur cap, pursued by the hue and cry of the rabble, and sometimes by their stones. Several times, when passing in front of the houses, I heard those inside say, "Bring me my gun: let me fire at him." I did not walk any faster, and this only increased their fury; but they always confined themselves to threats, at least as far as firearms were concerned.

[Rousseau is encouraged by a visit from Madame de Verdelin and her daughter. This gives him a better opinion of her.]

It was during her stay, in fact, that I began to be subjected to nightly attacks in my own house. One morning, her lady's-maid found a number of stones in front of my window which had been thrown at it during the night. A large, heavy bench, which stood in the street by the side of my door and was securely fixed, was torn up, removed, and set up on end against the door; so that, unless someone had seen it, the first person who had opened the door to go out would have been knocked down. Madame de Verdelin knew all that was going on; for, in addition to what she could see for herself, her confidential servant made himself very well known in the village, talked to everybody, and was even seen in conversation with Montmoulin. However, she did not appear to take any notice of anything that happened, never mentioned Montmoulin or anyone else, and only replied briefly to remarks which I sometimes made about him. She only seemed to be convinced that England would be the best place for me to stay in. She spoke much of Hume, who was in Paris at the time, of his friendship for me, and of his desire to be of service to me in his country. It is time to say something about M. Hume.

He had acquired a great reputation in France, especially amongst the Encyclopaedists, through his commercial and political treatises, and, lastly, by his "History of the House of Stuart," the only one of his writings of which I had read something in the Abbé Prévost's translation. Not having read his other works, I felt convinced, from what I had heard of him, that he united a genuine republican spirit with the paradoxical English prejudices in favour of luxury. In accordance with this opinion, I looked upon the whole of his apology for Charles I. as a marvel of impartiality, and I entertained as high an opinion of his virtue as of his genius. The desire of making the acquaintance of this singular man and gaining his friendship, had greatly increased the temptation to cross over to England, which the earnest entreaties of Madame de Boufflers, his intimate friend, had aroused in me. On my arrival in Switzerland, I received from him, through her, an extremely flattering letter, in which after praising my talents most highly, he gave me a pressing invitation to cross over to England, and offered to use all his influence and that of his friends to make my stay agreeable. I went on the spot to my Lord Marshal, Hume's friend and fellow-countryman, who confirmed my good opinion of him, and told me a literary anecdote about him, which struck me as much as it had struck him. Wallace, who had written against Hume on the subject of the population of the ancient world, was absent while his book was being printed. Hume undertook to revise the proofs and superintend the publication of the work. Such conduct was after my own heart. In the same manner, I had sold copies of a song which had been written against me, at six *sous* each. I accordingly had every reason to be prejudiced in favour of Hume, when Madame de Verdelin came and spoke strongly of the friendship which he professed to entertain for me, and of his eagerness to do me the honours of England, to use her own expression. She strongly urged me to take advantage of Hume's enthusiasm and to write to him. As I had no liking for England, and did not wish to adopt this course until I was actually obliged to. I refused either to write or to make any promise; but I left it to her discretion to do whatever she thought fit, to keep Hume favourably disposed towards me. When she left Motiers, she left me fully persuaded, from all that she had said to me concerning this famous man, that he was one of my friends, and that she was a still greater friend of his.

After her departure, Montmoulin pushed on his intrigues, and the people became uncontrollable. However, I continued to take my walks quietly, undisturbed by their hue and cry; the taste for botany, which I had begun to acquire through Doctor d'Ivernois, gave a new interest to my walks, and made me roam the country collecting plants, undisturbed by the shouts of the rabble, whose fury was only increased by my indifference. One of the things which most affected me was, to see the families of my friends, or people who called themselves such, openly join the ranks of my persecutors. . . .

[The people of Geneva are particularly violent. He is attacked by his friend Vernes.]

In this letter I was accused of having exposed my children in the streets, of taking about with me a soldier's trollop, of being worn out by debauchery, rotten with the pox; and similar politenesses. It was easy for me to recognise my man. On reading this libellous production, my first thought was to estimate at its true value everything that is called renown and reputation amongst men; when I saw a man treated as a whoremonger who had never been in a brothel in his life, and whose greatest fault was a constant timidity and shyness, like that of a virgin; when I saw that I was supposed to be eaten up by the pox—I, who had not only never had the slightest attack of any venereal disease, but who, according to the physicians, was so formed that it would have been impossible for me to contract it. After careful consideration, I came to the conclusion that I could not better refute this libel than by having it printed in the town in which I had lived longest. I sent it to Duchesne to be printed just as it was, with a prefatory notice, in which I mentioned M. Vernes, and a few brief notes, in order to explain the facts.

[Rousseau suppresses this pamphlet on the advice of Du Peyrou, for Vernes has promised to prove he is not the author of the letter. This he never does.*]

It is time to proceed to the final catastrophe at Motiers, and my departure from Val-de-Travers, after a residence of two

---

* It was Voltaire—not Vernes—who had written this nasty attack on Rousseau. But Rousseau was never willing to acknowledge his injustice.

years and a half, and eight months of unshaken firmness in enduring most unworthy treatment. It is impossible for me to recall clearly the details of this unpleasant period of my life; but they will be found in the account of it published by Du Peyrou, of which I shall have to speak later.

After Madame de Verdelin's departure, the excitement became more violent; and, in spite of the repeated prescripts of the King, in spite of the frequent orders of the Council of State, in spite of the efforts of the lord of the manor and the magistrates of the place, the people seriously regarded me as the Antichrist; and, finding all their clamours useless, seemed at last inclined to proceed to acts of violence. In the streets, stones already began to roll after me, which had been thrown from too great a distance to be able to reach me. At last, on the night after the fair at Motiers, at the beginning of September, I was attacked in the house where I lived in a manner which imperilled the lives of the inmates.

At midnight, I heard a loud noise in the gallery which ran along the back part of the house. A shower of stones, thrown against the window and the door which led to this gallery, fell into it with such a noise that my dog, who slept in the gallery, and at first commenced to bark, was terrified into silence, and ran into a corner, where he scratched and gnawed the boards in his endeavours to escape. Hearing the noise, I got up. I was on the point of leaving my room to go into the kitchen, when a stone thrown by a powerful hand, smashed the window of the kitchen, flew across it, burst open the door of my room, and fell at the foot of my bed; and, if I had been a second sooner, I should have had it in my stomach. I concluded that the noise had been made in order to attract my attention, and the stone thrown to receive me when I left my room. I dashed into the kitchen. There I found Thérèse, who had also got up and ran trembling towards me. We stood close against a wall, out of the line of the window, to avoid being hit by the stones, and to think of what we should do; for to go out to call for help would have been certain death. Fortunately, the servant of a worthy old man, who lodged below me, got up at the noise, and ran to call the lord of the manor, who lived next door. He jumped out of bed, threw on his dressing-gown, and immediately came with the watch, who, on account of the fair, were making the round, and were close at hand. When he saw the havoc, he grew pale with affright; and, at the sight of the stones, of which the gallery was full, he exclaimed, "Good God! it is a regular quarry!" On going below, we found that the door of a small yard had been broken open, and that an attempt had been made to get into the house through the gallery. When inquiry was made, why the watchmen had neither perceived nor prevented the disturbance, it was found that, although those of another village ought properly to have done duty, those from Motiers had persisted in taking this watch out of their turn. On the following day, the lord of the manor sent in his report to the Council of State, who, two days afterwards, commissioned him to institute an inquiry into the matter, and to offer a reward, under promise of secrecy, to those who informed against the guilty parties. In the meantime, he was to set a guard, at Government expense, to protect my house and his own, which adjoined it. The next day, Colonel de Pury; Meuron, the *procureur-général;* Martinet, the lord of the manor; Guyenet, the receiver of taxes; D'Ivernois, the treasurer, and his father—in a word, all the persons of importance in the district, came to see me, and united their entreaties to induce me to bow to the storm, and to leave, at least for a time, a parish in which I could no longer live with safety or honour. I even noticed that the lord of the manor, terrified by the fury of the frenzied populace, and alarmed lest it might extend to him, would have been very glad to see me leave at once, that he might be relieved from the responsibility of protecting me, and might be able to leave the place himself, as in fact he did, after my own departure. I accordingly yielded, and even with little reluctance; for the sight of the hatred of the people caused me such heart-breaking anguish, that I could no longer endure it.

[Rousseau is offered refuge by "a certain M. Walpole." Keith suggests Potsdam. But he decides on the little isle of Saint-Pierre, in Switzerland.]

The island of Saint-Pierre, called the Ile de la Motte at Neufchâtel, in the middle of the Lake of Bienne, is only about half a league in circumference; but within this small space it produces all the chief necessaries of existence. It contains fields, meadows, orchards, woods, and vineyards; the whole, thanks to the diversified and mountainous nature of the ground, exhibits a variety that is the more agreeable, since its different aspects, not disclosing themselves all at the same time, mutually set each other off, and cause the island to seem larger than it really is. The western portion of it, which faces Gleresse and Bonneville, is formed by a very lofty terrace. This terrace has been planted with a long row of trees, intersected in the middle by a large *salon*, where, during the vintage, the inhabitants assemble on Sundays from the neighbouring shores, to dance and enjoy themselves. There is only one house in the island, where the receiver of taxes lives; but it is large and commodious, and situated in a recess, which shelters it from the wind.

Five or six hundred yards from Saint-Pierre, in a southerly direction, is another island, much smaller, uncultivated, and uninhabited, which appears to have been at some time separated from the larger one by the violence of the storms; its gravelly soil produces nothing but willows and persicaria, but it contains some rising ground, covered with turf and very pleasant. . . .

Such was the refuge which I had secured for myself, where I made up my mind to settle on leaving Val-de-Travers.° This choice was so entirely suited to my quiet tastes and to my solitary and indolent disposition, that I reckon it as one of the delightful dreams for which I have conceived a most passionate affection. It seemed to me that, in this island, I should be

---

* It is perhaps not irrelevant to observe that I left behind me a personal enemy in a certain M. de Terraux, mayor of Verrières, who was not held in particular esteem in the country, but who has a brother, who is said to be an honourable man, in M. de Saint-Florentin's offices. The mayor had paid him a visit some time before my adventure. Little remarks of this kind, which in themselves are quite insignificant, may subsequently assist in the discovery of many underhand proceedings.

more removed from the society of men, more sheltered from their insults, more completely forgotten by them, and, in a word, more at liberty to abandon myself to the delights of idleness and a life of contemplation. I should have liked to be shut up in this island so completely as to have no further intercourse with any living man; and I certainly took all possible steps to relieve myself of the necessity of having any.

[Rousseau arranges to do a complete edition of his works, in return for an annuity, but this was later to fall through.]

The reader will be able to judge whether, without degrading myself to the lowest depths of infamy, I could have adhered to arrangements which others have always been careful to make disgraceful for me, by at the same time depriving me of all other resources, in order to compel me to consent to my dishonour. How could they have felt any doubt as to my course of action in such an alternative? They have always judged my heart by their own.

My mind being easy in regard to my means of livelihood, I had no other anxiety. Although, in the world, I left the field free for my enemies, I was leaving behind me, in the noble enthusiasm which had prompted all my writings, and in the consistent uniformity of my principles, a testimony on behalf of my soul which corresponded to that which my whole course of behaviour rendered to my character. I needed no other defence against my calumniators. They might, under my name, represent a totally different man; but they could only deceive those who wanted to be deceived. I could leave them my life to criticise, from one end to the other; I felt certain that, amidst all my faults and weaknesses, and my unfitness for submitting to any yoke, they would always find a man who was just, good, free from bitterness, hatred and jealousy, ever ready to acknowledge his own injustice, and still more ready to forget that of others, who sought all his happiness in loving and gentle emotions, and displayed in everything sincerity even to the extent of imprudence and the most incredible disinterestedness.

Accordingly, I in a measure took leave of my generation and my contemporaries, and said farewell to the world, by confining myself within this island for the remainder of my days; for such was my resolution, and it was there that I hoped at last to be able to carry out the grand scheme of a life of idleness, to which I had hitherto devoted in vain all the little energy which Heaven had bestowed upon me. . . .

As the age for romantic schemes was over, and the incense of vainglory had rather made me giddy than flattered me, there remained nothing for me, as a last hope, but a life free from restraint, spent in perpetual leisure. This is the life of the blessed in the next world, and, from this time forth, I fixed upon it my supreme happiness in this.

Those who reproach me with so many inconsistencies, will not fail here to reproach me with another. I have said that the idleness of society made it unendurable to me; and yet, here was I seeking solitude with the sole object of abandoning myself to idleness. And yet such is my disposition; if there is any inconsistency in this, the fault is in nature and not in me; but it is so trifling, that it is just that which makes me always consistent. The idleness of society is tedious, because it is obligatory; that of solitude is delightful, because it is free and voluntary. In company it is a cruel task for me to do nothing, because I am under compulsion. I am obliged to remain there, nailed to my chair, or standing bolt upright like a sentinel, without moving hand or foot, afraid to run, to jump, to sing, to cry out, or gesticulate when I have a mind to, afraid even to dream. I feel at once all the weariness of idleness and all the torture of constraint. I am obliged to listen attentively to all the silly things that are said and the compliments that are interchanged, and to rack my brains incessantly, that I may not fail in my turn to bring in my pun or my lie. And that is called idleness! It is the work of a galley-slave!

The idleness that I love is not that of an idler who remains with folded arms in a state of total inactivity, no more thinking than acting. That which I love is the combined idleness of a child who is incessantly in motion without ever doing anything, and that of a dotard, who wanders from one thing to another while his arms are still. I love to busy myself about trifles, to begin a hundred things and finish none, to come and go as the fancy takes me, to change my plans every moment, to follow a fly in all its movements, to try and pull up a rock to see what is underneath, to undertake with eagerness a work that would last ten years, and to abandon it without regret at the end of ten minutes—in a word, to spend the day in trifling without order or sequence, and, in everything, to follow nothing but the caprice of the moment.

Botany, such as I have already regarded it, and such as it began to be a passion for me, was exactly the kind of idle study which was calculated to fill up the void of my leisure time, without leaving room for the extravagances of imagination or the weariness of absolute idleness. To wander carelessly in the woods and in the country, to pluck mechanically, here and there, sometimes a flower, sometimes a branch, to munch my food almost haphazardly, to observe the same things thousands and thousands of times, and always with the same interest, because I always forgot them—that was the way to spend eternity without a moment's weariness. However delicate, however admirable, however different the structure of plants may be, it never strikes an ignorant eye sufficiently to interest it. The consistent analogy and, at the same time, the enormous variety which characterises their organism, only delights those who already have some idea of the system of the vegetable world. . . .

I sent for Thérèse with my books and belongings. We boarded with the receiver of the island. His wife's sisters, who lived at Nidau, came to see her in turns, and this was company for Thérèse. Here I first experienced the pleasures of a life which I could have wished might last out my own; but the taste which I acquired for it only served to make me feel more keenly the bitterness of that life which was so soon to succeed it.

I have always been passionately fond of the water, and the sight of it throws me into a delightful state of dreaminess, although often without any definite object. When it was fine weather, I always hastened to the terrace as soon as I was up, to inhale the fresh and healthful morning air, and let my eyes roam over the horizon of this beautiful lake, the shores of which, surrounded by mountains, formed an enchanting prospect. I can think of no worthier homage to the Divinity than the mute admiration which is aroused by the contemplation of His works, and does not find expression in outward acts. I can understand how it is that the inhabitants of cities, who see nothing but walls, streets and crimes, have so little religious belief; but I cannot understand how those who live in the country, especially in solitude, can have none. How is it that their soul is not lifted up in ecstasy a hundred times a day to the Author of the wonders which strike them? As far as I am concerned, it is especially after rising, weakened by a night of sleeplessness, that I am led by long-standing habit to those upliftings of the heart, which do not impose upon me the trouble of thinking. But, for this to take place, my eyes must be smitten by the enchanting spectacle of nature. In my room, my prayers are not so frequent or so fervent; but, at the sight of a beautiful landscape, I feel myself moved without knowing why. I remember reading of a wise bishop, who, during a visit to his diocese, came upon an old woman who, by way of prayer, could say nothing but "Oh!" "Good mother," said the bishop, "continue to pray in this manner; your prayer is better than ours." This better prayer is also mine.

After breakfast I hastily wrote a few miserable letters, with a sulky air, longing eagerly for the happy moment when I need write no more. I bustled about my books and papers for a few moments, more for the sake of unpacking and arranging than of reading them; and this, which became for me the task of Penelope, afforded me the pleasure of idling away my time for a few moments, after which I became tired of the task, and spent the three or four remaining hours of the morning in the study of botany, especially the system of Linnaeus, of which I became so passionately fond that I have never been able to give it up entirely, even after discovering its deficiencies. This great observer is, in my opinion, with the exception of Ludwig, the only man who has as yet considered botany from the point of view of a naturalist and a philosopher; but he has studied too much from gardens and collections of dried plants, and too little from nature herself. . . .

In the afternoon I abandoned myself entirely to my idle and careless disposition, and followed, without any system, the impulse of the moment. Frequently, when the weather was calm, immediately after dinner, I jumped by myself into a little boat, which the receiver had taught me how to manage with a single oar, and rowed out into the middle of the lake. The moment at which I left the bank, I felt ready to leap for joy. It is impossible for me to explain or understand the reason for this feeling, unless it was a secret self-congratulation on being thus out of the reach of the wicked. I rowed by myself all over the lake, sometimes near the bank, but never landing. Frequently, leaving my boat at the mercy of the wind and water, I abandoned myself to aimless reveries, which, although foolish, were none the less delightful. I sometimes exclaimed with emotion, "O Nature! O my mother! behold me under thy protection alone! Here there is no cunning or knavish mortal to thrust himself between me and thee." In this manner I got out half a league from land. I could have wished that this lake had been the ocean. However, in order to please my poor dog, who was not so fond of long excursions on the water as I was, as a rule I followed a definite plan. I landed on the small island, walked about for an hour or two, or stretched myself on the grass at the top of the rising ground, to sate myself with the pleasure of admiring this lake and its surroundings, to examine and anatomise all the plants within my reach, and to build for myself, like a second Robinson, an imaginary dwelling on this little island. I became passionately attached to this hillock. When I was able to take Thérèse, the receiver's wife and her sisters, for a walk there, how proud I felt to be their pilot and their guide! We solemnly took some rabbits to it, to stock it. Another gala for Jean-Jacques! This colony made the little island still more interesting to me. I visited it more frequently and with greater pleasure from that time, to look for signs of the progress of the new inhabitants.

To these amusements I united another, which reminded me

of the delightful life at Les Charmettes, and for which the season was particularly suitable. This was the occupation of a country life; and we gathered in the fruit and vegetables, which Thérèse and myself were delighted to share with the receiver and his family. I remember that a Bernese, named M. Kirchberger, when he came to see me, found me perched on the branches of a tall tree, with a bag tied round my waist, so full of apples that I could not move. I was not at all sorry that he and others should find me thus. I hoped that the Bernese, seeing how I employed my leisure time, would no longer think about disturbing its tranquillity, and would leave me in peace in my solitude. I should have preferred to be shut up there by their will than by my own; for, in that case, I should have felt more certain of not seeing my rest disturbed.

I am now again coming to one of those confessions, in regard to which I feel sure beforehand that those readers will be incredulous, who are always determined to judge me by their own standard, although they have been compelled to see, throughout the whole course of my life, a thousand inner emotions which have not the least resemblance to their own. The most extraordinary thing is that while denying to me all the good or indifferent feelings which they do not themselves possess, they are always ready to attribute to me others so utterly bad that they could not even enter into the heart of a man. They find it perfectly simple to put me into contradiction with nature, and to make me out a monster such as cannot possibly exist. No absurdity appears incredible to them, if only it is calculated to blacken me; nothing that is at all out of the common seems to them possible, if only it is calculated to bring honour upon me.

But, whatever they may believe or say, I will none the less continue faithfully to set forth what Jean-Jacques Rousseau was, did, and thought, without either explaining or justifying the singularity of his sentiments and ideas, or inquiring whether others have thought as he. . . .

I was in the habit of going every evening to sit upon the shore, especially when the lake was rough. I felt a singular pleasure in seeing the waves break at my feet. They represented to me the tumult of the world and the peacefulness of my own abode; and I was sometimes so touched by this delightful idea, that I felt the tears trickling down from my eyes. This repose, which I passionately enjoyed, was only troubled by the apprehension of losing it; but this feeling of uneasiness spoilt its charm. I felt my position to be so precarious that I could not reckon upon its continuance. Ah! said I to myself, how gladly would I exchange the permission to leave the island, for which I do not care at all, for the assurance of being able to remain there always! Instead of being allowed here by sufferance, why am I not kept here by force? Those who only leave me here on sufferance, can drive me away at any moment; can I venture to hope that my persecutors, seeing me happy here, will allow me to continue to be so?

[Suddenly Rousseau receives an official letter expelling him from his island. The weather is severe. Rousseau is angry, bewildered.]

If I had listened to the first impulse of my indignation, I should have set out at once. But where was I to go? what was to become of me, at the beginning of winter, when I had made no plans or preparations, and was without a guide or conveyance. Unless I was prepared to leave everything in confusion, my papers, belongings, and affairs generally, I required time to see to them, and it was not mentioned in the order whether this was to be allowed me or not. My continued misfortunes began to weaken my courage. For the first time in my life, I felt my natural pride bend beneath the yoke of necessity; and, in spite of the murmurings of my heart, I was obliged to humiliate myself by asking for delay. It was to M. de Graffenried, who had sent me the order, that I addressed myself for an explanation of it. In his letter, he expressed strong disapproval of this order, which he had only communicated to me with the greatest regret; and the evidences of sorrow and esteem, of which it was full, seemed to me a kindly invitation to speak to him with perfect frankness, which I did. I had no doubt that my letter would open the eyes of these unjust men to their barbarous conduct, and that, even if they did not revoke so cruel an order, they would at least grant me a reasonable delay, perhaps the whole winter, to make preparations for retreat, and to select another place of refuge.

While awaiting their reply, I began to consider my situation, and to reflect upon the course of action which I had to adopt. I saw so many difficulties on all sides, my sorrow had so greatly affected me, and my health, at this moment, was so bad, that I allowed myself to give way altogether, and the effect of my despair was, to deprive me of the few expedients, which might possibly remain in my head, for getting out of my melancholy situation as successfully as was possible. In whatever asylum I might take refuge, it was clear that I could not avoid being exposed to the two methods which had been employed in order to drive me out; the one, to stir up the people against me by underhand intrigues; the other, to expel me by open force, without assigning any reason for it. Thus, I could not reckon upon any refuge where I should be safe from attack, without going further to look for it than my own strength and the weather seemed to permit me. All these considerations led me back to the ideas with which I had just been busying myself; I ventured to desire and to propose that I should rather be imprisoned for life than driven incessantly as a wanderer over the face of the earth, expelled in succession from all the places of refuge which I might choose. Two days after my first letter, I wrote a second to M. de Graffenried, asking him to lay my proposal before their Excellencies. The reply from Berne to both these letters was an order, couched in most harsh and formal terms, to leave the island and all the territory belonging directly or indirectly to the Republic within the space of twenty-four hours, and never to enter it again, under pain of the severest penalties.

It was a terrible moment. Since then I have often been in greater distress, never in greater embarrassment. But what afflicted me most was, to be obliged to give up the scheme which had made me wish to spend the winter in the island. It is now time to relate the fatal circumstance which has crowned my disasters, and which has involved in my ruin an unfortunate people, whose growing virtues already gave promise of some day equalling those of Sparta and Rome. In the "Contrat Social" I had spoken of the Corsicans as a new people, the only one in Europe which had not yet been ruined by legislation; and I had pointed out the great hopes which might be entertained of such a people, if it should be fortunate to find a wise instructor. My work was read by some Corsicans, who appreciated the terms of respect in which I had spoken of them; and, finding themselves obliged to devote their energies to the establishment of their republic, some of their chiefs bethought themselves of asking my opinion upon this important work. A certain M. Buttafuoco, who belonged to one of the chief families of the country and was a captain in the French Royal Italian regiment, wrote to me on the subject and furnished me with a number of documents, which I had asked him for, to make myself acquainted with the history of the nation and the state of the country. M. Paoli also wrote to me several times; and, although I felt that such an undertaking was beyond my strength, I thought that I could not refuse my assistance in so great and noble a task, after I had procured all the information which I required. It was to this effect that I replied to both; and this correspondence continued until my departure from Saint-Pierre.

Exactly at the same time, I heard that France was sending troops to Corsica, and had concluded a treaty with the Genoese. This treaty and this despatch of troops made me uneasy, and, without imagining that I was in any way connected with it, I considered that it would be impossible, and even absurd, to devote my attention to a work, which requires such profound tranquillity—the organisation of a people, at the moment when it was perhaps on the point of being brought under the yoke. I did not conceal my uneasiness from M. Buttafuoco, who calmed me by the assurance that, if this treaty had contained anything detrimental to the liberty of his country, a good citizen like himself would not remain, as he did, in the service of France. In fact, his zeal for the legislative arrangements of Corsica, and his intimate connection with M. Paoli, prevented me from entertaining any suspicions in regard to him; and, when I heard that he made frequent journeys to Versailles and Fontainebleau, and had interviews with M. de Choiseul, I could only conclude that he had assurances in regard to the real intentions of the French Court, which he left me to understand, but about which he did not desire to express himself openly in a letter. . . .

The longer I thought over the proposed undertaking, and the more I studied the documents I had in my hands, the more I felt the necessity of studying on the spot both the people who were to be legislated for, and the country which they inhabited, and of examining, in all their relations, the circumstances, the aid of which was necessary for them, in order to adopt such legislation. I understood more clearly every day, that it was impossible for me to acquire from a distance all the information necessary for my guidance. I wrote to this effect to Buttafuoco: he agreed with me, and, if I did not exactly make up my mind to go over to Corsica, I thought a good deal about the means of undertaking the journey. . . .

But, when the persecutions to which I was subjected at Motiers made me think of leaving Switzerland, this desire was revived by the hope of at last finding amongst those islanders the tranquillity which was denied me everywhere else. One thing only alarmed me in regard to the journey—my unfitness for, and the aversion which I had always felt to, the active life to which I should be condemned. Fitted by nature to meditate at leisure by myself, I was utterly unfitted to speak, act, and conduct affairs amongst men. . . .

Tormented, buffeted by storms of every kind, worn out by journeys and persecutions for many years past, I strongly felt the need of the repose of which my barbarous enemies, by way of amusing themselves, deprived me. I sighed more than ever for the delightful idleness, for the sweet repose of body and soul, which I had so longed for, to which the supreme happiness of my heart, now cured of its idle dreams of love and friendship, was limited. I only regarded with alarm the task which I was on the point of undertaking, the stormy life to which I proposed to abandon myself. . . .

I thought of an expedient, which seemed to me well adapted to settle everything. Pursued, wherever I took shelter, by the underhand intrigues of my secret persecutors, and seeing no other place but Corsica where I could look forward, in my old age, to the repose which they refused to allow me anywhere, I decided to go there, in accordance with the instructions of Buttafuoco, as soon as it should be possible for me to do so; but, in order to live quietly there, I made up my mind to abandon, at least to all appearance, the work of legislation, and in order to repay my hosts in some measure for their hospitality, to confine myself to writing their history on the spot, with the reservation of quietly acquiring the information necessary to make me of greater use to them, if I saw any prospect of success. By thus binding myself to nothing at first, I hoped to be able to think, by myself and at greater leisure, of a suitable plan, without either abandoning my cherished hopes of solitude, or adopting the kind of life which was unendurable to me, and for which I had no qualifications.

[But Corsica is far, and life there is hard, the people barbarous. He decides on Berlin, but then receives an invitation from the citizens of the free city of Bienne. The French ambassador urges Rousseau to accept it.]

This behaviour on the part of Barthès upset all my conjectures. I had always suspected M. de Choiseul of being the secret author of all the persecutions to which I had been subjected in Switzerland. The behaviour of the French Resident at Geneva and of the ambassador at Soleure confirmed these suspicions only too strongly. I saw the secret influence of France in all that had happened to me at Berne, Geneva and Neufchâtel, and I thought that the only powerful enemy I had in France was the Duc de Choiseul. What, then, was I to think of the visit of Barthès and of the tender interest which he seemed to take in my destiny? My misfortunes had not yet destroyed my natural trustfulness, and experience had not yet taught me to see a snare in every demonstration of affection. Greatly surprised, I tried to discover the cause of this kindness on the part of Barthès. I was not foolish enough to believe that he was acting on his own initiative. I saw in his behaviour an ostentation and even an air of affectation, which was evidence of some hidden purpose, and I was far from ever having found in these inferior agents that high-spirited intrepidity, which, when I held a similar position, had often made my heart throb. . . .

When I left the island, Kirchberger accompanied me as far as Bienne, where I found Wildremet and some other Biennese waiting for me. We all dined together at the inn; and the first thing I did, on arriving, was to order a conveyance, as I intended to set out on the following morning. During dinner, these gentlemen renewed their entreaties to me, to remain amongst them, with such warmth and such touching assurances, that, in spite of all my resolutions, my heart, which has never been able to resist affection, felt moved by theirs. As soon as they saw that I began to hesitate, they redoubled their efforts, and with such success that I finally allowed myself to be overcome, and consented to remain at Bienne, at any rate until the following spring.

Wildremet immediately made haste to find me a lodging, and highly recommended to me, as a great find, a wretched little room, on the third floor back, looking upon a yard, where I could feast my eyes upon the stinking skins of a leather-dresser's establishment which were displayed there. My landlord was a little, low-looking man, a tolerable rascal, of whom I heard the next day, that he was a rake and a gambler, and in very bad repute in the district. He had neither wife nor children nor servants; and I, shut up in melancholy confinement in my solitary room, and in the most pleasant country in the world, was lodged in a manner calculated to make a man die of melancholy in a few days. What affected me most, in spite of all that I had been told as to the eagerness of the inhabitants to have me amongst them, was, that I did not observe, when walking through the streets, any politeness in their behaviour, or friendliness in their looks. However, I had quite made up my mind to remain there, when, even on the next day, I learned, saw, and perceived nyself, that the town was in a terrible state of excitement on my account. Several persons were obliging enough to hasten to inform me that, on the next day, I should be told, as harshly as possible, to leave the State, that is to say, the town, immediately. I had no one in whom I could trust; all those who had urged me to stay had dispersed. Wildremet had disappeared; I heard nothing more of Barthès, and it did not seem as if his recommendation had done much to ingratiate me with the "patrons" and "fathers" of whom he had boasted to me. A certain M. de Vau-Travers, however, a Bernese, who had a nice house near the town, offered me a refuge in the meantime, in the hope, as he said, that I might escape being stoned. This recommendation did not seem to me sufficiently enticing to tempt me to prolong my stay amongst this hospitable people.

Having lost three days by this delay, I had already considerably exceeded the twenty-four hours which the Bernese had allowed me to leave their States, and, as I knew their harshness, I was not free from some anxiety as to the manner in which they would allow me to pass through them, when the *Bailli* of Nidau most opportunely relieved me of embarrassment. As he had openly expressed his disapproval of the violent measures adopted by their Excellencies, he believed, in his generosity, that it was his duty to testify publicly, that he had nothing to do with them, and he had the courage to leave his bailiwick and pay me a visit at Bienne. He came the day before I left, by no means *incognito*, but even with a certain amount of ceremony; he came in state in his carriage, accompanied by his secretary, and brought me a passport in his name, which would enable me to cross the State of Berne without fear of being molested. The visit touched me more than the passport. I should have been equally sensible of it, if it had been paid to anyone else. I know nothing which exercises a more powerful influence upon my heart than an act of courage, performed at an opportune moment, on behalf of the weak who are unjustly oppressed.

At last, having with difficulty procured a conveyance, I set out on the following morning from this murderous land, before the arrival of the deputation, with which it was proposed to honour me, even before I was able to see Thérèse again, to whom, when I thought that I was going to stay in Berne, I had written to join me, and whom I had hardly time enough to put off by a few lines, in which I informed her of my fresh misfortune. It will be seen, in the third part of my Confessions, if I ever have strength to write it, how, when I thought that I was setting out for Berlin, I was really setting out for England, and how the two ladies who were anxious to control my movements, after having driven me by their continued intrigues from Switzerland, where I was not sufficiently in their power, at last succeeded in delivering me into the hands of their friends.

I added what follows on the occasion of my reading these Confessions to M. and Madame la Comtesse d'Egmont, M. le Prince Pignatelli, Madame la Marquise de Mesmes, and M. le Marquis de Juigné.

"I have told the truth; if anyone knows things that contradict what I have just related, even though they be proved a thousand times over, he knows what is false and an imposture; and, if he declines to investigate and inquire into them together with me while I am still in the land of the living, he loves neither justice nor truth. As for myself, I declare openly and fearlessly: whosoever, even without having read my writings, after examining with his own eyes my disposition, my character, my manners, my inclinations, my pleasures, and my habits, can believe me to be a dishonourable man, is himself a man who deserves to be choked."

Thus I concluded the reading of my Confessions, and everyone was silent. Madame d'Egmont was the only person who appeared to be affected; she trembled visibly, but she quickly recovered herself and remained silent, like the rest of the company. Such were the results of this reading and my declaration.

[Rousseau's Confessions end in 1765. He did go to England, accepted Hume's hospitality, quarrelled with everyone and returned to France more convinced than ever of a gigantic plot against him. By now he had probably gone beyond the edge of sanity. Once more he wandered from one place to another, always quarrelling with his host. In 1770, he came back to Paris, married Thérèse, lived quietly as a music copyist. But in 1778, he moved again, this time to the enchanting estate of M. de Girardin, at Ermenonville. All his old suspicions and torments spring to fresh life. There death overtook him on July 2, bringing peace at last to the unhappiest of men.]